Other Books in This Series:

Family Walk: Love, Anger, Courage, and 49 Other
Weekly Readings for Your Family Devotions

Youthwalk: Sex, Parents, Popularity, and 49 Other
Topics for Teen Survival

365 DAILY DEVOTIONALS TO READ THROUGH THE BIBLE IN A YEAR

YOUR DAILY WALK

BRUCE H. WILKINSON
EXECUTIVE EDITOR

JOHN W. HOOVER
EDITOR

PAULA A. KIRK
GENERAL EDITOR

WALK THRU THE BIBLE MINISTRIES, INC.
ATLANTA, GEORGIA

ZONDERVAN PUBLISHING HOUSE
GRAND RAPIDS, MICHIGAN

This Zondervan edition of *Your Daily Walk* is published by arrangement with
Walk Thru the Bible Ministries.

Requests for information should be addressed to:

Walk Thru the Bible Ministries   or   **Zondervan Publishing House**
P.O. Box 80587   **Grand Rapids, Michigan 49530**
Atlanta, GA 30366

Library of Congress Cataloging-in-Publication Data

Your Daily Walk
    p. cm.
    ISBN 0-310-53651-0
    1. Devotional calendars. 2. Bible—Devotional use.
    I. Walk Thru the Bible (Educational Ministry).
BV4810.Y68   1991
242'.2—dc20   90—26142
                                                      CIP

Cover design by Foster Design Associates

Printed in the United States of America

00 01 02 /DC/ 31 30 29 28 27 26 25 24 23 22 2120 19

This devotional volume is affectionately dedicated to the Walk Thru the Bible Board of Directors who for years have served with courageous vision and loyal love. *Your Daily Walk* and the Walk Thru the Bible board members complement one another in humble fashion. Sending out a book about the Bible is a venture truly befitting the life goals of these men and women.

I will be forever indebted to them for keeping Walk Thru the Bible (and me, its Founder and President!) on the path of obedience to God's call for us as a ministry. We would not be encouraging believers in more than 30 countries and 21 languages around the world were it not for the patient and focused direction of this group. Their commitment to God's glory through the pursuit of excellence in their own lives and ministries has spilled over into Walk Thru the Bible's board room time and time again. For their faithfulness and their constant encouragement to us, my wife, Darlene, and I give heartfelt thanks to both them and to our Lord:

Paul (Chairman) and Marilyn Johnson
Ron and Judy Blue
Robert F. and Sara Boyd
Howard and Jeanne Hendricks
John and Mary Isch
Ryland and Carol Scott
John and Pat Van Diest

Acknowledgments

Your Daily Walk is a fresh, new compilation of daily Bible studies from *The Daily Walk* devotional guide, published by Walk Thru the Bible Ministries. We are grateful to everyone who worked so faithfully on this magazine during the past 13 years. We especially appreciate the vision and leadership given WTB in publishing, first by Harvey Warner, then by Don Holloway, and more recently by Calvin Edwards.

We've also been blessed by the valuable input from and support of other Christian organizations and churches who use *The Daily Walk* as a ministry tool. We thank Jim Gabrielson, Cathy Gates, Bob Westfall, and their team in WTB's Specialized Publishing Group for encouragement and support.

Our gratitude also goes to Jill Milligan and Libby Purvis whose desire is that every Christian read God's Word on a daily basis and draw closer to Him. They keep this vision before us all.

Finally, special thanks goes to our Daily Walk production team: Michelle Beeman, Martha Comeaux, Randy Drake, Tamilyn Hightower, Robyn Holmes, Stuart McLellan, Ruth Swanson, Peter Wallace, and Myra Wilkinson. The groundwork they laid by their dedication and commitment to excellence has made this book a joy to produce.

Index to the Books of the Bible

Introduction

Your Daily Walk is carefully designed to help in your spiritual walk. With this book you can spend a fruitful time each day in God's Word. Day by day you can read the Bible at an easy, manageable pace, gaining insights related to the Scripture you read. Gradually you will grasp the holy grandeur of God's plan for humanity, and you will find your understanding of the Lord deepening as you meditate on His Word.

As you find practical answers in *Your Daily Walk* to the perplexing problems you face each day, you will see the Bible in a new light. You will learn how to handle your heartaches, how to praise God, and how to draw upon God's power moment by moment.

Your Daily Walk will help you establish the Scriptures as your foundation for living in this chaotic and insecure world. As you grow stronger and more confident in God's love and His sovereignty, you will also have a platform from which to share the eternal truth of salvation with family members and friends.

We at Walk Thru the Bible Ministries are thrilled to join with Zondervan Publishers to make this Bible reading guide available to you. The common purpose of our ministries is to help Christians become grounded in the Scriptures.

Bruce H. Wilkinson
President and Executive Editor
Walk Thru the Bible Ministries

How to Get the Most Out of Your Daily Walk

Your Daily Walk is conveniently arranged for daily Bible reading 365 days of the year. Each section is dated with the month and day. You can start reading Genesis in January by using the dated track or just jump in any time during the year using the optional reading track ("Day 195"). Simply put a checkmark in the accompanying box to keep your place.

Your Daily Walk introduces each of the 66 books of the Bible with a summary of the theme and a chart showing the content of the book. Most days are divided into these three sections:

 Overview reviews the Bible reading for the day and touches on the major themes. The chart allows you to see at a glance how the Biblical action progresses or the theme unfolds.

 Your Daily Walk encourages you to think carefully about one theme from the day's reading. It shows how to apply principles from God's Word to your own life in the clamor and chaos of today's world.

 Insight builds factual Bible knowledge by highlighting a fascinating fact or historical incident.

From time to time, you'll have an opportunity to pause in your "walk" with a special devotional based on a theme or a topic that you've just read. The suggested Scriptures for these pages are shorter and are drawn from a number of Bible books. With shorter readings, these pages provide opportunities to do three things:

 Step Back and review the broad sweep of your reading for the previous week. Or catch up on reading from the past few days.

Look Up to the Creator in worship and praise, using these topics as a springboard.

Move Ahead with practical application.

Every feature of *Your Daily Walk* is designed to help you get the most out of your devotional times as you meet the Lord and draw closer to Him through the pages of His Word.

Walk Thru the Bible Ministries

Walk Thru the Bible Ministries (WTB) unofficially began in the early 1970s in Portland, Oregon, with the teaching of Old and New Testament surveys of the Bible. Dr. Bruce H. Wilkinson was looking for a way to innovatively teach the Word of God so that it would change people's lives.

Dr. Wilkinson officially founded WTB in 1976 as a nonprofit ministry. In 1978 WTB moved to its current home in Atlanta.

From these small beginnings WTB has grown into one of the leading Christian organizations in America with an international ministry extending to 30 countries and in 21 languages. International branch offices are located in Australia, Brazil, Great Britain, Singapore, and New Zealand.

By focusing on the central themes of Scripture and their practical application to life, WTB has been able to develop and maintain wide acceptance in denominations and fellowships around the world. In addition, it has carefully initiated strategic ministry alliances with over one hundred Christian organizations and missions of wide diversity and background.

WTB has four major outreach ministries: seminars, publishing, leadership training, and video training.

Since it began its seminar ministry two decades ago, WTB has instructed more than one million people worldwide through seminars in over 30 languages taught by more than two hundred highly qualified, well-trained teachers. People of all ages and religious persuasions have developed a deeper understanding of the Bible through these unique Old and New Testament surveys, and many have come to know Christ in a new and more personal way. WTB's seminars actively involve the audience in the learning process through memorable hand signs, and note-taking is prohibited!

WTB's publishing ministry began in 1978 with the launching of *The Daily Walk* magazine. Since then, WTB Publishing has continued to develop additional publications that enable individuals, families, and churches to maintain a regular, meaningful habit of daily devotional time in the Word of God. The publications include

Closer Walk, Family Walk, LifeWalk, and *Youthwalk.* WTB is one of the largest publishers of devotional magazines in the Christian community.

The third strategic ministry of WTB is the training of Christian leaders and communicators. Launched in the late 1980s, The Applied Principles of Learning (APL) training conference for teachers, pastors, and parents has rapidly become the most widely used interdenominational teacher training program in North America. Dozens of certified WTB instructors regularly conduct this life-changing course in schools, churches, businesses, and colleges. In addition, WTB's Leadership Dynamics curriculum is an integral part of the regular and ongoing discipleship training in hundreds of churches.

The newest and fastest growing ministry of WTB is the Video Training curriculum outreach. In just a few short years, the WTB creative team has developed a number of leading video courses that have enjoyed widespread distribution. "The Seven Laws of the Teacher" featuring Dr. Howard G. Hendricks equips church school teachers to effectively prepare and teach Bible lessons that capture attention and motivate lifechange. "Master Your Money" weaves a contemporary drama through the six-part presentation by Christian financial planner Ron Blue as he trains people to maximize their effectiveness as stewards. Thousands of churches use these and other fine WTB video series with their congregations each year.

Walk Thru the Bible Ministries has had a consistent history of strategic ministry since its beginning more than fifteen years ago. The call of the Lord has been clear and consistent on the organization as it strives to help fulfill the Lord's Great Commission. The highest ethics and standards of integrity are carefully practiced as Walk Thru the Bible lives out its commitment to excellence not only in ministry but also in its internal operational policies and procedures. No matter what the ministry, no matter where the ministry, WTB focuses on the Word of God and encourages people of all nations to grow in their knowledge of Him and in their unreserved obedience and service to Him.

For more information about Walk Thru the Bible's publications, videos, or seminars in your area, write to Walk Thru the Bible Ministries, P.O. Box 80587, Atlanta, GA 30366 or call (404) 458-9300.

Genesis

Genesis begins "in the beginning" and traces the inception of the universe, man, woman, marriage, worship, sin, judgment, civilization, and redemption. The first portion (chapters 1–11) presents a wide-angle view of God's dealings from Creation to Babel—a period characterized by human faithfulness. But chapters 12–50 focus on God's relationship with one man (Abraham) and his descendants over the next four centuries, during which a nation is founded and salvation is promised for the fallen race of man.

Focus	Foundation Events				Foundation People			
Divisions	Creation of the Universe	Fall of Man	Flood of Noah	Tower of Babel	Abraham's Faith	Isaac's Family	Jacob's Conflicts	Joseph's Calamity
	1 2	3 5	6 9	10 11	12 24	25 26	27 36	37 50
Topics	History of the Human Race				History of the Jewish Race			
	Faithfulness of Mankind				Faithfulness of One Man's Family			
Place	Eastward: From Eden to Ur				Westward: From Canaan to Egypt			
Time	2,000+ Years (20% of Genesis)				About 350 Years (80% of Genesis)			

1 Six Days of Creation / Genesis 1–2

Heart of the Passage: Genesis 2:4-25

Overview: The first two chapters of the Bible begin at "the beginning." Chapter 1 gives a concise overview of the progress of creation, climaxing in the creation of man. Chapter 2 takes a zoom-lens look at day six. There the details emerge of how God's image-bearers were created—man from the dust of the ground and woman from his rib. The stage is set, the characters are in place, the drama can begin.

Chapter 1	Chapter 2
Six Days Through a Telescope	Sixth Day Through a Microscope
Creation of the Universe	Creation of Man

The creation is both a monument of God's power and a looking glass in which we may see His wisdom.

Your Daily Walk: "When all else fails, follow the directions." That belated advice is based on a law as universal as gravity —the Law of Design, which states: "Things work well when they function according to the way they were designed; they work poorly (or not at all) when that design is violated." God, the Master Designer, made the water, sky, and land; then He made creatures suited for each environment. So it should not surprise you to discover that birds make terrible submarines, or that fish have trouble climbing trees.

The same design apparent in both solar system and desert flower is built into humans and their relationships. The husband is the head of the home; the wife is his helper by design. Violate the design and there's trouble. Follow it and there's harmony and fulfillment.

Grab a sheet of paper and see how many ways you can complete this sentence: "By God's design, I am _____"; (1-3, good start; 4-7, borderline Bible genius; 8 or more, you must be a design engineer!). If you got stuck, consult Psalm 139:14; 1 Corinthians 11:3; Ephesians 2:10; 5:21–6:9; Titus 2:14 for some help. With God's help, you can become all you were created to be!

Insight: Big Questions, Bigger Answers

The first verse in the English Bible uses only 10 words to answer four of the most basic questions thinking individuals ever ask: (1) What is there? (2) How did it get there? (3) Did it have a beginning? (4) What or who is responsible? These answers have been graciously supplied by the only One who was there at the time. (The correct answers are: 1. The heaven and the earth; 2. It was all created; 3. Yes; 4. God.)

Entrance and Extent of Sin / Genesis 3–5   2

Overview: The perfect environment into which man was placed is now shattered by the entrance of sin. Satan, posing as the subtle serpent, challenges God's only prohibition on man's use of the garden. Disobedience follows as the first family eats from the forbidden tree and is expelled from the garden. The results of their sin spread quickly as humankind and the whole creation fall under the penalty of death. Cain becomes the first murderer, and the downward spiral continues from Adam to Noah, paving the way for God's sweeping judgment upon the wickedness of the world.

Heart of the Passage: Genesis 3

Chapter 3	Chapter 4	Chapter 5
Root of Sin: Adam's Rebellion	Fruit of Sin: Cain's Evil Line	Fruit of Faith: Seth's Godly Line
Entrance of Sin	Extent of Sin	

Your Daily Walk: Has this ever happened to you? You turn on your radio or TV and hear glowing reports of a new "miracle product." Convinced, you go out and buy it, only to discover it fails to live up to its billing.

Satan has been in the business of overselling his "product"—sin—for thousands of years. He first tried this approach with Eve in the Garden of Eden. Notice the promise: "In the day ye eat thereof, then your eyes shall be opened, and ye shall be as gods, knowing good and evil" (3:5). Eve believed his claim and tried his product. The result? Pain . . . bitter disappointment . . . and expulsion from the garden.

Where has *your* resistance to temptation been tested by Satan? What are some of the false promises he would like you to believe in order to sell you on sin? "If it feels good it must be right. . . . Everyone else is doing it, so it must be okay. . . . If you haven't tried it, you can't know what you're missing. . . . It won't hurt to do it just once."

When tempted today to fall for one of Satan's false promises, respond instead with this scriptural promise from James 4:7: "Resist the devil, and he will flee from you."

The one who falls into sin is a human; the one who grieves at sin is a saint; the one who boasts of sin is a fool.

Insight: Same Scheme, Different Results

Compare Genesis 3 with Matthew 4:1-11 and you'll notice an interesting fact. Satan tempted Jesus in the same three ways that he tempted Eve (lust of the flesh, lust of the eyes, and pride of life; 1 John 2:16). But in Christ's case, Satan failed on every count!

3 *Stewards of God's Creation*

Scripture Reading: Colossians 1:16; Isaiah 45:18

Occasionally you'll be given the opportunity with these special pages to pause in your daily walk through the Bible. You can use these days to catch up on your regular reading. But more important, you can step back and take a look at the big picture, contemplating the broad themes from the passages you're reading, and worship their Author—God Himself.

Step Back

One of the most immense themes of Scripture is the one that starts it all: the Creation. Despite the debate that has raged especially in recent years over the origin of the universe, the Bible firmly and clearly proclaims God the Creator of all.

And not only in the early chapters of Genesis. The New Testament echoes this truth while shedding even brighter light on it. There it is revealed that God the Son, the Lord Jesus Christ, was the agent of creation: "For by him [Jesus Christ] were all things created, that are in heaven, and that are in earth, visible and invisible, whether they be thrones, or dominions, or principalities, or powers: all things were created by him, and for him" (Colossians 1:16; see also John 1:3 and Hebrews 1:2).

Go to your nearest window and take a careful look at the outside world. What does it mean to you that God Himself fashioned the natural elements you see—as well as the supernatural elements you can't see—for Himself?

Look Up

Make this Scripture the basis for prayer to your all-creative, all-powerful God: "For thus saith the LORD that created the heavens; God himself that formed the earth and made it; he hath established it, he created it not in vain, he formed it to be inhabited: I am the LORD; and there is none else" (Isaiah 45:18).

Just as a book requires an author, creation requires a God.

Move Ahead

God said He created the world "not in vain," but for a purpose: "to be inhabited." Realizing that God made this world, and realizing that you are an inhabitant of it, ask yourself: how responsibly are you caring for it? What actions are you taking as a steward of God's creation? Recycling newspapers, aluminum cans, and other materials . . . keeping check on your use of natural resources . . . getting involved in conservation activities . . . the list is endless. Determine today to be an informed and active caretaker of all that God has given you. His creation deserves special care.

Noah's Ark / Genesis 6–9

4

📖 **Overview:** In the course of its rebellion, humanity becomes so sinful that God prepares to execute the death sentence on the entire race. In grace He directs Noah—a just man who walks with God—to build a great ship in order to escape the coming judgment. Noah obeys God, and while the flood waters purge the earth, the ark preserves human and animal life for a fresh start. After a safe landing on Mount Ararat, God gives new directions and makes new commitments to Noah and his descendants: "I will remember my covenant" (9:15).

Heart of the Passage: Genesis 6

Chapter 6	Chapter 7	Chapter 8	Chapter 9
Preparation for Judgment	Deluge of Judgment	Aftermath of Judgment	Promise of Unrepeated Judgment
Building the Ark	In the Ark	Leaving the Ark	

👣 **Your Daily Walk:** Just imagine:

"You say you sometimes get tired of waiting for God to right the wrongs in your day? Maybe you should quit your job and sign on with Noah & Sons Shipbuilders. They're short of help, and you will be doubly welcome if you know anything about building triple-decker cargo ships.

"Seems nobody's ever tried this kind of thing before. But Noah is convinced God told him to do it. Says he's working against a deadline too.

"The contract calls for 120 years—no more, no less. Ol' Noah figures the Lord wants to give people another chance to turn back to Him. God's not in any hurry. That's because He's long-suffering. But the Lord won't wait forever. When the time comes, it's going to get real wet around here. God always keeps His word—and just at the right time too.

"Well, you can start by sawing those gopher logs into planks. . . ."

Make a list of the faith-inspired steps that Noah took in chapters 6–9. Noah obeyed God by picking up a hammer and saw. What is God asking you to do to join Noah's faithful ranks?

It is character rather than separate acts that will be rewarded or punished.

📄 **Insight:** When Came the Rainbow?

God decreed the rainbow a tangible sign of His promise never again to destroy the earth by flood. However, Scripture does not indicate whether the rainbow had previously existed, and was then chosen by God as a sign; or whether it was a new phenomenon, suggesting a changed climate after the Flood.

5 Babel and the Spread of Nations
Genesis 10–11

Heart of the Passage: Genesis 11:1-9, 27-32

Overview: Chapters 10 and 11 explain the origin of nations after the Flood. Beginning with Noah and his three sons, God repopulates the world. But since the root of sin has not been removed from individuals' hearts, the fruit of sin soon becomes apparent once again in proud, disobedient actions. God deals with human failure by scrambling the languages, causing humanity to disperse over the face of the earth—as God had originally commanded! After describing generations of self-serving humans in general, the narrative shifts to one man in particular—Abram—from whom God will build a new nation.

Chapter 10			Chapter 11		
Descendants of			Old Problem: Pride	New Problem: Languages	New Focus: Abram
Japheth	Ham	Shem			
1 5	6 21	22 32	1 4	5 9	10 32
Family Tree of Noah			Tower of Babel		

Your Daily Walk: What's so important about obeying God? He's patient and forgiving. And He will always give you another chance. Right?

There are no new sins—we just keep rerunning the old ones.

Think back over the opening chapters of Genesis. In the Garden of Eden, God gave Adam and Eve a forest of trees to enjoy, and only one tree to avoid. What happened? They ate fruit from the forbidden tree and were promptly evicted.

After the Flood God gave Noah's descendants one command: "Replenish [fill] the earth" (9:1). Spread out and repopulate the world. How did they respond? "Let us build us a city and a tower . . . lest we be scattered abroad upon the face of the whole earth" (11:4). Once again, divine judgment followed disobedience.

God means business when He gives a command. It is not there to be analyzed or debated or disregarded. It is there to be *obeyed*. Do you believe that? Then complete this sentence: "I will save myself some grief if I obey God today [how?] _____ ."

Insight: 4,000 Years After Babel

How many languages are there in the world today? According to Wycliffe Bible Translators, there are nearly 6,170—only 262 of which have the entire Bible. Some countries represent enormous challenges for Bible translators. There's Papua, New Guinea, with 849 languages; Indonesia with 669; India with 381; Mexico with 241. On the African continent alone there are 1,918 different languages!

The Call and Travels of Abram
Genesis 12–14

6

Overview: Chapters 12–14 describe God's call of Abram to leave his home in Ur (near the Persian Gulf) and travel to a distant but unspecified new land. Abram faces many potential distractions along the way: the death of his father in Haran, a severe famine, the worldly pursuits of his nephew Lot. But God is looking for a man of faith who will trust Him completely to keep His promises. For Abram and his descendants, those promises include receiving a great name, becoming a great nation, and experiencing great blessing in the face of impossible odds.

Heart of the Passage: Genesis 12:1-9; 13:14-18

Chapter 12		Chapters 13–14
Call of Abram in Ur	Travels of Abram in Canaan	Troubles of Abram with Lot
1 3	4 20	
"Get thee out . . . "	" . . . unto a land that I will show thee" (12:1)	

Your Daily Walk: How much room have you allowed in your life for God to redirect your steps? Would you be available to do what Abram did?

Close your eyes and imagine for a moment that you are Abram. God has just told you to pack your belongings and prepare to move. "Move where?" you respond. "To a place I'll show you at the proper time." So you obey. You quit your job, load up your furniture, pack up your family, and head out of town.

Destination: Unknown!

If this sounds farfetched, go back and reread the opening verses of chapter 12, for that is precisely the challenge Abram faced!

What if God should come calling at your house today and say, "Get ready to move!" Or He told you to do something else that just didn't fit into your own master plan for your life. Would you be willing to respond by faith and trust Him one step at a time—for finances, a place to live, a new church, a new circle of friends? During a quiet moment today, take a walk and get alone with God. Be candid with Him. If you're available, tell Him so. If you're not but you want to be, tell Him that too. Then relax and let Him lead.

It is not enough to want to be a useful tool for God: you must be willing to sit still for the grinding that produces the edge.

Insight: Walking in Abram's Sandals

While Abram's *faith* was growing, so was his *stamina*. After walking 600 miles from Ur to Haran, Abram set out at the age of 75 for the land of Canaan—400 miles away. He later made a 400-mile round trip to Egypt for a total of 1,400 miles. Now *that's* a *Daily Walk!*

7 *Covenant with Abraham / Genesis 15–17*

Overview: Today's reading describes the Abrahamic covenant as it was given, confirmed, and symbolized. God's promises to Abraham are given in great detail, confirmed with a unilateral treaty, repeated, and established by the sign of circumcision. But as the years pass with no evidence of fulfillment, Abraham acts in foolish impatience. The result is a son, Ishmael, who will forever cause the heartbreak of his father, constantly reminding Abraham of the price of his unbelief.

Heart of the Passage: Genesis 15

Chapter 15	Chapter 16	Chapter 17	
Abrahamic Covenant Given	Abram's Impatience	Abrahamic Covenant Repeated	Abraham's Obedience
		1 21	22 27
Isaac Promised	Ishmael Born	Isaac Promised	Ishmael Blessed

Your Daily Walk: How would you spend *today* if you thought you might have no *tomorrow*? For Abram this was more than an academic question. With his little army of 318 men, he had just thrashed a band of warring kings, rescued his nephew Lot, and brought back the kidnapped people and goods. Now, in the long, lonely night hours that follow, he is scared. Scared that his enemies might return to continue the battle. Scared that his life might be snuffed out while he is yet childless.

God never promises us an easy time, only a safe arrival.

In his moment of deepest need, with fear eating away at his faith in God, he hears a voice: "Fear not, Abram; I am thy shield" (15:1). God surrounded Abram with His presence, removed Abram's fears, and confirmed His promise. And Abram "believed in the Lord."

What fear paralyzes you most often? Fear of failure? Fear of the unknown? Fear of the past returning to haunt you? Write it down on a large piece of paper, along with the words of Genesis 15:1. Thank God that He can—and will—exchange that fear for His strength and comfort. Then tear that sheet of paper into tiny pieces as you, in an act of faith, give your fear to God and appropriate His peace (Philippians 4:6-7).

Insight: Hagar's Treatment—Abusive or Acceptable?
After 10 years of fruitless waiting for a son, Sarah offered Abram her personal Egyptian maid, Hagar, hoping to produce a son by her. The Hurrian laws from that period describe this as a customary practice. If a son was born, he was regarded as the wife's. But the painful lesson from Ishmael's birth is clear: God's will done in any way but God's way is not God's will!

Destruction of Sodom / Genesis 18–20 **8**

Overview: Chapters 18–20 relate crises arising in the lives of two of Abraham's family members: his wife, Sarah, and his nephew Lot. Lot's life of compromise and worldly pursuits stands in stark contrast to the life of faith demonstrated by his uncle. In response to Abraham's fervent prayers, God spares Lot while destroying his home town for its wickedness and perversion. And yet, even a man of faith like Abraham can stumble when he takes his eyes off God. On a trip to Gerar, Abraham lies about his beautiful wife, Sarah, calling her his sister in order to save his skin from King Abimelech.

Heart of the Passage: Genesis 18

Chapter 18	Chapter 19	Chapter 20
Abraham Prays for Lot	God Destroys Sodom and Gomorrah	Abraham Lies About Sarah
Lot Saved from Destruction		Sarah Saved from Defilement

Your Daily Walk: For the next minute, try to imagine the most difficult miracle God could ever perform. If you were to select the "Miracle of All Time," what would it be? Jot down what comes to mind and, if possible, exchange answers with a friend or family member.

How does your miracle compare with the one described in 18:9-15? *God promised Abraham and Sarah a son.* At first, that may not appear very spectacular, but consider the obstacles God had to overcome. Abraham was 99 years old at the time, and Sarah was 90. For her whole life, Sarah had never been able to bear children. She was now beyond childbearing years. And yet, even the exact time of conception was pinpointed by God. No wonder God posed the question, "Is anything too hard for the LORD?" (18:14).

If you could ask God for one miracle today, what would it be? Help you overcome a past failure? Conquer a dismal self-image? Rebuild a shattered marriage? Write that miracle in the margin of your Bible next to Genesis 18:14. Then stake your claim daily to the warming truth that God specializes in impossible cases.

What could be impossible for the God who created the universe and everything in it?

Insight: Where Is Sodom Today?
After its destruction by brimstone and fire (19:24-28), Sodom never occurs again in the Bible as an occupied city. Today its location lies somewhere beneath the waters at the southern end of the Dead Sea. A nearby free-standing pinnacle is appropriately named "Lot's Wife."

9 *The Abrahamic Covenant*

Scripture Reading: *Hebrews 8:6-12; Galatians 3:6-9*

Step Back

When God first spoke to the humble man of Ur, it marked a new dimension in His relationship with humankind.

Out of His great grace, God made Abram a specific promise regarding his future (Genesis 12). And when He put that promise in the form of a covenant with Abram (Genesis 15, 17), He made it clear to all throughout the ages that He is a God of His word. A God who works through His people to bring His blessing to the world He created. A God whose love and mercy is unyielding, unshakable, and even unfathomable.

Understandably, Abram was a bit doubtful. So when years had passed and God's promised blessing still had not yielded tangible fruit, Abram and Sarai attempted to help Him along. But the results of their efforts would haunt them and their descendants for generations to come.

Look Up

All I have seen teaches me to trust the Creator for all I have not seen.

If only Abraham and Sarah could have trusted God to come through as He promised—in His way, in His time.

Of course, they acted as we would have, didn't they? And yet we have a great advantage over them: They did not have the benefit of the extensive record of God's activities with humanity that we have in the Bible. But we can learn from that record, and trust our sovereign God. His promises are new every morning. And they are for you.

Take a moment to meditate on the promises God has made to you, His child. Read carefully Hebrews 8:6-12 to learn more about the covenant in force right now. And praise Him for His trustworthy love and grace for you.

Move Ahead

As those who believe, we are children of Abraham and inheritors of his blessing, according to the apostle Paul in Galatians 3:6-9. "And the scripture, foreseeing that God would justify the heathen through faith, preached before the gospel unto Abraham, saying, In thee shall all nations be blessed. So then they which be of faith are blessed with faithful Abraham" (Galatians 3:8-9).

Child of God, you are blessed with Abraham. And God intends for you to be a blessing to the world. Is your life an encouragement to those around you? Your family, your fellow workers, your neighbors? Are you showing them the way to your trustworthy God?

Isaac's Birth; Sarah's Death
Genesis 21–24

10

📖 **Overview:** The climax of more than 20 faith-stretching years for Abraham and Sarah comes in the birth of Isaac, their miracle son and heir. But soon Abraham's faith is tested again as God calls upon him to sacrifice that treasured son upon an altar. Abraham obeys, showing that the experiences of the past two decades have not been in vain. For his faithfulness to the point of death, God rewards Abraham with further assurances of blessing. In the closing years of Abraham's life, a time saddened by Sarah's death, there remains one important detail: finding a suitable bride for Isaac.

Heart of the Passage: Genesis 21:1– 22:19

Chapter 21	Chapter 22	Chapter 23	Chapter 24
Isaac's Birth	Isaac's Sacrifice	Sarah's Death	Isaac's Bride
Abraham's Faith Vindicated		Abraham's Faith Verified	

✔️ **Your Daily Walk:** Have you ever wished you had a "timer" that would tell you exactly when God was going to fulfill His promises in your life? A way to tell with assurance when your prayer would be answered for a helpmate . . . the salvation of a loved one . . . the end of an extended illness? Abraham must have wished for such a timer on many occasions as he waited year after year for the son God had promised to give him. But in the birth of Isaac God demonstrated that, though His promises may not come *speedily*, they will come *certainly*. "At the set time of which God had spoken" (21:2), He fulfilled His long-standing covenant.

It's easy to impose your own preconceived timetable upon God's promises . . . and difficult to deal with the frustration and anxiety that result when God doesn't answer "on time" according to your expectations. Try this instead: Copy the words of Genesis 21:1-2 onto an index card and place it next to a clock or calendar you glance at regularly. Let it refresh your memory throughout the day that the timing of the Creator of time is always *perfect*.

Only in obedience can we discover the great joy of the will of God.

📗 **Insight:** The Issue Was Obedience
God's commands to Abraham to offer Isaac did not mean that God was condoning human sacrifice (a common pagan practice in Abraham's day). Rather, God was testing Abraham's faith in His covenant promises. Check Hebrews 11:17-19 and James 2:21-23 for added insight into this event.

11 Isaac's Family and Works / Genesis 25–26

Heart of the Passage: Genesis 25:19– 26:5

Overview: The story of Isaac continues, focusing on his family and work. Though Abraham has died, God's promises to him live on in the persons of his son Isaac and his twin grandsons, Esau and Jacob. Sin, too, lives on—as demonstrated by Jacob's theft of his brother's birthright and by Isaac's imitation of his father's deception. Yet, despite human failings, God's covenant remains sure, as testified in His words to Isaac: "I will perform the oath which I sware unto Abraham thy father" (26:3).

Chapter 25			Chapter 26		
Abraham's Death	Jacob's Birth	Esau's Birthright	Isaac the Deceiver	Isaac the Farmer	Isaac the Well Digger
1 11	12 26	27 34	1 11	12 16	17 35
The Family of Isaac			The Work of Isaac		

Learn to put your hand on all spiritual blessings in Christ and say "Mine."

Your Daily Walk: "God has no grandchildren." Perhaps you've read that statement on a bumper sticker or poster. It means each generation must be personally related to God by faith. It's not enough that your parents trusted Christ as their Savior; *you* must make a commitment yourself. Similarly, your children are not saved simply because you are. It is a personal, individual decision. You become a child of God by faith in Christ. So do your children . . . and your grandchildren. Seen that way, it's clear that God has no grandchildren!

And so it is with the promises of God. Each succeeding generation must learn to claim them personally in order to enjoy their benefits. God has promises for you today that Christians have been claiming for centuries.

Check up on your relationship with Christ. Is it strictly firsthand, based on personal faith in Christ's finished work on the cross? Or are you relying on secondhand knowledge from your parents, your church, or your friends to get you through? You can become a child of God right now by believing on His Son (John 1:12). And then you can discover the joy of finding God's timeless promises true in your own life. But the choice is yours. God said, "I will . . ." What do *you* say? Say it to your heavenly Father right now!

Insight: A Family Tradition
The Cave of Machpelah in Hebron, originally purchased by Abraham from Ephron the Hittite as a tomb for Sarah, would soon become the burial place for Abraham himself (25:9); Isaac, Rebekah, and Leah (49:30-31); and Jacob (50:13).

Jacob's Birthright and Dream
Genesis 27–31

12

Overview: Chapters 27–31 introduce the third major character of the patriarchal period: Jacob ("deceiver"), a man who truly lives up to his name! The theft of the family blessing intended for his twin brother, Esau, demonstrates his scheming character. But it is through Jacob that God's promises—made more than a century and a half earlier—begin to be fulfilled in greater degree. During a 20-year stay in Haran, Jacob works for one wife and gets three more in the bargain, fathers 11 sons and a daughter, and amasses huge quantities of livestock and servants—the nucleus from which God will fashion a new nation.

Heart of the Passage: Genesis 27, 29

Chapter 27	Chapter 28	Chapters 29–30	Chapter 31
Jacob's Stolen Blessing	Jacob's Dream	Jacob's Wives and Children	Jacob's Quick Exit
Jacob's Spiritual Life		Jacob's Family Life	

Your Daily Walk: For every Jacob, you'll usually find a Laban. For every individual who insists on doing things his own way, giving God a helping hand, there is often a painful head-on collision with someone who is at least his equal as a schemer.

Laban became God's rod of discipline in Jacob's life. There's no doubt God was accomplishing His purpose with Jacob despite his stubbornness and conniving (28:15), but Jacob could have spared himself 20 years of grief if he had learned to wait on God in Canaan.

Waiting for an answer to prayer is often part of the answer.

Have you noticed "The Laban Principle" at work in your own spiritual life? God's stroke of discipline may be applied by a family member, a fellow employee, a creditor. But the goal is always the same: to help you develop spiritual maturity.

Write out a one-paragraph description of exactly what you are going to do the next time you feel like rushing ahead of God. Chances are, before the week is out you'll need it . . . and use it!

Insight: Marital Bliss . . . or Marital Blisters?
The wisdom of God's original one man/one woman blueprint for marriage is illustrated in the sad example of Jacob's household, where jealousy, bickering, and scheming between Leah and Rachel were regular occurrences. Refresh your memory of family life God's way by rereading Genesis 2:23-24. Then look up 1 Kings 11:1-8 to discover another man for whom *multiple wives* meant *multiplied woes.*

13

13 Struggles of Jacob and Esau
Genesis 32–36

Heart of the Passage: Genesis 32

 Overview: In chapters 32–36 Jacob the *schemer* becomes Jacob the *servant* of God. After leaving his uncle Laban, Jacob fears the inevitable reunion with his estranged brother Esau. But before he can be reconciled to Esau, he must first be reconciled to God. At the Jabbok River he wrestles with the angel of Jehovah, insisting on a blessing before he will release him. The angel assures him of God's continued presence, and leaves him with a new name (Israel, "God strives") and a permanent limp. After an emotional reunion with Esau, Jacob returns to Canaan, where God confirms His promises to Abraham and Isaac—promises of a large posterity and a new homeland.

Chapter 32	Chapter 33	Chapter 34	Chapters 35–36
Jacob's Encounter with an Angel	Jacob's Encounter with Esau	Dinah's Encounter with Shechem	Jacob's Encounter with God
Jacob's Struggles with Esau		Jacob's Family Struggles	

Your Daily Walk: Is it possible to be a rich Christian in the will of God?

A steward is one who owns nothing, yet is responsible for everything.

That question would have brought a chuckle from Abraham or Jacob. Both men were fabulously wealthy in their day. Jacob in particular shows how a person, blessed by God, can gain great amounts of earthly goods. His own personal testimony is found in 32:10: "I am not worthy of the least of all the mercies, and of all the truth, which thou hast showed unto thy servant; for with my staff I passed over this Jordan; and now I become two bands [caravans]." When he first crossed the Jordan, all Jacob owned was the staff in his hand and the clothes on his back. Now, some 20 years later, it takes two companies of men to carry all of God's blessings back across.

Reflect on the material possessions God has given you. Could it be that God has prospered you so that you in turn might be a blessing to others? And if so, who are the "others" God has brought into your life for that purpose? If God brings someone to mind, write that individual's name in the margin. Then let Jesus' own words in Acts 20:35 spur you to action today!

Insight: When God Prospers Someone, Look Out!

Beginning with nothing, Jacob amassed such wealth over 20 years that when he left for Canaan he could afford a gift of 580 animals to his brother Esau without straining the family budget!

Placing the Books of Genesis & Exodus

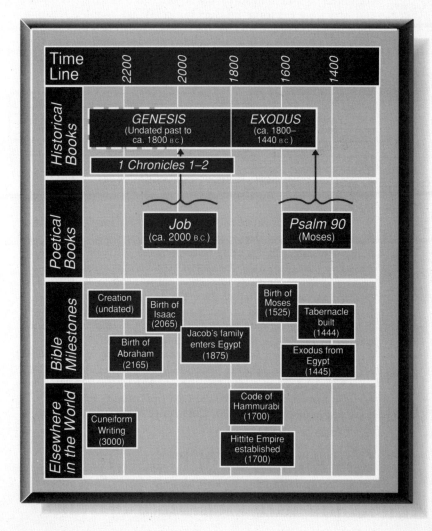

Time Line	2200	2000	1800	1600	1400
Historical Books		GENESIS (Undated past to ca. 1800 B.C.)	EXODUS (ca. 1800–1440 B.C.)		
	1 Chronicles 1–2				
Poetical Books		Job (ca. 2000 B.C.)		Psalm 90 (Moses)	
Bible Milestones	Creation (undated); Birth of Abraham (2165)	Birth of Isaac (2065)	Jacob's family enters Egypt (1875)	Birth of Moses (1525); Exodus from Egypt (1445)	Tabernacle built (1444)
Elsewhere in the World	Cuneiform Writing (3000)		Code of Hammurabi (1700); Hittite Empire established (1700)		

15

14 *Joseph's Enslavement / Genesis 37–40*

Heart of the Passage: Genesis 37, 39

Overview: Beginning with chapter 37, the narrative focuses on the next generation: Joseph, dreamer of dreams. Though the favorite son of his father Jacob, Joseph alienates himself from his brothers by his forthrightness. Envy grows into hatred, until finally the brothers sell him into slavery. Taken to Egypt, Joseph continues to suffer injustices, first at the hands of Potiphar's wife, and later from the forgetful chief butler. While Joseph is resisting the temptation of immorality, his brother Judah falls prey to the same sin. Clearly something is needed to insulate the chosen family from moral corruption for the next four centuries while it multiplies into a mighty nation.

Chapter 37	Chapter 38	Chapter 39	Chapter 40
Joseph Sold	Judah Shamed	Joseph Framed	Joseph Forgotten
Beloved Son in Canaan		Trusted Steward in Egypt	

Your Daily Walk: "I know some of the things I do to be accepted by my friends are wrong. But if I don't go along, they'll laugh at me!"

The best of saints have borne the worst of sufferings.

Joseph could relate to that statement. He learned firsthand the consequences of doing what was right. He could have avoided much discomfort by deciding to disobey his father or give in to Mrs. Potiphar. Loyalty to his convictions carried a price tag.

But faithfulness had its compensations too. Note the repeated expression in chapter 39: "The LORD was with Joseph." Now, which would you rather be: a guilt-ridden brother trying to explain Joseph's disappearance, Judah trying to untangle the mess created by his lack of restraint, Potiphar's frustrated wife, or Joseph? Only one of those individuals was truly free. (Which one?)

Where is compromise threatening to dull the cutting edge of your faith? Ask God to give you the courage to stand true to Him with love and tact. Then take the next opportunity to set the record straight and make your convictions known to all parties involved.

Insight: Clothes Mark the Man

Joseph's famous "coat of many colors" was probably an ornamented, ankle-length coat with long sleeves. It identified the wearer as a favorite son and perhaps indicated Jacob's intent to make Joseph chief heir of the family fortune.

Joseph's Egyptian Rule / Genesis 41–44 15

Overview: A difficult dream sent by God to Pharaoh jars the memory of the chief butler, and Joseph is promoted from prisoner to prime minister because of his God-given insight. The dream is a reliable forecast of the prosperity and famine in the years ahead. The worldwide famine prompts Jacob to send 10 sons to Egypt for grain, where Joseph, recognizing them immediately, proceeds to teach them a painful lesson. A series of confrontations builds up to the climax in chapter 44, where the brothers unknowingly fulfill the boyhood dreams of Joseph.

Heart of the Passage: Genesis 43–44

Chapter 41		Chapter 42	Chapter 43	Chapter 44
Pharaoh's Vision	Joseph's Vindication	Brothers' Visit	Benjamin's Visit	Joseph's Vengeance
1 36	37 57			
Joseph Exalted from Prison		Brothers Humbled in the Palace		

Your Daily Walk: There has yet to be a truly "secret sin."
For years, Joseph's brothers had lived with their cunning deception of Jacob. The secret was so complete that Jacob probably blamed himself for the loss of his favorite son. And the other sons, though seeing the agony of soul experienced by their father, maintained their conspiracy of silence at his expense.

Sins concealed by man are never canceled by God.

But they overlooked one witness to their crime—God. As Judah discovered, "God hath found out the iniquity of thy servants" (44:16). God gave them time to set things right on their own. Then He applied pressure. The result was a band of frightened men who seemed to be haunted by the memory of their lost brother. Guilt, anxiety, and uncertainty were their constant companions until their wrong was set right through confession and restoration.

As a sinner in the presence of God, you have two choices. You can carry the anxiety of your "secret" sins until God chooses to expose them. Or you can confess those sins to God and to those you've wronged, and as a result find forgiveness and peace. Because of Christ's death, you can take steps today to make things right with a brother or sister, pastor or neighbor, spouse or roommate. Will you do it?

Insight: Whatever Happened to the Tribe of Joseph?
Joseph's sons, Manasseh and Ephraim, were later "adopted" by Jacob (48:5). Consequently, the descendants of Joseph would later comprise two tribes of Israel, named respectively for his two sons.

16 *Joseph's Family Honored / Genesis 45–47*

Heart of the Passage: Genesis 47

Overview: Joseph, no longer able to maintain the masquerade, reveals his true identity to his terrified brothers. His explanation of recent events (45:5-8) reveals the spiritual perspective that sustained him through years of heartache and uncertainty. In keeping with the prophecy given to Abram (15:13), God assures Jacob that a sojourn in Egypt is divinely approved. And so the entire Jewish population (70 in number) moves to Goshen, which will become home for the fledgling nation for the next 400 years.

Chapter 45	Chapter 46	Chapter 47
A Brother Resurrected	A Family Reunited	A Father Rewarded
Joseph's Secret	Jacob's Sojourn	Jacob's Satisfaction

When God measures the greatness of an individual, He puts the tape measure around the heart, not the head.

Your Daily Walk: The contrast must have been striking. Into the court of the most powerful king on earth hobbled an old man dressed in the rough garb of a Bedouin tent dweller. Pharaoh was granting an audience to Jacob out of respect for Joseph. And Jacob, the seemingly insignificant old man, blessed the king (47:7-10)!

Pharaoh didn't know it, but he was being blessed by none other than Israel, the Prince of God. For all his supposed importance, Pharaoh would subsequently fade into oblivion. Even his name would disappear from historical records. Yet this old shepherd would continue to occupy a place of honor throughout the centuries. God's people would be called the "children of Israel," and God would identify Himself henceforth as "the God of Jacob." From Jacob's line would come the King of Kings, who "shall reign over the house of Jacob forever."

Appearances can be deceiving. You, like Jacob, may not look like a V.I.P. in the eyes of the world. But you are. Your importance, like Jacob's, does not stem from what *you* have made of yourself, but what *Christ* has made of you. On a sheet of paper, see if you can complete this sentence 10 ways: "Because I am a child of God, I am _____ ." Then live out your identity today as a child of the King!

Insight: "You Did It . . . He Did It!"
The words "ye sold me . . . God did send me" (45:5) form a classic statement of God's providence. Looking backward, Joseph could clearly see both elements—human and divine—at work in God's plan.

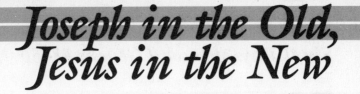

Joseph in the Old, Jesus in the New

In many ways Joseph foreshadows the life and ministry of Jesus Christ. Notice the many similarities between the two.

JOSEPH	JESUS
Was the well-beloved son of his father (Genesis 37:3).	Was the well-beloved Son of His Father (Matthew 3:17).
Testified against his brothers' sin and they hated him for it (Genesis 37:2, 4-5).	Testified against men's sin and they hated Him for it (John 15:18).
Was tempted and did not yield (Genesis 39:7-12).	Was tempted by Satan and did not yield (Matthew 4:1-11).
Judah sold him for 20 pieces of silver (Genesis 37:26-28).	Judas sold Him for 30 pieces of silver (Matthew 26:15).
Was put in the dungeon (the place of death) with two other criminals (Genesis 40:1-3).	Was put on the cross (the place of death) with two other criminals (Mark 15:27-28).
One of the criminals died and the other lived (Genesis 40:21-22).	One of the criminals died and the other lived (spiritually) (Luke 23:39-43).
Was raised from the place of death by the king of the land (Genesis 41:14).	Was raised from the place of death by the King of the universe (Colossians 2:12).
Became the deliverer of his people (Genesis 47:25).	Became the Savior of His people (1 Timothy 4:10).

17 *Final Days of Jacob / Genesis 48–50*

Overview: Chapters 48–50 conclude the book of Genesis by recording the final acts of Jacob and Joseph, along with their deaths and burials. Jacob's blessing upon Joseph's two sons, announcing that the younger would be more honored than the older, is in keeping with the pattern established in Genesis (Isaac instead of Ishmael, Jacob instead of Esau, Joseph instead of Reuben). As his final earthly act, Jacob blesses each of his 12 sons, giving a divinely guided pronouncement of their future history. Jacob's body is embalmed and taken back to Canaan for burial, while Joseph's body remains in Egypt until the release of the newly born nation of Israel.

Heart of the Passage: Genesis 50

Chapter 48	Chapter 49	Chapter 50	
Joseph's Sons Blessed	Jacob's Sons Blessed	Jacob's Death and Burial	Joseph's Death
		1 21	22 26
Jacob's Last Days		Joseph's Last Days	

Your Daily Walk: Do you sometimes wish your life could count more for God . . . that you could have more of an impact for good in the lives of those around you? You plod along faithfully, but nothing much ever seems to come of it. In fact, you're tempted to throw in the spiritual towel.

All Christ's blessings are like Him, spiritual and heavenly.

God's plan is larger than any one person. In an amazing way He weaves together the lives of many different people to accomplish His will. Joseph is a good example. Torn from his family, ill-treated and imprisoned, he later emerges as ruler in Egypt. And why? "God meant it unto good, to bring to pass, as it is this day, to save much people alive" (50:20). Joseph's family and the entire nation of Egypt soon owed their survival to Joseph's leadership.

How many lives do you touch every day? Make a mental list. The number might surprise you! Your spouse, your parents, the kids, the boss, the teacher. Don't forget the neighbors, the people in your office, the mailman, the cashier.

Select one name and one way God could use you to touch that life with a smile, a kind word, a thoughtful act. Then allow God to use you today . . . for good.

Insight: Egyptian Mortuary Service
Embalming usually took 40 days and was available in several different price ranges. When completed, the coffin was left standing upright against the wall of the burial chamber.

Exodus

During the nearly 400 years since the close of Genesis, the descendants of the patriarchal family have experienced good news and bad news. The good news: They have grown into a nation numbering several million. The bad news: They have become oppressed slaves in the land of Egypt. Exodus is thus the book of redemption from bondage to Pharaoh into a covenant relationship with God. From Egypt to Sinai, Israel learns of the might and power of God, and of the importance of national worship.

Focus	Slavery		Salvation				Sanctification			
Divisions	Birth of Moses	Call of Moses	Conflict with Pharaoh	Exodus from Egypt	Red Sea Crossing	Journey to Sinai	Laws and Ceremonies	Tabernacle Blueprint	Golden Calf	Tabernacle Dedication
	1	2 3	6 7	10 11	12 13	15 16 18	19 24	25 31	32 34	35 40
Topics	Deliverance from Oppression						Preparation for Worship			
	Getting Israel out of Egypt						Getting Egypt out of Israel			
Place	In Egypt		On the March				At Sinai			
Time	430 Years (15% of Exodus)		2 Months (30% of Exodus)				10 Months (55% of Exodus)			

18 *Israel's Bondage / Exodus 1–2*

Heart of the Passage: Exodus 1:8–2:10

Overview: As Jacob's descendants continue to multiply and prosper in Goshen, they pose a growing threat to the new Egyptian ruler. His plan to kill all newborn Hebrew boys is thwarted by the courageous midwives, and in this context of danger the child Moses is born. Destined to become the deliverer of God's people, Moses enjoys the finest of education in Pharaoh's court. But when he seeks to deliver Israel in his own time and way, Moses finds himself fleeing for his life to the desert of Midian. There he spends the next 40 years tending sheep and awaiting God's instructions for freeing His people.

Chapter 1		Chapter 2	
Israel's Growth in Egypt 1　　　　　6	Israel's Groaning in Egypt 7　　　　　22	Moses' Birth in Egypt 1　　　　　15	Moses' Training in Midian 16　　　　　25
Egypt the Oppressor		Moses the Deliverer	

Patience is a virtue that carries a lot of wait!

Your Daily Walk: Where are you currently enrolled in God's "School of Patience"? Put a check next to the "classroom" where you are learning the most right now about bearing up under difficult circumstances:

_____ Home _____ School _____ Work
_____ Church _____ Marriage _____ Hospital

Moses learned patience in the desert as he tended sheep. Unknown to him, God was using those years as part of a tailor-made program to prepare Moses for shepherding a much larger flock—the emerging nation of Israel. Only when Moses was truly ready did God appear to him in the burning bush and send him back to Egypt.

God's patience-building process may seem agonizingly slow to you, but remember, your response to God's "tutoring" is all-important. How fast are you learning the lessons you need to master in order to be ready for greater service when He calls? Right now, complete this prayer. "Dear Lord, because I know You want to use me in a significant way, please help me to learn the lesson in patience You have set before me today as I _____."

Insight: A Deadly Law for Men Only

Pharaoh's plot to kill all newborn Hebrew males not only would have curtailed the rapid growth of the Israelites, but would later have encouraged intermarriage between Hebrew women and Egyptian men, causing the people of Israel to lose their national identity.

Moses' Call and Credentials / Exodus 3–6 **19**

Overview: With his long period of desert exile drawing to a close, Moses becomes God's choice to lead the people out of bondage. When confronted by God in the burning bush, Moses is far from convinced he is the right man for the job! But once his objections have been answered, Moses goes forth to confront Pharaoh, armed with supernatural signs. True to God's prediction, Pharaoh not only refuses to let the people go, but increases their labors as well. As the people react with anger, God responds with assurance that His nation will indeed be redeemed.

Heart of the Passage: Exodus 3; 5:1– 6:13

Chapter 3		Chapter 4	Chapter 5	Chapter 6
Moses' Call	Moses' Commission	Moses' Companion	Moses' Confrontation	
			with Pharaoh	with God
1 8	9 22			
God's Man for Deliverance			God's Plan for Deliverance	

Your Daily Walk: Put yourself in Moses' sandals. You have been sent by God to deliver a people who have groaned under the burden of slavery for centuries. Upon your arrival, you encounter their oppressor, Pharaoh, and deliver the message God gave you. But instead of making things better, you only make them worse! You watch helplessly as Pharaoh increases the burden on your countrymen. What is your response?

Probably you'd do the same as Moses: Cry out to God in frustration. Perhaps you *have* been in Moses' sandals before if you have experienced the failure of a project you attempted for God. If so, God's fresh revelation of Himself—who He is, what He has done in the past, and what He promises to do in the future—should be as much of an encouragement to you as it was to Moses! God's *promises* are grounded in God's *character*. That's all Moses needed to know.

The same never-changing God who sustained a discouraged shepherd can do the same for you in difficult times. Find a hymnbook and browse through some of the faith-building refrains composed by those who learned firsthand that God is faithful. Their God is your God—and aren't you glad!

It is God's resound- ing "I AM" that drowns out our weak "I can't."

Insight: Take Away the Stubble, and You've Got Trouble
Bricks made with straw are stronger than those lacking it, because chemicals released by the decomposing straw make the clay more pliable and homogeneous. Archaeologists report that numer- ous structures built in biblical times with sun-dried bricks are still standing today.

20 *First Nine Plagues / Exodus 7–10*

Heart of the Passage: Exodus 7

📖 **Overview:** When a person will not obey God *willingly*, God will often bring to bear circumstances that force him to obey God *unwillingly*. Such is the case with the reluctant Pharaoh of Egypt. God sends a series of nine national calamities involving insects, disease, and nature, in order to impress upon Pharaoh the importance of obedience. In halfhearted rebellion, Pharaoh repeatedly refuses to honor his promises and release the people. The stage is set for the tenth and climactic plague.

Ch. 7	Chapter 8			Chapter 9			Chapter 10	
Nine Good Reasons to "Let My People Go":								
Blood	Frogs	Lice	Flies	Murrain	Boils	Hail	Locusts	Darkness
	1　　15	16　　19	20　　32	1　　7	8　　12	13　　35	1　　20	21　　29
The gods of Egypt vs. the God of Israel (12:12)								

Those who say "No!" to God shouldn't be surprised when the locusts come calling.

✔️ **Your Daily Walk:** Darkness and hail . . . locusts and flies . . . frogs and blood—what possible connection could there be between the 10 plagues? Did God have a reason for selecting those particular calamities? Why didn't He use high taxes . . . air pollution . . . inflation . . . "chariot recalls"—you know, the kinds of things we wrestle with today?

The key is found in 12:12: "Against all the gods of Egypt I will execute judgment." *Every one of the 10 plagues represented an attack on an object of worship in Egypt:* the Nile River, the sun god Re, the frog-goddess Haqt, the fly-god Uatchit, the protector-god Seth (who supposedly kept away locusts), the Pharaoh himself. The Egyptians had forsaken the Creator and in His place substituted the creation. So God used 10 "visual aids" to turn their eyes (and their worship) back to Him.

And that raises a penetrating question: If God were to bring 10 plagues upon your nation today—10 attacks upon objects of worship in your land—what might He use? Is there any evidence that He is doing precisely that? If so, what should your response be in the light of Pharaoh's sad experience?

📰 **Insight:** If You Thought *Yesterday's* Plague Was Bad . . .
Each succeeding plague was more intense and severe than its predecessor. The first four plagues produced only discomfort for the people. The fifth brought death to the cattle; the sixth produced physical pain; the seventh and eighth brought economic chaos; the ninth induced mental and emotional panic; and the tenth brought death to every Egyptian household.

The God *of* Israel
vs. the "gods" of Egypt

"Against all the gods of Egypt I will execute judgment; I am the LORD" (Exodus 12:12). (See Exodus 18:11; Numbers 33:4.)

Plague (Reference)		Special Features	Object of Egyptian Worship*
1.	Polluted Nile (7:14-25)	Dead fish, putrid smell, undrinkable water. Egyptian magicians duplicated plague on small scale but could not reverse it. Lasted seven days.	The Nile itself; Khnum (guardian of river's source); Hapi (spirit of Nile); Osiris (Nile was his bloodstream); various fish dieties; Hapi (crocodiles)
2.	Frogs (8:1-15)	Magicians duplicated plague but could not reverse it.	Hapi and Heqt (frog goddesses both related to fertility)
3.	Dust and Gnats (8:16-19)	No warning given. Magicians unable to duplicate plague. They attributed it to "the finger of God" (8:19).	Seb (earth god)
4.	Swarms of Flies (8:20-32)	Did not affect Goshen, the region where the Israelites lived. Pharaoh first offered two compromises.	Uatchit (fly god)
5.	Death of Domestic Animals (9:1-7)	No warning given. First plague directly affecting personal property. Israelite animals unaffected.	Ptah, Hathor, Mnevis, Amon (gods associated with bulls and cows)
6.	Boils (9:8-12)	No warning given. First plague directly affecting personal health. Magicians unable to appear at court because of boils.	Sekhmet (goddess of epidemics); Serapis and Imhotep (gods of healing)
7.	Hail and Fire (9:13-35)	Most of Egypt gets little or no rain. This storm had no historical parallel. Goshen again left untouched. First of Pharaoh's "confessions."	Nut (sky goddess); Isis and Seth (agricultural dieties); Shu (atmosphere)
8.	Locusts (10:1-20)	Egypt's crop loss: 100%. Pharaoh offers third compromise, second "confession."	Serapia (protector from locusts)
9.	Darkness (10:21-29)	Israel apparently had light in Goshen. Lasted three days.	Re, Amon-Re, Aten, Atum, Horus, Harakhte (sun gods); Thoth (moon god)
10.	Death of the First-born (11–12)	Specifically designated by God as the final plague. Firstborn slain in every Egyptian household. Pharaoh expels Israel unconditionally.	All of Egypt's gods, including Pharaoh himself

*The religion of ancient Egypt is very difficult to analyze, for the Egyptians were one of the most polytheistic people of antiquity. The total number of their gods is uncertain, but most lists include at least 80. Most living creatures and many inanimate objects became the embodiment of some deity (Romans 1:23), and even Pharaoh himself was considered to be divine, on a par with other deities in the Egyptian pantheon (Exodus 5:2).

21 Tenth Plague, Passover, and Exodus
Exodus 11–12

Heart of the Passage: Exodus 12:1-28

Overview: Nine devastating plagues, and still Pharaoh will not budge! But the tenth and last plague, the slaying of the firstborn (of both man and animal) in every Egyptian household brings about the long-awaited deliverance of Israel. To escape the terrible judgment on the firstborn, each Israelite household observes the Passover by substituting the death of a lamb for the death of a child. With no further resistance from Pharaoh, all Israel begins its Exodus from Egypt.

Chapter 11	Chapter 12		
Final Plague	First Passover	Firstborn Destroyed	Final Goodbye
	1 28	29 36	37 51
"Go, serve the Lord, as ye have said" (12:31).			

Insight: Christ, Our Passover Lamb

Notice how the details of the Passover parallel the events surrounding the death of Christ.

The blood of Christ is the seal of the testament.

Passover	Christ
The sacrifice must be a lamb (12:3).	Christ was the Lamb of God (1 Corinthians 5:7).
The lamb must be without spot or blemish (12:5).	Christ was without spot or blemish (1 Peter 1:18-19).
The lamb must be in the prime of life when offered (12:5).	Christ was in the prime of His manhood when He died (John 8:57).
Lamb's blood was shed that Israel might have life (12:23).	Christ's blood was shed that the world might have life (John 3:16).

Your Daily Walk: Death is never pleasant. Multiple deaths are considered disasters. So imagine the national impact when at least one member of each family in Egypt died overnight. But it was all necessary to prove to a stubborn Pharaoh that there is one true God. Deliverance for the Israelites came through faith in the blood applied to their doorposts.

Centuries later, Jesus Christ, the Lamb of God, gave His life to free men from bondage to sin. The question remains: Has His blood been applied to the doorposts of your heart? If so, thank Him again for the suffering He endured for you. If not, what better time than right now to pray: "Jesus, thank You for Your death on the cross. I receive You as my Redeemer from sin and as my Passover Lamb."

Crossing the Red Sea / Exodus 13–15   *22*

Overview: Delivering the people from Egyptian bondage is only the first step in God's plan to bring the Israelites to the Promised Land of Canaan. Many obstacles lie ahead. Pharaoh, whose heart is again hardened, sends his armies in pursuit of Moses and the people. Trapped between the Red Sea and the rapidly approaching chariots of Egypt, the people cry out in desperation— and God answers in a miraculous fashion. The Red Sea parts, the nation crosses over on dry ground, and shouts of panic turn to hymns of praise as the Egyptian army disappears in a watery grave.

Heart of the Passage: Exodus 13:17– 14:31

Chapter 13	Chapter 14	Chapter 15
A Pillar of Cloud and Fire	A Path Through the Red Sea	A Psalm of Moses
Provision	Protection	Praise

 Your Daily Walk: Little children don't always know what's best for them. If you don't believe that, just turn a child loose in an unfenced yard near a busy intersection . . . or leave your medicine cabinet unlocked. No, children don't have the wisdom of adults. That's why God provides parents: to help children survive to adulthood.

When the Israelites left Egypt, they were like a large band of children, not knowing what was best for them. But, like a loving father, God provided guidance, protection, food, water, and instruction to teach them how to enjoy a "grown-up" relationship with Him. Patiently and thoroughly He showed them what it meant to rely on God in every facet of life, to depend upon His daily provision.

Has God placed you in a wilderness situation? Remember, you are there to learn a lesson in trusting God. Attach a safety pin to your lapel or collar today as a reminder of your dependence upon the Father. (It might even give you an opportunity to witness!)

I need never distrust my God for cloth or bread while the lilies flourish and the ravens are fed.

Insight: What Color Is the Red Sea?
The Red Sea is a narrow body of water that stretches in a southeasterly direction from Suez to the Gulf of Arden for about 1,300 miles. Surprisingly enough, the Red Sea is usually bright turquoise in color. However, periodically algae grow in the water. When they die, the sea becomes reddish-brown, thus giving it the name Red Sea.

23 *A Living Sacrifice*

Scripture Reading: Romans 12:1

Step Back

Redemption.

It's unfortunate that word has such a heavy theological ring to it, because it captures the heart of God's work on our behalf.

God redeemed His people from Egypt. And that incident illustrates how He redeems us from slavery to sin, from captivity to the ways of the world.

The word *redeem* means to "obtain release by means of a payment." God illustrates the process with the Passover lamb—the spotless sacrifice shedding its blood as a covering so that God's angel of death might pass over His people. That innocent death was the required payment for the release.

In the same way, Jesus Christ offered the required payment for our release from sin, enabling us to become His children for all eternity. Because of His death on our behalf, we have been redeemed. Purchased for a price. Delivered from slavery. Set free to walk with Him.

And we need not pay the price again. In fact, since the death penalty has been paid, we are now to be consecrated by our life, not by our death. As Paul puts it, "I beseech you therefore, brethren, by the mercies of God, that ye present your bodies a living sacrifice, holy, acceptable unto God, which is your reasonable service" (Romans 12:1).

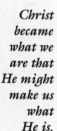

Look Up

Believer, Jesus Christ is your Redeemer. Because of the Father's love for you, He has provided the way out of slavery to sin.

Christ became what we are that He might make us what He is.

But just as the Israelites would face hardships and heartaches after they left Egypt, so you too may face tough times in your walk with your Redeemer. Even so, the Israelites had a pillar of fire and smoke to guide them; you have the Holy Spirit in your heart and the Word of God in your hands to guide you.

In prayer, thank God for redeeming you, and for providing all you need as you continue along life's path.

Move Ahead

Today, anytime you pay for an item with cash or by writing a check, let that action remind you of the payment God has made for you. Your debt has been paid in full by the Savior in His redeeming sacrifice on the cross.

And why not take the opportunity to share a word of testimony to the person you're paying?

Journey to Sinai / Exodus 16–18

Overview: When Israel left Egypt, there were two things the people could do well: make bricks and complain. They now develop the latter ability to a fine art. As supplies decrease, complaints increase. When their resources run out, God supplies manna, quail, and water in abundance to demonstrate that He is now their reliable source of supply. Israel fights (and wins) its first military battle. And Moses, following the advice of his father-in-law, delegates some of his responsibilities to 70 capable assistants.

Heart of the Passage: Exodus 16:1– 17:7

Chapter 16	Chapter 17		Chapter 18
Hunger in the Wilderness	Thirst in Rephidim	Victory over Amalek	Victory over Exhaustion
1	7 8	16	
Grumbling	Fighting		Delegating

Your Daily Walk: Start with a basic, two-door sedan loaded with luggage. Add a father, mother, and three children under the age of 10. Aim the car at a destination 500 miles down the road (such as Grandma's house). After 350 miles have passed, examine the scene. What shape is the "traveling circus" in now?

Com- plaining is the art of collecting petty annoy- ances.

Magnify that basic situation 600,000 times over, move it back some 3,500 years, and you begin to understand Moses' predicament in Exodus 16. The thrill of freedom and the excitement of the Exodus were soon erased by the discomforts of travel. Gratitude gave way to grumbling during the long desert trek.

Are you inclined to complain when things don't go as you think they should? Moses' words to Israel are timeless: "Your murmurings are not against us, but against the LORD" (16:8).

On the other hand, one of the best indicators of your love for God is a contented spirit that expresses itself in thanksgiving. Get out your best stationery and write a thank-you note to God for some of the blessings you may have been taking for granted: health, peace, family, friends, employment, personal freedoms. Then mail it to yourself. In a day or two, you'll be twice blessed to read it again!

Insight: What's on the Menu?
Though God faithfully provided manna for 40 years, it should not be assumed that manna was the sum total of Israel's diet. They took numerous herds and flocks out of Egypt (12:38; 17:3) and were able to buy other food and water along the way (Deuteronomy 2:6-7).

25 *The Ten Commandments / Exodus 19–20*

Heart of the Passage: Exodus 20:1-17

Overview: For the first time in four centuries, the Israelites are free to worship and walk with their holy God. But how do they approach God? What are His righteous demands? At Mount Sinai Moses prepares the people to receive the Commandments, a body of law which they promise to obey—even before it is delivered! After two days of purification, the nation witnesses an awesome display of God's majesty as He descends in a thick cloud to deliver the Ten Commandments, the broad moral principles which will guide the new nation and set it apart from its pagan neighbors.

Chapter 19		Chapter 20	
Cleansing the People	Cautioning the People	Commanding the People	Comforting the People
1 15	16 25	1 17	18 26
Thunder and Clouds		Ten Commandments	

Your Daily Walk: What is missing in the following story?

If God had wanted a permissive society, He would have given us the Ten Suggestions.

A brain surgeon is at home planting a garden when he receives word that an emergency case needs his immediate attention. He jumps in his car, drives to the hospital, strides into the operating room, and immediately begins to operate on the dying man. . . .

Two items are clearly missing: (1) the all-important step of scrubbing up before the surgery, and (2) the name of a good lawyer to handle the almost certain malpractice suit!

Just as a doctor must scrub up before surgery, so must the Christian "scrub up" before entering the presence of a holy God in worship and prayer. The Israelites participated in symbolic acts of cleansing (19:10) in preparation for God's descent on Mount Sinai. The same God who desired purity from the Israelites requires pure hearts from those who approach Him today (Psalm 66:18; 1 John 1:9).

Is unconfessed sin soiling your relationship with God and keeping you from fellowship with Him? Talk to Him about that now. Then put a bar of soap by your Bible to remind you of the importance of scrubbing up regularly in your walk with God.

Insight: When It Comes to God's Law, Take It Personal!

Though the Law was designed to govern the conduct of a nation, Exodus 20 uses *thou* (singular), not *ye* (plural), showing that the character of a nation depends upon the proper conduct of its citizens.

Civil and Ceremonial Laws
Exodus 21–24

26

Overview: At Mount Sinai God delivers to Israel's leader not just the Ten Commandments, but also an extensive body of civil and ceremonial laws designed to regulate all aspects of Israel's life. The section you will read today contains the civil and social regulations which comprise "the book of the covenant" (24:7). Levites and priests, offerings and feasts, services and sacrifices—all are dealt with in meticulous detail. After receiving assurances from the people, "All that the LORD hath said will we do" (24:7), Moses returns to the mountain, where for 40 more days he receives additional instructions from the Lord.

Heart of the Passage: Exodus 24

Chapter 21	Chapter 22	Chapter 23	Chapter 24
Law of Relationships	Law of Restitution	Law of Priests and Feasts	Law on Tablets of Stone
Civil		Ceremonial	Certain

Your Daily Walk: What does the Bible have to say about television? How about Sunday football? Where would you turn in your Bible to find day-care centers discussed? Or movies? Or smoking? What about birth control? Or rock music? Or recreational vehicles? Or horoscopes?

If you go to your Bible expecting a detailed answer for every situation you encounter today, you will come away disappointed and discouraged. Even the seemingly exhaustive regulations of chapters 20–23 leave as much unsaid as they do said! But where God has seen fit not to provide particulars (either in Moses' day or in yours), He has supplied principles which help you to determine God's mind in every situation. His Word, though ancient, is always relevant!

Prove it to yourself. Start with the list of 20th-century activities from the opening paragraph of "Your Daily Walk" (and add it to other activities you may be wrestling with). Can you suggest a principle from your reading of chapters 20–23 that will help you determine your level of participation in each of those activities? (Caution: Wives, football is not included under Exodus 20:13.)

Expedients are for the hour; principles for the ages.

Insight: The Mosaic Law, Expanded Version
In Exodus 20:1-17 God gives the law in summary fashion, and in 20:22–23:19 He provides a detailed amplification. In the first section God lays down broad moral principles; in the second He gives specific applications of those principles to everyday life.

27 *Plan for the Tabernacle / Exodus 25–27*

Heart of the Passage: Exodus 26

Overview: What exactly was it that took Moses 40 days to write down while on Mt. Sinai? As you read today's section (and the chapters that follow), you will discover the answer! Moses is receiving from God the detailed blueprint for the "church in the wilderness"—the tabernacle which would be Israel's place of worship. In minute detail Moses learns about the furnishings, coverings, curtains, and courtyard. Everything is to be built "according to the fashion . . . which was shewed thee in the mount" (26:30). The description moves from the inside out, reflecting not the perspective of man looking in, but of God looking out. True religion originates with a holy God.

Chapter 25	Chapter 26	Chapter 27
Blueprint for the Tabernacle . . .		
Furnishings	Coverings	Courtyard
Pattern of Worship	Place of Worship	

Life ought not merely to contain acts of worship; it should be an act of worship.

Your Daily Walk: Put down this devotional guide. Close your eyes. Visualize the living room in your house, and make a mental list of every piece of furniture and decorative item in it. Now can you do the same with the furniture in the tabernacle? (Hint: There are four pieces inside and two outside.) Can you recall the *function* of each? More important, can you identify one *picture* which each *piece* suggests regarding the person and work of Jesus Christ, who came to "tabernacle" with men and women forever? (If you have time, reading Hebrews 8–10 will make the tabernacle unforgettable!)

Insight: Arrangement of the Tabernacle

HOLY PLACE
Altar of Incense
Candlestick
Table of Shewbread

Bars and Boards

Inner Veil

HOLY OF HOLIES
Ark of the Covenant

Coverings and Curtains

Gate

Laver

Brazen Altar

The Way to the Father

28

Scripture Reading: Hebrews 10:1-39

Step Back

As you read through Exodus 25–27 yesterday, you may have had a difficult time relating to all the details about Israel's mobile worship center, the tabernacle. But step back for a moment to view the big picture—a picture of our relationship with God.

The various aspects of the tabernacle—the furnishings, the coverings, the courtyard, the furniture—all symbolize some aspect of our life with God. We enter the sphere of spiritual life, approaching the Holy One through the sacrifice, being cleansed by the water, and entering the Holy Place in worship and commitment.

Today there is no tabernacle in which to worship. For Israel, the temple became the seat of spiritual life. Today, we may consider our church to be our worship center.

But the tabernacle in its essence pictures the relationship we have as believers with God through His Son, Jesus Christ, who is our High Priest. Moses' tabernacle served as the place where God met with His people, and it symbolized the perfect approach to God we have been given through the blood of Christ, who "tabernacled" with us while on earth (see John 1:14).

Because of His perfect offering of Himself—an unblemished, perfectly acceptable sacrifice made once for all time—we have redemption and eternal life. And because of that, we can enter boldly the Holy of Holies to fellowship intimately with our God.

Look Up

Jesus Christ fulfilled the requirements of God on our behalf, empowering us to live holy lives, enabling us to draw upon His strength and peace. "Having therefore, brethren, boldness to enter into the holiest by the blood of Jesus, by a new and living way, which he hath consecrated for us, through the veil, that is to say, his flesh; and having an high priest over the house of God; let us draw near with a true heart in full assurance of faith, having our hearts sprinkled from an evil conscience, and our bodies washed with pure water" (Hebrews 10:19-22).

Put that passage into practice right now . . . on your knees.

God often visits us, but most of the time we are not at home.

Move Ahead

Through Jesus Christ, you have entered the heavenly tabernacle, to dwell there eternally in the glorious presence of God.

But don't keep that great blessing to yourself. After you read through Hebrews 10 today, look for an opportunity to tell someone else today about the salvation available to them through Jesus Christ, the great High Priest.

29 *Blueprint for the Priests / Exodus 28–31*

**Heart
of the
Passage:
Exodus
28**

📖 **Overview:** After describing the place of worship (the tabernacle), Moses goes on to detail the people of worship (the priests, Israel's representatives before God). Everything about them is special, from the clothing they wear to the elaborate rituals they perform in leading the worship of the nation. Both they and the implements of worship they use require special purification, as befitting those in the service of a holy God. Even the builders who are selected to follow the divine blueprint for the tabernacle are handpicked by God for their skill and Spirit-filled craftsmanship.

Chapter 28	Chapter 29	Chapter 30	Chapter 31
Priestly Clothing	Priestly Consecration	Priestly Conduct	Tabernacle Craftsmen
Preparation for the Minister		Preparation for the Ministry	

**Does God
seem far
away?
Guess
who
moved.**

🗝️ **Your Daily Walk:** Apart from the symbolism found in the tabernacle, its foremost significance was this: The tabernacle represented God come to dwell among men and women, the beacon of God's presence among His people. In addition, the priest's role was to act as a go-between, a bridge-builder, someone who could stand on behalf of sinful mankind before a holy God.

In the New Testament there is a beautiful blending of these two themes. Where does God dwell today? He continues to dwell among people. How has He seen fit to do this? By indwelling those who have turned their lives over to Him (1 Corinthians 6:19). And whom has He called to be priests today, bringing sinful people back to their holy God? The very ones He indwells (1 Peter 2:9)! You are both the tabernacle God indwells, and the priest God empowers to call men and women back to Himself.

If God were to give you the privilege of building a "gospel bridge" into someone's life today, would you be ready? willing? able? Tell Him so . . . right now!

📖 **Insight:** And Don't Forget the Sabbath Day
The commandment concerning the Sabbath had already been given in the Law. It is interesting that this fourth commandment is mentioned again in conjunction with instructions for the workmen (31:12-17). God had commissioned the people to a work especially sacred; He had provided for carrying out the work by especially equipped men. How easy it would have been for them to imagine that in doing this work they might dispense with the Sabbath observance. God's work must be done in *His* way.

Israel's Idolatry and Moses' Intercession *Exodus 32–34*

30

📖 **Overview:** While Moses receives God's laws on the mountain, the Israelites are busy on the plains below. Concluding that their leader has died in the presence of God, they fashion their gold jewelry into a replica of an Egyptian god and turn the camp into a grotesque pagan party. Moses returns and in righteous anger shatters the two stone tablets, destroys the golden calf, and orders the Levites to purge the camp of the guilty Israelites. But though the newly adopted covenant between God and His people has been shattered (as illustrated in the two broken tablets), repentance and restoration are only a prayer away.

Heart of the Passage: Exodus 32

Chapter 32	Chapter 33	Chapter 34
Worshiping the Golden Calf	Moving the Tabernacle	Renewing the Ten Commandments
Idolatry and Intercession		Recommitment and Renewal

✔️ **Your Daily Walk:** Could it be the golden calf episode (Chapter 32) is also a 15th-century B.C. parable of a 20th-century A.D. phenomenon?

With assurances of the nation's obedience and love (24:7), Moses left to be with God on the mountain. No sooner was he gone than false worship and gross wickedness replaced the flimsy promises which the people had made. Though their lips vowed allegiance, their hearts were far from God. And as soon as their leader departed, the people's true character emerged.

In the same way, the church's Leader has gone to be with God for a time, leaving His church behind to carry out His commands. But worldliness and sin, idolatry and preoccupation, have dimmed His final words to "go . . . preach the gospel to every creature" (Mark 16:15). Idolatry couldn't happen in your life . . . in your family . . . in your church . . . could it? What should you do if it has (1 Corinthians 10:11-14)?

If your face reflected your God, what would you see when you looked in the mirror?

🔦 **Insight:** Reflecting God to the Nation (34:29-35)

Moses remained on Mount Sinai 40 days longer (34:28), receiving additional instructions from the Lord, and again God carved the Ten Commandments onto tablets of stone. When Moses returned to the camp, it was impossible for him to conceal the fact that he had been in the presence of the Lord. His face made that clear to all those around him! Today your task is the same: to reflect the glory of Jesus Christ to others around you. How are you doing with your assignment?

35

31 Tabernacle Erected and Occupied by God
Exodus 35–40

Overview: The book of Exodus closes with the record of how the tabernacle and priestly garments are completed exactly as God instructed. The people donate the materials, and the chosen artisans do the work. Moses inspects the finished product, the furnishings are set in place, and Aaron and his sons are anointed for service. Finally, God declares His satisfaction by filling the tent with His glory. For the next 480 years, the tabernacle will remain the focal point of the nation's worship.

Heart of the Passage: Exodus 36, 40

Chapter 35	Chapters 36–38	Chapter 39	Chapter 40	
Contributions by the People	Construction by the Craftsmen	Consecration by Moses	Finishing the Tabernacle ₁ ₃₃	Filling the Tabernacle ₃₄ ₃₈
Tabernacle Organized			Tabernacle Occupied	

Your Daily Walk: Today you will complete your first month (and the first two Old Testament books) of this year's journey through the Bible. But today's reading will require extra discipline! You have already read much of this material before—in chapters 25–28. There Moses set forth the plan for constructing and erecting the tabernacle. Now in chapters 36–39 you'll study the performance of that plan as Moses' instructions are carried out to the letter, making the tabernacle a reality.

But don't miss the point. *The requirement was 100 percent compliance.* It's like baking a cake. Follow the recipe to the letter and you get a delicious dessert; omit some ingredients or instructions and you get a culinary catastrophe. When it comes to holiness or obedience, halfway measures will not do. You are not to love the Lord with most of your heart, a portion of your soul, and a tithe of your mind.

Revival is nothing more, or less, than a fresh commitment to obey God.

As you carefully read through these last chapters of Exodus, ask God to reveal any areas in your life where you have become halfhearted or sloppy. The ongoing construction of your life as God's temple demands no less care than the building of Israel's tabernacle if your life is to radiate His glory and bear witness of His name to the community around you.

Insight: What Do You Do with Too Much Gold?
In view of the fact that the weight of the precious metals used in building the tabernacle ran into the tons (38:24-29), it is an even greater marvel that the budget for this building project was exceeded by the donations (36:3-7).

Leviticus

I n Exodus, Israel was redeemed and established as a kingdom of priests and as a holy nation. Taking its name from the priestly tribe of Levi, Leviticus shows God's people how they are to fulfill their priestly calling. Led out of slavery and into the sanctuary of God, Israel must now move from salvation into service, from deliverance into dedication. This move involves animal sacrifice for the atonement of the people's sins, and a series of strict laws to govern all aspects of daily life, worship, and service.

Focus	Worship			Walk				
Divisions	Sweet Savor Sacrifices	Nonsweet Savor Sacrifices	Priestly Role in the Sacrifices	Personal Purity for God's People	Day of Atonement	Distinctiveness in the Nation	Holy Priests and Yearly Feasts	Holiness in the Promised Land
	1 3	4 7	8 10	11 15	16 17	18 20	21 23	24 27
Topics	Sacrifice			Sanctification				
	Access to God			Fellowship with God				
Place	Mount Sinai							
Time	About 1 Month							

1 Offerings of Praise / Leviticus 1–3

Heart of the Passage: Leviticus 1

Overview: With the tabernacle completed, God now gives Moses instructions regarding the five types of sacrifices that would be offered in the tabernacle. Three of them—the sweet savor offerings—were voluntary expressions of worship tailored to the person's ability to give. Two—nonsweet savor offerings—were required when sin had broken fellowship with God. In the burnt offering, the worshiper declared his total commitment to God. Through the meal offering he acknowledged that his material possessions belonged wholly to the Lord. By means of the peace offering, the worshiper publicly expressed his thanks or made a vow of spiritual service to God.

Chapter 1	Chapter 2	Chapter 3
Burnt Offering	Meal Offering	Peace Offering
Sacrifices for Those in Fellowship with God		

Insight: Sacrifices for the 20th Century
Animal sacrifices, so essential to Old Testament worship, ceased with Christ's once-for-all-time sacrifice on the cross. Yet Peter tells us that all believers are priests who should continually offer up spiritual sacrifices acceptable to God (1 Peter 2:5).

God knew all about the wicked-ness of the world, and still thought it worth saving.

Your Daily Walk: Today you will read about three Old Testament sacrifices prescribed for each Israelite. But did you know that the New Testament describes at least three "sacrifices" prescribed for each believer—three ways for you to offer a sacrifice to God today?

Instead of a whole burnt offering, you can offer your body as "a living sacrifice . . . unto God" (Romans 12:1). In place of a meal offering, you might offer from your material possessions "an acceptable sacrifice" by helping someone in financial need (like the Philippians did for Paul; see Philippians 4:18). Instead of the peace offering, you could offer the "sacrifice of praise" to God (Hebrews 13:15), a verbal expression of thanksgiving for His care and provision in your life.

Today would be a good time to offer a sweet savor sacrifice to God. Take one of the three sacrifices described above and put it to work by committing each part of your body to God's service (living sacrifice), sharing publicly God's goodness in your life (sacrifice of praise), or writing a check to someone in need (accept-able sacrifice).

Offerings for Restoration / Leviticus 4–7 2

📖 **Overview:** In addition to the three sweet savor offerings, God gives the Israelites two nonsweet savor sacrifices. Both are required when sin has broken fellowship with God. The sin offering—covering sins of uncleanness, neglect, or thoughtlessness—provided restoration for the sinner while teaching the seriousness of sin and its consequences. The trespass offering—covering sins of injury to God and to others—provided not only for the restoration of the sinner, but for compensation to the injured party as well.

Heart of the Passage: Leviticus 4–5

Chapter 4	Chapter 5	Chapters 6–7
Sin Offering	Trespass Offering	A Second Look at the Offerings
Sacrifices to Restore Fellowship		Sacrifices Reviewed

🐾 **Your Daily Walk:** In the margin, list five unpleasant but beneficial experiences from daily life—things you dislike doing, but know they are good for you. (Hint: You might want to start in the dentist's office.)

Life is a long lesson in humility.

If you're normal, you probably don't enjoy the whine of the dentist's drill; but after all the poking and drilling and bitter taste, you find you feel a lot better. Being corrected by a boss when you've made a mistake isn't pleasant either, but afterwards you're glad your boss cared enough to confront you with the truth.

In the Christian life there are some equally painful but profitable exercises—like obeying the biblical principle of restitution. When an Israelite caused injury to another, God's command was clear: "Make it up to him." You, as a Christian, likewise have an obligation to repay those whom you have injured.

Think back over the past week. Is there someone whose character or possessions you have damaged? Have you asked for forgiveness? (That's hard!) Have you repaid what you owe? (That's harder still!) Take the initiative today to offer a trespass offering to God. You'll find the peace of mind and restored relationship well worth the pain.

📓 **Insight:** And If You Need a Model to Follow . . .
Zacchaeus, the tax collector who trusted Christ (Luke 19:1-10), beautifully illustrates restitution at work. The law told a sinner to restore what he had taken or damaged, plus 20 percent. Zacchaeus in his gratitude offered to restore what he had taken *fourfold!*

3 *Israel's High Priest and Yours*

Scripture Reading: Hebrews 7:25-28; 9:1-28

 Step Back

Israel's high priest was the most important man in the religious life of the nation, for only he could offer the atoning sacrifice which God demanded. God still requires an atoning sacrifice for the sins of humanity, but in place of the temporary priesthood of Aaron He has installed Jesus Christ, His own Son, as our High Priest by virtue of His perfect sacrifice of Himself for our sins.

There are a number of striking comparisons between Israel's High Priest and ours:

• For Israel, the *person* was Aaron or one of his descendants; for us, it is Christ Himself (Leviticus 16:3, 32; Hebrews 4:14).

• For Israel, the *place* was the Holy of Holies in the tabernacle; for us, it is heaven itself (Leviticus 16:15-17; Hebrews 9:24).

• For Israel, the *offering* was animal blood; for us it is Christ's own blood (Leviticus 16:14-15; Hebrews 9:12).

• For Israel, the *frequency* was once a year; for us it is once for all time (Leviticus 16:34; Hebrews 9:12).

• For Israel, the *effectiveness* was for the nation of Israel; for us it is effective to save "to the uttermost" (Leviticus 16:34; Hebrews 7:25).

• For Israel, the *duration* was one year; for us Christ's offering provides eternal redemption (Leviticus 16:34; Hebrews 9:12).

• For Israel, in terms of *purity* the high priest needed purification himself; but Christ "is consecrated for evermore" (Leviticus 16:6; Hebrews 7:26-28).

Look Up

The best way to remember people is in prayer.

In the heavenly sanctuary, our great High Priest Jesus Christ dwells forever. Think of Him mediating between you and the Father. Meditate on Hebrews 7:25-28. Remember that Jesus "ever liveth to make intercession" for you.

What concerns will you take to Him today in prayer? What joys and praises? What heartaches or disappointments?

Move Ahead

As Jesus is your Intercessor to God, you can be an intercessor for others, bringing to the Lord in prayer the needs and concerns of your family, friends, and neighbors.

Make a list of the prayer requests you're familiar with. You may even want to contact a few people to learn best how to pray for them. Then take time to pray over the items you've listed.

Remember, "The effectual, fervent prayer of a righteous man availeth much" (James 5:16).

Holy Office of the Priest / Leviticus 8–10 **4**

 Overview: Israel's tabernacle, the place of communion with God through sacrifice, is entrusted to the custody of Aaron and his sons. The priestly corps must undergo a 10-step consecration process and a seven-day dedication period before they can begin their ministry of mediation. God's blessing—made visible by His fiery presence—suddenly turns into a curse as judgment falls on two of Aaron's disobedient sons. Their deaths remind all Israel of the solemn responsibility of serving a holy God. *Obedience*, not *expedience*, should mark the people of God.

Heart of the Passage: Leviticus 9:23– 10:7

Chapter 8	Chapter 9	Chapter 10
Consecration of the Priestly Ministry	Inauguration of the Priestly Ministry	Regulation of the Priestly Ministry
Dedication	Duty	

Your Daily Walk: Nothing is as hard to gain, and as easy to lose, as a good reputation. One philosopher has observed, "To have lost your reputation is to be dead among the living." Perhaps as a child you heard your parents say, "Remember now, what you do and say reflects on us." Your parents were telling you that the family's reputation was either being tarnished or enhanced by your actions.

No one can build a reputa- tion on what he's going to do tomorrow.

Perhaps that is why God responded with such frightening judgment upon Nadab and Abihu. By their carelessness and disobedience, they threatened God's very reputation both inside and outside the nation of Israel—a grave sin indeed.

Your life as a Christian is the only "Bible" some people will ever read. Do you reveal to others a holy God by your commitment to holiness, or do you smear the reputation of God with an inconsistent life? Write out this thought on an index card and carry it with you today:

"God's reputation is at stake in my life. I want to *maintain* it, not *stain* it."

Then each time you are tempted to stray from God's holiness, pull out that card. Read it; think about it; then let God strengthen you to be wholly—and holy—His!

Insight: The Danger of Failing to Live Up to Your Name
Nadab ("noble, virtuous") and Abihu ("God is my father") were in danger of damaging more than the reputation of their God. If allowed to continue in their sinful ways, they would have besmirched both their families and the godly names they carried.

5 Holiness in Daily Life / Leviticus 11–15

Heart of the Passage: Leviticus 11:44-47; 13:59; 14:54-57

Overview: Worshiping a holy God demands a holy people. For this reason God gives Israel a series of regulations dealing with ceremonial uncleanness. Four areas are specified: dietary laws (describing edible and nonedible animals); childbirth matters; leprosy and other skin disorders; and bodily discharges. Each set of commands follows a general pattern. The worshiper's defilement is first described, then the means for regaining his purity are prescribed. It's a lengthy, detailed section—because holiness demands attention to detail.

Chapter 11	Chapter 12	Chapters 13–14	Chapter 15
Purity in Diet	Purity in Delivery	Purity in Disease	Purity in Discharges
Avoidable Defilement	Unavoidable Defilement		

Your Daily Walk: A popular ballad opened with the words, "It's impossible. . . ." And when you read the command in 11:44, "Be holy; for I am holy," you're probably ready to croon right along with the singer!

The Lord has two heavens to dwell in, and the holy heart is one of them.

Isn't God demanding something impossible and unattainable from His people? Isn't He being unreasonable when He says, "Be holy"? Why, from a human point of view, the task seems impossible.

That is precisely the point! It is impossible by human efforts alone to live up to the righteous demands of a holy God. But rather than frustrate you, God wants to teach you. The law was designed to teach the Israelites to be dependent upon God. Just as He provided sacrifices and rituals for cleansing His less-than-perfect people, so He wants to teach you that only through the supernatural provision of a sinless Savior, Jesus Christ, can you hope to achieve holiness.

Paul puts it this way: "As ye have therefore received Christ Jesus the Lord [by faith, trusting in Him], so walk ye in him [by faith, trusting in Him]" (Colossians 2:6). In Christ's strength you can live a holy and pure life. Complete this thought from Leviticus 11:44: *"Ye shall be holy* [how? when? where? with whom?]; *for I am holy."* Then work today on developing the habit of holiness in one area of your life.

Insight: Leprosy Then and Now

It is doubtful that modern-day leprosy (which cripples and disfigures) is the same as Levitical or New Testament "leprosy" (which was a white scaly disease, much like eczema or psoriasis).

Holiness in National Life 6
Leviticus 16–17

Overview: The great Day of Atonement observed each year was Israel's most significant act of worship. On that day, the nation gathered to watch in expectation as the high priest entered the Holy of Holies with the blood atonement which would cover the sins of the entire nation for another year. Because blood was the central ingredient in Israel's national and personal forgiveness, God prohibited the use of blood for any purpose other than sacrifice to Him.

Chapter 16	Chapter 17
Day of Atonement	Defilement by Blood
Holiness of the Nation	

Your Daily Walk: What would you do if God gave you the responsibility of atoning for your own sins? What would *you* offer as payment to satisfy His righteous demands: the deed to your house? your savings account? your awards and achievements? your spotless reputation? As sincere as these offerings might be, they would never be adequate to make amends for your sins.

Each year, as the nation of Israel stood in front of the tabernacle on the Day of Atonement and watched the high priest carry the blood of the sin offering into the Holy of Holies, the people were reminded again that atonement was God's idea. It was *His* provision for forgiveness of sinful men. *He* took the initiative to establish a sacrifice of atonement which provided a blood substitute for the guilty nation.

Just as God provided the way to cover Israel's sins, so too He has sent His own Son as the once-for-all-time atonement for your sins (1 John 2:2). As you rejoice over that wonderful truth, make a list of three friends who need to experience Christ's forgiveness of sins. Pray today for each of the three names . . . and be ready to share a word of testimony when God opens the door.

Insight: No Private Sacrifices Allowed!
The restrictions against private sacrifices outside the tabernacle (17:3-4) were to prevent the people from copying their pagan neighbors, who often poured their blood sacrifices into the ground as food for their gods. Only properly ordained priests in the proper location (the tabernacle) could offer Israel's sacrifices.

7 Holiness for the Individual
Leviticus 18–20

Heart of the Passage: Leviticus 19

Overview: In addition to the regulations governing national holiness, God provides Israel with laws governing personal conduct and purity in relation to the family, the community, and society in general. Because obedience is His primary concern, God requires that violators of His laws be punished, and that the punishment be appropriate to the crime committed. God's strict guidelines for living reflect His desire that His people "be holy . . . for I the LORD am holy, and have severed you from other people, that ye should be mine" (20:26).

Chapter 18	Chapter 19	Chapter 20
Purity in Morals	Practice of Love	Penalty for Disobedience
Holiness for the Individual		

The primary test of life is not service but love for both man and God.

Your Daily Walk: "Thou shalt love thy neighbor as thyself" (19:18) rolls off the tongue with a familiar ease. But putting it into practice is another matter. Of all God's commands, it may be one of the most difficult to keep. The reason? Because *loving* your neighbor means you must be *involved in the life* of your neighbor. That's hard to do because a human being's natural tendency is toward *selfishness*, not *selflessness*.

The Old Testament law was a challenge to keep because it made very specific demands on the individual. If an Israelite had questions about how to relate to his neighbor, the law provided the answers (19:9-18). The New Testament is just as demanding—especially when it speaks of your relationship to your "neighbor." Jesus' story of the Good Samaritan (Luke 10:25-37) makes it clear that your "neighbor" is anyone near you who needs your help and whose need God has equipped you to meet.

Even if you live alone, there are people around you who need your loving involvement. Put God's command to love your neighbor into practice today by seeking out someone who needs help with yardwork, housework, or homework. Assist them in love . . . and treat them as you would yourself!

Insight: "Do Like Me to Be Like Me"
Nearly 30 times in chapters 18–22 we read God's words: "I am the LORD," and, "Be holy . . . for I the LORD your God am holy." Without a doubt, the holiness of the Redeemer is the all-compelling reason for His insistence on practices of purity by the redeemed.

A Deeper Look at Israel's Feasts

8

Step Back

Israel's religious festivals—which you'll read about tomorrow in Leviticus 23—provided God's people with an annual opportunity to look back on the great epochs of their national history, and to look ahead to the time when Messiah would come to fulfill the events pictured in the feasts.

Scripture Reading: Psalm 145

The annual festivals were seven in number. Four were bunched together at the beginning of the year; they portrayed events Christ fulfilled in His first coming. The other three occurred in the seventh month, and pictured events Christ will fulfill at His second coming. The interval between the feasts on Israel's calendar corresponds to the time gap between Christ's first and second comings. This chart summarizes the feasts and their significance:

	Mon.	Day(s)	Feast	Looks Back On . . .	Looks Ahead To . . .
Christ's First Coming	1st	14	Passover	Redemption of Firstborn	Christ's Redeeming Death
		15–22	Unleavened Bread	Separation from Other Nations	Communion of the Saints
		16	Firstfruits	Harvest in the Land	Christ's Resurrection
	3rd	50 days after First-fruits	Pentecost	Completion of Harvest	Sending of Holy Spirit
Second Coming	7th	1	Trumpets	New Year for Israel	Regathering of Israel
		10	Day of Atonement	Israel's National Sin	Israel's National Repentance
		15–22	Tabernacles	Israel in the Wilderness	Israel's National Blessing

Look Up

Our God is a lover of celebration, a giver of joy. The festivals demonstrate clearly the need humans have to gather in triumph and enjoy the life God has given them. Redemption . . . harvest . . . forgiveness . . . the new year—whatever the event, God set forth a way to observe it. And celebrate it.

Let Psalm 145 serve today as your prayer of celebration, honoring the God who gives you life and joy.

There is no such thing as the pursuit of happiness, there is only the discovery of joy.

9 Holy Priests and Holy Feasts
Leviticus 21–23

Heart of the Passage: Leviticus 21

Overview: Privilege often carries with it responsibility, and in the case of Israel's priests, the responsibilities of serving a holy God become quite demanding. The priests must avoid defilement which others might ordinarily experience. They must be without physical defect in order to serve in the sanctuary. They must bear the responsibility for maintaining purity in Israel's sacrificial worship. They must preside at Israel's yearly feasts and sacred assemblies. It is indeed a demanding assignment to lead a nation in corporate worship of a holy God—a privilege not to be taken lightly or entered into casually.

Chapter 21		Chapter 22	Chapter 23
Disqualification of a Priest Through		Duties of a Priest in	
Defilement	Defect	Ceremonies	Celebrations
1 15	16 24		
Holy Priests			Holy Feasts

Your Daily Walk: If you discovered that your dining room had been "bugged," would you have some embarrassing conversations to explain?

It is easier to follow the leader than to lead the followers.

Unfortunately, in many Christian homes the main course for Sunday dinner is often "roast preacher." It's an easy habit to slip into, but one which can produce harm and bitterness.

In Israel's system of worship, the priests carried much of the responsibility for leading corporate worship. Today the church no longer has a "priestly class," but it does have those specially gifted, trained, and set apart for the work of the ministry (1 Timothy 3; Titus 1). Like the priests of Old Testament times, these leaders have given freely of their time and energy in order to lead you in worship.

How often do you "remember them which have the rule over you" (Hebrews 13:7)? Take a few minutes to write a thank-you note to your pastor or church leader, expressing gratitude for the consistent spiritual investment that person makes in your life.

Insight: Probing a Priestly Prohibition

Priests with physical handicaps were excluded from offering sacrifices (21:17-21), though they were entitled to the privileges of priesthood such as eating the priestly portion (21:22). God was not relegating them to second-class status, but merely showing that the special service of sacrificing unblemished animals before a holy God required unblemished priests.

Holiness in the Land / Leviticus 24–27 **10**

📖 **Overview:** The closing chapters of Leviticus contain a variety of instructions for Israel when the people occupy the Promised Land. Oil and bread must be provided for the sanctuary. The death penalty must fall on those who blaspheme the name of God. The land must be given periodic rest during the Sabbatical and Jubilee years. God promises to honor obedience to His commands, and reward disobedience with stern judgment. The work of the Lord must be faithfully supported by the tithes of God's people, and vows must not be entered into lightly.

Heart of the Passage: Leviticus 25

Chapter 24	Chapter 25	Chapter 26	Chapter 27
Provision for the Sanctuary	Protection for the Land	Obedience and Disobedience	Vows and Tithes
Honoring God's Property		Honoring God's Program	

✔ **Your Daily Walk:** Ownership is always a sensitive issue. People are born with an innate desire to possess. Children at play argue loudly, "That's mine!" Though adults usually tend to be more civilized about it, you'll find the same sentiment voiced repeatedly: "I want what's mine!"

God recognized this tendency in His people and instituted the Year of Jubilee to help teach them a crucial spiritual truth. Every fiftieth year, all land that had been sold was to be returned to its original owner. And every acre of land was to remain uncultivated in order to remind the nation that the land belonged not to them, but to God. He would give it to them (25:2), and they would enjoy it—not as owners but as aliens and tenants (25:23).

How do you view your possessions? Do you hold on to them tightly, or have you recognized them as something graciously "loaned" to you by God? Remember, a steward is someone who owns nothing, but is responsible for everything entrusted to his care. To reinforce that truth, take one room of your house and inventory everything in it. Then across the list, write these words: "Mine by stewardship, His by ownership!" Get the picture?

If you owned every-thing your heart desired, chances are your heart would desire some-thing else.

📓 **Insight:** Captivity Foretold
One of the earliest predictions of the Assyrian and Babylonian captivities occurs in today's reading (26:33-35). Israel knew from the start what would happen if the people disobeyed God's word. Yet, centuries later it would come true—to the letter!

Numbers

Numbers is the chronicle of Israel's 40 years of wilderness wandering between Sinai and Moab. Named for the two numberings of the nation, the book begins in the second year after the people left Egypt and ends as the new generation prepares to cross the Jordan River and occupy the Promised Land. Detailing the lives of such men of God as Moses, Caleb, and Joshua, the book of Numbers teaches that while God's discipline may sometimes be severe, He patiently waits to reward those who obey His Word.

Focus	Walking			Wandering			Waiting		
Divisions	Counting and Camping	Cleansing and Congregating	Carping and Complaining	Twelve Spies and Death in the Desert	Aaron and Levites in the Wilderness	Serpent of Brass and Story of Balaam	Second Census and Laws of Israel	Last Days of Moses' Leadership	Sanctuaries, Sections, and Settlements
	1 4	5 8	9 12	13 16	17 20	21 25	26 30	31 33	34 36
Topics	Law and Order			Rebellion and Disorder			New Laws for the New Order		
	Moving Out			Moving On			Moving In		
Place	En Route to Kadesh			En Route Nowhere			En Route to Canaan		
Time	2 Months			38 Years			A Few Months		

Counting the People / Numbers 1–4

11

Overview: The book of Numbers might well be called "the Book of Censuses," for that is how it begins and ends. With the nation of Israel poised at Mount Sinai ready to begin its march to Canaan, God commands Moses to number the fighting men and Levites. A detailed blueprint is given for arranging the people both on the march and in the camp. In the intervening 430 years since Joseph and his brothers moved to Egypt (Exodus 12:40), the nation's fighting force has grown to an impressive 603,550, suggesting a total population of several million.

Heart of the Passage: Numbers 1:1-3, 45-46

Chapter 1	Chapter 2	Chapter 3	Chapter 4
Counting the Nation	Arranging the Camp	Arranging the Levites	Assigning the Levites
Numbering the People		Numbering the Priests	

Your Daily Walk: Censuses are prominent throughout the pages of Scripture. How many different censuses can you recall, excluding the two in Numbers? (If you think 0–1, numbers must leave you numb; 2–3, you can be counted on; 4 or more, you must work for the Census Bureau!)

Even more important than the presence of censuses in the Bible is the purpose behind them: to show that God is a God of order and detail. Confusion and disorder in your home, church, or private life are a sure sign that God-honoring principles are being overlooked (1 Corinthians 14:40). Pick an area of your Christian life where the goal of doing all things "decently and in order" has proven elusive. Write it in the margin, and make it the target of your prayer and planning this week. Remember, if you aim at nothing, you will hit it every time.

Your life can't go according to plan if you have no plan.

Insight: On Your Mark . . . Get Set . . . March!

Leviticus prepared the people for worship; Numbers prepares them for war. After reading today's section, summarize the census and the preparations for the march to Canaan.

- Census of the warriors: _____(total)
- Census of the workers: _____ Levites (1 month upward)
  _____ Levites (30–50 years)
- Largest tribe: _____ Its population: _____
- Smallest tribe: _____ Its population: _____
- Who takes care of the tabernacle? _____
- Who transports the tabernacle? _____

49

Placing the Books of
Leviticus, Numbers, & Deuteronomy

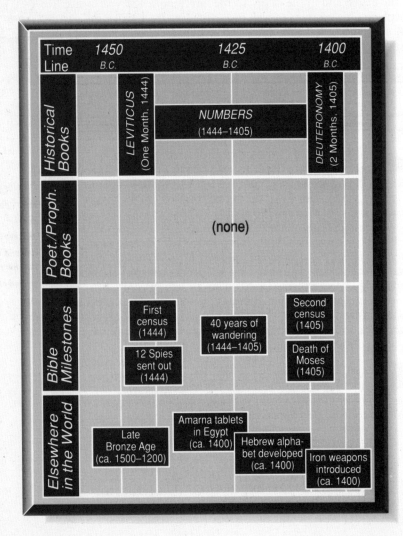

Time Line	1450 B.C.	1425 B.C.	1400 B.C.
Historical Books	LEVITICUS (One Month, 1444)	NUMBERS (1444–1405)	DEUTERONOMY (2 Months, 1405)
Poet./Proph. Books		(none)	
Bible Milestones	First census (1444); 12 Spies sent out (1444)	40 years of wandering (1444–1405)	Second census (1405); Death of Moses (1405)
Elsewhere in the World	Late Bronze Age (ca. 1500–1200)	Amarna tablets in Egypt (ca. 1400); Hebrew alphabet developed (ca. 1400)	Iron weapons introduced (ca. 1400)

Cleansing the People / Numbers 5–8 *12*

Overview: Three weeks remain before the people leave Sinai to begin the last leg of their journey to Canaan. During this time Moses receives certain commands from God designed to cleanse the people and prepare them to enter the Promised Land. They must be free from immorality and jealousy; they must understand the binding nature of vows made to God; the Levites must realize the sacred nature of their calling. Through the generous gifts of the tribal leaders, the tabernacle implements and supplies are provided for the worship of the Lord.

Heart of the Passage: Numbers 6:1–7:11

Chapter 5	Chapter 6	Chapter 7	Chapter 8
Clean Morals	Commendable Vows	Consecrated Offerings	Clean Levites
Defilement	Dedication		

Your Daily Walk: What is the most important tool you will ever use in your service for God? (Write in the margin the first that comes to mind.)

Perhaps you thought of a book, or the Bible, or a God-given ability. Here's another tool you may not have considered: your body.

Any service you render for God in this life will be done through the use of your body. And while you may pride yourself on the way you discipline your mind, your body may be one of the most neglected tools God has entrusted to you.

The Old Testament man or woman who wanted to be used in God's service but was not eligible as a Levite or priest could take the Nazirite vow—a vow that involved abstaining from certain hindrances to holiness in order to be wholly devoted to the service of the Lord. It was a voluntary vow, difficult to get into and equally difficult to get out of. And yet it held the promise of personal blessing for those who successfully fulfilled it.

Is your body available to God today, cleansed and prepared for His use? Romans 12:1–2 will show you how, but only you can volunteer!

The best exercise for strengthening the heart is reaching out and lifting people up.

Insight: No Wine, Hair Cuts, or Corpses Allowed

The requirements of the Nazarite vow might seem strange unless understood in their symbolic sense. Wine symbolized comfort and enjoyment. Death represented defilement. Long hair stood for God-given strength and dignity. By avoiding the former and maintaining the latter, the Nazarite declared his total devotion to God.

13 The People Complaining / Numbers 9–12

Heart of the Passage: Numbers 10:11-13; 11:1-15

Overview: The time has come for the final journey to Canaan. After a special celebration of the Passover, the people watch as the pillar of cloud begins to move. Trumpets blare forth the exciting news: It is time to march! But the thrill of expectation soon gives way to the tedium of travel, and Moses is faced with numerous problems: complaints about the travel conditions and the food, longings for the good old days in Egypt, greedy hoarding of the quail God supplies, and jealousy by Miriam and Aaron toward his position of leadership. In spite of the difficulties, the people finally arrive at Kadesh-barnea—on the doorstep of Canaan!

Chapter 9	Chapter 10	Chapter 11	Chapter 12
A Cloudy Pillar	A Call to March	A Complaining People	A Covetous Miriam
Preparations for the Journey		Problems on the Journey	

Your Daily Walk: How do you react when God's will for you turns out to be inconvenient? Do you think, *Maybe later, God, but not right now.*

Some people ask the Lord to guide them; then they grab the steering wheel.

For Israel, God's will was easily determined by the movement of the cloud covering the tabernacle. When it moved, they moved. When it lingered, they camped. At first glance that may seem like an exciting way to live—but consider the possibilities!

It is 3 A.M. You are sound asleep after a difficult 14-hour march when the quiet desert air is shattered by the blast of a trumpet. Time to march! Or consider another scene. For three days now the cloud has hovered motionless. You sense that any minute it is going to move, so instead of unpacking that bulky tent and all those cooking pots, you just "live off the camel." Another day goes by. And another. Finally, you give in and begin the arduous task of unpacking. No sooner do you drive in the last tent peg when . . .

Obedience to God's will is not always convenient, but it is always profitable! Do you see a pillar of cloud moving in your life? What is it? And what do you suppose you ought to do about it?

Insight: Quail Dinner—All You Can Eat!

When God sent quail in response to the people's complaining, the least amount gathered by one person was 10 homers. One homer is 11 bushels. One bushel is 8 gallons. That makes a total of 880 gallons!

Spying Out the Land / Numbers 13–16 *14*

 Overview: Following the Lord's instructions, Moses selects one representative from each of the 12 tribes to form a scouting party. Their assignment: to spy out the defenses of the land and bring back a sample of the produce grown there. The 12 obey and, like many a committee, return with a divided report! Ten see only the obstacles; two see the opportunities. The nation, disheartened and faithless, threatens to stone Moses and return to Egypt rather than face what lies ahead. As a result, God condemns that unbelieving generation to 40 years of fruitless wandering the wilderness.

Heart of the Passage: Numbers 13:1-2, 26-33; 14:20-35

Chapter 13	Chapter 14	Chapter 15	Chapter 16
A Divided Report	A Deadly Result	A Divine Code of Law	A Premature Death for Korah
Twelve Spies	Wandering	Regulations	Rebellion

Insight: . . . 8 . . . 9 . . . 10 . . . You're Out! (14:22)
On 10 separate occasions the Israelites grumbled and murmured against God. Can you find what prompted each complaint?

Exodus 5:20-21 _____
Exodus 14:10-12 _____
Exodus 15:24 _____
Exodus 16:2-3_____
Exodus 16:20, 27_____
Exodus 17:2-3_____
Exodus 32:1-4_____
Numbers 11:1_____
Numbers 11:4-5_____
Numbers 13:26–14:3_____

So often the first screw that works loose in a person's head is the one that holds the tongue in place.

Your Daily Walk: Every part of the human body gets tired eventually . . . except the tongue! It is no accident the Bible describes the tongue as sharp (Psalm 140:3), biting (Proverbs 25:23), and untamable (James 3:8).

Do you (like the Israelites) have trouble bringing your tongue under control? Then enlist the aid of your spouse or a close Christian friend in "Operation Salty Speech" (Colossians 4:6). Every time he or she catches you in an ungracious remark during the next seven days, you must pay 25 cents. Try it! What you lose in material wealth you'll more than regain in spiritual maturity!

15 Dying in the Wilderness
Numbers 17–20

Heart of the Passage: **Numbers 20:1-13**

Overview: Throughout their wilderness wanderings, the children of Israel are reminded of two things: death and hope. Death as the result of their unbelief at Kadesh-barnea, and hope in the promise that God would still give His people a land of their own. God's authority continues to rest with Moses and Aaron, as demonstrated in the miracle of Aaron's budding rod. And the priests and Levites are still God's chosen servants to lead the nation in corporate worship. But death becomes the constant companion of the Israelites on their march: death in the sacrifices, death of the red heifer for purification, and the death of the high priest Aaron.

Chapter 17	Chapter 18	Chapter 19	Chapter 20
Rod of Aaron	Responsibilities of the Levites	Red Heifer	Rebellion of the People
Establishing the Priesthood		Enforcing National Purity	

Your Daily Walk: Find a hammer, nail, and piece of wood. Drive the nail halfway into the wood; then remove it carefully. What do you have left? (To make this a truly memorable experience, drive the nail into your front door, or substitute your favorite piece of furniture!)

Sin produces a moment of gratification and an eternity of remorse.

That illustration from the world of carpentry provides a parable of the permanent results of sin. Once confessed, sin receives God's full forgiveness (1 John 1:9)—like removing the nail from the piece of wood. But you may not be able to erase fully the scars which that sin has left behind.

Are you, like Moses, tempted to "strike a rock" when God has told you to "speak softly"? Weigh the consequences ahead of time! Christ not only died that sin might be forgiven; He died that sin might be avoided. Thank Him for a scar or nail hole you'll never have to carry because you were willing to say no to sin and yes to Him!

Insight: Heifer in the Old, Savior in the New
Chapter 19 describes God's provision for the people's uncleanness by using water mingled with the ashes of a red heifer. This curious rite becomes clearer in the light of Hebrews 9:11-14 as a foreshadowing of Jesus Christ. Just as the ashes of the sin offering had a purifying effect when applied by water, so Christ's offering for sin purifies all to whom it is applied by the Holy Spirit.

The Brass Serpent and Brash Seer
Numbers 21–25

16

Overview: As the Israelites march to Canaan, they meet and defeat three enemies: the Canaanites, Amorites, and Bashanites. But on the heels of victory they suffer defeat at the hands of a peculiarly persistent foe: grumbling. Because of the people's constant complaining, God sends fiery serpents to chasten His rebellious nation. The threat of Israel's advance prompts the neighboring pagan nations to hire the prophet Balaam to bring down a curse upon God's people. But instead of a curse, Balaam delivers a sweeping witness to the glorious future of Yahweh's nation. What Balaam could not do with his voice, however, is accomplished by his evil influence, as the Israelites give in to idolatry and mixed marriage in defiance of God's law.

Heart of the Passage: Numbers 21–22

Chapter 21	Chapters 22–24	Chapter 25
Conquest and Complaint	Call and Prophecies of Balaam	Calamity in the Camp
Success	Sovereign Blessing	Sin

Your Daily Walk: Find a small piece of sandpaper and tuck it in your pocket or purse. Then read the next few paragraphs thoughtfully . . . prayerfully.

In chapter 21 the nation Israel conquered three national powers. Smashing victories! Stunning triumphs! But for some of the people it wasn't enough. After all, they were still on the wrong side of the Jordan and didn't possess even a spadeful of the Promised Land. Their impatience led to criticism—and criticism to fiery judgment.

One key to consistency in the Christian life is simply giving God time to work. Rough edges take time to smooth. Growth to maturity never occurs overnight. But each day can be a step in the right direction.

Is God using a little sandpaper on your life right now? How can you cooperate with—rather than oppose—the work of the Master Carpenter?

When opportunity knocks, a grumbler complains about the noise.

Insight: Jesus and Numbers—They Go Together!
Look up the following verses to discover how each Old Testament passage provides a preview of Jesus Christ centuries before His birth:
- Serpent of brass (21:4-9; cf. John 3:14)
- Water from rocks (20:11; cf. 1 Corinthians 10:4)
- Manna (11:7-9; cf. John 6:31-33)

17 *Second Census / Numbers 26–30*

Heart of the Passage: Numbers 26:52-56; 27:18-23

 Overview: Now that the journey is virtually over, it is time for a second census—both to assess Israel's military strength and to apportion the soon-to-be conquered territory of Canaan. In addition, it is time to appoint Moses' successor—the one who will lead the people in their conquest. God's choice is Joshua, one of the only two members of the generation which left Egypt to survive the wilderness wanderings and enter the Promised Land. Under Joshua's leadership, the nation will enjoy both military victory and spiritual vitality as they obey God's commands and fulfill their holy obligations.

Chapter 26	Chapter 27	Chapters 28–30
Another Numbering of the Nation	Another Leader for the Nation	Another Code of Worship for the Nation
Census	Succession	Ceremony

Insight: Tallying Up the Second Census (Fill It In!)

Every great person has first learned how, when, and whom to obey.

Tribe	1st Census	2nd Census	Tribe	1st Census	2nd Census
1. Reuben	46,500		7. Ephraim	40,500	
2. Simeon	59,300		8. Manasseh	32,200	
3. Gad	45,650		9. Benjamin	35,400	
4. Judah	74,600		10. Dan	62,700	
5. Issachar	54,400		11. Asher	41,500	
6. Zebulun	57,400		12. Naphtali	53,400	
			Total:	603,550	

Your Daily Walk: After multiplying from a family of 70 to a nation of 600,000 fighting men in the space of about 400 years, Israel actually declined in population during the next 40 years. In part, the lack of growth was because of the numerous judgments God sent to discipline Israel's disobedience: 14,700 dead after Korah's rebellion (16:49); 24,000 dead after following Balaam's teaching (25:9).

Is God enlarging or shrinking your sphere of influence? Jabez, an obscure figure in 1 Chronicles 4:10, prayed, "Oh that thou wouldest bless me indeed, and enlarge my coast. . . . And God granted him that which he requested." God delights in blessing obedient children. Talk to Him about an "expanded border" you want to be entrusted with!

Preparing to Possess the Land
Numbers 31–33

18

Overview: During the final days of his life, Moses is active in at least three roles: commander-in-chief of Israel's army; administrator of the nation's internal affairs; and travel guide, bringing the people to the plains of Moab. The Israelite army, using only a token force of troops, exterminates Midian for its idolatrous influence. Later Moses must deal with the request by the tribes of Reuben, Gad, and Manasseh that they be allowed to settle east of the Jordan. The section closes with a review of the travel route from Egypt to Moab.

Heart of the Passage: Numbers 33

Chapter 31	Chapter 32	Chapter 33
Destruction of Midian	Decision of Reuben and Gad	Description of the Journey
Warfare	Wisdom	Wandering

Your Daily Walk: Numbers chapter 33 is both one of the darkest and one of the brightest chapters in the Bible. It is a dark chapter because it chronicles the journey from Egypt to Moab—a journey that should have taken weeks, but instead consumed four decades plus the lives of an entire generation.

But the picture is not all dark, for chapter 33 also portrays the nation's movement under the watchful eye of God. Guided through barren wilderness, provided with manna from heaven, protected from marauding bands, the people experienced God's tender care daily, even as they felt the sting of His discipline.

Christian, do you view God's discipline in your life as "pain with a purpose"? God loves you too much to allow your disobedience to go unpunished. Having read chapter 33, write these words in the margin of your Bible: "A chapter that should have read differently."

There is a chapter being written in your life today as well. How will it read? Learn a lesson from Israel's mistake—take God at His word. This week's memory verse will remind you to do just that!

The real problem is not why some pious, humble, believing people suffer, but why some do not.

Insight: The End . . . of Balaam, That Is!
Israel's conquest of Midian included the execution of Balaam (31:8). This judgment may seem unduly harsh for the one who had blessed the nation, until it is learned that Balaam masterminded the scheme to defile the Israelites with Midianite women (31:16).

19 *Instructions for Entering the Land*
Numbers 34–36

Heart of the Passage:
Numbers 34:1-15

Overview: The book of Numbers closes with a list of the geographic boundaries of the Promised Land and the names of those who will apportion the land to the 9 1/2 tribes still awaiting the inheritance. Since the Levites are allotted no land, they are given 48 cities scattered throughout Canaan. Laws are established to provide for justice in cases of manslaughter and to protect the inheritance of families who have no surviving male heir.

Chapter 34	Chapter 35	Chapter 36
Borders of the Land	Cities of Refuge	Laws of Inheritance
Geographic Boundaries	Legal Boundaries	

Your Daily Walk: *You cannot enjoy what you do not possess.*

We cannot rely on God's promises without obeying His commands.

God had promised to give His people a great land. You'll find the description of its borders in chapter 34. It extended as far north as Mount Hor and Hamath, as far south as Kadesh-barnea and the river of Egypt (Wadi el-Arish), and as far east as the Jordan River. Sadly, Israel would seldom enjoy the full extent of these promised boundaries. Only briefly in the reigns of David and Solomon would the nation encompass that much territory.

Was God's promise no good? Or was there something else that kept the people from enjoying the full blessing God intended? Every promise has two parts: the promise itself, and the possession of that promise by the person for whom it is intended. God told His nation repeatedly, "Go in and possess the land. It's all yours!" But because of unbelief and indifference, the people settled for God's second best. They could not enjoy what they did not possess.

Thumb back through the Daily Walk sections you've already read this month. Is there a promise you've yet to possess—a blessing from God you've yet to stake your claim to? What are you waiting for?

Insight: Obscure Names, Outstanding Truths

Of those selected by God to allot the land (34:16-29), only Caleb is familiar. But consider the names of others: Shemuel, "name of God"; Elidad, "God has loved"; Hanniel, "favor of God"; Elizaphan, "my God protects"; Paltiel, "God is my deliverance"; Pedahel, "God has redeemed." Names can carry timeless truths, can't they!

Deuteronomy

C omposed mainly of three great orations by Moses, Deuteronomy (which means "second law") is a review of the law given in Exodus. Here Moses recounts God's past dealings with His people and prepares the nation for its arrival in the Promised Land. In Deuteronomy Moses stresses holiness as a way of life and reminds the people of the necessity of obedience to God in every action. Whether possessing the land, defeating the enemy, or simply enjoying life in a new homeland, God's people must exhibit complete obedience to His commands.

Focus	Remembrance			Reminder			Refrain	
Divisions	Motives for Obedience	Measures of Obedience	Mentality of Obedience	Ceremonial Regulations	Civil Regulations	Societal Regulations	Commitment to the Covenant	Culmination of Moses' Ministry
	1 4	5 7	8 11	12 16	17 20	21 26	27 30	31 34
Topics	Learning from the Past			Looking to the Future			Legacy of a Leader	
	Israel's History			Israel's Holiness			Israel's Hero	
Place	Moab (East of Jordan)							
Time	About 2 Months							

20 Motives for Obedience / Deuteronomy 1–4

📖 **Overview:** In his first of three sermons to the nation, Moses begins with a review of the past. God had promised His people a new homeland, but Israel failed to possess it because of unbelief. For 40 years they had wandered and died. Now, with the passing of that unbelieving generation, God has led the nation in smashing victories over Sihon and Og, bringing them to the threshold of the land once again. But before they are ready to enter, they must learn a crucial lesson from the past—the lesson that obedience brings victory and blessing, while disobedience results only in defeat and judgment.

Heart of the Passage: Deut. 1, 4

Chapter 1	Chapters 2–3	Chapter 4
Israel's Past Failure	God's Persistent Faithfulness	Israel's Promising Future
Example	Encouragement	Exhortation

✔️ **Your Daily Walk:** Preaching at its finest involves godly persuasion. When you listen to a preacher, you will often hear him make three painfully pointed statements: (1) "God says to do this: _____ ." (2) "You are doing this: _____ ." (3) "Therefore, you need to change _____ now." That's why preaching can make you uncomfortable! It shows you from God's Word where you are wrong and tries to persuade you to change your attitudes or actions to conform with God's commands.

It requires great listening as well as great preaching to make a great sermon.

Moses' first sermon to Israel is a masterpiece of godly persuasion as he points out to the people the past, present, and future dealings of God. Israel should obey God because of her *past* experience of God's deliverance, provision, and judgment; Israel should obey God because of her *present* experience of God's sufficiency in supplying her needs and in fighting her battles; and Israel should obey God because of her *future* promises of blessing or cursing, all hinging on her proper response to God's pointed commands.

If you were preaching Deuteronomy 1–4 instead of Moses, which of God's past, present, or future dealings in your life could you point to as proof positive that God ought to be obeyed?

🔍 **Insight:** Standing on the Promises of Old
Moses' confidence in God is largely rooted in God's promises to Israel's forefathers. The phrase "the Lord sware unto your fathers" (1:8) is repeated at least 25 times in Moses' three sermons!

The Influence of Deuteronomy

21

Step Back

If you were to determine which book of the Old Testament had the greatest influence on the rest of the Bible, Deuteronomy would prove to be a finalist. The New Testament writers alone quote it directly in 17 of the 27 New Testament books and allude to it more than 80 times.

Jesus turned back each of Satan's three temptations in the wilderness with words from Deuteronomy (Matthew 4:1-11). And when He summarized the entire Old Testament Law (Matthew 22:37), He quoted Deuteronomy again.

Here is a chart showing how extensively the writers of Scripture have drawn upon the fifth book of the Old Testament:

Scripture Reading:
Matthew 4:1-11

JOSHUA
6:17-18 (13:15)
7:25 (13:10; 17:5)
8:27 (20:14)
8:29 (21:22-23)
8:30-31 (27:3; 8)
8:33-35 (11:29; 27:11-13)

JUDGES
1:17 (7:2; 20:16)
7:1-7 (20:1-9)
17:13 (18:1-8; 33:8-11)

HOSEA
4:4 (17:12)
5:10 (19:14)
8:13 (28:68)
11:13 (1:31; 32:10)

AMOS
3:2 (7:6; 9:12)
2:6-8 (24:12-15; 23:17)

MATTHEW
4:1-11 (6:13, 16; 8:3)
22:37 (6:4-5)

MARK
10:5 (24:1)

ROMANS
10:6-9 (30:12-14)

GALATIANS
3:10, 13 (27:26; 21:23)

HEBREWS
10:28 (17:6)

Look Up

As you read Matthew 4:1-11, ask yourself how you would fare if you were in a situation in which you needed to draw on the truths of God's Word—truths that could strengthen you against temptation or comfort you in distress.

Move Ahead

Skim again through Matthew 4:1-11 and select one of the passages from Deuteronomy which Jesus quoted. Then take a few moments to memorize it. As you continue to read through the Bible with *Your Daily Walk*, ask God to help you memorize significant passages from His Word.

In the Old Testament the New lies hidden; in the New Testament the Old is laid open.

22 *Measures of Obedience* *Deuteronomy 5–7*

Overview: Moses' second sermon begins in chapter 5 and extends through chapter 26. He opens with a repetition of the Ten Commandments (hence the name Deuteronomy— "second law") and exhorts the people to obey the Lord from a heart of love, to teach their children obedience, and to be careful not to forget the Lord in times of prosperity. Victory over the pagan occupants of Canaan is assured as long as the people faithfully obey God's commands. They will prevail, not because of their strength, but because of their all-conquering God.

Heart of the Passage: Deut. 7

Chapter 5	Chapter 6	Chapter 7
Old Law for a New Generation	New Law for a New Generation	New Hope for a New Generation
Ten Commandments	Greatest Command	Future Conquest

Your Daily Walk: Reading today's section, you may be reminded of the fairy tale about the goose that laid the golden egg. (If your childhood memories are fuzzy, the story goes this way: A farmer, upon discovering a most remarkable golden-egg-laying goose, got impatient about having to wait for the daily quota of eggs. He chopped off the goose's head to find the source of the eggs . . . and in a fit of impatience destroyed the very source of his prosperity.)

Most of modern man's troubles stem from too much time on his hands and not enough on his knees.

"I want it all—and I want it now!" is the cry of the day, even among many Christians. But God is not limited by our impatient timetables. He gave the Israelites a principle for conquest which still applies today: "little by little" (7:22). God's methods often take time. He could have given the land to Israel in a day, but instead He instructed them to move step by step, trusting Him each "cubit" of the way.

Where are you hoping for instant results in your Christian life: victory over a habit . . . knowledge of God's Word . . . spiritual maturity? God's way is not rush, rush, rush but little by little. Look for a small but significant step of growth you can take today: a verse to memorize, a command to obey, a promise to treasure.

Insight: Sour Milk and Sticky Fingers, or Something Else! The description of the Promised Land as "the land that floweth with milk and honey" pictures it as a land of prosperity and abundance. Milk was part of the Hebrews' staple diet, and so a rich supply of milk indicated vast pasturelands. Honey was considered a delicacy.

Mentality of Obedience
 Deuteronomy 8–11   *23*

Overview: Moses continues his review of Israel's history as an illustration to the people of God's faithfulness throughout their 40-year wilderness trek. God's provision in the past provides confidence for the future. He will continue to do great things for His people if they continue to walk in obedience to Him. But if they are disobedient, ignore His commands, and worship other gods, God will judge their rebellion. The facts are clear: If Israel loves and obeys God, she will experience blessing. If she disobeys, God's judgment will be sure.

Heart of the Passage: Deut. 8–9

Chapter 8	Chapter 9	Chapters 10–11
Remember God's Goodness	Remember the Golden Calf	Remember to Obey
Reminders from the Past		Responsibilities for the Future

Your Daily Walk: Spend a few minutes walking through the rooms of your house and noting all the items you own that you did not purchase yourself, but received as gifts. As you look at each item, try to remember who gave it to you and when. If you are like most people, you'll have a difficult time with the assignment.

How happy a person is depends upon the depth of his gratitude.

Moses' review of Israel's history was a verbal recollection of all the good things Israel possessed as a result of God's blessing. The manna in the wilderness and God's other provisions merely foreshadowed what lay ahead: a land flowing with milk and honey. But the promise of prosperity in Canaan pointed to a potential problem. The people of future generations might forget who gave them these good gifts, and take personal credit for their own prosperity. Moses drove home the message that the Israelites were never to forget it was God who supplied their needs and gave them their abundance.

Have you forgotten who gave you the gifts you possess? Write a thank-you note to God, expressing your gratitude for something He has given you in recent days. He loves to hear you say, "Thanks."

Insight: "Remember to Forget Not"
Moses reminds his people not to make God's goodness a basis for personal pride. Complete these important thoughts:
Remember how the Lord _____ (8:2).
Remember that God gives you _____ (8:18).
Don't forget how you _____ (9:7).

24 *Ceremonial Regulations*
Deuteronomy 12–16

Heart of the Passage: Deut. 12:1-16; 14:22–15:11

Overview: Following his review of the past and preview of the future, Moses turns to the more specific and detailed statutes which will be in effect as Israel takes up residence in the land. Desiring that His people be separate from the nations around them, God commands that Israel's religious life be free from all associations with idolatry. God's chosen people must be characterized by only the highest standards of purity, hygiene, and treatment of the poor—actions which will demonstrate Israel's unique relationship with God. In addition, Israel's feasts must be times of consecration as well as celebration.

Chapter 12	Chapter 13	Chapter 14	Chapter 15	Chapter 16
Religious Laws Concerning . . .			
Food	Idols	Animals	Debts	Feasts
Regulations Designed to Demonstrate Israel's Uniqueness				

Your Daily Walk: Are you a grudging or a generous giver? When you hear of some need, do you look for an avenue of giving or an excuse for not giving?

When it comes to giving, some people stop at nothing.

Yesterday you learned that everything you own is a gift from God's hand. Today there is a companion lesson: God expects those whom He has blessed to reflect the same generosity He has shown to them. God specified to Israel that they were to be openhanded with their possessions if they saw a brother or sister in need. Since God was the source of their supply, it was almost as if He were doing the giving Himself. Therefore His people could give generously, knowing their needs would also be met by the Giver of every good gift.

When seen in the light of Christ's command, "Freely ye have received, freely give" (Matthew 10:8), your giving can take on new depth and meaning. You can be a source of blessing to someone else, and at the same time receive a blessing yourself. Tap into God's vast storehouse and help someone you know who needs financial assistance this week. Remember, "freely . . . received, freely give"!

Insight: A Painful (and Prohibited) Funeral Ritual (14:1)
The practices of self-inflicted wounds and baldness were signs of mourning for the dead which the Canaanites used as part of their pagan worship. God strictly forbade such activities for His consecrated people. Does He expect any less from you? (See 1 Peter 2:9.)

Civil Regulations / Deuteronomy 17–20 **25**

📖 **Overview:** In addition to the religious laws regulating national worship, Moses sets forth civil laws to govern the selection and application of civil authority in the land. How do you choose a king? How do you prove the trustworthiness of a prophet? How do you protect innocent manslayers? How do you treat captured peoples humanely and impartially? You'll find the answers in today's section, along with a collection of regulations for prophets and priests, kings and kingdoms.

Heart of the Passage: Deut. 17

Chapter 17	Chapter 18	Chapter 19	Chapter 20
Choosing a King	Proving a Prophet	Providing a Refuge	Providing for Peace
Civil Laws		Humanitarian Laws	

✏️ **Your Daily Walk:** If it is indeed true that "righteousness exalteth a nation: but sin is a reproach to any people" (Proverbs 14:34), how would you grade your nation in its efforts to promote righteousness in the following areas (A = Excellent, C = Average, etc.)?

If someone calls you "forth-right," be careful; he may mean you're right a fourth of the time.

- Dealing with idolatry (objects of worship other than God, 17:2-5)
- Promoting justice (impartiality and fairness, 17:8-11)
- Prohibiting occult practices (witchcraft, horoscopes, 18:9-14)
- Practicing truthfulness (in government, in the courts, 19:15-19)

As a concerned Christian, you cannot do *everything* to promote national righteousness, but you can do *something*. Prayer . . . fasting . . . phone calls . . . letters . . . a fresh commitment to Christian principles—all are powerful deterrents to evil in your nation, but only if you use them. Will you pick one and put it to work today?

🖎 **Insight:** Three Don'ts, One Do for Future Kings

In 17:14-20 you'll find four specific commands directed to future monarchs who would reign over God's people. Complete each command, and compare the performance of Solomon (one such future monarch) as recorded in the book of 1 Kings.

God's Command (Deut.)	Solomon's Response (1 Kings)
"Don't multiply_____ " (17:16).	_____ (4:26).
"Don't multiply_____ " (17:17).	_____ (11:3).
"Don't multiply_____ " (17:17).	_____ (10:14).
"Do make _____ " (17:18).	_____ (11:11).

26 Societal Regulations
Deuteronomy 21–26

Heart of the Passage: Deut. 23:1-8; 26:16-19

Overview: How do you promote peace and stability in the land and at the same time deal with unsolved murders, alien settlers, divorce, family inheritance, stray livestock, sanitation problems, territorial disputes, and a host of other matters? Moses seeks to answer many of these "What if?" situations before they arise in order to ensure the orderly management of God's holy people in the Holy Land.

Chapters 21–22	Chapters 23–24	Chapters 25–26
Holiness in the Home	Holiness Toward the Helpless	Holiness in Human Relations
Domestic Laws	Humane Laws	Societal Laws

Your Daily Walk: Have you ever approached the door to a restaurant, there to find the words, "No bare feet allowed"? What was the reason behind that prohibition? Why would restaurants pick on people with bare feet?

Cleanliness is next to godliness; but for some, it is next to impossible.

Under the Mosaic Law, some people were excluded from the assembly: those with certain defects, those born illegitimately, those of Ammonite or Moabite descent (23:1-3). Why this seemingly arbitrary exclusion of parties from Israel's religious community? Because, just like the bare feet in the restaurant, each represented a potential source of defilement for all the others in the community.

Mutilation of the body, brazen immorality, and pagan intermarriage were common practices in the Canaanite community. If these defilements were to be kept out of the Israelite camp, certain exclusions had to be enforced.

The church today is often both inclusive and exclusive. Carefully and thoughtfully read Ephesians 2:1-7. Then write down your answer to this question: "Because of my inclusion in the body of Christ, what is one source of defilement I need to exclude from my life of service to God?"

Ask God to give you the strength you need to completely eliminate that sin from your life.

Insight: Buried Like a Common Criminal

The burial of a criminal who is crucified (21:22-23) foreshadows the ignominious death suffered by our Lord. In the New Testament verse 23 is quoted in reference to Christ's taking the curse of our sins upon Himself: "Cursed is every one that hangeth on a tree" (Galatians 3:13). Also see John 19:31.

Commitment to the Covenant *Deuteronomy 27–30* 27

📖 **Overview:** Moses has come to a solemn, climactic moment in his address to the nation—the time for a recommitment of the people to the covenant. He reminds the new wilderness generation that the potential for God's richest blessing awaits them in the land, as well as the potential for His severest judgment. It all depends on their submissive response to the demands of the covenant. Dramatically Moses delivers the challenge: "I have set before you life and death . . . choose life."

Heart of the Passage: Deut. 27–28

Chapter 27	Chapter 28	Chapter 29	Chapter 30
Prescribed Ceremonies	Promised Blessings	Conditions of the Covenant	Commitment of the Nation
The Covenant Reviewed		The Covenant Renewed	

🏃 **Your Daily Walk:** "I wish I were dead!" Perhaps at an unguarded moment of despair or shame, you vented your frustration with such words. But you didn't really mean them literally. Most people want to live! In fact, they will do just about anything to preserve their life. But that strong survival instinct doesn't always carry over into the spiritual realm.

Moses made the choice transparently clear for Israel with these two simple (and unalterable) formulas:

OBEDIENCE = LIFE
DISOBEDIENCE = DEATH

And yet, in the months ahead you will read the tragic national consequences of Israel's decisions.

You are facing similar decisions today . . . with equally far-reaching consequences. You, like Israel, can choose a deathlike lifestyle by rebelling against God's will. Or by obeying you can choose life—and daily fellowship with the God of life. Which will it be?

Take a 3x5 card and write the two formulas on it. Tape the card to your refrigerator, bathroom mirror, or dashboard. Let it remind you often of God's timeless principle of life and death. The choice is yours.

We make our decisions, and then our decisions turn around and make us.

📑 **Insight:** The Day the Slave Markets Were Glutted

The horrible curse of 28:68 literally came true! After the fall of Jerusalem in A.D. 70, the slave markets of Egypt became so glutted with captive Israelites that there were not enough buyers for them all. God always keeps His promises—both good and bad alike.

28/29 *Culmination of Moses' Ministry*
Deuteronomy 31–34

Heart of the Passage: Deut. 32, 34.

Overview: With the covenant reestablished and the nation poised at the Jordan River, Moses completes his duties as leader of God's people. He commissions Joshua as his successor with a sober warning of Israel's future rebellion. In order for the people to remember his message of life, Moses records his final words as a song and teaches the melody and message to the nation. After pronouncing blessings on each of the 12 tribes, Moses climbs Mount Nebo for a final glimpse of the Promised Land. There he dies, physically strong in spite of his 120 years. And though his final resting place remains a mystery to this day, he has the finest of Undertakers to arrange his funeral!

Chapter 31	Chapter 32	Chapter 33	Chapter 34
Moses' Successor	Moses' Song	Moses' Blessing	God's Benediction
The Final Days of Moses			

Your Daily Walk: You've heard of fair-weather friends—the kind who flock to you when everything is going right, and disappear when things start going wrong. But have you ever heard of "foul-weather friends," the kind who cling to you when things are going badly, and ignore you when everything is running smoothly?

If you are reading in leap year, read two chapters on February 28 and two more on February 29.

"Foul-weather friends" is a perfect description of the children of Israel. During their times of need in the wilderness, Israel followed after God despite occasional grumblings and rebellions. But God warned the nation that coming prosperity would bring indifference toward Him. When the Promised Land was conquered and occupied, the nation would abandon God for idols (31:16; 32:15, 18).

When you're face to face with a crisis, it's natural to cry out to God for help. But what about when things are running smoothly? When the wind is at your back . . . your health is excellent . . . there's money in the checkbook and the bills are all paid—what then? Try singing a few verses from the "Song of Moses" (chapter 32), expressing your devotion to God in the good times as well as the bad!

Insight: A Fitting Epitaph for Moses' Tombstone
"The eternal God is thy refuge, and underneath are the everlasting arms" (33:27).

Joshua

I n the book that bears his name, Joshua
succeeds Moses as commander-in-chief of
Israel and leads the people across the Jordan
into the Promised Land. This is a book of war
and peace, detailing Israel's conquering of
Canaan and marking their beginning as a
settled nation. The first half of the book
(chapters 1–12) recounts three military cam-
paigns spanning seven years, in which Joshua
meets and defeats more than 30 enemy armies.
The second half (chapters 13–24) relates the
settlement of Canaan, the fulfillment of God's
age-old promise to Abraham.

Focus	Conquest			Consolidation		
Divisions	Preparing for War	Beginning the Conquest	Completing the Conquest	Allocations for 5 Tribes and Caleb	Allocations for 7 Tribes and Levites	Joshua's Final Challenge and Death
	1 5	6 8	9 12	13 17	18 21	22 24
Topics	Securing the Land			Settling the Land		
	Warlords in Canaan			Landlords in Canaan		
Place	Both Sides of the Jordan					
Time	7 Years			18 Years		

1 *Preparing for War / Joshua 1–5*

Heart of the Passage: Joshua 1:1-8; 3

Overview: Moses has died, and Joshua is appointed by God to take the reins of leadership. The people are poised within view of the land promised to their ancestors and denied their unbelieving parents. The time has come to cross over, conquer, and possess! But will they succeed where their fathers failed? The task seems impossible: a swollen, turbulent river to ford; foreign terrain to cross; mighty walled cities to conquer. So God begins to prepare His people for the days of warfare just ahead. He reminds Joshua that careful attention to His Word brings blessing and success. Spies are sent to survey Jericho, the first obstacle in the land. The priests, bearing the ark of the covenant, lead the people across the rampaging Jordan without even getting their sandals wet! The stage is set for conquest.

Chapter 1	Chapter 2	Chapter 3	Chapter 4	Chapter 5
Preparing the People for Battle . . .				
Spiritually	Militarily	Geographically	Historically	Ceremonially
"Be Strong"	"Go View"	"Cross Over"	"Remember"	"Circumcise"

God will lead you to no waters He cannot part, no brink He cannot cross, no pain He cannot bear.

Your Daily Walk: God specializes in dry sandals. He loves to start with an impossible situation in your life . . . and then do the impossible.

When the nation of Israel approached the Jordan, God demanded a step of obedience before they could cross. The priests, like drum majors leading a three-million-member marching band, had to hike to the brink of the flood-swollen Jordan and take that first step into the water. Then—and only then—would God perform a miracle, roll back the waters, dry up the puddles, and send the people across kicking up dust at every step! Dry sandals followed trusting obedience.

Where in your life is God waiting for you to take that first step of faith? In the margin at the left of the page, write down the *obstacle* you are facing (your Jordan) and the step of *obedience* God is asking you to take (your dry-sandals experience). Trust Him for the unexpected, and let Him surprise and delight you by doing the unexplainable!

Insight: A Mighty Little River

The Jordan, a winding, muddy river 250 miles long (and only waist-deep in some places) carries biblical significance much greater than its size. It is mentioned 67 times in Joshua and a total of 175 times in the Old Testament.

Beginning the Conquest / Joshua 6–8 2

Overview: Joshua employs a textbook strategy for military victory: "Divide and conquer!" He attacks the middle of the country first, dividing the enemy forces in half, before mopping up resistance among the isolated troops in the south and north. His stunning victory at Jericho shows the importance of following God's directions down to the smallest detail, no matter how trivial they may seem! The lesson is painfully reinforced at Ai, where disobedience leads to defeat and death. But after disciplining His overconfident people, God patiently encourages them and leads them to victory in the rematch with Ai.

Heart of the Passage: Joshua 6:1–7:13; 8:1, 25

Chapter 6	Chapter 7	Chapter 8
Obedience Brings Victory	Disobedience Brings Defeat	Restoration Brings Victory
Jericho	Ai (Round One)	Ai (Round Two)

Your Daily Walk: The true test of an obedient child comes, not when the parent's orders make good sense ("Don't touch the stove or you'll burn yourself"), but when there seems to be no good reason for the command ("Be home by 11 . . . eat your spinach . . . don't sleep with your shoes on"). A parent's wishes may be changeable or based on a whim, but God's will is never that way (Hebrews 13:8; James 1:17).

True obedience has no lead at its heels.

God's command to Israel at Jericho to destroy what was not consecrated to Him contradicted "good human judgment." It seemed wasteful to the people and unnecessarily cruel. Joshua did the "sensible" and "prudent" (but disobedient) thing by sending only a small army against Ai. And the result was a rout for Israel and the needless death of 36 soldiers.

Pick a command from God's Word that you have been tempted to label impractical, unnecessary, or irrelevant (you might try Ephesians 5:22, 25; 6:1; or 6:5). Write it on a slip of paper along with these words: "Where I understand the will of God, I will do it; where I do not understand the will of God, I will trust Him . . . and do it anyway!"

Insight: The High Cost of Covetousness
The gold and silver pieces Achan took (7:21) were worth only a few thousand dollars. In exchange, they cost the lives of 36 soldiers, a humiliating defeat for the nation of Israel, and death by stoning for Achan and his entire family.

3 *The Servant Leader*

Scripture Reading: Hebrews 4:1-11

Step Back

Like Joseph in Genesis, Joshua foreshadows the life and work of Jesus. In fact, they even share the same Hebrew name, "Yeshua."

As Moses' trusted right-hand man who assumed the reins of leadership for the Hebrew nation, Joshua lived an exciting and fulfilling life, filled with success and honor. God entrusted him with the vast responsibility of leading His people into the Promised Land. And Joshua fulfilled that responsibility with vision and vigor.

But his achievements were not simply the work of a shrewd man following sound leadership principles. Joshua's success instead was sourced in his deep and abiding trust in God. As Numbers 27:18 puts it, Joshua was "a man in whom is the spirit."

Joshua's humble, Spirit-directed leadership skill was recognized early, when he was chosen to represent his tribe when the 12 spies reconnoitered in Canaan. Only Joshua and Caleb were determined to follow God's clear direction to take possession of the land, despite the threat of resistance. So only Joshua and Caleb were allowed to enter the land after 40 years of wandering.

Joshua was a brilliant military strategist, a wise and worthy statesman. But more than that, he was God's chosen servant/leader who fulfilled the work Moses began, establishing Israel in the Promised Land. In this way, he foreshadowed the work of Christ.

Look Up

With his faith firmly set in the promise of God, Joshua led the people of Israel into a period of physical rest in the Promised Land. In the same way, we can experience the peaceful rest of salvation when we have placed our faith in the person and work of our Savior, Jesus Christ. God invites each of us to enter into His rest— a rest that was pictured physically in Canaan.

Take rest; a field that has rested gives a bountiful crop.

As you meditate through Hebrews 4:1-11, thank God for the eternal rest He has graciously given you. Ask Him to build your patient faith and enable you to experience that rest, now and forever.

Move Ahead

Flip back through the first eight chapters of the book of Joshua and pull out a few leadership insights from the life of Joshua. Perhaps it's God's admonition to "be strong and of a good courage" (1:6), or Joshua's commitment to obey God completely (5:14), or his willingness to expose sin (7:19).

Ask yourself how you can apply those insights in any leadership role you may play—with your family, at work, at church. Remember, it all starts with a humble and obedient heart.

Completing the Conquest / Joshua 9–12 **4**

📖 **Overview:** In many ways, Joshua's military strategy is dictated more by the actions of his enemies than by his own plans. First, the king of Jerusalem forms an alliance of kings in the south and attacks Gibeon (the nation which had tricked Israel into a treaty of protection). True to her pact, Israel comes to Gibeon's defense, smashing the southern coalition. A similar alliance now forms in the north, led by Jabin, king of Hazor. And once again, "The LORD [delivers] them into the hand of Israel" (11:8). Finally, Joshua squelches resistance throughout the entire land until "the hills . . . valley . . . plain, and . . . mountain" (11:16) are secure, ready to be allotted to the waiting tribes.

Heart of the Passage: Joshua 9, 12

Chapter 9	Chapter 10	Chapter 11	Chapter 12
Deception of Gibeon	Destruction of the South	Defeat of the North	Description of the Battle Plan
Compact	Coalition		Conquest

✒️ **Your Daily Walk:** Nothing is as exasperating to a parent as the newfound independence of a three-year-old. "Let me do it . . . don't help . . . I can do it myself" are all expressions of a dependent child exercising his awakening sense of independence. The parent's help may no longer be wanted by the child, but that doesn't mean it isn't needed!

When faced with the unexpected problem of Gibeon (chapter 9), the leaders of Israel responded in immature independence. "We can handle this one on our own. No need to consult God about such an elementary matter. After all, we've made tougher decisions than *this* before!" The foolish peace pact with Gibeon, made without consulting God, was based on false appearances and deceiving words. In the years ahead it would be a source of heartache to Israel.

Peace is such a precious jewel that I would give anything for it but truth.

What decision are you tempted to make without giving God a single thought? Talk to Him first. God delights in guiding those who acknowledge their need of Him (Proverbs 3:5-6). And the consequences of ignoring Him can't be ignored!

📖 **Insight:** A Hungry Homeland
Earlier the spies described Canaan as "a land that eateth up the inhabitants thereof" (Numbers 13:32). During the seven-year conquest, Joshua's army destroyed 31 kings and most of the Canaanites, making the spies' statement ironically prophetic!

Placing the
Books of
Joshua –
2 Samuel

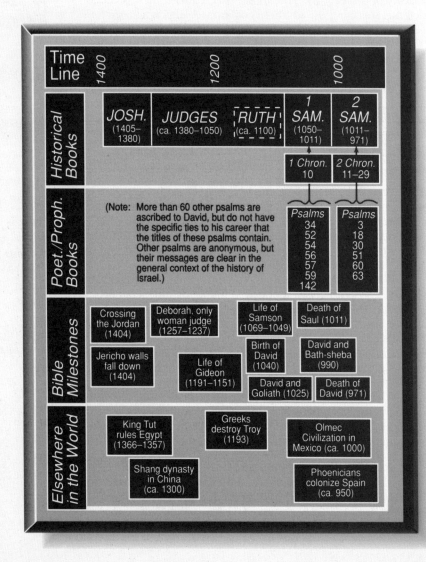

Time Line	1400		1200		1000	
Historical Books	JOSH. (1405–1380)	JUDGES (ca. 1380–1050)	RUTH (ca. 1100)	1 SAM. (1050–1011)	2 SAM. (1011–971)	
				1 Chron. 10	2 Chron. 11–29	
Poet./Proph. Books	(Note: More than 60 other psalms are ascribed to David, but do not have the specific ties to his career that the titles of these psalms contain. Other psalms are anonymous, but their messages are clear in the general context of the history of Israel.)			Psalms 34 52 54 56 57 59 142	Psalms 3 18 30 51 60 63	

Bible Milestones

- Crossing the Jordan (1404)
- Deborah, only woman judge (1257–1237)
- Life of Samson (1069–1049)
- Death of Saul (1011)
- Jericho walls fall down (1404)
- Life of Gideon (1191–1151)
- Birth of David (1040)
- David and Bath-sheba (990)
- David and Goliath (1025)
- Death of David (971)

Elsewhere in the World

- King Tut rules Egypt (1366–1357)
- Greeks destroy Troy (1193)
- Olmec Civilization in Mexico (ca. 1000)
- Shang dynasty in China (ca. 1300)
- Phoenicians colonize Spain (ca. 950)

Allocations for Five Tribes
Joshua 13–17

5

📖 **Overview:** Although Israel under Joshua's leadership has conquered Canaan by destroying key cities and their kings, "there remaineth yet very much land to be possessed" (13:1). To complete the task, Joshua assigns territories to each individual tribe with instructions to clear out the remaining pagan influence and possess the land completely. Territories have already been assigned to Reuben, Gad, and half the tribe of Manasseh on the east side of Jordan. But before any allotments are made on the west side, Caleb asks for and receives the area promised him by Moses: Mount Hebron, a known Canaanite stronghold!

Heart of the Passage: Joshua 14

Chapter 13	Chapter 14	Chapter 15	Chapters 16–17
Allotment to 2-1/2 Tribes	Allotment to Caleb	Allotment to Judah	Allotment to Joseph's Sons
East of Jordan	West of Jordan		

🗡️ **Your Daily Walk:** Probably as a child you either played with model planes, boats, and trucks or knew someone who did. Take a sheet of paper and list as many characteristics of a model as you can think of. (If you thought of 8 or more, you're still a kid at heart; 4–7, you could use a second childhood; 3 or less, you are probably from an all-girl family!) Now think about some outstanding characters who emerge from the pages of Scripture, and ask yourself this question: "Apart from the Lord Jesus Himself, which individual would I most like to model my life after?"

Did the name Caleb cross your mind? Here is a man of whom it is said three times in seven verses that he "wholly followed the Lord" (14:8-9, 14). Caleb knew what it meant to claim the promises of God, then move out by faith to possess what God had promised.

As you read chapter 14 today, did you notice what was said about Caleb—his age, physical condition, godly ambitions, steps of obedience? Select one way in which Caleb's life can become a model for your life today, and put it to work!

The single most important characteristic of a Christian is not how much of God's Word he knows, but how much he lives.

📖 **Insight:** God's People and Long Life—Fact or Fluke?
It is interesting that life expectancy charts show ministers as a group live longer than most other occupational groups, and Christians generally outlive non-Christians. Discuss with a group of friends whether or not they find that observation to be true.

6 Allocations for Seven Tribes
Joshua 18–21

Heart of the Passage: Joshua 18:1-10; 21:43-45

Overview: With the moving of the tabernacle to the territory of Ephraim, Shiloh becomes the new center of Israel's worship. The remaining seven tribes now receive their inheritance by lot. But for the tribe of Levi there will be no territorial allotment, for their inheritance is the priestly service of God (13:14; 18:7). Instead, 48 cities are assigned to the three families of Levites (Kohath, Gershon, Merari), and six cities are reserved as places of refuge for accidental manslayers. At last, the task of dividing and distributing the land is complete.

Chapter 18	Chapter 19	Chapter 20	Chapter 21
Allotment to Benjamin	Allotment to Other Tribes	Cities for the Innocent	Cities for the Levites
Reward		Refuge	

Make this simple rule the guide of your life: to have no will but God's.

Your Daily Walk: Use your imagination for a moment. Try to envision 22 godly men gathered together in a tent with 8,000 square miles of real estate at stake (18:4, 10). And how are they making the weighty decision as to which tribe receives which parcel of land? They are "casting lots"—the Old Testament equivalent of throwing dice!

Does it bother you that Joshua would leave such an important matter as the partitioning of the land to the "chance" roll of the dice? Then remember that in Bible times God often made His will known in the casting of lots (Leviticus 16:8; 1 Samuel 10:19-21; Jonah 1:7; Acts 1:15-26). Notice the repeated phrase "before the LORD" in 18:6, 8, 10. This was no accidental division of the land, but a public acknowledgment that God's will extended even to the parceling of the land.

God's will for your life today can be known with just as much certainty as Joshua enjoyed thousands of years ago. Only now, God has specified other ways of finding it besides the roll of the dice. Make a study of the following verses to learn how He wants to reveal His will to you today: Psalm 119:105; Romans 12:2; 1 Thessalonians 4:2-7; 5:18. If God cares enough about a piece of real estate to guide Joshua's lots, then how much more must He care about you?

Insight: The End of a Six-Century Wait (21:43-45)
In the space of these three short verses, at least five promised blessings are fulfilled for the nation Israel. How many can you find? (Hint: Watch for and circle the word *all*.)

76

Joshua's Final Challenge / Joshua 22–24 7

Overview: After being commended for their faithful service in conquering the land of Canaan, the warriors of the tribes east of Jordan are sent home. They recognize that the Jordan River (which forms a natural barrier between the tribes) may one day form a spiritual barrier as well. To prevent this, a memorial altar is built on the riverbank—an act misunderstood and viewed with horror by the tribes west of Jordan. Civil war nearly breaks out before the real motives behind the altar are revealed. The book closes with Joshua's farewell address in which he gives the people an ultimatum: "Choose you this day whom ye will serve . . . as for me and my house, we will serve the LORD" (24:15).

Heart of the Passage: Joshua 2:10-34; 24:29-33

Chapter 22	Chapter 23	Chapter 24
A Memorial for the Future	A Challenge for the Present	A Commitment for All Time
Witness to Unity	Call to Consecration	

Your Daily Walk: Try your hand at a little detective game. Analyze the following situation, then select the correct response: A woman running breathlessly down the road is being hotly pursued by an equally breathless man who is gaining on her at every step. The man is: (a) a criminal, (b) a bill collector, (c) a sports enthusiast. Correct answer: (c) The fellow is a jogger, and so is his wife. They are out for their morning run, and he is just about to pass her. If you had been an onlooker would you have assessed the situation correctly?

Snap judgments would be all right if they didn't come unsnapped so often.

Motives are hard to read, but easy to misread. How can you avoid the kind of mistake made by the tribes west of Jordan? When tempted to think the worst about another's actions or attitudes, stop and ask yourself these two questions: (1) What would I want others to believe about *me* if *I* were in the same situation? (2) What damage might result if I don't get all the facts and jump too quickly to the wrong conclusion?

Insight: "Just Look at His Track Record!"
Joshua wanted to ensure that his people would continue following the Lord wholeheartedly after his death. So he wove an incontrovertible argument for his God by recalling numerous instances of His goodness to Israel in the past, ending it with a personal exhortation to "choose for yourselves whom you will serve." Did his plea bring results? Reread 24:31.

Judges

I n Joshua, an obedient people conquered the land through trust in God's power. By contrast, in Judges a disobedient and idolatrous people are often defeated because of their rebellion against God. In seven cycles of sin, Judges shows how the nation sets aside God's laws and replaces them with "that which was right in [their] own eyes" (21:25). Time after time God disciplines the nation with foreign oppression. But national repentance leads to national deliverance as God raises up Deborah, Gideon, Samson, and others to overthrow their oppressors.

Focus	Conditions	Cycles				Conclusion
Divisions	Review and Preview of the Judges	Deborah and Four Judges	Gideon and the Midianites	Seven Judges and Civil War	Samson and the Philistines	Idolatry and Immorality During the Judges
	1 2	3 5	6 8	9 12	13 16	17 21
Topics	Israel's Need for Judges	Israel's Judges				Failure of Israel's Judges
	Defeat and Deliverance					Decay and Decline
Place	Canaan and Transjordan					
Time	About 350 Years					

Review and Preview of the Judges
 Judges 1–5

8

📖 **Overview:** In spite of God's persistent commands and Joshua's constant warnings, the people choose to accommodate, rather than annihilate, the Canaanites, thereby surrounding themselves with godless and immoral influences. Because of the nation's compromising attitude, God allows neighboring powers to test Israel by war to find out if they will obey the commandments of the Lord (3:1-4). Failing these tests, Israel settles into a downward spiral spiritually, politically, and morally. Seven recurring cycles of sin show that indeed the period of the judges is one in which "Every man [does] that which [is] right in his own eyes" (17:6; 21:25).

Heart of the Passage: Judges 2

Chapter 1	Chapter 2	Chapter 3	Chapters 4–5
		Five Early Judges	
Military Failure	Spiritual Failure	Othniel, Ehud, and Shamgar	Deborah and Barak
Israel in the Land		Confusion in the Land	

✔️ **Your Daily Walk:** If you've ever planted a garden or tried to maintain a lawn, you have no doubt encountered weeds, which are not only ugly but can ruin your crop or turf.

The worst part about weeds is weeding, an unpleasant chore that can be accomplished in two ways: (1) by pulling out the weed, roots and all; or (2) by lopping off the weed at the ground level. Both methods appear to accomplish the same purpose, but only one really works.

For the Israelites, the land of Canaan could be likened to a garden full of weeds. For a while, the people diligently uprooted their enemies. But as time passed and the recollection of God's urgent commands grew fuzzy, the people became halfhearted in the task. At first there were no visible consequences. But later, the devastation would be evident to all as immorality and idolatry flourished in the nation.

Look at the "garden" of your life. Do you see any weeds that need pulling? A nagging habit . . . a negative attitude. Resist the urge to "plow them under," hoping they will disappear. Instead, deal with the root of the problem. You'll be glad you did.

Be careful that your victories do not bring with them the seeds of future defeats.

✍️ **Insight:** Half a Victory Is No Victory at All

The seeds of Israel's downfall are visible throughout chapter 1. Read verses 19, 21, 27-33 and watch for the common element that would later lead to Israel's undoing. (Hint: Watch for the word *but*.)

9 *Gideon and Midianites / Judges 6–8*

Heart of the Passage: Judges 7

 Overview: Gideon, Israel's fifth judge, receives God's call while hiding in a winepress secretly threshing wheat. Midian's oppression is indeed severe, and Gideon is God's man to lead the people in throwing off that yoke of bondage—an assignment Gideon is not anxious to accept! But once convinced of his calling through two miraculous signs, Gideon leads a humble army of 300 men, equipped only with pitchers, torches, and trumpets, in a stunning victory against the mighty Midianite forces. Israel's unconventional weapons and unusual battle plan leave no room for doubt: The victory is the Lord's!

Chapter 6		Chapter 7	Chapter 8
Israel's Oppression	Gideon's Objection	Gideon's Army Decreased	Midian's Army Destroyed
Gideon's Call		Gideon's Conquest	

The first step on the way to victory is to recognize the enemy.

Your Daily Walk: "It's not the size of the dog in the fight; it's the size of the fight in the dog that counts."

Think about the many Old Testament accounts where the size of the army or individual did not determine the outcome of the battle: David vs. Goliath . . . Moses vs. Pharaoh . . . Joshua vs. Jericho . . . Gideon vs. Midian. Truly, in Israel's case it can be said, "It's not the size of the army in the fight, but the size of the God in the army!"

Though Gideon and his army were woefully undermanned and ill-equipped by human standards, their victory was total because their obedience was total. God specifically commanded them to use unconventional military tactics so that it would be clear to all *who* was responsible for their smashing triumph!

Where are "Midianites" gathering in your life—those intimidating, seemingly unconquerable problems you face? Pick one and write it down. Then spend some extra moments in today's passage seeking God's strategy for confronting and conquering it. Remember to give Him credit when the victory is won!

Insight: Wherefore the Midianites (Genesis 25:1-6)?

The Midianites descended from Midian (Abraham's son by his concubine Keturah) and Midian's five children. Abraham "sent them away from Isaac his son, . . . eastward, unto the east country" (Genesis 25:6), where they multiplied into a nation.

Seven Judges and Civil War
Judges 9–12

10

Overview: Often when a ruler dies, his son succeeds him to the throne. But what happens when the ruler has 70 sons? Trouble! Especially when one of the sons has such strong aspirations for his father's position that he attempts to murder all his brothers. Gideon's son Abimelech attempts just such a coup. His rash actions are a prelude to three stormy years in power—a reign cut short by a divinely guided millstone. By contrast, Jephthah, the illegitimate son of a harlot, zealously leads Israel in the ways of God—though his zeal also gets him into trouble!

Heart of the Passage: Judges 9, 11

Chapter 9	Chapter 10	Chapter 11	Chapter 12
A Corrupt Ambition	A Cruel Enemy	A Committed Leader	A Critical Test
Abimelech	Tola/Jair	Jephthah	Ibzan/Elon/Abdon

Your Daily Walk: "The measure of a man is what he does with power." Those words, written centuries ago by a Greek philosopher, have more than a grain of truth, especially when applied to Abimelech. If his character were measured solely by what he did with power, the score would be low indeed. Abimelech's tactics were both brutal and foolish. He first murdered his brothers, then surrounded himself with people of like mind. The result was predictable—and lamentable.

It is easy to look at Abimelech's actions and conclude, "I could never do something like that!" But think for a moment about all the subtle ways you can use (and abuse) power: telling half-truths, being seen only with the "right" people, using others as stairsteps to success. Though these actions aren't as violent as Abimelech's, they violate the spirit of Christ's teaching, "He that is greatest among you shall be your servant" (Matthew 23:11).

As you conclude your devotional time today, look for a positive principle from the life of Gideon, and a negative principle from the life of Abimelech, regarding how to use the power and influence God has given you to bring glory to Him.

No statue was ever erected to the memory of a man or woman who thought it best to leave well enough alone.

Insight: Oh, Those Terrible Tongue Twisters
After defeating the Ephraimites, the Gileadites seized the fords of the river to prevent the retreating army from returning home. One by one, men who came to the crossing were asked to say the word *Shibboleth*. Those who pronounced the *sh* as *s* were identified by their dialect as Ephraimites and were executed.

11 *Trapped in the Cycle of Sin*

Scripture Reading: 1 Corinthians 15:56-58

◀ Step Back

You could let the book of Judges depress you, or you could let it be a determining factor in your spiritual growth.

As you read the book, you'll note that Israel fell progressively away from God as they repeated a deadly cycle seven times. The cycle would begin with rebellion from God's direction, followed by retribution on the sin by God—usually in the form of enemy conquest of the land. Then would follow the people's repentance from their sin, and God's restoration of their walk with Him. After that, the nation would experience a time of rest . . . only to be followed by another period of rebellion.

Another way to view the cycle is with the words sin, servitude, supplication, salvation, and silence.

But with each cycle, the nation was dragged deeper into depravity. Until finally, as Judges 21:25 puts it, "In those days . . . every man did that which was right in his own eyes"—the ultimate expression of self-centered sinfulness.

Why did this happen? Why was Israel so spiritually weak that she became mired in the muck of degradation?

The answer is simple: It's a lack of faith, a lack of obedience to God's clear direction. More specifically, God instructed the nation to drive out the Canaanites and destroy any remnant of their pagan religions. But they compromised. That compromise led to conflict, and ultimately to chaos. The cancer of paganism spread . . . and the result was spiritual death.

▲ Look Up

First Corinthians 15:56-58 speaks not only of the power sin has over us, but the power God has given us over it: "Thanks be to God, which giveth us the victory through our Lord Jesus Christ."

We are as human as the Israelites were in the days of the Judges. But as believers, God has given us the opportunity to claim victory over sin through Jesus Christ.

Ask God to show you if you may be trapped in the cycle of sin. If so, turn to God in repentance—changing your mind, your heart, and your direction—and claim His victory in Christ.

God wants us to be victors, not victims, to soar, not sink; to overcome, not to be overwhelmed.

➡ Move Ahead

Make 1 Corinthians 15:58 your plan of action today—be "steadfast, unmoveable, always abounding in the work of the Lord." That's not to say you won't ever sin again. But when you do, you can deal with it immediately, taking it to the cross, accepting God's forgiveness and cleansing, and moving ahead in His power. There's no more fulfilling way to live than that.

82

Samson and the Philistines
Judges 13–16

12

 Overview: Even before his birth, Samson's destiny is clearly announced. He is to be separated unto the Lord for a divine mission—a mission requiring him to abstain from certain defilements. Miraculous in his birth and equipped with supernatural strength for the task of delivering Israel from Philistine domination, Samson instead spends much of his life violating his Nazirite vow. Because of his lack of control, he loses his secret, his hair, his strength, his sight, and eventually his life—but not before God uses him in a mighty way to avenge the Israelites of their Philistine oppressors.

Heart of the Passage: Judges 13, 16

Chapter 13	Chapters 14–15	Chapter 16
Samson, the Miracle Child	Samson, the Mighty Champion	Samson, the Man of Passion
Destiny	Dominance	Downfall

Your Daily Walk: Certain Bible characters seem to receive more than their share of "bad press": Jacob for his conniving ways, Samson for flirting with (instead of fighting with) the Philistines, David for his sin with Bathsheba. But the remarkable thing is this: All these men are memorialized in the "Believer's Hall of Faith," Hebrews 11! In spite of their shortcomings, they, like so many other men and women in the Bible, lived their lives by faith, "standing on the promises of God." They were not perfect, but were being perfected day by day into "vessels [of] honor, sanctified, and meet [fit] for the master's use" (2 Timothy 2:21). And God used them greatly to His glory.

Failure is something we can avoid by saying nothing, doing nothing, and being nothing.

A history of failure in your life, like that in the lives of Jacob, Samson, and David, need not disqualify you from God's service, provided you continue to grow up—not merely grow old—in your walk with Him. On one side of an index card, write the words of Hebrews 10:38; on the other, a "Lesson from Samson's Life" that with God's help you will seek to put to work in your life, beginning today.

Insight: Samson, the Judge like No Other
Unlike the other judges of Israel, Samson led no army, but rather performed his valiant deeds singlehandedly. His up-and-down career paralleled the up-and-down conditions in his nation during a time when "there was no king in Israel: every man did that which was right in his own eyes" (21:25).

13 *Idolatry and Immorality / Judges 17–21*

Overview: Chronologically, today's section fits after chapter 3. But thematically it provides a fitting conclusion to the entire book of Judges. What happens to a nation when "every man [does] that which [is] right in his own eyes"? The grisly details contained in these chapters will provide the answer: gross idolatry, perversion, brutality, immorality, and total disregard for the Word of God. When at last Israel's national conscience is pricked by a shocking "telegram" sent to the 12 tribes, the response is brutal outrage.

Heart of the Passage: Judges 17; 19; 21:25

Chapter 17	Chapter 18	Chapter 19	Chapters 20–21
A Priest for Hire	An Idol for Worship	A Grisly Murder	A Violent Revenge
Gross Idolatry		Gross Immorality	

Your Daily Walk: If something is worth saying, it is worth repeating. Look at the first verse of chapters 18 and 19, and the last verse of chapter 21 to discover a "key" to the book of Judges. Write it in the space provided:

Collapse in the Christian life is seldom a blowout; it is usually a slow leak.

There is more to that phrase than the simple fact that Israel had yet to crown her first king. It is an acknowledgment that the nation had forsaken her true King—the God of her forefathers. In God's own words, "They have rejected me, that I should not reign over them" (1 Samuel 8:7; 10:19); and the result was national chaos and corruption.

There is something more important than the system a nation is governed by, and that is the people's attitude toward the Supreme Governor, the Lord of heaven and earth. Select a day this month and declare it a personal or family "day of fasting and prayer." Pray that God will bring revival to your nation, your community, your family—and that He will let it begin with you!

Insight: A Man and a Tribe, Two Sad Stories
As you read chapters 17 and 18, the accounts of Micah and the tribe of Dan, watch for some striking contrasts:
• Micah wanted more of God's favor (17:13); Dan wanted more of God's land (18:9).
• Micah set up images (17:5); the Danites stole images (18:17).
• Micah returned to his house without his gods (18:26); the Danites worshiped new gods but not in the house of God (18:31).

Ruth

S et in the context of unrest during the time of the judges, the story of Ruth is a bright gem of redemption and hope. Faced with famine and poverty, Ruth, a young widow, leaves her native land to travel with her mother-in-law to Bethlehem. There she gleans in the field of Boaz, who grows to love her and becomes her kinsman-redeemer. In their marriage, Ruth and Boaz become ancestors of the Messiah, Jesus. With its twin themes of faithfulness and redemption, the book of Ruth pictures God's redeeming love and His faithful devotion to all of mankind.

Focus	Ruth's Faithfulness Revealed		Ruth's Faithfulness Rewarded	
Divisions	Ruth's Decision	Ruth's Devotion	Ruth's Deliverer	Ruth's Delight
	1:1 1:18	1:19 2:23	3:1 3:18	4:1 4:22
Topics	Ruth and Naomi		Ruth and Boaz	
	Going with Naomi	Gleaning for Naomi	Loved by Boaz	Married to Boaz
Place	Moab	Fields in Bethlehem	Threshing Floor in Bethlehem	Home in Bethlehem
Time	About 30 Years			

14 *Ruth: Interlude of Love / Ruth 1–4*

**Heart
of the
Passage:
Ruth 1, 4**

 Overview: The book of Ruth provides a beautiful "interlude of love" in the period of the judges in Israel—an era marked by immorality, idolatry, and war. This heartwarming account of devotion and faithfulness tells the story of Ruth, a Moabite widow who leaves her homeland to live with her widowed Jewish mother-in-law in Bethlehem. God honors her commitment by guiding her to the field of Boaz (a near kinsman), where she gathers grain and eventually finds a husband! The book closes with a brief genealogy in which Boaz's name is prominent as the great-grandfather of King David, and an ancestor of Jesus.

Chapter 1	Chapter 2	Chapter 3	Chapter 4
Ruth's Resolve: "I Will Go"	Ruth's Response: "Let Me Glean"	Ruth's Request: "Redeem Me"	Ruth's Reward: "A Son . . . Obed"
Ruth and Naomi		Ruth and Boaz	

**Duty
makes
us do
things,
but love
makes us
do things
beauti-
fully.**

Your Daily Walk: *Love is a many-splendored thing.
Love makes the world go around.*

Love . . . (How many more ways can you think of to complete the sentence?)

Love is difficult to define because it is a quality of life more readily demonstrated than described. Ruth demonstrated the true character of love when she willingly and steadfastly pledged her allegiance and devotion to Naomi. Clearly, by traveling to a foreign country she had more to lose than gain. She was still young and easily could have remarried someone of her own nationality. But her primary concern was not for her own well-being, but rather for the well-being of Naomi. Ruth exemplifies sacrificial love—the kind that Christ portrayed when He "[gave] his life for the sheep" (John 10:11).

How can you give of yourself sacrificially to someone around you—your spouse, roommate, employer, neighbor, or friend? Jot down a name in the margin, a specific act of selfless love you can do for that person, and the date when you will do it. Don't let your love be "Ruthless," or it will soon become useless (1 Corinthians 13:1-3).

Insight: Ruth and Esther—Alike and Yet So Different
Ruth and Esther are the only two books in the Bible named after women. Ruth, a Gentile, lived among Hebrews and married a Hebrew. Esther, a Hebrew, lived among Gentiles and married a Gentile. However, both women were greatly used by God to bring glory to Him.

Our Kinsman-Redeemer **15**

⬅ Step Back

Against the dark, depressing backdrop of the book of Judges, Ruth shines with the beauty of simple faith and devoted love.

Contrary to the trend of paganism in Israel at the time, Ruth—a young widow from the land of Moab—forsakes her pagan heritage to cling to the people of Israel and the God of Israel. And because of her faithfulness in an era of faithlessness, God rewards her by giving her a faithful husband, a son, and the privilege of being the great-grandmother of King David . . . and an ancestor of Christ Himself.

Scripture Reading: Ephesians 5:23-32

Within the story of Ruth is found a concept that portrays the work of Christ on our behalf. It's the concept of the kinsman-redeemer (or *goel*, "close relative"; 3:9). A goel must be related by blood to those he redeems (Deuteronomy 25:5, 7-10; John 1:14; Romans 1:3; Philippians 2:5-8; Hebrews 2:14-15). Second, he must be able to pay the price of redemption (Ruth 2:1; 1 Peter 1:18-19). Third, he must be willing to redeem (Ruth 3:11; Matthew 20:28; John 10:15, 18; Hebrews 10:7). And finally, he must be free himself (as Christ was free from the curse of sin).

Just as Boaz served as a kinsman-redeemer to Ruth, so also did Christ serve as the mediator who redeemed us from our bondage to sin. And He loves us even more than Boaz could ever love Ruth.

⬆ Look Up

Just as Ruth became the bride of Boaz, so also the church is the bride of Christ (see, for example, Matthew 9:15; John 3:29; Romans 7:4; 1 Corinthians 6:15; Revelation 19:7-9; 21:2).

To understand better what that means, spend a few moments reading Ephesians 5:23-32. Then thank your loving Savior for His sacrificial love for you—a love that will last throughout eternity.

It is easier to love humanity as a whole than to love one's neighbor.

➡ Move Ahead

Just as Christ loved us, we are to love others. That means wholeheartedly. Sacrificially. Preeminently.

In Ephesians 5, Paul paralleled the love of Christ for His bride, the church, with the love of a husband and wife. If you're married, consider your relationship with your spouse. If you're not, broaden the application to your close friends or family members. Are your relationships illustrations of the love of Christ for His church? They can be, in His power, and for His glory.

1 Samuel

Following the destructive period of the judges, Samuel—prophet and king-maker—is called by God to rebuild Israel spiritually and politically. In time he anoints Saul as Israel's first king. But Saul soon proves unable to rule even his own heart. Because Saul lacks a heart for God, he is rejected by God. Samuel anoints the young David to take Saul's place, which causes a fierce rivalry resulting in David's flight into the wilderness to escape the jealous king. The book ends with Saul's death—clearing the way for David's glorious reign.

Focus	Samuel		Saul		David			
Divisions	Samuel's Call	Israel's Defeat	Saul's Selection	Saul's Rejection	David in the Court	David on the Run	David's Mercy	Saul's Downfall
	1 3	4 8	9 12	13 15	16 19	20 23	24 26	27 31
Topics	Last Judge		First King		King-Elect			
	Transition		Rise of Saul		Decline of Saul and Rise of David			
Place	Israel in Canaan							
Time	At Least 60 Years							

Samuel's Call and Childhood
1 Samuel 1–3

16

Overview: The period of the judges is nearly at an end. One last judge remains: Samuel, a man of godly character and integrity who will guide the nation from judgeship to kinship. Samuel's early life parallels that of another famous judge—Samson. Both are the offspring of barren women and the answer to fervent prayer; both are consecrated to the Lord's service from birth; both enter a society marked by moral decline and spiritual apathy. But while Samson spent much of his life avoiding his calling, Samuel does just the opposite. Even as a child he is quick to hear and obey the word of the Lord.

Heart of the Passage: 1 Samuel 1:1-20; 3:1-21

Chapter 1	Chapter 2		Chapter 3
Hannah's Petition	Hannah's Praise	Eli's Rejection	Samuel's Selection
1	11	12	36
Samuel's Childhood		Samuel's Call	

Your Daily Walk: Everything in the modern home is run by a switch . . . except the children! Discipline—once considered standard operating procedure for parents—is becoming rare; in its place permissiveness reigns.

But that is nothing new! A thousand years before Christ, the Bible paints a picture of the ruin and rejection of a family because the father failed to discipline his children. Eli, high priest of God, allowed his two sons to do that which was right in their own eyes. In shameless greed they stole for themselves the best parts of the sacrifices being offered to God. In response, God said He would "judge [Eli's] house for ever for the iniquity which he knoweth; because his sons made themselves vile, and he restrained them not" (3:13).

Parents, your role as a discipliner is not just a good idea; it is your God-given duty. God has a blueprint for you to follow in your child-rearing assignment (Proverbs 19:25; 23:13-14). Read about it, build upon it; and watch God bless!

Parents who are afraid to put their foot down usually have children who step on toes.

Insight: A Four-Question Quiz (with Only One Answer!)
 1. Who was the last judge in Israel? _____
 2. Who was the first prophet in Israel? _____
 3. Who anointed the first two kings in Israel? _____
 4. Who was the only man in the Old Testament to have two books of the Bible named after him? _____

17 *Israel's Defeat / 1 Samuel 4–8*

Heart of the Passage: 1 Samuel 4, 6, 8

Overview: When faith in God wavers, faith in man-made objects increases. In a scene reminiscent of the golden calf at Mount Sinai, the people of Israel carry the ark of the covenant into battle, confident that its presence will ensure victory over the Philistines. Instead, they suffer a shattering defeat in which 30,000 lives are lost (including the two sons of Eli) and the ark of the covenant is captured. Upon hearing the news, Eli falls backward and breaks his neck—a pathetic picture of a broken man and a broken nation. It remains for Samuel to assume the reins of leadership and guide the people back to repentance. But his declining years prove no more successful than Eli's as Samuel's sons once again corrupt the priesthood, causing the nation to clamor for a king "that we may be like all the nations" (8:20).

Chapter 4	Chapter 5	Chapter 6	Chapter 7	Chapter 8
The Ark Captured	The Ark Unwanted	The Ark Returned	The People Repenting	The People Demanding
Returning the Ark			Rebuilding the Nation	

Your Daily Walk: True or False: The desire to keep up with the Joneses began with the Joneses' neighbors.

Answer: False! It was present thousands of years ago when the people of Israel demanded a king just like their neighbors had.

It's a human tendency to want what someone else has. Call it what you may—covetousness, lust, envy, the "grass-is-greener-on-the-other-side" syndrome—God calls it sin. *Contentment,* not *covetousness,* should mark the lifestyle of God's children.

Check up on your *"CQ"*—your "Contentment Quotient." What purchases made in the last 30 days were prompted more by envy than by genuine need? Has a desire for material things diverted funds that should be going into the Lord's work? If so, what needs to change about your spending habits and attitudes if you are to be a good steward of the resources God has given you? Remember what Jesus said: "But seek [you] first the kingdom of God, and his righteousness . . ." (Matthew 6:33)!

Discontent makes rich men poor, while contentment makes poor men rich.

Insight: An Inglorious Birth at an Infamous Moment
Moments before her death, Phinehas's wife gave birth to a son and named him Ichabod ("where is the honor?")—a fitting title for a child suddenly left orphaned by disobedient parents (4:19-22).

90

Saul's Selection / 1 Samuel 9–12

18

Overview: From all outward appearances, Saul's selection as the first king of Israel is an outstanding choice. His kingly demeanor and imposing presence make him a promising candidate —from a human perspective. But while "man looketh on the outward appearance, the LORD looketh on the heart" (16:7). Saul is anointed by Samuel, installed as king at Mizpeh, proven in battle against the Ammonites, and confirmed as king at Gilgal. But the fact remains (as pointed out by Samuel in his final address to the nation) that God—not Saul—should be King over Israel.

Heart of the Passage: 1 Samuel 10; 12:6-25

Chapter 9	Chapter 10	Chapter 11	Chapter 12
Choosing a King	Crowning a King	Confirming a King	Cautioning a King
Saul's Administration			Samuel's Admonition

Your Daily Walk: What does it take to lead a nation? In the margin, see if you can compose a list of "Five Indispensable Qualities of a Leader."

Perhaps you thought of things like a commanding presence . . . eloquent speech . . . an aura of authority . . . toughness of character. But study the early years of Saul's reign—the only part of his life which received God's commendation—and you'll discover something interesting about Saul's leadership style. He held his peace with dissenters and refused to make examples of them when proven wrong; he gave God the credit for his successes; he didn't think of himself more highly than he ought; he was sensitive to the needs of people. In short, he was a true servant of God . . . and of the people he was trying to lead.

What is your leadership style in your home? your church? your office? your social and civic relationships? Do you seek to serve or be served? to meet needs or have your own needs met? Remember, man looks at (and applauds) the external appearance; God looks at (and rewards) the internal attitude. Which leadership role will you turn into an opportunity to serve this week? And as you contemplate your leadership of others, memorize Isaiah 48:17, a verse describing *God's* leadership of *you!*

Before following a leader, it is wise to see if he is headed in the right direction.

Insight: God Doesn't Act out of Character

God's promise that he would "not forsake his people for his great name's sake" (12:22) simply meant that to abandon Israel would have been a violation of His covenant and a contradiction of His character. God is always true to His Word . . . and His name.

19 Saul's Rebellion and Rejection
1 Samuel 13–15

Heart of the Passage:
1 Samuel 13:1-14; 15:1-23

Overview: Only two years into his reign, Saul is faced with a critical test. Confronted by a Philistine onslaught, would he obey God's word as delivered by Samuel? The answer is a resounding "No!" Saul enters the priest's office at Gilgal and offers sacrifices which only a Levite is permitted to offer—thus blatantly disregarding God's law. Samuel's announcement that God will take the kingdom from him only spurs Saul on to greater efforts at doing God's work—but not in God's way. By ignoring Samuel's specific command from God to annihilate the Amalekites, Saul seals the fate of his kingship.

Chapter 13	Chapter 14	Chapter 15
God's Curse upon Saul	Saul's Curse upon Israel	God's Rejection of Saul
War with Philistia		War with Amalek

Your Daily Walk: Is God pleased when you use company time to prepare your Sunday school lesson? How about driving 65 m.p.h. in a 55 m.p.h. zone so you won't be late for church? Is it okay to cheat on your income tax if you give the benefits of your "creative arithmetic" to God?

Only he who believes is obedient; only he who is obedient believes.

There is a fundamental question behind these situations and countless others you may face during your lifetime: How important is obedience to the Word of God? Is keeping His commands more important than trying to do something else you think will please Him more?

For King Saul, the question carried life-or-death importance. He concluded that God would overlook his incomplete obedience because of the generous sacrifices he offered, the money he gave to God's service, the time he spent in God's house. The decision cost him his kingdom—and eventually his life.

When God speaks, do you listen? And then do you act? You cannot learn too well the lesson which Saul failed to learn at all: "Hath the LORD as great delight in burnt offerings and sacrifices, as in obeying the voice of the LORD? Behold, to obey is better than sacrifice, and to hearken than the fat of rams" (15:22). Obeying God with half a heart can only lead to a broken heart—every time!

Insight: Glossary of Terms in the Blacksmith Shop (13:20-21)

share = sickle	mattock = hoe
coulter = plow	pim = file for sharpening

David in the Court of Saul
1 Samuel 16–19

20

Overview: The rejection of a king after the people's heart (Saul) sets the stage for the choice of a king after God's own heart (David). A young shepherd with a disposition more suited to the pasture than the palace, David possesses few claims to fame. He is a good marksman with a sling, an excellent lyre player, and the youngest of eight sons from an insignificant family in Bethlehem. But his heart attitude is one of undivided devotion—a quality readily visible in the way David dispatches the Philistine giant Goliath and handles Saul's jealous attacks.

Heart of the Passage: 1 Samuel 16–17

Chapter 16	Chapter 17	Chapter 18	Chapter 19
David the Musician	David the Giant Killer	David the Groom	David the Fugitive
David in Saul's Favor		David in Saul's Fury	

Your Daily Walk: Do you see life from God's perspective? Here's a quick way to find out. Simply answer these three questions honestly:

1. Do you see a calamity in every opportunity, or an opportunity in every calamity?

2. When confronted with a Goliath-size problem, do you respond, "He's too big to hit," or like David, "He's too big to miss"?

3. Do you feel that you've been put out to pasture, or do you see your present circumstances as proving grounds?

If you chose the second response to each question, then you see life from David's (and God's) perspective—the perspective that views one plus God as a majority in any situation—the perspective that enables you to walk with God in castles and caves, in pastures and palaces, when you are at peace and when you are pursued.

If you discover that your perspective needs sharpening, then spend some extra moments today reading Psalm 139—a page from David's diary that shows the heart attitude God delights to find.

Sometimes only a change of viewpoint is needed to convert a seemingly tiresome duty into an interesting opportunity.

Insight: David, the King Without a Crown
In 16:13 Samuel anoints David as the second king in Israel's history. But not until 2 Samuel 5:3 will David assume the reins of leadership over all 12 tribes—a wait of about 15 years! During that interval God has many important lessons to teach the young king-elect about how to shepherd His people.

21 *David on the Run from Saul* 1 Samuel 20–23

Overview: Today's section paints a peculiar picture: David, the king-elect of Israel—anointed, approved in battle, and awaiting the inauguration of his reign—is fleeing for his life from the deranged Saul, the king-rejected. Saul's pursuit drives David to desperate measures such as eating the forbidden shewbread at Nob and feigning insanity at Gath. But Scripture records that David's confidence in God never slackens, as his frequent petitions to God for direction and protection clearly testify.

Heart of the Passage: 1 Samuel 20–21

Chapter 20	Chapter 21		Chapter 22	Chapter 23
Saul's Deadly Plot	David's Frantic Flight . . .			
	to Nob	to Gath	to Adullam	to the Wilderness
	1 9	10 15		
David Endangered	David Estranged			

Your Daily Walk: Do you find yourself attracted to great individuals? Do you find something magnetic about a gifted athlete who performs effortlessly on the playing field, or a musician who plays an instrument or sings with consummate skill? If so, then you've also probably felt a sense of defeat and frustration, for you knew you could never be like the great individual you so admired.

Great occasions do not make heroes or cowards; they merely reveal them to others.

David was a great man of God in the truest sense of the word. He excelled as a warrior, writer, administrator, and musician. Perhaps you wish your life could be like his. But that isn't possible, is it?

When the Bible paints a picture of a believer, it paints it in human tones—blemishes and all. Victory and defeat, joys and heartaches, faith and faithlessness—it's all there. And it's there so you can identify with David, and know that the same quality of life he learned to experience with God day by day, you can experience.

Believers aren't perfect, they're just forgiven. But they're growing. How about you? Are you mired in a situation as David was? Then learn from it and move on. Get back in stride with God. Pick a quality you admire from David's life and work on it today.

Insight: Psalms Written in the Crucible of Experience

The Psalms are sacred songs of worship and praise, written by David and others as emotional responses to crisis experiences. Some of David's most moving psalms flowed from his pen during Saul's murderous pursuit. For an inside look, read Psalms 34, 52, 54, 57, 142.

David's Mercy Toward Saul
1 Samuel 24–26

Overview: After a brief delay to deal with a Philistine threat, Saul returns to take up the pursuit of David. His renewed zeal nearly pays off as (unknowingly) he traps David and his men in a cave. Then, miraculously, the tables are turned as David stands poised over King Saul with the power of life and death in his hand. And though vengeance is within his reach, David refuses to end the life of God's anointed. Again in chapter 26 the scene is repeated, this time in the wilderness of Ziph. Once again David must make a choice. Once again the source of David's anxiety is only a sword's thrust away. And once again David resists the temptation to assume God's role by ending the life of Saul prematurely.

Heart of the Passage: 1 Samuel 24

Chapter 24	Chapter 25	Chapter 26
David Spares Saul's Life	Abigail Spares Nabal's Life	David Spares Saul Again
In the Cave	On the March	In the Trench

Your Daily Walk: Patience is accepting a difficult situation without giving God a deadline for removing it. It means waiting without worrying.

Picture in your mind the tall, youthful figure of David standing over King Saul, who is finally at his mercy. What thoughts must David be wrestling with? Hatred for his mistreatment . . . pity for the demented king . . . exhilaration that at last his moment of revenge has come? No, there is no hint of animosity or vengeance. Rather, David's only desire is that Saul spare his life until God fulfills His promise.

Are you biding your time, waiting for a chance to avenge a wrong suffered? God wants to replace that spirit of bitterness with a spirit of love and forgiveness. But, as in David's case, the choice is yours. Are you willing? Then let Ephesians 4:31-32 show you the way!

Patience is accepting a difficult situation without giving God a deadline for removing it.

Insight: Rest in Peace, Old Testament Style

You may have seen old gravestones marked with the letters "R.I.P."—Rest In Peace. The Old Testament analogy is found in 1 Samuel 25:29—"Bound in the Bundle of Life." This saying has long been applied to life beyond the grave, and the first letter of each Hebrew word is found on virtually every Jewish tombstone. The phrase is taken from the custom of binding up valuable things in a bundle to prevent them from being damaged or lost (Genesis 42:35).

23 *Saul's Downfall / 1 Samuel 27–31*

Heart of the Passage: 1 Samuel 27–28, 31

 Overview: After months of running for his life, David concludes that leaving Israel entirely is the only way to escape Saul's relentless pursuit. By convincing the Philistines he is a true defector, David is given the city of Ziklag as his base of operations. But instead of aiding the enemy, David and his army methodically destroy Philistine strongholds. Meanwhile, Saul's desperate attempts to counter the Philistine threat finally lead him to consult with a medium from Endor. Instead of the promise of victory, Saul hears frightening predictions of death and defeat— forecasts which come true the very next day as he and his sons die on the field of battle.

Chapter 27	Chapter 28	Chapter 29	Chapter 30	Chapter 31
David at Ziklag	Saul at Endor	David Dismissed	Ziklag Defended	Saul Destroyed
End of Saul's Pursuit			End of Saul's Dynasty	

God has linked two things together which cannot be separated: obedience and power.

 Your Daily Walk: "When the going gets tough, the tough get going!"

That's a well-known slogan originally describing the grit and determination of a certain branch of the military. But despite the slogan, even a good soldier knows when it is best to get going . . . in the opposite direction.

David was a first-rate soldier. Consider his military accomplishments: He whipped Goliath with one stone, led a rout of the Philistine army, and leveled several Philistine cities while living in Ziklag. If anyone could hold his own against an enemy, it was David. Why then did he decide to run from Saul's army and hide in Ziklag? Because he knew that sometimes it is wiser to get *out* than to get *tough*. Fighting with Saul would have only served to reduce David to Saul's level of petty jealously and revenge.

Are you in the midst of defending your rights against someone who has wronged you? Instead of "fighting it out," let God fight for you. Meditate today on Psalm 37:1-8: "Fret not . . . Trust . . . Delight . . . Commit . . . Rest . . . Fret not."

Insight: No Middle Ground with a Medium

Saul's visit with the witch of Endor not only violated God's law (Leviticus 19:31), but contradicted Saul's actions in 1 Samuel 28:3 in which he expelled all witches and mediums from Israel.

2 Samuel

David, the king-elect in 1 Samuel, becomes the king-enthroned in 2 Samuel, ruling first over Judah and then over all Israel. Characterized at first by victory and success, David leads Israel to world prominence. But his reign is soon marred by the dual sins of adultery and murder. The aftershocks of turmoil, trouble, and unrest rock the kingdom for the rest of his life and beyond. Despite his personal weaknesses, David remains "a man after God's own heart" because of his repentant attitude and his responsiveness to God's will.

Focus	David's Triumphs			David's Troubles			
Divisions	Divided Nation	United Nation	Expanded Nation	Adultery and Murder	Absalom's Revolt	Unrest and Violence	David's Last Words
	1 4	5 7	8 10	11 14	15 18	19 20	21 24
Topics	Civil War			Crimes	Conflict		
	Obedience and Blessing			Disobedience and Judgment			
Place	Hebron	Jerusalem					
Time	7 1/2 Years	33 Years					

24 David's Divided Nation
2 Samuel 1–4

Heart of the Passage:
2 Samuel 1:1–2:7

📖 **Overview:** The books of 1 and 2 Samuel are actually a single continuous story. In 1 Samuel, the mood is one of death and despair; in 2 Samuel, a ray of hope shines. In 1 Samuel, Saul's dynasty is destroyed; in 2 Samuel, David's dynasty is established. But the transition of power is not a simple one. Proper mourning for the departed monarch, the inauguration of the leader, the purging of the former regime's influence, and the putting down of rival factions and rebellious elements—all must be done before David can rule in peace.

Chapter 1	Chapter 2	Chapter 3	Chapter 4
David's Lament	Saul's Lingering Influence	Abner's Defection	Ish-Bosheth's Death
Mourning Saul's Death		Fighting Saul's House	

You can judge a man by his enemies as well as by his friends.

🖊 **Your Daily Walk:** Make a mental list of three candidates for the title, "My Least Favorite Person on Earth." Pick one name that seems to emerge as the prime contender. Now ask yourself this question: "How would I react to the news that _____ had met a violent death?"

In a sense, David's prayers had finally been answered. Without raising a finger against God's anointed, David had at last been vindicated in his claim to the throne of Israel. The man who had tried so long and hard to snuff out his life was now dead. And yet, instead of rejoicing over the misfortunes of Saul, David wept unashamedly at the news. He even composed a beautiful song of testimony as a perpetual memorial to Israel's first king.

Do you love your enemies? Can you highlight their virtues and strengths—and minimize their faults and failings—without bitterness or envy? That's what divine love is all about (1 Corinthians 13:4-7). If you are still "enemies with your enemies," ask God to give you a heart like David's. Then turn your list of "Least Favorite People" into a prayer list. It will revolutionize your prayers; it may even turn some of your enemies into friends!

🖊 **Insight:** The Irony of David's Tears
Deep mourning for Saul (1:11-12) came from the people he had hated and persecuted most severely. Compare the weeping of Jesus over the city of Jerusalem just days before its inhabitants would nail Him to a cross (Matthew 23:37-39).

David's United Nation / 2 Samuel 5–7   25

 Overview: With the death of Ish-Bosheth, the people of Israel transfer their allegiance to David as their rightful king. As his first official act, David conquers the strategic Jebusite stronghold of Jerusalem and makes it the new capital of the nation. But something more than political and military reform is necessary. The worship of God must be returned to its place of primacy. Knowing this, David makes plans to bring the ark of the covenant to Jerusalem and build a fitting place for it to reside. In the process he learns some hard lessons about doing God's will in God's way and in God's timing.

Heart of the Passage: 2 Samuel 5:1-5; 7:1-29

Chapter 5	Chapter 6	Chapter 7
David Unites the Nation	David Returns the Ark	David Receives a Covenant
Consolidation	Jubilation	Expectation

Your Daily Walk: Think carefully about each statement and decide whether it is true or false:

T F 1. If God has placed a desire in my heart, then it must be His will for me to accomplish it.

T F 2. If my goal is to please and glorify God, then it is really insignificant how I go about it.

T F 3. Doing God's will in something other than God's way cannot truly be God's will.

David had two ambitions in the early years of his reign: to bring the ark to Jerusalem, and to build a house for God there. To accomplish the first, David chose the expedient—rather than the obedient— mode of transportation, and it cost an unsuspecting man his life. David's wish to build a majestic temple for God was commendable, but it simply wasn't God's plan for David's life.

It's wonderful to dream big dreams for God. But be sure those dreams are implemented in God's way, in God's timing, and with the people God intends to use. It was David's son Solomon whom God wanted to build the temple—and who penned these fitting words well worth memorizing: "A man's heart deviseth his way; but the LORD directeth his steps" (Proverbs 16:9).

Choosing the expedient way instead of the obedient way can be a hindrance to your furtherance.

Insight: Learning a Life-and-Death Lesson (6:3-7)

For perhaps 50 years the ark had been considered little more than a piece of furniture. God's stern judgment upon Uzzah for touching it marked the beginning of a new era in Israel's worship in which the people recognized again the sanctity of God's presence.

26 David's Expanding Nation
2 Samuel 8–10

Heart of the Passage: 2 Samuel 8–9

Overview: Once the internal opposition against his rule has been silenced, David is free to secure his new kingdom against foreign invasion. In quick succession the Moabites, Syrians, Edomites, and Ammonites fall to David's troops, causing the other neighboring powers to surrender without a fight. Extensive new territory and enormous amounts of tribute are added to David's kingdom. But David nurses no spirit of revenge, as evidenced in his dealings with Mephibosheth.

Chapter 8	Chapter 9	Chapter 10
David Extends His Kingdom	David Extends His Kindness	David Exterminates His Enemies
Moab	Mephibosheth	Ammon

God's part we cannot do; our part He will not do.

Your Daily Walk: Here's another true/false quiz to take. According to 8:1-14:

T F 1. David defeated the enemies of the Lord.
T F 2. The Lord defeated the enemies of David.

To check your answers, simply reread the passage, circling all the verbs describing David's actions ("David smote . . . subdued . . . took . . . put to death . . . slew") and all the verbs describing God's actions ("The Lord preserved [literally, gave victory to] David whithersoever he went," 8:6, 14).

Who fought the battle? David did! Who gave the victory? God did! David could not do God's part, but neither would God do David's part. It was a cooperative effort from start to finish, with God providing the power and protection, and David swinging the sword and smiting the enemy. For David to go forth in his own strength—or sit idly by and expect the job to get done in God's strength—would have proven disastrous. But by teaming up with God, David was invincible.

The attitudes, "God, You don't need me" and "God, I don't need You," are twin formulas for disaster. Check up on your own battle plan for today. Then jot down a challenge you are facing, and the strategy you will use to ensure that you come out a winner.

Insight: Half Shorn, Fully Shamed (10:4)
Even to this day, cutting off a person's beard is regarded by the Arabs as the height of indignity, comparable to that of flogging or branding. Many would rather die than have their beards shaved off, which shows the severity of the insult to David's men.

David's Adultery and Its Aftermath
2 Samuel 11–14

📖 **Overview:** At a time when David should have been on the field of battle, he finds himself instead on the roof of the palace. A casual glance . . . a lustful thought . . . an inquiry . . . and the king of Israel set in motion a chain of events that culminates in adultery and murder. David's sinful acts continue to ripen for years within David's family in the form of murder, incest, treachery, and open revolt.

Heart of the Passage: 2 Samuel 11–12

Chapter 11		Chapter 12	Chapters 13–14
Adultery in the Palace	Murder on the Battlefield	David's Heartfelt Confession	David's Family Consequences
Recklessness	Reaction	Repentance	Regret

🖊 **Insight:** The Subtle Slide from Sin to Sin
   The leap from a single covetous thought (11:2) to the coldly calculated murder of one of David's most loyal soldiers would probably have been unthinkable to the king. But because one "little" sin relentlessly dragged him into another—idleness, selfishness, covetousness, adultery, treachery, murder—the net result was the same.

Secret sins won't stay secret for very long.

✓ **Your Daily Walk:** Do you use . . . or abuse . . . the authority God has given you?
   Scan chapter 11 and circle the word sent every time you discover it (hint: it occurs a dozen times), for therein lies the key to David's downfall.
   While it was common practice for the king to send others to do his bidding, such practice was subject to abuse. David "sent Joab" to the battle front (11:1), when in fact David should have accompanied him there. David "sent and inquired" after Bathsheba (11:3), though he had no business doing so. David "sent messengers, and took her" (11:4), though she belonged to another man. David "sent . . . by the hand of Uriah" (11:14) that loyal soldier's own death certificate. Small wonder that when David's wicked plan was at last complete, God "sent Nathan unto David" (12:1) to uncover the whole ugly scheme.
   Using God-given authority for your own convenience may seem expedient now, but in the long run it will prove bitterly expensive. In the margin, list the roles of authority you fill today (e.g., parent, deacon, vice-president, teacher, club leader). Then turn your list into a prayer project as you ask God to make you a "sanctified sender"!

28 *Sins of the Fathers*

Scripture Reading: Psalm 51

⬅ Step Back

In the Ten Commandments, God instructed His people to keep from making, serving, or worshiping any graven image or idol. "For I the LORD thy God am a jealous God, visiting the iniquity of the fathers upon the children unto the third and fourth generation of them that hate me; and shewing mercy unto thousands of them that love me, and keep my commandments" (Exodus 20:5-6).

Ironically, one of the Bible's most piercing examples of the sins of a father carrying through to the next generation is one of the Bible's brightest lights: David.

Though David is called a man after God's own heart, he still had feet of clay. His sin with Bathsheba, followed by a murderous cover-up, revealed his humanity. And that sin haunted him as his sons Amnon and Absalom fell into degradation and treachery—in fulfillment of God's promised judgment (2 Samuel 12:11).

The truth is clear: Sin may be forgiven, but one will still reap its inevitable consequences. You'll read of those consequences in David's life in the next few days. Incest, murder, intrigue, rebellion—the story of David's family from chapter 12 on reads like a horror story.

⬆ Look Up

The course of a person's life can pivot on one small event. Such was the case with David. But David's sin with Bathsheba was no sudden collapse of his moral values. Rather it was the outgrowth of an undisciplined life given to passion, polygamy, and idle pleasure. So when temptation confronted him, David had no willpower to resist. And the crash was heard for generations, in the form of treachery, immorality, jealousy, and murder in David's family.

You simply can't put your sins behind you until you face them.

➡ Move Ahead

There is light in the darkness of David's sin. Second Samuel 12 shows us that David's heart was broken by his sin, and he immediately responded to Nathan's rebuke with wholehearted repentance. Psalm 51 captures that heartfelt cry for forgiveness. But though David experiences God's forgiveness, the seeds of sin have been planted—and the harvest will be reaped.

Face up to your areas of weakness today. Confess them honestly to your forgiving God; turn from them with your whole heart; draw new strength from Him to move forward.

And if you have children, be sure you pray for them every day. For protection, for guidance, for mercy. You can leave them a wonderful spiritual heritage—one that will last them a lifetime.

Revolt Against David / 2 Samuel 15–18 *29*

📖 **Overview:** Of all the sons mentioned in the Bible, none is as physically handsome and yet so emotionally and spiritually scarred as Absalom. Of Absalom, Matthew Henry writes, "In his body there was no blemish, but in his mind nothing but wounds and bruises." Today's reading describes the fulfillment of Nathan's prophetic judgment upon David. While his own transgression had been done in secret, the shame, dishonor, and murder within his own family circle would be done before all Israel. But the greatest headache would be the rebellious attempt by Absalom to usurp his father's throne. David's faith in God and love for his wayward son never diminish, though they are severely tested. Driven from Jerusalem, cursed by his countrymen, and disgraced by his son, David is eventually vindicated and restored, though at tremendous personal and national cost.

Heart of the Passage: 2 Samuel 15, 18

Chapter 15		Chapter 16	Chapters 17–18
Absalom's Crafty Revolt	David's Hasty Retreat	Absalom's Grand Entrance	Absalom's Sorry End
1 12	13 37		
David's Rule Threatened			David's Rule Restored

✒️ **Insight:** Diary of a Disgraced Dad

What thoughts must David have been thinking, what emotions must he have been feeling, as he saw his favorite son make a mockery of the kingship and openly disgrace the family name from the rooftops of the palace? What tears must he have shed in private and before God at seeing his own trespasses come to fruition? There is no need to conjecture—David's thoughts and prayers are written down in his "diary" for you to read! They're found in Psalms 3, 4, 62, and 63.

✔️ **Your Daily Walk:** Mankind has yet to invent a glue that can mend a broken heart. But God can. Psychologists can probe your past, tell you why your heart is broken, and help you cope with a broken heart. They aren't in the business, however, of fixing broken hearts. But God is. He specializes in reconstructive surgery on shattered lives—taking the pieces of an empty shell and turning them into something beautiful and purposeful and glorifying to Himself. Prodigal children, fractured marriages, splintered homes —they're His specialty.

Laugh at your troubles; that way you can be sure you'll always have something to laugh at.

Do you have a job for the Mender of broken hearts? His office is open 24 hours a day, seven days a week. No appointment necessary.

30 *Unrest and Violence in the Land*
2 Samuel 19–20

**Heart
of the
Passage:
2 Samuel
19**

 Overview: Overcome with grief for his slain son Absalom, David mourns so loudly and long as to seem ungrateful for those who risked their lives to return him to the throne. This stinging insight, delivered by David's field marshal Joab, shakes David from his fit of depression and stirs him to resume the reins of power. However, his homecoming is not a particularly pleasant one. By addressing his own tribe (Judah) and inviting them to restore him as their king (which they readily agree to do), David isolates the other tribes in a national display of jealousy. A revolutionary named Sheba stages an untimely rebellion, and only after it is crushed can David rule a united kingdom.

Chapter 19		Chapter 20	
A Jolt from Joab	A Journey to Jerusalem	Sheba's Defection	Sheba's Death
1 14	15 43	1 3	4 26
David's Restoration in Judah		Further Rebellion in Judah	

**Two
quick
ways to
disaster
are to
take
nobody's
advice
and to
take
every-
body's
advice.**

Your Daily Walk: Yesterday you read how Absalom ignored the wise counsel of Ahithophel and followed the foolish counsel of Hushai. Today you read how David avoided a mass mutiny of his friends by listening to the wise words of General Joab.

Advice is one commodity of which there will never be a shortage! Everyone from the mailman to the meter maid is quick to give advice on a variety of problems. But such counsel is only as good as its source. "Blessed is the man that walketh not in the counsel of the ungodly" (Psalm 1:1). There is counsel you should avoid. "Hear counsel and receive instruction, that thou mayest be wise in thy latter end" (Proverbs 19:20). There is counsel you should seek and apply. And how do you tell the difference? "The counsel of the LORD standeth for ever, the thoughts of his heart to all generations" (Psalm 33:11). Counsel that is true to the heart of God, true to His Word, is the kind you should seek and follow in your life.

Take a decision you are facing today, and share it with a godly man or woman from your church or community. Listen carefully to the counsel that's given. Then do it. God will honor you for it.

Insight: And Speaking of Wise Counselors . . .
Don't miss the story of the wise woman of Abel (20:14-22) who saved her hometown from destruction by confronting Joab!

David's Last Words and Deeds
2 Samuel 21-24

31

📖 **Overview:** Today's reading covers six topics which, though out of strict chronological order, form an appendix to the main body of 2 Samuel: (1) a severe famine sent in judgment for Saul's treatment of the Gibeonites; (2) a series of wars with the Philistines; (3) a beautiful psalm of deliverance and praise; (4) a list of David's mighty men of valor; (5) a sinful census; (6) the severe punishment that followed. The closing paragraph of the book portrays David in his most natural pose: worshiping the Lord in humility.

Heart of the Passage: 2 Samuel 22; 24:18-25

Chapter 21	Chapter 22	Chapter 23	Chapter 24
David's Rescue	David's Refrain	David's Roster	David's Roll Call
David's Life on the Line		David's Life in Review	

✍ **Your Daily Walk:** How do you respond when you have failed God—and you know it? Do you find yourself running to Him . . . or from Him?

In the closing days of David's life, he ordered a census of his troops—a census motivated by pride, not necessity . . . a census which angered God and forced David to select his own punishment.

In most pagan religions today, the emphasis is on appeasing —rather than approaching—an angry god. But notice David's reaction after ordering his sinful census.

He knew his actions were wrong and that he deserved the chastening of the Lord. But he saw more mercy in God than in man. And so he responded, "Let us fall now into the hand of the LORD; for his mercies are great: and let me not fall into the hand of man" (24:14). Even in the midst of chastening, the arms of the Lord are the safest place to be, and David knew it.

Pain is never pleasant, because pain hurts. But there is a pain that comes from your Father in heaven who cares too much to allow you to sin with impunity. Read Hebrews 12:5-11—and thank God for His chastening in your life. It's a sure sign you are His child.

Mercy does not always express itself by with- holding punish- ment.

📷 **Insight:** From Threshing Floor to Something More
Araunah was known as a Jebusite (24:18), one of the original inhabitants of the city of Jerusalem. Many believe his threshing floor is to be identified with the rock formation preserved under the Dome of the Rock, on or near the site of Solomon's temple.

1 Kings

K ing Solomon's illustrious life is set
forth in the first half of 1 Kings.
Under his leadership, Israel rises to its peak
of power and glory. The crowning touch
comes with the construction of the temple in
Jerusalem. But Solomon's zeal for God cools
as pagan wives turn his heart away from
godly worship. Solomon dies a man divided
religiously, leaving behind a nation divided
physically. The next century sees the decline
of two nations, each growing indifferent to
God's prophets and precepts.

Focus	United Kingdom			Divided Kingdom		
Divisions	Solomon's Rise	Solomon's Temple	Solomon's Fame	A Nation Torn	Ministry of Elijah	Reign of Ahab
	1 4	5 8	9 11	12 16	17 19	20 22
Topics	Expansion and Glory			Division and Decline		
	One King			Many Kings		
Place	Jerusalem			Northern Kingdom (Israel) Southern Kingdm (Judah)		
Time	About 40 Years			About 90 Years		

Solomon's Rise to Glory / 1 Kings 1–4

1

Overview: As David's life draws to a close, his son Adonijah attempts to usurp the throne from the rightful heir, Solomon. But the plot is foiled when David publicly proclaims Solomon his true successor. In the final hours before his death, David charges Solomon to walk before the Lord in integrity and truth—a request which Solomon fulfills in the early days of his administration by ruling with justice, discernment, humility, and honesty before God and man. Presented with a "blank check" by God, Solomon asks for wisdom to rule skillfully rather than for wealth to live lavishly. In return, God gives him both!

Heart of the Passage: 1 Kings 2:1-4; 3:1-15

Chapter 1	Chapter 2	Chapter 3	Chapter 4
Solomon's Competition	Solomon's Confirmation	Solomon's Counsel	Solomon's Cabinet
Anointing a King		Administration of a King	

Your Daily Walk: Humility is a paradox: The moment you think you've finally found it, you've lost it! There has yet to be written a book entitled *Humility and How I Achieved It.* And yet, God expects—and rewards—an attitude of servantlike humility in His children.

Solomon had everything going for him: godly heritage, distinguished family name, financial security, and the one true God on his side. But he also had a realistic view of himself. He knew his own weaknesses: partiality, insensitivity, impatience—weaknesses which, if left uncorrected, might doom his reign from the start. In childlike humility he asked for what he needed from God, not merely what he wanted.

Here is a sentence to complete, and a project to begin: "I know I am weak in the area of [what?]; but this month with God's help, I'm going to strengthen that area of weakness [how?]." As you ponder what steps to take, claim the promise of Isaiah 41:10 and count on God to strengthen you.

One way to build spiritual strength is to commit God's Word to memory.

Insight: Following in His Father's Footsteps
David became known as the "sweet psalmist of Israel" for his skill in composing half of the psalms in Israel's hymnbook. But Solomon was not far behind! According to 4:32, he composed more than a thousand songs himself, of which Psalm 127 is an example.

2 *Solomon's Temple / 1 Kings 5–8*

Overview: Before his death, David had charged his son Solomon with the responsibility of building a house for God in Jerusalem. Now at last it is time to make that dream a reality. Nothing is too good for the place where God's glory will dwell: cedar trees from Lebanon, costly stones, tons of precious metals. For seven long years Solomon plans and prepares the temple. When at last the ark of the covenant is installed in the Holy Place, the cloud of God's presence fills the house of the Lord. Once again, God's glory dwells in the midst of His people.

Heart of the Passage: 1 Kings 6:1-14; 8:12-61

Chapter 5	Chapter 6	Chapter 7	Chapter 8
Buying for the Temple	Building the Temple	Furnishing the Temple	Finishing the Temple
Preparation	Construction	Decoration	Dedication

Your Daily Walk: The reason people may sometimes feel like complete failures is because they fail to complete! Look around your home or office and make a list of all the jobs, projects, and assignments you have begun—but never have brought to completion. Wouldn't you agree that one worthwhile task carried to a successful conclusion is worth 50 half-finished tasks? It wasn't until the temple was *completed* that God's glory took up residence there—God's stamp of approval upon a job well done.

The root of all steadfastness is in consecration to God.

On a sheet of paper, jot down three of your "unfinished tasks." Perhaps it's a Christian book you never finished reading . . . an unsaved neighbor you've been meaning to get to know . . . a family project that never got off the ground. Next to each one, write a realistic date for completion and mark your calendar. By finishing those half-done tasks, you just might receive God's "well done" (Matthew 25:21)!

Insight: The Tabernacle and Temple—a Study in Contrasts

Detail	Tabernacle (Exodus 26)	Temple (1 Kings 6)
Dimensions	45x15x15 feet	90x30x45 feet
Porch	no	yes, 30 feet long
Windows	no	yes
Divider between two rooms	veil	veil and doors (2 Chronicles 3:14)
Items in Most Holy Place	ark with two cherubim (Exodus 25:18-20)	ark and two separate cherubim (2 Chron. 5:7-8)

Fame, Fortune, and Failure
1 Kings 9–11

3

📖 **Overview:** Under Solomon's able leadership, the nation's boundaries expand to five times the area ruled by David. Financially, Solomon enjoys unparalleled prosperity as tribute from neighboring nations flows into the national treasury. But even as the nation prospers, the seeds of spiritual decay are being sown. Solomon's passion for pagan women, of whom he takes hundreds to be his wives and concubines, turns his heart from the God of heaven to the gods of men. Result: God tears most of the kingdom away from Solomon's son.

Heart of the Passage: 1 Kings 9:1-9; 11:1-13

Chapter 9	Chapter 10		Chapter 11	
Increasing Frontiers	Increasing Fame	Increasing Fortune	Pagan Wives	Persistent Enemies
1	13	14 29	1 13	14 43
Solomon's Assets			Solomon's Liabilities	

🖊 **Your Daily Walk:** Find a flashlight, some aluminum foil, and a piece of black paper. Take them into a dark room. Lay a piece of foil on the paper and shine the flashlight on it. Then move the beam of light so that it hits the paper but not the foil. Which is brighter: light hitting the paper (and being absorbed) or light hitting the foil (and being reflected)?

When the queen of Sheba heard of Solomon's vast wealth and wisdom, she had to learn firsthand if the reports were true. Notice what she concluded: "Blessed be the LORD thy God, which delighted in thee . . . because the LORD loved Israel for ever, therefore made he thee king" (10:9). Rather than absorbing the glory for himself, Solomon had become a reflector of God's glory. When others saw the king's greatness, they gave glory not to the king but to the King of Kings!

Tear off small pieces of the black paper and the aluminum foil and carry them with you today. Ask yourself frequently which one represents your life at that time. Meditate on Matthew 5:16 throughout the day, looking for creative ways to reflect, rather than absorb, the glory of God.

A humble talent that is used is worth more than one of a genius that is idle.

📖 **Insight:** Developing Your Talent for Talents

Though the precise weight (and therefore the value) of Old Testament monetary measures is unknown, the *talent* was approximately 75.6 pounds, the *shekel* about .403 ounces, and the *pound* about 1.25 pounds. Using these numbers and a gold price of $475 per ounce, the total value of the gold mentioned in 10:14 was about $380 million!

4 *A Nation Torn in Two / 1 Kings 12–16*

Heart of the Passage: 1 Kings 12

Overview: Solomon's great wealth results partly from the soaring taxes he exacts from his countrymen. After his death, his son Rehoboam must decide if he will continue or cancel the harsh taxation policies of his father. Following foolish advice, Rehoboam increases the tax burden—and spawns a national "tax revolt." When the dust settled, the united kingdom is no more, and in its place stands a divided kingdom of two distinct nations (Israel and Judah) ruled by two decadent kings (Jeroboam and Rehoboam).

Chapter 12	Chapter 13	Chapter 14	Chapters 15–16
Rehoboam's Insensitivity	Jeroboam's Idolatry	Jeroboam's Illness	Judah's Wars with Israel
Division	Defilement	Disease	Disaster

For parents to allow a child to grow up without Christ is a far greater dereliction of duty than for parents to have children who grow up without learning to read or write.

Your Daily Walk: A grade school class wrote essays on the subject "What's Wrong with Parents Today?" One child said it all: "We get our parents so late in life that it is impossible to do anything with them."

Parents, most of you received your children when they were only minutes old—but at what age will they receive you? Parents are prone to give their children everything except the one thing they need most: time. Time for listening, time for understanding, time for helping, time for guiding. Taking time away from your own concerns and focusing on those of your children sounds simple. In reality it is the most difficult and sacrificial task of parenthood.

Whatever spiritual legacy Rehoboam received from his father Solomon, it apparently did not help him learn to love the God of Israel. As a result, the spiritual vacuum that resulted after Solomon's death led to the fracturing of the nation. Will your home be any different? Call a family council this evening to evaluate (with input from every family member) how you spend time together as a family—and how often!

Insight: The Divided Kingdom Doubly Divided

Most readers will be familiar with the divided kingdom—10 tribes in the north (Israel), and 2 tribes in the south (Judah). But did you know there was a time when the northern 10 tribes nearly divided again? Two power blocks, led respectively by Tibni and Omri, struggled for control of the northern kingdom. And in the end, who prevailed as "king of the north" (16:22)?_____

The Curse of the Kings

5

← Step Back

In the days of the Judges, the people of Israel had clamored for a king (1 Samuel 8:6). Displeased with their rebellious spirit, Samuel turned to the Lord in prayer. And God assured him, "Hearken unto the voice of the people in all that they say unto thee: for they have not rejected thee, but they have rejected me, that I should not reign over them" (v. 7).

Scripture Reading: 1 Samuel 8:6-18

The Lord pointed out that the Israelites had been stubborn since the day He brought them out of Egypt: "They have forsaken me, and served other gods, so do they also unto thee" (v. 8).

As a result, God instructed Samuel to give them the king they wanted. But Samuel also was to warn of the problems having a king would bring . . . including the drafting of young people, taxation of crops and flocks, appropriation of private property, and the loss of personal liberty (see 1 Samuel 8:10-18).

By now, you've read that all those warnings have come back to haunt the Israelites. And their situation will only grow worse.

Was it God's will for Israel to have a king? Obviously the Lord knew that Israel would have a king (see the prophecies of Genesis 49:10; Numbers 24:17; Deuteronomy 17:14-20). In His sovereignty, God allows even evil deeds to fulfill His purposes (see, for instance, Genesis 50:20; Acts 2:23).

As you continue your daily reading, you'll see time and time again the degrading results of Israel's choice. God allowed that choice. But He also allowed its consequences.

↑ Look Up

Unlike the world's monarchies, Israel was to be a theocracy—literally, a nation under God's rule. God was to reign over their affairs, working through His people. But Israel chose the world's ways by installing a human king. As you'll note as you read through the Bible, humanity is prone to consider its ways superior to God's —even though the results of such an attitude are always disastrous.

One step of obedience is better than a hundred sermons.

Could you be prone to do the same? Is there an area of your life in which you think you're in control, rather than God? What can you learn from Israel's decision to go her own way?

→ Move Ahead

It's easy for us to read the Bible and shake our heads over the selfish, ungodly choices of God's people. But we may be blind to our own failures to follow God's Word in our daily lives.

Today, think about your true King, the Lord Jesus Christ (John 1:49). Pledge yourself to Him in loyal obedience, and be prepared to serve Him faithfully today. He deserves nothing less.

6 *Elijah and Ahab / 1 Kings 17–19*

Heart of the Passage: 1 Kings 18:20– 19:21

 Overview: Chapter 15 begins a pattern that will extend throughout the rest of 1 and 2 Kings. The writer flip-flops in his account between the nations of Israel and Judah, first describing the reigning power in the North, then moving to the South, and so on. He traces the parallel stories of two nations in spiritual decline, taking time occasionally to highlight a prophet (such as Elijah) or a king (such as Ahab) who contributes significantly to the spiritual rise or fall of one of the nations. Today's reading centers around the mysterious (yet very human) person of Elijah, the prophet who courageously faces a heathen Israelite king and 850 pagan prophets of Baal, only to flee for his life from the murderous Queen Jezebel.

Chapter 17	Chapter 18	Chapter 19
Prediction in the Palace: "Drought"	Contest on Carmel: "The Lord Is God"	Hiding on Horeb: "Anoint Elisha"
Elijah Confronts Ahab	Elijah Confronts Baal	Elijah Confronts God

We cannot expect to live defectively and pray effectively.

Your Daily Walk: How often do you pray the prayer of inconvenience?

In the book of James (5:17-18), Elijah is held up as a model of prayer. He was no "super saint" but rather "a man subject to like passions as we are." He got tired, discouraged, and anxious on occasion, but his first reaction was to take it to God in prayer.

But the remarkable thing about his prayer life was how often he prayed inconvenient prayers. He prayed for a drought, then watched as God answered his prayer . . . and dried up his only source of water! He prayed for fire from heaven, knowing it would make him a marked man in Jezebel's eyes. His constant prayer was, "God, do something great . . . and I'm available if You need me."

Examine your prayer life. Which do you pray: "God save my heathen neighbor," or "God, use me to help lead that neighbor to You"? "God comfort that heartbroken family" or "God use me to bring comfort to that family"? Take a situation you are facing today, and write out your own prayer of inconvenience to God.

Insight: And Speaking of Jogging Enthusiasts . . .
With his life on the line, Elijah ran from Mount Carmel to Jezreel to Beersheba—a distance of about 110 miles! When Elijah "went for his life" (19:3), he took no chances.

Reign of Ahab / 1 Kings 20–22

7

Overview: If you expect a climactic finish to the book of 1 Kings today, you will be disappointed! Originally 1 and 2 Kings were a single continuous account, and the division between them in the English Bible is only literary, not historical. Today you will read about the conclusion of Ahab's wicked reign in Israel, and take a brief look at Jehoshaphat's righteous reign in Judah. Ahab's life is one long illustration of a man with no heart for God. In spite of God's powerful display on Mount Carmel, and two heaven-sent victories over the Syrians, Ahab shows utter disregard for God's commands.

Heart of the Passage: 1 Kings 20; 22:29-40

Chapter 20	Chapter 21	Chapter 22
Ahab's Smashing Victories	Ahab's Stealing of a Vineyard	Ahab's Shameful Death
Conquest	Covetousness	Calamity

Your Daily Walk: Fighting against God can be dangerous business. Ahab tried it, and it cost him his life.

In today's reading, notice how many times God made Himself known to Ahab. Patiently but persistently, He showed Israel's king that the God of heaven rules in the affairs of men. But in spite of fire from heaven, two divinely provided victories over superior foes, and the ringing declaration of the prophets, Ahab would not be swayed from his wicked ways. Refusing to be convinced that there are no "accidents" with God, Ahab became the object of one such "accident." Disguising himself to avoid the prophetically decreed end of his life, he was struck by an arrow sent flying "at a venture" and guided by a higher hand straight to the one chink in his armor.

Think back over the first week of this month. How has God been demonstrating His reality and His power to you through daily displays of protection or provision? And how have you responded? Write in the margin an appropriate response that Ahab never gave—but you will!

The only kingdom that will prevail in this world is the kingdom that is not of this world.

 Insight: Murder Without a Weapon

Ahab cared nothing for the law of God, a fact clearly seen in his disregard for the divine restriction on transferring land from one tribe to another (21:1-3; Leviticus 25:23-28; Numbers 36:7-8). In shameless greed he allowed Jezebel to mastermind Naboth's murder—a crime for which he would later be held responsible by God (21:18-19).

2 Kings

T he author of 2 Kings weaves the historical threads of two nations into one fabric. In Israel, 19 wicked kings in succession ascend the throne, leading the people even farther from God. In spite of the efforts of Elisha and other prophets judgment can no longer be stayed. Israel finally receives her reward: captivity and dispersion by the Assyrians. To the south, Judah survives 150 years longer. But in the end the damage done by her corrupt leadership again brings a bitter harvest: 70 years of exile in Babylonia.

Focus	Last Days of Israel and Judah					
Divisions	Elisha, God's Mouthpiece	Elisha, God's Miracle Worker	Jehu, Destroyer of Ahab's House	Assyria, Destroyer of Israel	Hezekiah, the Reformer in Judah	Babylonia, Conqueror of Judah
	1 3	4 8	9 12	13 17	18 21	22 25
Topics	Israel's Captivity				Judah's Collapse	
	Dispersion				Displacement	
Place	Israel and Judah				Judah	
Time	About 300 Years					

Elisha, God's Mouthpiece / 2 Kings 1–3 **8**

📖 **Overview:** The book of 2 Kings can be summarized in a single verse: "In those days the LORD began to cut Israel short" (10:32). The downward spiral begun in 1 Kings now accelerates as one bad king after another accedes to the throne. Standing in the path of this downward trend are the prophets who speak for God. Elisha takes up the mantle—and ministry—of his master Elijah. Calling upon the God of Elijah, Elisha watches as God sends waterlogged valleys as a sign to Jehoram, and blood-red water signaling defeat for Moab.

Heart of the Passage: 2 Kings 2

Chapter 1	Chapter 2		Chapter 3
A Consuming Fire	A Chariot of Fire	Water for a City	Water for a Sign
1	18	19 25	
Elijah's Ministry Ends	Elisha's Ministry Begins		

🐾 **Your Daily Walk:** Elijah and Elisha. Have you ever gotten their names mixed up? If so, don't be too hard on yourself. Their names sound so much alike and their careers are so closely associated, it is hard to tell them apart. But don't miss the lesson of their lives!

Elijah shows what God can do through the life of a person willing to stand alone; Elisha shows what God can do through someone who is willing to stay in the shadows. Elijah was known for his strength on Mount Carmel; Elisha gained a reputation for his service as the man who "poured water on the hands of Elijah" (3:11). Elijah was an outspoken declarer of God's righteousness; Elisha was a soft-spoken demonstrator of God's righteousness. Elijah exhorted; Elisha encouraged. And God used them both!

Who are you more like in your temperament and talents: Elijah or Elisha? Don't try to be a poor imitation of what you aren't. With God's help, become the best you can possibly be to God's glory. Select one quality from the life of Elijah or Elisha that you will seek to emulate in your service for God this week. Ask God to open doors of opportunity to make that quality a reality in your life.

The world is full of willing workers; some willing to work, and others willing to let them work.

🗝 **Insight:** A Fiery Testimony to Truth

In addition to Elijah's blazing rhetoric indicting Israel for her sins, the 500 prophets of Baal mentioned in 1 Kings 18 and the 153 soldiers of 2 Kings 1 surely would have acknowledged that he was the prophet of fire. His spectacular departure into heaven in a chariot drawn by horses of fire was a fitting climax to his career.

9 *The Ministry of Encouragement*

Step Back

The stories of Elijah and Elisha are among the most exciting and intriguing in the entire Bible. Elisha enters the scene to shine the light of friendship and encouragement during a distressing time in the elder prophet's life.

First Kings 19 records the story of the confrontation between God and Baal on Mount Carmel. It was Elijah versus 450 priests of Baal in a showdown to end all showdowns. And God's miraculous power was demonstrated with no room for doubt.

That incredible scene was followed by God's answer to Elijah's prayer for rain after a three-and-a-half-year drought . . . even though there was no cloud in the sky.

Yet when Elijah heard that Israel's evil queen Jezebel was determined to kill him, he panicked in fear and discouragement. Exhausted and depressed, he begged God to end his life.

That's when God instructs Elijah to seek out and anoint Elisha as his companion and successor as prophet. For 10 years, until Elijah was taken into God's presence, Elisha served the elder prophet as his helper and friend. And then he assumed the prophet's mantle himself as a servant of God.

Scripture Reading:
1 Samuel 20:1-4;
Acts 11:19-26

Look Up

The ministry of encouragement is a common theme in the Bible. Jonathan encouraged David (1 Samuel 20:1-4). Barnabas encouraged many in the early church, including the apostle Paul (Acts 11:19-26).

Who has been an encourager to you? Perhaps a pastor, Sunday school teacher, student, or friend. Take a moment to bring those special people to your mind, then take them to God in prayer. Thank Him for their loving support to you over the years, and ask His special blessing on them—that they might receive the encouragement they need when they need it.

Believe there is nothing too small to do well.

Move Ahead

The ministry of encouragement may seem like a minor gift or a lesser calling. You may never achieve the fame of an Elijah, a David, or a Paul. But that's irrelevant. You see, the bottom line is whether you are faithful to God's calling on your life. That faithfulness will be evaluated at the judgment seat of Christ.

At that awesome time, many who play "starring roles" on earth will step back in humility and thanks, as another emerges from the shadows to receive the applause of heaven for their faithful ministry of encouragement. That person could be you. Be faithful to serve; be quick to encourage.

Elisha, God's Miracle Worker
2 Kings 4–8

10

📖 **Overview:** Elisha, the great miracle worker of God, performs no fewer than eight miracles in the space of today's section: providing an "oil well" for a destitute widow, giving new life for a dead boy, making poisoned stew harmless, multiplying bread for a hungry crowd, curing a leprous army captain, making an ax head defy the law of gravity, reading the mind of an enemy king, opening the eyes of a servant to see the angels of God, and closing the eyes of the enemy to the same spectacle. In each case, God's power at work in the *individual* shows His readiness to do the same in the *nation* He has called His own.

Heart of the Passage: 2 Kings 4:1-7; 5:1-14; 6:1-7

Chapter 4					Ch. 5	Ch. 6	Chs. 7–8
Elisha's Miracles Involving . . .							
Oil	Birth	Death	Poison	Bread	Leprosy	Ax Head	Deliver-ance
1 7	8 17	18 37	38 41	42 44			
A Shunammite Woman					The Syrian Army		

🏃 **Your Daily Walk:** If you wear glasses, then you're probably familiar with the term *myopia*. Myopia, simply defined, is improper focus. Images appear fuzzy or blurred because the eye is incapable of bringing the light to a sharp focus. Physical myopia can be detected and corrected quite easily.

But there is a similar visual problem in the spiritual realm. Let's call it "spiritual myopia." The symptoms: clear focus when it comes to identifying problems, obstacles, and difficulties in everyday life, but great difficulty in focusing on the reservoir of power and protection which God has provided to meet those problems head-on. Spiritual myopia is the condition Elisha's servant suffered from when he focused on the *problem* (6:15) but not the *provision* (6:17). He saw only a horde of Syrians, while Elisha saw the host of angels.

On a 3 x 5 card, draw a small eye chart (similar to what you would find in an ophthalmologist's office) using the words of 2 Kings 6:16 and place it on your mirror or mantel. Let it remind you often of the importance of proper spiritual focus in your walk with God.

The devil's No. 1 tool is not an active sinner, but an inactive Christian.

🖊 **Insight:** Two Kingly Books Compared

1 Kings describes	2 Kings describes
• Elijah's ministry	• Elisha's ministry
• God's longsuffering of sin	• God's sure punishment of sin
• progress of unbelief	• consequences of unbelief
• blessing of obedience	• curse of disobedience
• consecration of the temple	• desecration of the temple

117

11 *Jehu and Joash / 2 Kings 9–12*

Heart of the Passage: 2 Kings 9–10

Overview: Jehu, newly anointed king of Israel, carries out his instructions to "smite the house of Ahab thy master, that I [God] may avenge the blood of my servants the prophets" (9:7). In quick succession, Jehu dispatches Jehoram (king of Israel), Ahaziah (king of Judah), Jezebel (wicked wife of Ahab), the entire family of Ahab, and finally the false prophets, worshipers, and priests of Baal. Meanwhile in the southern kingdom of Judah, intrigue and bloodshed also prevail. After Ahaziah's death, his mother Athaliah usurps the throne and seeks to secure her position by killing all the royal offspring. Only the infant Joash survives, and in time becomes one of the greatest reforming kings of Judah.

Chapters 9–10		Chapter 11	Chapter 12
Assassinations by . . .			Achievements of Joash
Jehu	Athaliah		
Revenge of a King		Refuge of a King	Reform of a King

Your Daily Walk: Here is a one-question quiz. Place a check (✓) by the *most correct* answer: Spiritual change in the life of a Christian is . . .

Many Christians have enough religion to make them decent, but not enough to make them dynamic.

_____ a. all right if you don't overdo it.

_____ b. very beneficial for my friends.

_____ c. something to be pursued wholeheartedly.

Although "b" is a true statement, the best response is "c": something to be pursued diligently. God desires continual, whole-hearted conformity "to the image of his Son" (Romans 8:29). It's not enough merely to begin a program of change. God wants to complete what He begins. That's why Jehu, though he started out well in handling his God-given assignment, lost God's full commendation because he did a halfway job (10:28-29).

Think back to the last major area of change you began to work on in your life: a bad habit, a new priority, a neglected relationship. Did you approach the assignment *wholeheartedly* or *halfheartedly*? Are there still unwritten chapters in your story of "How God Helped Me to Change"? If so, what needs to be written today?

Insight: A Grim Prophecy Fulfilled to the Letter

In 1 Kings 21:23 Elijah prophesied that dogs would devour Jezebel in the district of Jezreel. Second Kings 9:30-37 gives a detailed description of how God's judgment on wicked Jezebel came true . . . right to the last bone!

Assyria, Destroyer of Israel *12*
2 Kings 13–17

📖 **Overview:** Time is running out for the nation of Israel. Though God's patience with His wayward people is enormous, His hand of judgment is poised and will not be stayed much longer. Following the death of Elisha, the nation's downward spiral accelerates. In spite of the able rule of Jeroboam II, who revives the nation every way but spiritually, the kings who succeed him lead the people ever deeper into idolatry and immorality. Not a single one of the last nine monarchs looks to God for direction in his earthly affairs. At last the nation of Assyria administers the "knock-out punch" by capturing and dispersing God's disobedient people and bringing the northern kingdom to an end.

Heart of the Passage: 2 Kings 13, 17

Chapter 13	Chapter 14	Chapter 15	Chapters 16–17
Death of Elisha	Decline of Jeroboam II	Decadence of Five Kings	Dispersion of Israel
"Assyria . . . carried Israel away" (17:6)			

📝 **Your Daily Walk:** Is it possible to be both prosperous and bankrupt at the same time? (Discuss this question with your spouse, friend, or tax lawyer until you come to a consensus!)

From the outside looking in, conditions had never been better for Israel than during the reign of Jeroboam II. Prosperity and prominence marked every area of the nation's secular life. The glorious splendor of Israel was at its zenith. But strip away the trappings of materialism, and what do you find? Beneath the radiance was rottenness. To borrow from the words of Jesus, the people and their leaders were like "whited sepulchers"—beautiful on the outside, but dead and decaying on the inside. Beneath the thin veneer of seeming prosperity were spiritual bankruptcy and moral corruption.

The poorest man is he whose only wealth is money.

Get alone sometime today and look at your life from God's perspective. Are you, on the *inside*, what you show yourself to be on the *outside*? Does your walk match your talk or has a particle or two of rottenness crept behind the radiant Christian exterior you show to others? The time to deal with it is *now*, and the place to begin is 1 John 1:9.

📷 **Insight:** A Rash of Assassinations in the North
During the final 30 years of Israel's history, a total of six kings reigned—four of whom were brutally murdered in office. A fifth was carried off to captivity, never to be heard from again.

Placing the Books of 1 Kings – 2 Chronicles

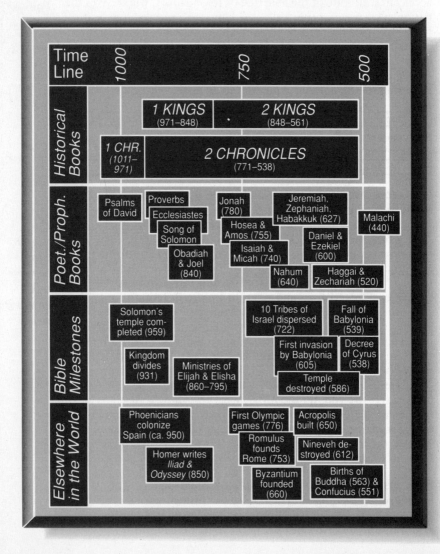

Time Line	1000		750		500
Historical Books		**1 KINGS** (971–848)		**2 KINGS** (848–561)	
	1 CHR. (1011–971)		**2 CHRONICLES** (771–538)		
Poet./Proph. Books	Psalms of David	Proverbs / Ecclesiastes / Song of Solomon / Obadiah & Joel (840)	Jonah (780) / Hosea & Amos (755) / Isaiah & Micah (740)	Jeremiah, Zephaniah, Habakkuk (627) / Daniel & Ezekiel (600) / Nahum (640) / Haggai & Zechariah (520)	Malachi (440)
Bible Milestones		Solomon's temple completed (959) / Kingdom divides (931) / Ministries of Elijah & Elisha (860–795)		10 Tribes of Israel dispersed (722) / First invasion by Babylonia (605) / Temple destroyed (586)	Fall of Babylonia (539) / Decree of Cyrus (538)
Elsewhere in the World		Phoenicians colonize Spain (ca. 950) / Homer writes *Iliad* & *Odyssey* (850)	First Olympic games (776) / Romulus founds Rome (753) / Byzantium founded (660)	Acropolis built (650) / Nineveh destroyed (612) / Births of Buddha (563) & Confucius (551)	

Hezekiah, the Reformer / 2 Kings 18–21 **13**

Overview: The epitaph over the tomb of King Hezekiah might well have read: "Hezekiah, Best King of Judah." Taking the throne at the young age of 25, he soon establishes himself as a reformer par excellence by destroying all traces of heathen worship among the people, including the bronze serpent Moses had made (and the people had cherished for centuries). Choosing to put his trust in God rather than in armies and horses, Hezekiah often finds himself on his knees. In response to the king's prayers, God strikes 185,000 Assyrians dead and extends King Hezekiah's life an additional 15 years. But the king's godly influence and reforms scarcely outlive him as his son Manasseh introduces abominable practices once again, returning the nation to its pagan ways and downward spiritual slide.

Heart of the Passage: 2 Kings 18–19

Chapters 18–19	Chapter 20	Chapter 21
Confrontation with Assyria	Continuance of Hezekiah's Life	Contamination of Hezekiah's Son
"He removed the high places" (18:4)		"He [rebuilt] the high places" (21:3)

Your Daily Walk: What deeds and character qualities do you want to be remembered for after you die? Try on a few of Hezekiah's biblical epitaphs for size:

"He did that which was right in the sight of the LORD" (18:3).

"He trusted in the LORD God of Israel" (18:5).

"[He] departed not from following [the LORD]" (18:6).

"The LORD was with him" (18:7).

"He prospered whithersoever he went" (18:7).

What a perpetual testimony to a great man of God! What would you like others to write about you after you are gone? Remember, before it can be penned, it must be practiced. Write your own epitaph the way you would like it to read someday. Then look for ways to live out your epitaph today to God's glory.

What you possess in this world will go to someone else when you die, but what you are will be yours forever.

Insight: The Eleven-Chapter Champion

Only a handful of characters are given 10 or more chapters in the pages of the Bible: Moses, David, Paul, and Hezekiah, to name a few. The 11 chapters given to Hezekiah's life span three books of the Old Testament. Can you name the books? Better yet, can you name the chapters? _____

_____

14 Babylonia, Conqueror of Judah
2 Kings 22–25

Heart of the Passage: 2 Kings 22, 25

Overview: Hezekiah, perhaps the best king in Judah's history, is succeeded by Manasseh, quite possibly the worst! Manasseh's 55-year reign of terror sends the nation into a spiritual stupor from which it will never fully recover. Even godly King Josiah is powerless to reverse the wicked trends in his nation, though his crusade for righteousness postpones the inevitable for a few more decades. After Josiah's death, there can be no escaping the long-delayed consequences of Judah's idolatry and immorality. The black cloud of God's judgment sweeps down upon the nation in the form of Nebuchadnezzar and the armies of Babylon. Judah, who had refused to learn from the sad example of her northern sister Israel, now experiences the same calamities: death, destruction, and deportation to a new "home" in exile.

Chapter 22	Chapter 23	Chapters 24–25
Recovering the Word of God	Reinstating the Worship of God	Removing the People of God
Josiah's Crusade		Judah's Captivity

Give me a Bible and a candle, shut me up in a dungeon, and I will tell you what the world is doing.

Your Daily Walk: Next time you visit your church, take a minute to stop by the lost and found area and notice the large number of Bibles that have become separated from their owners. Now imagine that some day no one is able to find a Bible. Through neglect or indifference, the Word of God simply disappeared from pew racks and purses, classrooms and coat pockets. Not a copy can be found in the entire church. Would that affect the way your church conducts its services, or would anyone notice the loss?

Perhaps the saddest commentary on Josiah's day is that the Word of God was missing—but nobody missed it. Brainstorm for a few minutes on ways you can make the Bible more visible and vital in your home, office, church, or school. Lost or found, the choice is yours.

Insight: 1 and 2 Kings, the Beginning and the End

1 Kings begins with	2 Kings ends with
• David, king of Israel	• Nebuchadnezzar, king of Babylon
• Solomon's glory	• Jehoiachin's shame
• the temple consecrated	• the temple desecrated
• blessing for obedience	• judgment for disobedience
• the growth of apostasy	• the consequences of apostasy
• the united kingdom divided	• the divided kingdom destroyed

1 Chronicles

T he books of 1 and 2 Chronicles describe the same period of Jewish history as 2 Samuel through 2 Kings, but from a different perspective. Chronicles provides a priestly commentary or "divine editorial" on the people of God during this historical period. After tracing King David's royal line back to the beginning, 1 Chronicles outlines the spiritual significance of David's righteous reign, demonstrating how the nation prospers when its leaders honor and obey God. The emphasis is on proper worship of the one true God—a worship David's life exemplifies.

Focus	Line of David		Reign of David			
Divisions	Genealogies of David and Israel	Ark of God	Covenant with God	Temple for God	Final Words	
	1 9	10 16	17 21	22 27	28 29	
Topics	Genealogy	History				
	Ancestry of David	Administration of David				
Place	United Kingdom of Israel					
Time	Thousands of Years	About 40 Years				

15 *Genealogies of David / 1 Chronicles 1–9*

Heart of the Passage: 1 Chron. 1

📖 **Overview:** Chronicles does more than merely recount the same political history contained in the books of Samuel and Kings. It gives a priestly perspective on the history of God's people, a sort of "divine commentary" on the kingdom period. It carefully weds the nation's history with the active hand of God in Israel's affairs. Chronicles centers on the southern kingdom of Judah. First Chronicles opens with a lengthy series of genealogies tracing the line of David all the way back to Adam. The genealogies provide clear evidence of God at work throughout history, by selecting a people for Himself and then protecting a family within that people to provide leadership.

Chapter 1	Chapters 2–4	Chapters 5–8	Chapter 9
	Descendants of . . .		
Patriarchs	Judah	10 Tribes & Levites	Exile Returnees
	Genealogies of David and Israel		

History is just the accumulated stories of how God is working in the lives of all the individual people on the earth.

🪶 **Your Daily Walk:** Today's section is definitely not a candidate for "Favorite Devotional Passage of the Year"! Apart from providing some dubious practice in Hebrew pronunciation, it seems to serve little purpose except to fill nine chapters of the Bible. Why is it there?

It is there to show you the historical basis for your faith! The opening chapters of 1 Chronicles form the skeletal framework of the entire Old Testament. They bind the Old Testament together into a unified whole, showing that it is in fact history and not merely legend or myth. From Adam to Abraham, Boaz to Benjamin, the generations are all there in their proper order to show the outworking of God's plan and purposes through the years and in the lives of men and women of faith.

Don't fall asleep during today's reading (though it is a great cure for insomnia). Stay with it until the point of the passage sinks in: God has a plan for history; He has a plan for Israel; He even has a plan for you!

📓 **Insight:** The End (of the Hebrew Bible, That Is)
Chronicles was originally the last book of the Hebrew Old Testament. That is why Christ in Luke 11:51 spoke of all the martyrs from Abel (in the first book, Genesis 4:8) to Zechariah (in the last, 2 Chronicles 24:21). He was speaking of all the martyrs from A to Z, first to last, in the Old Testament!

The Ark of God / 1 Chronicles 10–16

16

Overview: The ark of the covenant is a prominent feature of Chronicles, being mentioned more than 40 times. So it should not come as a big surprise that events surrounding the journey of the ark to Jerusalem consume three full chapters. The lesson is clear: The right action done with the right motives but carried out in the wrong way produces deadly consequences. Three months elapse before the journey can be completed. But when the ark is at last installed in Jerusalem, David leads the people in national celebration.

Heart of the Passage: 1 Chron. 11:1-9; 13:1-14; 15:1-3

Chapter 10	Chapters 11–12	Chapters 13–15	Chapter 16
Postscript on Saul	Proclaiming David King	Plans to Move the Ark	Praise for David's God
David the Warrior		David the Worshiper	

Your Daily Walk: The flashing blue lights and wailing siren make it clear that something is wrong. The motorist pulls over to the side of the road, stops, and listens in amazement as the patrol officer announces: "I'm giving you a ticket for running a green light."

Preposterous? Consider this: David, given a "green light" from the Lord to bring the ark to Jerusalem, was leading a joyous procession. Suddenly the merriment was cut short by God's displeasure.

An uneven spot in the road . . . a jostling of the cart . . . Uzzah's steadying hand . . . and what began like a wedding march ended like a funeral procession—all because David overlooked God's clear instruction in Numbers 4:15 regarding how to transport the ark.

How about you? Are you doing the right things with the right motives in the right way? Try this little test. Pick one area of Christian service you engage in regularly, and probe it with these two questions: (1) Are my motives right for doing what I do? (2) Am I seeking to do God's work in God's way? If the answer to either question is no, talk to Him about it. If the answers are yes, follow the injunction of 1 Chronicles 16:8 and praise God for His work in your life.

He who obeys sincerely endeavors to obey thoroughly.

Insight: A Thoroughly Anointed King
David's anointing as king over all Israel (11:3) was in fact his *third* anointing. The first was done privately by Samuel (1 Samuel 16:13), the second publicly as king over Judah (2 Samuel 2:4).

17 Covenant with David
1 Chronicles 17–21

Heart of the Passage: 1 Chron. 17

Overview: David's greatest dream—one he will nurture throughout his life—is to build a house for God. The prophet Nathan encourages David in this God-honoring ambition. But God soon makes it clear to Nathan—and through Nathan to David—that only in the lifetime of Solomon will the dream actually come to fruition. Though David is not permitted to build a house for God, God will build a house for David—a perpetual dynasty and eternal kingdom. In peacetime and war, through times of faithfulness and faltering in David's life, God remains true to His promise by preserving the line of David.

Chapter 17	Chapter 18	Chapters 19–20	Chapter 21
David's Covenant	David's Kingdom	David's Conquests	David's Census
Eternal	Enlarged	Extensive	Evil

Before you do something great for God, let Him do something great in you.

Your Daily Walk: Grab a sheet of paper, divide it in half, and for the next five minutes make two lists. On the left write "All the things I want to do for God in my lifetime." On the right list "All the things God wants to do for me in my lifetime." Now compare lists. Are some of the items the same?

David experienced the death of a dream. He had his heart set on doing something great for God. In spite of the prophet's words of prohibition, David could have insisted on his way. He could have gone ahead with his plans, built the temple anyway, and fulfilled his dream. But in the end the temple would have stood silent and empty, for God was not in the plans and would not have blessed the work. And in the process, David would have missed the far greater blessing that God had in store for him.

God may want you to attempt something great for Him. Then again, He may simply want to do something great for you. Are you available for either option? Take your "dream list" and pray each part of it back to God. Consecrate your dreams . . . then watch God work in and through you!

Insight: General David, Man of War

David's life in chapters 18–20 reads like a chapter from World War II. In the space of these 44 verses can be discovered at least a dozen different battles! How many can you find? How might this explain why God wanted Solomon—not David—to build the temple?

Pursuing God's Heart

⬅ Step Back

David's life touches everyone who reads about it in the Bible. His wholehearted devotion to God encourages us to press forward in faith; his dark times of pain and sin give us hope when our own humanity stifles us.

Scripture Reading: Acts 13:20-23; Psalm 139:23-24

When David was a young shepherd, he had ample opportunity to contemplate His loving God. In the process of spending hours shepherding his flocks in the wilderness, his love of God grew. And God loved him. Acts records God's feelings clearly: "I have found David the son of Jesse, a man after mine own heart, which shall fulfil all my will" (Acts 13:22).

Their unique relationship is revealed in David's intimate wordsongs. Psalms like 7–8, 23, 51 . . . the list goes on. It was a relationship of openness and honesty. Of confession. Of utter trust. And God delighted in it.

So when the storms of life hit—the tragedies, the failures, the questions—the relationship was strong enough to endure. Even when David reached the depths of despair, having committed adultery and murder, his heart remained tender enough to respond to Nathan's strong rebuke by turning to God in complete repentance.

What sets David's heart apart? It was a heart that reached boldly toward God. There was no room for lukewarm love. He wanted God's companionship more than anything else in life. So he got it.

⬆ Look Up

You may be thinking your relationship with God would be a lot more like David's if all you had to do was lie on a hillside and watch sheep all day and night. There's no way David could have coped with the stresses of *your* life and maintained such a vibrant companionship with God—he wouldn't have had time. Right?

Christianity is not a religion, it's a relationship.

Wrong. David's relationship with God came from his heart. No matter where you are, what you're doing, your heart is with you. If your heart doesn't hunger for God no matter what your circumstances, then it won't hunger for God under other circumstances. Search your heart before God right now. As a springboard for your time of prayer and meditation, read Psalm 139:23-24.

➡ Move Ahead

If you find that your relationship with God is shallower and emptier than you'd like, take this opportunity to make a change. Carve out time to spend with God alone; you can do it if you make it a priority.

A relationship with God like David had won't just happen. But with God's help, you can make it happen.

19 *David's Temple for God*
1 Chronicles 22–27

*Heart
of the
Passage:
1 Chron.
22–23*

 Overview: David's dream of a house being built for God is not denied—merely postponed. It will remain for Solomon his son to erect the structure. But David is given the joyful privilege of planning and preparing for that great architectural feat. A suitable site must be found, building materials secured, "blueprints" drawn, and priests, musicians, and officers organized for the orderly management of the worship services. After passing on the vision and responsibility of the project to Solomon, David passes on the reins of leadership as well.

Chapter 22	Chapters 23–24	Chapter 25	Chapters 26–27
Instructions for Solomon	Levites	Arrangements for . . . Musicians	Officers
Temple Plans	Temple People		

*If you
don't
know
where
you're
going,
you'll
probably
end up
someplace
else.*

Your Daily Walk: "Plan ahead. After all, it wasn't raining when Noah built the ark."

That humorous motto stresses the importance of short-and long-range planning. There are many services you can render for God on a moment's notice: witnessing at a bus stop, visiting a shut-in, extending hospitality to a stranger. But there are many more acts of service that demand planning and long-range goal setting. If you are going to build a new church, become an overseas missionary, or begin a new degree program, it won't happen by accident—or overnight!

Presumptuous living in the future is wrong (James 4:13-17), but careful planning for the future is right (2 Corinthians 9:1-8). Plan a get-together tonight with your spouse or friend to set at least one new goal in your ministry for God. *Those who fail to plan, plan to fail.*

Insight: David's Lasting Legacy to the Levites

Almost unnoticed among David's other achievements—but of enormous spiritual significance—were his efforts to organize the tribe of Levi for effective ministry. As you read chapter 23, capture your insights regarding the Levites' divisions and duties:

Division	Size	Principal Duty	Reference
Workers	24,000	Minister in the temple	23:4
Officers	6,000	_____	23:4
_____	____	_____	23:5
Musicians	____	Sing and play instruments	23:5

David's Final Words and Deeds
1 Chronicles 28–29

20

Overview: Compare the opening chapters of David's life with the closing ones, and you will come to a startling conclusion: David ends his life the same way he began it—with humble confidence in God. In spite of his numerous accomplishments, David never lets greatness go to his head. Rather, his final words to Solomon and the nation reflect the same wholehearted devotion to God that characterized the young shepherd in the pasturelands of Judea. With the dream of a temple entrusted to his son, and the tokens of God's blessings all around him, David dies "in a good old age, full of days, riches, and honour: and Solomon his son [reigns] in his stead" (29:28).

Heart of the Passage: 1 Chron. 29:20-30

Chapter 28		Chapter 29	
David's Sayings . . .		David's Supplication	David's Successor
to Israel 8 | 9 to Solomon 21	1	19 20	30
Exhortation		Exaltation	Epitaph

Your Daily Walk: There's an amazing epitaph inscribed over the life of King David. But to discover it, you'll need to look in an unlikely place—Acts 13:36. There you'll read these words: "David served his own generation by the will of God."

In the 40 years David ruled the nation of Israel, several things were true of his administration:

(1) *He lived to serve.* Instead of the pride, revenge, and self-seeking that characterized so many of Israel's kings, David's reign was marked by mercy, justice, and humility. Further,

(2) *He lived to do God's will.* Pleasing God was David's daily passion; obeying God was David's greatest delight. And the result?

(3) *He followed God's purpose for his life.* There was a job to be done in David's day and, by God's strength, David did it.

You can't have (3) without (1) and (2), for God's will for His children involves the path of service (Ephesians 6:6). But as David learned, there's no more delightful calling in life!

Whom God sends He employs, for He sends no one to be idle.

Insight: Three Kings Two Times Crowned

The double coronation of Solomon (23:1; 29:22) followed a pattern that began with Saul (1 Samuel 10:1; 11:15) and continued with David (2 Samuel 2:4; 5:3). In each case, the second coronation was a public confirmation of the first.

129

2 Chronicles

The book of 2 Chronicles spans four centuries of Judah's history from the glory days of Solomon and the building of the magnificent temple to the conclusion of the Babylonian Exile. Following the death of Solomon, a succession of good and bad kings rises to power. As go the leaders, so go the people, until finally the spiritually bankrupt nation is carried off into captivity. But the final verses of 2 Chronicles sparkle with hope. After 70 years, the Persian King Cyrus decrees the rebuilding of God's house and the return of God's people.

Focus	A Priestly View of Judah's Demise								
Divisions	Solomon's Temple Erected	Solomon's Temple Dedicated	Rehoboam's Kingdom Divided	Asa's Reforms	Jehoshaphat's Reforms	Judah's Kings & Queens	Ahaz's Corruption	Hezekiah's Reforms	Judah's Last Days
	1 5	6 9	10 12 13	16	17 20 21	25	26 28	29 32	33 36
Topics	A King's Glory	A Kingdom's Disgrace							
	Judah's Zenith	Judah's Ruin							
Place	Southern Kingdom of Judah								
Time	About 40 Years	About 400 Years							

Solomon's Temple Erected
2 Chronicles 1–5

21

Overview: A father's dream becomes a son's delight as Solomon undertakes the greatest architectural feat of his lifetime: building the temple in Jerusalem. Great quantities of men and materials, plus seven years of Solomon's life, are invested in the task of completing the house of the Lord. When at last the temple stands finished with the ark of the covenant in place, Solomon leads the people and musicians in heartfelt praise to God. "And when they lifted up their voice with the trumpets and cymbals and instruments of music, and praised the LORD . . . then the house filled with . . . the glory of the LORD" (5:13-14).

Heart of the Passage: 2 Chron. 1, 5

Chapter 1	Chapter 2	Chapter 3	Chapters 4–5
Promoting the King	Planning the Temple	Building the Temple	Furnishing the Temple
Solomon's Wisdom	Solomon's Works		

Your Daily Walk: When commissioned by God to do a job, Solomon allowed nothing to stand in the way of completing his God-given assignment. With breathtaking speed he organized more than 150,000 workers and tons of materials to ensure that the task went ahead smoothly.

Solomon's zeal and enthusiasm for God left scant time for coffee breaks as long as there was still work to be done!

If you were to evaluate the degree of your own enthusiasm for God's service, where would it fall on the following scale?

By the time you get your shoulder to the wheel, your nose to the grind-stone, and your ear to the ground, it's usually time for lunch.

```
0            30                70              100
|---|---|---|---|---|---|---|---|---|---|
Sorry, not    Do I            It's my      It's my
available.    have to?        duty.        delight!
```

Earlier this month you learned that whatever you do, you should do it *heartily* "as to the Lord" (Colossians 3:23). Now add another thought from 1 Corinthians 10:31—whatever you do, do it *honorably*, "to the glory of God." That's service both you and God can delight in.

Insight: Gold, Gold, Everywhere
Nearly every feature of the temple, including the walls, doors, nails, and furnishings, involved gold or gold overlay—a fact made possible by the enormous preparations of King David (1 Chronicles 22:14) in which he set aside 100,000 talents (3,750 tons) of pure gold!

131

22 *The Temple Today*

Scripture
Reading:
1 Corin-
thians
6:19-20;
Matthew
5:14-16

◄ Step Back

It took seven years and the skilled labor of 153,000 workers. And the end result was magnificently breathtaking.

Solomon's temple depicted God's majesty and glory like nothing made by human hands ever had. As the spiritual home of the nation, its presence in the capital said more than mere words. It declared to the nations that the God of the universe reigns over Israel.

The temple was an irony—a house for the God of the universe. As Solomon put it, "The house which I build is great: for great is our God above all gods. But who is able to build him an house, seeing the heaven and heaven of heavens cannot contain him?" (2 Chronicles 2:5-6).

No, four walls could never surround the infinite God. But it could reflect in a small way His majesty and glory. And it could cause those who saw it to respond in worshipful awe to the God who commissioned it.

You may not have realized it before, but God has commissioned you to play the same role in your world. You are called to reflect the glory of God, who dwells in you. As Paul explained, "Know ye not that your body is the temple of the Holy Ghost which is in you, which ye have of God, and ye are not your own? For ye are bought with a price: therefore glorify God in your body, and in your spirit, which are God's" (1 Corinthians 6:19-20).

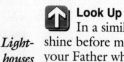 Look Up

*Light-
houses
don't fire
cannons
to call
attention
to their
shining—
they just
shine.*

In a similar vein, Jesus told His disciples, "Let your light so shine before men, that they may see your good works, and glorify your Father which is in heaven" (Matthew 5:16). Ask God in prayer right now to intensify your life's light for His glory. The key here is "good works." Meditate with Him on what good works you might pursue this week with Him, to shine the light of His love on those who need its warmth and brightness in their own lives.

► Move Ahead

How can you reflect God's majesty and glory in your own "temple"? Think about it. The clothes you wear. The words you speak, the habits you practice, the places you go. Those things either reflect or detract from the glory of God in your life.

Today, place a candle in a prominent place in your home or at work. Throughout the day, let it remind you of the importance of your life's light. It's what God has called you to do. Nothing is more fulfilling.

The Temple Dedicated / 2 Chronicles 6–9 23

Overview: In a setting fit for a king's inauguration, Solomon now leads the nation in dedicating the newly completed temple to the glory and worship of the God of Israel. Kneeling on a specially constructed bronze scaffold, Solomon prays one of the most majestic and moving invocations found anywhere in the Bible. He overflows with praise to God, thanking Him for His unchanging character and unfailing promises on behalf of the nation. When Solomon finishes, the glory of God fills the temple, prompting the people to respond, "He is good; for his mercy endureth for ever" (7:3). But even in the midst of worship and rejoicing, there is cause for concern. By night, God appears to Solomon to warn him that if the nation fails to remain true to God, He will uproot the people from their beloved homeland and will destroy the magnificent temple which they have labored so long to complete.

Heart of the Passage: 2 Chron. 6, 9

Chapter 6	Chapter 7	Chapter 8	Chapter 9
A Prayer of Dedication	A Promise of Forgiveness	A King's Reputation	A King's Vast Riches
Solomon's Relationship to God		Solomon's Relationship to Goods	

Your Daily Walk: What do these three words all have in common: *salt, magnet, light*? (Hint: They all end in *t*, but that's not it!)

Answer: They are all descriptions of your task as a Christian.

Each day God leaves you here on earth, you are to be like salt (making others thirsty for God), a magnet (drawing others to God), and light (showing the way to God). The queen of Sheba came hundreds of miles to learn firsthand of the wisdom and wealth of Israel's king (9:1). Notice her conclusion: "Blessed be the LORD thy God . . . because thy God loved Israel" (9:8). After looking at Solomon's life, the queen gave glory to Solomon's God! Is that what happens from day to day when others rub shoulders with you?

If the service of God is worth anything, it is worth everything.

Carry a packet of salt, a small magnet, or a book of matches with you today. Then every time you reach into your pocket or purse, remember your God-given role—and practice it!

Insight: Great Achievements of a Great Monarch
Chapter 8 describes more than a dozen of the major accomplishments of Solomon's reign militarily, architecturally, religiously, and commercially. How many can you find?

24 *A Divided Kingdom*
2 Chronicles 10–12

Overview: Solomon is barely cold in his grave when the nation turns from worship to waywardness in its commitment to God. Solomon's son Rehoboam imposes a foolish tax increase, prompting a bitter division of his kingdom. On the verge of civil war with Jeroboam (the newly established king of the northern 10 tribes), Rehoboam obeys the word of the prophet and breaks off the conflict. But once his kingdom is established, he forsakes the law of the Lord yet again. God sends a stinging rebuke in the person of Shishak, king of Egypt, who defeats Rehoboam's army and plunders the wealth of the Lord's house.

Heart of the Passage: 2 Chron. 10

Chapter 10	Chapter 11	Chapter 12
Rehoboam Follows Bad Counsel	Rehoboam Follows the Lord	Rehoboam Forsakes the Lord
Divided Kingdom	Devoted King	Disciplined King

Your Daily Walk: Is your religion . . .

. . . like a spare tire? (You only use it in an emergency.)

. . . like a wheelbarrow? (Easily upset and must be pushed.)

. . . like a bus? (You ride it only when it goes your way.)

. . . or like a pacemaker? (Something you rely on constantly.)

The person who is ashamed of his religion probably has a religion of which he ought to be ashamed.

Rehoboam's up-and-down spiritual life could well be likened to a spare tire! When times were tough, he turned to God; when things were running smoothly, he forsook the Lord. It may remind you of God's words through the prophet Hosea: "They were filled, and their heart was exalted; therefore have they forgotten me" (Hosea 13:6).

Take stock of your own life at this time. Are things going smoothly? All bills paid? Enjoying good health? No major conflicts in your family, church, or neighborhood? Job secure? Refrigerator full? Then watch out! Now is the time Satan would love to trip you up by turning your eyes away from the Source of your supply. On the memo line of each check you write today, add the words "Don't forget!" This might even provide an opportunity to witness for your Lord.

Insight: "Dear Diary, Today I Plundered a Temple. . . ."

Inscriptions found on Egyptian temple walls show Shishak's military success in plundering the Jerusalem temple during Rehoboam's reign (12:9). One picture shows Shishak holding a group of Israelites by the hair and hitting them with a club—a painfully accurate rendering.

Asa's Reforms / 2 Chronicles 13–16

25

📖 **Overview:** Abijah, king of Judah, is used by God to discipline and defeat Jeroboam, king of Israel. During their battle, 500,000 Israelites fall—a shattering defeat from which Jeroboam will never fully recover. What Abijah accomplishes in the military sphere, Asa attempts to duplicate in the spiritual realm. He removes all traces of foreign religion from the land and commands the people to return to the careful observance of God's statutes. But toward the end of his reign, Asa faces a threat from Baasha (king of Israel) and seeks an alliance of protection with the king of Syria. Even on his deathbed he puts his trust in earthly physicians alone, rather than in the Great Physician.

Heart of the Passage: 2 Chron. 15–16

Chapter 13	Chapters 14–15	Chapter 16
Abijah's Spiritual Recession	Asa's Spiritual Reforms	Asa's Spiritual Regression
Reliance on an Army	Reliance on God	Reliance on Syria

✔️ **Your Daily Walk:** Stand in the middle of the floor, reach down, grasp your shoelaces (straps, buckles, or whatever else is holding your shoes on), and see how far off the floor you can lift yourself. Try it three times.

Things were looking bad for King Asa. Baasha, king of Israel, had sealed off all escape routes, and the situation looked hopeless. So Asa grabbed hold of his own bootstraps and gave them a good yank. He turned to Ben-hadad, king of Syria, and bribed him to come to his rescue. From all outward appearances, the strategy worked!

Weave in faith, and God will find the thread.

But God saw the situation differently. Previously, Asa had trusted in the Lord, not in foreign powers. Now he was turning from trust in God to trust in bootstraps, and God disciplined him for doing so.

What is the pattern of your life: belief or bootstraps? faith or footwork? trust or trickery? God or self? Each time you put on or change your shoes today remind yourself that it's always safe to trust the Lord.

✒️ **Insight:** The Prophet of Dubious Distinction (16:7-10)
Hanani the seer, who condemned Asa for his reliance on foreign armies rather than on the Lord, becomes the earliest "persecuted prophet" in the pages of the Bible. (But check Luke 11:47-51 for the name of one other man who, though seldom thought of as a prophet, might also lay claim to this rather dubious distinction!)

26 *Jehoshaphat's Reforms / 2 Chronicles 17–20*

Heart of the Passage: 2 Chron. 17, 20

Overview: Only 10 verses are given to godly King Jehoshaphat in 1 Kings, but the chronicler devotes a full four chapters to his life, and with good reason! Jehoshaphat knows that the key to spiritual revival in the nation is a renewed interest in and commitment to the law of the Lord. He institutes a nationwide "Bible study program," using as teachers the princes, Levites, and priests—an effort which God richly blesses with peace and prosperity. In contrast to his predecessors, Jehoshaphat manages to make peace with the king of Israel. But a friendly visit nearly costs him his life as he becomes entangled in a war between Israel and Syria. His reaction to divine rebuke, his appointment of judges to rule "not for man, but for the LORD" (19:6), and his Godward response in the face of crisis all point to the day-by-day reality of his faith!

Chapter 17	Chapters 18–19	Chapter 20
Seeking the Lord in Worship	Seeking the Lord in Ramoth-gilead	Warfare Against Moab and Ammon
Jehoshaphat's Righteous Reforms		

Regeneration has made our hearts a battlefield.

Your Daily Walk: Chapter 20 describes perhaps the most curious battle scene found anywhere in Scripture. Jehoshaphat leads his army out to confront the combined forces of Moab and Ammon. His battle plan is simple: "Set yourselves, stand ye still, and see the salvation of the LORD" (20:17). Then, as if to add insult to injury, Jehoshaphat selects singers to go before the army and chant choruses of praise. While the singers sing and the soldiers stand at attention, God produces a mighty victory for Judah as the enemy forces oblige and "every one [helps] to destroy [one] another" (20:23)!

Have you learned yet the lesson Jehoshaphat and the people of God learned? When the battle seems overwhelming, when the enemy is large and imposing, don't turn and run. Instead, stand still, sing out, and watch God work.

Insight: A Big Mistake

Jehoshaphat's alliance with Ahab (18:1–19:11) was a serious blunder, fully deserving the rebuke of the prophet Jehu (not to be confused with Jehu, grandson of Nimshi, who later wiped out the line of Ahab). The prophet's question, "Shouldest thou help the ungodly, and love them that hate the LORD?" (19:2) rebuked Jehoshaphat and prompted him to restore justice and priestly order in Judah.

136

The Kings of Israel   (North, 10 Tribes)

Name	Date of Reign B.C.	Relation to Predecessor	Yrs. of Reign	Char- acter	Manner of Death	1 Kings	2 Chronicles
Jeroboam	931–910		22	Bad	Stricken by God	11:26–14:20	9:29–13:22
Nadab	910–909	Son	2	Bad	Murdered by Baasha	15:25-28	
Baasha	909–886	None	24	Bad	Died	15:27–16:7	16:1-6
Elah	886–885	Son	2	Bad	Murdered by Zimri	16:6-14	
Zimri	885	Captain of Chariots	7 days	Bad	Suicide	16:9-20	
Omri	885–874	Army captain	12	Bad	Died	16:15-28	
Ahab	874–853	Son	22	Bad	Wounded in battle	16:28–22:40	18:1-34
Ahaziah	853–852	Son	2	Bad	Fell through lattice	22:40– 2 Kng. 1:18	20:35-37
						2 Kings	
Jehoram*	852–841	Brother	12	Bad	Murdered by Jehu	3:1–9:25	22:5-7
Jehu	841–814	None	28	Bad	Died	9:1–10:36	22:7-12
Jehoahaz	814–798	Son	17	Bad	Died	13:1-9	
Jehoash**	798–782	Son	16	Bad	Died	13:10–14:16	25:17-24
Jeroboam II	793–753	Son	41	Bad	Died	14:23-29	
Zechariah	753–752	Son	6 mo.	Bad	Murdered by Shallum	14:29–15:12	
Shallum	752	None	1 mo.	Bad	Murdered by Menahem	15:10-15	
Menahem	752–742	None	10	Bad	Died	15:14-22	
Pekahiah	742–740	Son	2	Bad	Murdered by Pekah	15:22-26	
Pekah	752–731	Army captain	20	Bad	Murdered by Hoshea	15:27-31	28:5-8
Hoshea	731–722	None	9	Bad	Deposed to Assyria	15:30–17:6	

The Kings of Judah   (South, 2 Tribes)

Name	Date of Reign B.C.	Relation to Predecessor	Yrs. of Reign	Char- acter	Manner of Death	1 Kings	2 Chronicles
Rehoboam	931–913	Son	17	Bad	Died	11:42–14:31	9:31–12:16
Abijam***	913–911	Son	3	Bad	Died	14:31–15:8	13:1-22
Asa	911–870	Son	41	Good	Died	15:8-24	14:1–16:14
Jehoshaphat	873–848	Son	25	Good	Died	22:41-50	17:1–20:37
						2 Kings	
Jehoram	853–841	Son	8	Bad	Stricken by God	8:16-24	21:1-20
Ahaziah	841	Son	1	Bad	Murdered by Jehu	8:24–9:29	22:1-9
Athaliah	841–835	Mother	6	Bad	Murdered by army	11:1-20	22:1–23:21
Joash	835–796	Grandson	40	Good	Murdered by servants	11:1–12:21	22:10–24:27
Amaziah	796–767	Son	29	Good	Murdered	14:1-20	25:1-28
Azariah****	792–740	Son	52	Good	Stricken by God	15:1-7	26:1-23
Jotham	750–732	Son	16	Good	Died	15:32-38	27:1-9
Ahaz	735–716	Son	16	Bad	Died	16:1-20	28:1-27
Hezekiah	716–687	Son	29	Good	Died	18:1–20:21	29:1–32:33
Manasseh	697–643	Son	55	Bad	Died	21:1-18	33:1-20
Amon	643–641	Son	2	Bad	Murdered by servants	21:19-26	33:21-25
Josiah	641–609	Son	31	Good	Wounded in battle	22:1–23:30	34:1–35:27
Jehoahaz	609	Son	3 mo.	Bad	Deposed to Egypt	23:31-33	36:1-4
Jehoiakim	609–598	Brother	11	Bad	Died in siege?	23:34–24:5	36:5-7
Jehoiachin	598–597	Son	3 mo.	Bad	Deposed to Babylon	24:6-16	36:8-10
Zedekiah	597–586	Uncle	11	Bad	Deposed to Babylon	24:17–25:30	36:11-21

*Joram, **Joash, ***Abijah, ****Uzziah

Note: Dates of some reigns overlap due to co-regencies

Taken from WALK THRU THE OLD TESTAMENT, copyright ©, Walk Thru the Bible Ministries, Inc.

27 *Judah's Kings / 2 Chronicles 21–25*

Heart of the Passage: 2 Chron. 21–22

Overview: Jehoram's life is living proof that a bad marriage can undo even the best of upbringings. Raised by a godly father and grandfather, Jehoram marries the wicked daughter of Ahab and Jezebel, embraces her pagan deities, and leads the nation into idol worship once again. The atmosphere of trust and affection which characterized his father's administration is replaced by a mood of suspicion and jealousy. As Jehoram's first public act, he slays all his brothers and many key rulers in the nation—a move designed to secure his position as king, but which in fact leads to an excruciating and premature death. In rapid succession, his son, wife, and grandson come to the throne in a tale of family intrigue that must be read to be believed! Joash and Amaziah both become long-reigning kings with halfhearted commitments.

Chapter 21	Chapter 22		Chapters 23–24	Chapter 25
Jealous Jehoram	Healed Ahaziah	Usurper Athaliah	Junior Joash	Immature Amaziah
	1 9	10 12		
Wicked Rulers			Righteous Rulers	

Sometimes the right enemies can do you more good than the wrong friends.

Your Daily Walk: Rotten apples have a curious property. No matter how many good apples you pack around a rotten one, you can't make the rotten one good. But you can ruin an awful lot of good apples.

The same is true in the relationships people have with each other. One corrupting friendship is enough to drive a person away from God, even in the presence of countless righteous lives . . . provided that friendship is close enough and lasts long enough to exert its corrupting influence.

That's why your close friends will mark you for life. That's why your choice of a lifemate is critically important. God states very clearly in His Word, "Be ye not unequally yoked together with unbelievers: for what fellowship hath righteousness with unrighteousness? and what communion hath light with darkness?" (2 Corinthians 6:14). Examine your relationships. And if you're courting disaster, make the necessary changes now—before the "rotten apple" becomes you.

Insight: The Unenviable Life of a Ruler in Judah

All five of the rulers discussed in today's reading met violent deaths. Four were murdered and one was stricken by God with an incurable disease. Of the 20 rulers in Judah's history, half died from "unnatural causes."

Ahaz's Corruption / 2 Chronicles 26-28 28

📖 **Overview:** King Uzziah does mighty things for the nation of Judah both militarily and architecturally. But spiritually his life resembles a roller coaster. "As long as he sought the LORD, God made him prosper. . . . But when he was strong, his heart was lifted up to his destruction" (26:5,16). Uzziah dies a leper's death for his halfhearted devotion to God. By contrast, his grandson Ahaz is wholehearted in his zeal for false gods and pagan practices! Ahaz introduces images of Baal, worship on the heathen high places, and infant sacrifice. Though God repeatedly tries to warn Ahaz of the danger of his ways and to turn the king's heart back to Him, there is no response. Only one question remains: How long will God's patience continue with His rebellious people?

Heart of the Passage: 2 Chron. 28

Chapter 26	Chapter 27	Chapter 28
Uzziah and His Battles	Jotham and His Building Projects	Ahaz and His Unbelief
Good and Evil	Good	Evil

✍️ **Your Daily Walk:** In the carpentry business, a 2 x 4 can come in many different lengths. But every 2 x 4 has one thing in common: It is about 2 inches thick and 4 inches wide.

When God disciplines an individual . . . or a family . . . or a church . . . or a nation, often He does so with a painful set of circumstances. And though it would be easy to liken such an experience to being "hit over the head with a 2 x 4," there is a fundamental difference: 2 x 4s used like that are for *punitive* reasons; God's discipline is *therapeutic*.

Think back over the life of Ahaz as you have seen it unfold in 2 Chronicles 28 and 2 Kings 16. How did God try to get his attention and change his course of action through . . .
. . . defeat in battle?
. . . the word of the prophet?
. . . enemy occupation?
Before you are too hard on Ahaz, is there a lesson God has been waiting patiently for you to learn as well?

God loves His people when He strikes them as much as when He strokes them.

📖 **Insight:** A Pagan Practice Punishable by Death
Infant sacrifice by fire was a brutal Canaanite ritual introduced into Judah by Ahaz. Not only was it abhorrent for human reasons, it was also a capital offense under the Mosaic law, punishable by stoning (Leviticus 20:1-5).

29 *Hezekiah's Reform / 2 Chronicles 29–32*

Overview: The Assyrian assault and dispersion of Israel are totally omitted at this point in the Chronicles account, though they have a profound impact on Hezekiah's life and rule in Judah. Inheriting a disorganized country and a heavy burden of tribute to Assyria, Hezekiah nevertheless puts first things first. In the very first month of his administration he reopens and repairs the house of the Lord, restores the long-neglected temple worship and Passover celebration, and declares war on idol worship and pagan practices. When the Assyrian King Sennacherib besieges Jerusalem and the situation looks hopeless, Hezekiah puts his faith to work once again in earnest prayer for deliverance. God answers his plea and crowns his life with prestige and power.

Heart of the Passage: 2 Chron. 29, 32

Chapter 29		Chapter 30	Chapter 31	Chapter 32
Revival of Righteousness	Restoration of Worship	Preparation for Passover	Provision for Priests	Protection for God's People
1 19	20 36			
Hezekiah's Righteous Reforms				

Insight: "Dear Diary, It Was a Bad Day in Jerusalem. . . ." Sennacherib's own account of this invasion has been found on a clay prism, which he himself had made. It is now in the Oriental Institute Museum in Chicago, and reads in part: "As for Hezekiah, king of Judah, who had not submitted to my yoke, 46 of his fortified cities . . . I besieged and captured. . . 200,150 people . . . I took as booty. Hezekiah himself I shut up like a caged bird in Jerusalem, his royal city. I built a line of forts against him, and turned back everyone who came forth out of his city gate."

You can expect God to intervene when you have taken time to intercede.

No Assyrian king would ever record a defeat, especially one as devastating as the Jerusalem debacle, but it is significant that Sennacherib did not claim to have taken Jerusalem—a most remarkable confirmation of biblical history!

Your Daily Walk: Wouldn't it be wonderful to know that someone like Hezekiah was praying for you every day? Here was a man whose every recorded prayer was answered. Wouldn't you like to have that kind of "clout" working for you? You would? Then read and ponder this sermon-in-a-sentence by Robert Murray McCheyne, Scottish missionary and preacher who didn't live to see his thirtieth birthday: *If I could hear Christ praying for me in the next room, I would not fear a million enemies. Yet distance makes no difference; He is praying for me.* Now what do you think?

Judah's Last Days / 2 Chronicles 33–36 **30**

📖 **Overview:** The final century of Judah's national history reads like a bad dream. After Manasseh's 55-year reign of terror and apostasy, even a godly reformer like Josiah is powerless to prick the hearts of the people, though for a time he is able to stem the external appearances of evil. But after his death the nation swiftly returns to its abominable ways. Oppressed and eventually overthrown by the Babylonians, the people of Judah are slaughtered, their homes and temple destroyed, their city walls leveled. The survivors are dragged off to Babylon, there to ponder their fate for 70 long years. But in the midst of this doom and destruction shines a ray of hope. Cyrus, king of Persia, issues a decree: The house of the Lord must be rebuilt in Jerusalem. Who among His people is willing to return?

Heart of the Passage: 2 Chron. 34; 36:17-23

Chapter 33	Chapters 34–35	Chapter 36
The Lawless Days of Manasseh and Amon	The Law-abiding Days of Josiah	The Last Days of Judah
Rebellion	Reform	Ruin

✍️ **Your Daily Walk:** For the Jews, Jerusalem represented their place of greatest failure. To stare at the rubble of what was once mighty Jerusalem—with its shattered temple and broken-down walls—must have broken the heart of even the most callous of God's people. They had failed Him. They had gone their own sinful ways. And they had been punished.

Now, through Cyrus, God was calling His people back to "the scene of the crime," back for a second chance.

Have you failed God in recent days, then gone off to your own personal exile? Take heart—you are in good company! Abraham, Moses, and Jonah (to name a few) suffered similar setbacks. But they emerged from failure to accomplish great things for God. And you can too.

Is God calling you back to repentance, back to your family, school, or job? Will you answer that call . . . right now?

Some people never change their opinion because, after all, it has been in the family for generations.

📝 **Insight:** Judah's Final Kings—Brothers in the Business
For more than three centuries the kingdom of Judah had passed in an orderly fashion from father to son, interrupted only briefly by the reign of Queen Athaliah. But now, in Judah's final frantic years, like a top winding down and toppling over, the kingdom passes quickly between three sons and a grandson of Josiah.

Ezra

I n the book of Ezra , the historical
narrative of 2 Chronicles continues.
After 70 years of exile, God fulfills His
promise to return His people to their homeland. Under His direction, King Cyrus of
Persia now rules Babylonia, and the Jews
are free to go home. The first group of
returnees rebuild the temple in Jerusalem
(chapters 1–6). Fifty-eight years later, Ezra
leads a second group (mostly priests and
Levites) back to Jerusalem to rebuild the
spiritual and moral character of the people
(chapters 7–10).

Focus	Rebuilding the Temple			Rebuilding the People	
Divisions	Temple Commission	Temple Completion	Book of Esther	Priests and Pilgrims	Pollution and Purging
	1 3	4 6		7 8	9 10
Topics	Return Under Zerubbabel		58-Year Interlude	Return Under Ezra	
	Material Restoration			Spiritual Restoration	
Place	Persia to Jerusalem			Persia to Jerusalem	
Time	23 Years (538–515 B.C.)			1 Year (457 B.C.)	

Temple Commission / Ezra 1–3 1

📖 **Overview:** The people of God have paid dearly for their indifference and idolatry. For 70 years they have languished in Babylonian exile. But though the situation looks bleak, God has neither forsaken nor forgotten them. At the appointed time He raises up a pagan Persian king named Cyrus, whose proclamation permits the Jews to return to Jerusalem and rebuild the temple—an event prophesied in remarkable detail fully two centuries in advance (Isaiah 44:28; 45:1-4). Sadly, only a relative handful of exiles respond to the invitation. Led by Zerubbabel and supported by the king's treasury, about 50,000 Jews begin the long trek to their shattered homeland, where together they begin to rebuild the nation's temple and the nation's future.

Heart of the Passage: Ezra 1:18; 3:1-13

Chapter 1	Chapter 2	Chapter 3
Proclaiming Release for the Exiles	Preparing to Build the Temple	Progress in Building the Temple
Cyrus	Census	Consensus

📝 **Your Daily Walk:** Try this experiment. Using a watch with a sweep second hand or digital counter, see how long it takes you to find a paper clip, a postage stamp, and last year's tax return. Ready? *Go!* (Less than a minute—your house is arranged "decently and in order"; between one and three minutes—you could use some help; more than three minutes—you probably have small children around the house.)

Have your tools ready; God will find work for you.

While you catch your breath, ponder this observation. The myriad of numbers in Ezra 1–2 is not there to overwhelm you, but to show you that God is a God of detail and orderliness. In fact, those priests who sought their family records and could not find them were excluded from the priesthood as unclean (2:62)! Take a moment right now to look up 1 Corinthians 14:40 then put it to work today in an area of your personal or spiritual life that needs attention.

📘 **Insight:** The Elusive Book of Ezra
In the English Bible, Ezra follows 2 Chronicles and continues the narrative where 2 Chronicles leaves off (compare 2 Chron. 36:22-23 with Ezra 1:13). In the Hebrew canon, Ezra and Nehemiah were originally one book and were located just before Chronicles. The first division into two books in the Hebrew Bible was not made until 1448, more than 18 centuries after the material was written.

2 *Temple Completion / Ezra 4–6*

Overview: Zerubbabel knows that the task of rebuilding the nation must begin at the altar, not the workbench. The challenge is primarily spiritual, not architectural. Accordingly, Zerubbabel's first priority is to erect the altar and reinstate Israel's national feasts, which recognize God's dealings in the life of the nation. Afterward, once materials are gathered and assignments made, the actual work of rebuilding the temple can commence. But it is not long before the local residents lodge complaints with the king, bringing the work to a halt. Not until Darius, a sympathetic new Persian ruler, comes to power 15 years later can the project be resumed and completed.

Heart of the Passage: Ezra 4:15, 24; 6:13-22

Chapter 4	Chapter 5	Chapter 6
Restraining the Builders	Reinstating the Builders	Reaching the Goal
Work Opposed	Work Resumed	Work Completed

Your Daily Walk: There has yet to be a work attempted for God that did not produce criticism. In fact, if you want to avoid criticism, there is only one way: *say* nothing, *do* nothing, and *be* nothing!

Zerubbabel's goal of rebuilding the temple in Jerusalem sprang from pure motives. He marched 900 miles through perilous wilderness. He labored neither for monetary gain nor public notoriety. But despite all that, he met with stiff criticism and opposition from the local Jewish population—who had embraced foreign wives and pagan ways.

Never be afraid to test yourself by your critic's words.

No one so thoroughly appreciates the value of criticism as the one who gives it. But consider these wise words from H. A. Ironside, American preacher and commentator in the first half of this century, on how to face criticism: "If what they are saying about you is true, mend your ways. If it isn't true, forget it, and go about the business of serving the Lord." Good advice to remember next time you are the target. After all, sticks and stones are only thrown at fruit-bearing trees!

Insight: How "Great" Can You Get?
According to Ezra 5:8, the rebuilt temple was constructed with "great stones" (literally, "stones of rolling" which could only be moved with the aid of rollers). The size of these stones is unspecified, but they were large enough to cause Jesus' disciples to respond in amazement (Mark 13:1)—great stones befitting a great God.

The Message of the Exile

3

⬅ Step Back

Exile. To many of us today that word refers to the involuntary removal of a political leader from his position as head of his homeland. But in the Bible, the word refers to the removal of an entire nation—the southern kingdom of Judah.

It's a sad story, the climax of years of degradation. God's people—and their leaders—continually refused to acknowledge His preeminent place in their nation. So God allowed Babylonia to decimate the nation and capture all the people. After the destruction of Jerusalem by Nebuchadnezzar in 587 B.C., the kingdom of Judah ceased to exist politically.

The people were forcibly removed from their homeland and made to live under social and economic hardships in a different land. But the years passed, and God's people grew to live comfortably. By the time of the end of the exile, 70 years later, most considered Babylon to be home.

God's prophets remained active through the years, keeping alive the hope of their homeland. For instance, Ezekiel and Daniel ministered in Babylon during the exile. And seventy years after their departure, God allowed Zerubbabel, Ezra, and Nehemiah to lead the captives back home.

Scripture Reading: Psalms 126, 137

⬆ Look Up

The exile tragically ended the political life of Judah. But it also proved that God was in no way confined only to the land of Palestine. He was God of the whole world. And the fact that His people were scattered and removed only extended the influence of His ways in the world. He was with His people in Babylon and cared for them there.

And in a way the experience shook the nation back to her spiritual senses. The prophets, they realized, were right. Their hardship and suffering, along with the direct contact with the realities of false religions, drove out of the people once and for all their idolatrous desire to follow false gods.

In the exile, God got the attention of His people. What will it take Him to get your attention? Are you blind in an area of disobedience or laxity? Turn to God in penitent prayer. Seek to be cleansed of self-will; invite Him to be God of your life once again.

The greatest of all faults is to be conscious of none.

➡ Move Ahead

Capture a bit of the joy of the return from the exile by reading Psalm 126 aloud to yourself. Do you know a fellow believer who is wandering away from his or her homeland? Perhaps God will use you to encourage their return to Him in joy.

4 *Priests and Pilgrims / Ezra 7–8*

Overview: A striking feature of the book of Ezra is that the name "Ezra" does not appear until chapter 7! The first six chapters chronicle the life and ministry of Zerubbabel in rebuilding the temple; now chapters 7–10 introduce a priest named Ezra whom God uses to rebuild the spiritual condition of the people. Ezra begins his task 58 years after the events of chapter 6. The people have a house for God, but not a heart for God. Ezra realizes revival must begin with a national return to the statutes and judgments of God as contained in the Mosiac law. With the support of the Persian King Artaxerxes, Ezra sets out with 1,753 of his countrymen to cover the 900 dangerous miles back to Jerusalem.

Heart of the Passage: Ezra 7:6-10; 8:21-36

Chapter 7		Chapter 8	
Ezra's Departure	Artaxerxes' Decree	Ezra's People	God's Protection
1 10	11 28	1 14	15 36
Provisions for a Journey		Priests for a Journey	

Your Daily Walk: Do you remember your first church school teacher? Are you currently, or do you ever hope to become, a teacher of God's Word?

The mediocre teacher tells; the good teacher explains; the great teacher inspires.

Those who devote themselves to the teaching of Scripture have accepted a staggering responsibility. According to Ezra 7:10 they are accountable in four ways: (1) They are to "prepare" their hearts for obedient service, (2) to "seek" the meaning of God's Word, (3) to "do" what they discover, and (4) to "teach" what they have learned. Far from being merely a classroom lecture, true Bible teaching is the overflow of one obedient life into the life of another.

Think of one teacher who has contributed to your spiritual growth over the past year by seeking, doing, and teaching God's Word. How can you honor that person today with a note, phone call, or special gift? (That's one good way to put 1 Timothy 5:17 to work!) Ezra 7:10 succinctly describes Ezra's pattern of life: "For Ezra had prepared his heart to seek the law of the LORD, and to do it, and to teach in Israel statutes and judgments." Why not memorize that verse and then ask God for the strength to make it your life pattern as well!

Insight: Slim Ranks for an Enormous Task

Ezra's goal was to rebuild the people spiritually. To do that, his primary need was not manpower (he took fewer than 2,000 men with him), but ministers. Many of those he took were priests and Levites.

Pollution and Purging / Ezra 9–10

5

Overview: The good news of Ezra's arrival in Jerusalem is tempered by the bad news of mixed marriages in the community. Jews are permitting their sons to marry heathen women from neighboring territories. Even the priests, Levites, and civic leaders are involved—a condition which the law of God condemns and which Ezra finds intolerable. The process of righting these wrongs is painful, difficult, and time-consuming. But even those "rainy skies" cannot dampen Israel's renewed commitment to personal and national purity.

Heart of the Passage: Ezra 9:1– 10:17

Chapter 9		Chapter 10	
Mixed Marriages	Anguished Acknowledgment	Repentance of the People	Roll of the Offenders
1 2	3 15	1 17	18 44
Confusion	Confession	Reconciliation	Registry

Insight: The Chronic Problem of Pagan Partners

Ezra 10:18-43 lists 111 men guilty of mixed marriages—the very sin condemned and forbidden in Deuteronomy 7:1-5. The history of Israel from the period of the judges onward illustrates the chronic nature of the situation (Judges 3:5-7) and its devastating consequences. Later, Nehemiah (13:23-28) and Malachi (2:11) would also deal with the recurring problem of mixed marriages.

Never be yoked to one who refuses the yoke of Christ.

Your Daily Walk: Marriage has been defined many ways— some humorous, some tragic. Which would you say best describes yours? *Marriage is*

... *the peaceful coexistence of two nervous systems.*
... *a school of experience where husband and wife are clashmates.*
... *a union that defies management.*
... *the world's most expensive way of discovering your faults.*

Add to that list one more: *Successful marriage always involves a triangle: a man, a woman, and God.* The prophet Amos asked the right question more than 2,700 years ago: "Can two walk together, except they be agreed?" The answer is obvious ... yet a tragic number of God's people ignore the clear warnings and prohibitions of Scripture.

If you are single, read 2 Corinthians 6:14 right now; if you are married, meditate on 1 Corinthians 7:10-16. Let those verses remind you again that Christian marriage is designed for three (you, your believing spouse, and God) for life!

147

Nehemiah

A rebuilt temple stands in Jerusalem, but only crumbled walls surround the Holy City. Clearly, there is much work to be done! For the task of rebuilding the city walls, God raises up Nehemiah to lead the third and last expedition of Jewish returnees from Persia. In spite of stiff opposition to the reconstruction efforts, Nehemiah and his band of bricklayers complete the job in only 52 days. Nehemiah's zeal extends not only to reconstructing the city, but also to reforming its citizenry—a task which demands inspired leadership.

Focus	Physical Reconstruction			Spiritual Reformation	
Divisions	Nehemiah's Plans for Rebuilding the Walls	Early Opposition to Rebuilding the Walls	Growing Opposition to Completing the Walls	Revival in the Rebuilt City	Protecting and Purifying the Rebuilt City
	1	2 3	4 5 7	8 10 11 13	
Topics	Construction of the City			Instruction of the Citizens	
	Israel's Restoration as a Nation				
Place	Jerusalem				
Time	About 25 Years (445–420 B.C.)				

Constructing the Walls / Nehemiah 1-2   6

Overview: In ancient times, a city was only as secure as its walls. In the case of Jerusalem, the temple stands in glistening splendor, but the walls lie in ruin and rubble. Enter Nehemiah, cupbearer to the king of Persia and God's choice to rebuild the city's defenses. After four months of prayerful intercession for his people and homeland, Nehemiah finds his opportune moment. Armed with both a blueprint and a burden, Nehemiah shares his request with the king—and receives even more than he asked for! After personally inspecting Jerusalem's precincts, Nehemiah rallies his countrymen with the faith-inspired cry, "The God of heaven, he will prosper us" (2:20).

Heart of the Passage: Nehemiah 1:1-2:8

Chapter 1		Chapter 2
Nehemiah's News from Jerusalem	Nehemiah's Prayer for Jerusalem	Nehemiah's Inspection
Pain	Preparation	Plans

Insight: Autobiography of a Powerful Prayer

Nehemiah's memoirs bear eloquent testimony to the power of prayer in the life of a child of God. As you continue reading the book, catalog Nehemiah's prayers and God's answers:

Reference	Nehemiah prayed for . . .	God answered with . . .
1:4-11		
2:4-8		
4:4-12		
6:9, 14-16		
13:14-31		

Prayer is not so much submitting our needs to God but submitting ourselves to Him.

Your Daily Walk: Look around your house and you will discover two kinds of corners: inside corners (the kind you sit in) and out-side corners (the kind you walk around). Think of that as a picture of your prayer life. There are two kinds of prayers you can pray: comfortable prayers ("Lord, meet that need") and commitment prayers ("Lord, use me to help meet that need").

Learn a lesson from the life of Nehemiah. Don't pray to be comfortable in your circumstances; instead pray to be available and ready to do the will of God in every situation. And in the process, some mighty important walls may get built! Find a quiet corner as you read Nehemiah's prayer of commitment in 1:5-11. Then make it yours!

7 *Rallying the Workers / Nehemiah 3–4*

Heart of the Passage: Nehemiah 4

Overview: Like the earlier reconstruction efforts under Zerubbabel and Ezra, Nehemiah's "rebuilding corps" faces opposition both from without and within. As the walls begin to rise, so does opposition from leaders in surrounding provinces. For each problem, Nehemiah seeks—and finds—a God-honoring solution: Ridicule is handled with prayer; threats of violence are dealt with by adequate preparation; discouragement is met with a personal example of faith in God's power.

Chapter 3	Chapter 4		
Repairing the Walls	Ridiculing the Workers	Rallying the Workers . . . Prayerfully	Militarily
Work Initiated	Work Interrupted		

Few things heal more than the laughter of delight; few things hurt more than the laughter of derision.

Your Daily Walk: Think of a time when you looked ridiculous. Perhaps it was at a costume party, or on a fishing trip, or in a school play. In any case, you dressed in such a way that others laughed at the way you looked.

Perhaps you never stopped to realize that ridicule is the act of making someone feel ridiculous. That's why it's so painful. Through taunts, coarse jesting, misrepresentation, or mocking, someone makes you (or what you believe) an object of derisive laughter.

One of the tests of your Christian character is the way you handle ridicule. Do you explode in anger and look for a quick way of retaliation? Or do you, like Nehemiah, leave the matter to God.

Jesus had some special words of comfort and encouragement for those suffering ridicule and persecution in their walk with God: "Blessed are ye, when men shall revile you, and persecute you, and shall say all manner of evil against you falsely, for my sake. Rejoice, and be exceeding glad: for great is your reward in heaven" (Matthew 5:11-12). Remember that the next time you or your godly views are laughed at. And if ridicule is not a problem you face often, perhaps you had better check to see if your light is really shining!

Insight: Nehemiah's Notorious Neighbors
Several of Nehemiah's persecutors are noted in historical sources other than the Bible. The pesky Sanballat (4:1) is identified as the governor of Samaria in the Elephantine Papyri. In addition, a rock inscribed with the name *Tobiah* (4:3) in ancient Aramaic script was discovered near present-day Amman, Jordan.

Completion of the Walls / Nehemiah 5–7 **8**

📖 **Overview:** With progress continuing on the rebuilding of the walls, Nehemiah's opponents shift their attacks from direct confrontation to subtle conspiracy. Sanballat and Geshem repeatedly try to sidetrack Nehemiah from his God-given assignment. Even a false prophet arises to lead Nehemiah into a potentially fatal trap—only to have his plan foiled by Nehemiah's keen discernment. In spite of "loan sharks," espionage, deceit, and attempted assassination, Nehemiah and his dedicated band of bricklayers complete the city walls in less than two months—a feat even Israel's enemies perceive is "wrought of God" (6:16). And now come new responsibilities for Nehemiah. As governor, he appoints (7:1), delegates (7:2), organizes (7:3), and utilizes the new leadership in the newly built city.

Heart of the Passage: Nehemiah 5, 6:15-19

Chapter 5	Chapter 6	Chapter 7
Oppression from Within	Completing the Walls	Cataloging the Workers
Usury	Victory	Authority

✍️ **Your Daily Walk:** What is your *Gullibility Index?* How much of what others tell you do you believe without question? Jesus told His disciples to be "harmless as doves," but He also cautioned them to be "wise as serpents" (Matthew 10:16). How are you doing?

Shemaiah was hoping Nehemiah would be gullible enough to ensnare himself and thereby ruin the building project (6:10-14). Would you have known that Shemaiah's suggestion was out of harmony with God's will? Nehemiah recognized the snare because he knew his Scriptures. Look up Numbers 18:7 and you'll see that what at first appeared to be a difficult decision for Nehemiah was actually quite simple *when he recalled what God had already said on the matter!*

Mastering your Bible is not just a good idea; it is essential if you are to make wise, God-honoring decisions. Read 2 Peter 3:18 out loud, and make it your personal growth project for today.

One of the Devil's tricks is to stop people from digging into the Bible.

📓 **Insight:** Whistle While You Work (7:1-3)

When the walls were finished, Nehemiah set up doors in the different gates. But because of the sparse population, those who usually worked in the temple ("the singers and Levites," 7:1) joined the "porters" (gatekeepers) in standing guard.

9 *Rebuilding Spiritual Walls*

⬅ Step Back

Scripture Reading: Luke 14:25-35

When Nehemiah discovered the plight of the exiles who had returned to Jerusalem to rebuild their homeland, he immediately sought the Lord for help. Without walls, their lives were in peril as they faced the possibility of enemy attack.

Actually, the walls of Jerusalem served many functions. Obviously they gave the city protection and security from outside attack. But more than that, they kept the people inside, enabling them to rebuild their spiritual lives without the degrading influence of the world around them.

In the same way, we believers need to build a wall to protect ourselves from the outside, and to build a relationship with our Lord inside. How are your walls? Do they need repairing? Have weeds begun to cause the mortar to disintegrate?

Charles Swindoll, in "Hand Me Another Brick," draws out several principles to apply from Nehemiah's life in this regard:

1. *Develop a genuine concern for the condition of your walls.* The rebuilding of Jerusalem's walls began with a burden in Nehemiah's heart. If our walls are to be repaired, we must be genuinely concerned about their condition.

2. *Pray specifically for guidance and protection.* When Nehemiah became aware of the situation, he immediately started to work—by praying to God. Lay the foundation for your walls first by asking God for His guiding, protecting hand in the process.

3. *Face the situation honestly and with determination.* The project is not easy. See it for what it is, and you will see more clearly what needs to be done.

4. *Recognize that you cannot correct the condition alone.* Rebuilding walls is tough work. It's easy to let it slide and never finish the project. Don't let that happen. Live dependently on God for strength to complete the task. Your survival depends on it.

⬆ Look Up

Let us pray not for lighter burdens, but for stronger backs.

Just as Nehemiah surveyed the walls before he got started, take time to survey the walls of your spiritual life. Ask God to show you specific areas that need work. Meditate thoughtfully on Luke 14:25-35 as you contemplate your personal rebuilding project.

➡ Move Ahead

The walls of protection are maintained through the spiritual disciplines. Prayerfully develop your own plan of action to rebuild your walls. Include the bricks of Bible reading and study, prayer, fellowship, and witnessing. Be specific about the ways you will maintain the strong walls of godly protection in your life.

Revival in the City / Nehemiah 8–10   **10**

📖 **Overview:** The first half of the book of Nehemiah teaches valuable lessons about working for God; the second half emphasizes worshiping God. Beginning with chapter 8 the account becomes biographical rather than autobiographical (no longer is it in the first person, "I"). Now it centers on the spiritual rather than physical well-being of the people. The public reading and explanation of God's Word bring a sweeping revival to the city. Rejoicing at the sound of God's precious laws as preached by Ezra the priest, the people respond with prayers of confession, worship to God, and a fresh resolve to live godly lives in keeping with their commitment.

Heart of the Passage: Nehemiah 8:1-12

Chapter 8		Chapter 9	Chapter 10
Reading the Law	in Rejoicing	Responding to the Law	
		in Repentance	in Resolve
1 12	13 18		
Revival in Jerusalem			

🗝 **Your Daily Walk:** Revival is the phenomenon perhaps most often discussed and yet the least experienced by Christians today! And the reason is not hard to find. Though the way to revival is simple, the price of revival is staggeringly high. And few are willing to pay it.

Nowhere in the Bible is the "formula" for revival presented more clearly than in today's reading. There were three main ingredients in Israel's revival: (1) reading of God's Word, (2) confession of sins, and (3) wholehearted commitment to God. The people made a solemn covenant to "walk in God's law" (10:29)—a promise which only a decade later would be shamelessly broken.

Think of an area in your life that needs a "revival": your marriage, your business ethics, your relationships with your children and other family members, your prayer life. Now count the cost. What good things will you have to give up in order to gain God's best? What sin will you have to forsake? What action can you take now to show God you mean business?

Every revival that ever came in the history of the world, or in the history of the church, laid great emphasis on the holiness of God.

📝 **Insight:** The First Old Testament Commentaries
Ezra and his assistants "read in the book of the law of God distinctly and gave the sense [that is, the interpretation], and caused them to understand the reading" (8:8). After their years of exile, many of the Jews no longer understood Hebrew, requiring interpretation and explanation in Aramaic—the vernacular of the common people.

11 *Resettlement / Nehemiah 11–13*

Overview: With the walls in place and the spiritual condition of the nation revived, Nehemiah now sets about the task of consolidating and organizing the populace. One-tenth of the people are chosen by lot to relocate within the city walls, while the rest remain in the suburbs. The walls are formally dedicated and temple officers commissioned to oversee the functions of national worship. After an extended leave of absence, Nehemiah returns from Babylon to find Tobiah living in a temple storeroom, and the people displaying a shocking disregard for God's laws concerning marriage and the Sabbath. Assuming again the role of reformer, Nehemiah labors to restore national purity.

Heart of the Passage: Nehemiah 13

Chapter 11	Chapter 12	Chapter 13
Deploying the Citizens	Dedicating the City Walls	Defending the City's Purity
Distribution	Celebration	Expulsion

Your Daily Walk: Life would be a simple assignment if you were the only person on earth! And therein lies the problem. People. You can't live without them, but how often have you yearned to try nonetheless? Nehemiah's greatest challenge came not from trying to lay bricks, but from trying to love bricklayers! Perhaps he pondered questions like the one expressed by Peter in Matthew 18:21: "Lord, how oft shall my brother sin against me, and I forgive him? till seven times?"

Slow forgiveness is not much better than no forgiveness.

If Nehemiah had stopped at seven, he never would have lasted through chapter 3 of his book! Notice Jesus' reply: "I say not unto thee, Until seven times: but, Until seventy times seven" (Matthew 18:22).

What Nehemiah did with bricks and mortar is well known; what he did with stubborn men and women, "forgiving their offenses against him," is just as well documented in God's Word. Nehemiah knew that forgiveness is our command from God; criticizing, grumbling, and condemning are not. Do *you* know that? Do you *show* that?

Insight: Malachi, a Prophetic Postscript on Nehemiah
Four centuries of divine silence follow the book of Nehemiah. No Scripture was written during that time span, possibly because of the hardheartedness of the people. Malachi, a contemporary of Nehemiah, left a brief record of the heedless attitude of their day.

Esther

L ike an exciting novel, the real-life drama of Esther pits a beautiful heroine against a hateful villain, builds to a life-threatening climax, then ends with a surprise twist. Beautiful Esther is among the many Jews whose family chooses to remain in Persia following the return of Israel to Jerusalem with Zerubbabel, Ezra, and Nehemiah. Selected as queen, she discovers a court official's plot to kill her and her countrymen. In a dramatic turn of events, God uses the roll of the dice and a king's sleeplessness to save the day and preserve His people.

Focus	Plotting Destruction		Preventing Destruction	
Divisions	Esther Ascends to the Throne	Haman Stoops to Vengeance	Haman Receives His Just Reward	The Jews Receive a Reprieve
	1　　　　　　2	3　　　　　　4	5　　　　　　7	8　　　　　　10
Topics	Conflict	Cunning	Courage	Conquest
	Vashti Deposed	Haman Defeated		Purim Decreed
Place	Persia			
Time	About 10 Years (483–473 B.C.)			

12 *Esther Ascends to the Throne / Esther 1–2*

Heart of the Passage: Esther 1:1-12; 2:8-23

📖 **Overview:** Esther is more than a story about heroism. It is the story of how God controls the destinies of people and nations in spite of harrowing circumstances and opposition. Esther reads like today's news: national intrigue, political unrest, attempted assassination. And over it all, the sovereign hand of God is at work in the lives of His people, placing Esther in the palace and Mordecai's name in the Persian chronicles "for such a time as this" (4:14).

Chapter 1		Chapter 2	
Ahasuerus's Debauchery	Vashti's Divorce	Esther's Coronation	Mordecai's Courage
1 9	10 22	1 18	19 23
An Old Queen Deposed		A New Queen Discovered	

Courage is not the absence of fear, but the conquest of it.

🖊 **Your Daily Walk:** Alone . . . in a strange place . . . no friends . . . scared. That's a good description of how Esther might have felt when she was taken to the palace by her cousin Mordecai.

How would you have liked her assignment? She is presented in the story as one who has been left alone in the world by the death of her parents (2:7). Although she was adopted into her cousin's home, her Jewish heritage placed her life in jeopardy when she found herself entered in King Ahasuerus's beauty contest. So there she was: without a home, without a friend, without a father . . . or was she?

Esther evidently trusted an unseen Father. When called to appear at the palace, she never faltered. Armed with her faith in God, she marched boldly into an unfamiliar place to assume unfamiliar duties. When Haman's plot was uncovered, Esther called for fasting among the Jews—a sign of humble intercession before God.

If you are a believer, then you are never alone. God is always present as your loving Father. In fact, Psalm 68:5 describes Him as a "father of the fatherless." Why not call or write your earthly father today and tell him what his fatherly role . . . and God's . . . have meant in your life. Fathers love to be loved!

⛏ **Insight:** The Palatial Palace at Shushan
The Pentagon is one of the world's largest office buildings, with room for 26,700 employees on its 30-acre site. Enlarge that 10 times and you'll have an idea of the size of King Ahasuerus's 300-acre acropolis, site of the first "Miss Persia" beauty contest!

156

Haman Stoops to Vengeance / Esther 3–4 13

Overview: As in a masterful novel, the plot now thickens. Esther has been elevated to queen without her nationality being discovered. And now the villain, Haman, steps onto center stage. A favorite of the court, Haman also rises to the top politically. His hatred for the Jews burns hot when Mordecai fails to pay homage to him. Haman persuades King Ahasuerus with words and money to issue an edict of destruction for the Jewish race. Superstitious by nature, Haman selects the date of the execution by the throw of the dice, thereby giving God yet another opportunity to work behind the scenes! Now Queen Esther is faced with a deadly decision. Should she risk revealing her nationality in an attempt to dissuade the king? Or should she protect her life—and silently watch while her countrymen are slaughtered?

Heart of the Passage: Esther 3:1-6; 4:13-17

Chapter 3	Chapter 4	
A Deadly Decree	A Desperate Fast	A Daring Decision
1	14	15 17
Haman's Plot	Esther's Promise	

Your Daily Walk: Is it difficult for you to believe you could hate someone enough to want to kill him? Enough to want to kill his entire family? Even enough to want to destroy his whole town? Then imagine the hatred that smoldered in Haman's heart toward Mordecai—a hatred strong enough to drive Haman to destroy an entire nation.

Vengeful hatred is the perfect picture of the villainous Haman, and the exact opposite of the forgiving attitude God desires for you. You may not harbor the kind of grudge that Haman did, but are you guilty of an unforgiving spirit toward someone who has hurt you? Would you want God's forgiveness of you to be proportionate to your forgiveness toward others (Matthew 6:12)?

Carry five pennies in your pocket or purse today. Then each time you are tempted to respond in anger to a person or circumstance, leave a penny—and the resentment it represents—at the point of the offense. By the end of the day you might be a nickel poorer, but you will have done what Jesus urged in Matthew 6:12!

In taking revenge, a man is equal to his enemy; in passing over it, he is his superior.

Insight: The High Price of Cold Blood
One commentator has valued the Hebrew talent of silver at $12,000. That means Haman was willing to pay $120 million to exterminate the Jews—a fabulous sum for a Persian hit man!

157

14 *God's Odds*

*Scripture
Reading:
Daniel
4:34b-35;
Psalm 46*

Step Back

Ironically, the book of Esther does not refer specifically to God. Yet His unseen hand is constantly at work in the events Esther relates. Esther's coronation, Mordecai's forgotten act of bravery, Haman's lots, Esther's uninvited audience with the king . . . the list goes on.

In the first seven chapters alone, at least a dozen events indicate that God was sovereignly at work behind the scenes. The odds of 12 events occurring in consecutive order by chance are 1 in 479 million. Of course, the odds of that happening in God's will are 1 in 1!

More than any other book of the Bible, Esther points to the invisible sovereignty of God. The book swells with a sense of confidence that He is in control, working skillfully to preserve His people from ultimate tragedy.

As you've read to this point in the Bible, ask yourself which events reveal God's handiwork most clearly. Perhaps you're thinking of the Creation, the Flood, the parting of the Red Sea. It's easy to see God in the dramatic events of life. But we live in the mundane, and here it's harder to see Him at work.

Nevertheless, He is at work. And the message of Esther is to be sensitive to His will. To listen to His quiet voice. And to respond to Him eagerly, faithfully, no matter how He directs.

Look Up

*God is too
great to
be
knocked
off course
by the
wickedness
of men.*

God is indeed sovereign. Meditate prayerfully on this attribute of your mighty God by reading Daniel 4:34b-35 and Psalm 46. Praise Him that He is God, and He will have His way. And thank Him that His way is perfect, full of grace, mercy, and love.

Move Ahead

Willing to put her life on the line for her people, Esther put her trust solidly in God. As events whirled around her, her faith in God's sovereignty was unshakable.

Is that a lesson you need to grab hold of yourself? It's easy to assume that we know best when it comes to living our own lives. God is not one to force His will and His way into our lives; but He is there, speaking gently to us to entrust our lives into His hands.

If you need a reminder of the role you've been called to play in the drama of life, consider these words of God from the book of Isaiah: "For my thoughts are not your thoughts, neither are your ways my ways, saith the LORD. For as the heavens are higher than the earth, so are my ways higher than your ways, and my thoughts than your thoughts" (Isaiah 55:8-9).

Haman Receives His Just Reward
Esther 5–7

📖 **Overview:** Esther boldly approaches the throne to ask a humble request: The king and Haman are invited to a special banquet. At the conclusion of the festive occasion, Esther makes another petition: The king and Haman are invited to yet another banquet! Esther's wise and timely delay allows the Divine Director to stage Haman's exit. As Haman returns home, he is insulted by Mordecai's presence in the king's gate and orders gallows built for the speedy execution of Mordecai. Meanwhile, King Ahasuerus has trouble sleeping and tries to cure his insomnia by reading the court records. To his surprise he discovers the unrewarded kindness of Mordecai and orders Haman to lead the regal procession in Mordecai's honor. Thoroughly humiliated, Haman returns to Esther's banquet, where she reveals both her nationality and his treachery. The king directs his servants to hang Haman on the very gallows prepared for Mordecai.

Heart of the Passage: Esther 5, 7

Chapter 5		Chapter 6	Chapter 7
Esther's Banquet	Haman's Boasting	Mordecai's Reward	Haman's Ruin
Hope		Honor	Hanging

(1 ... 8 | 9 ... 14)

✔️ **Your Daily Walk:** It has been well said: "Pride always demands that *I* be in the middle." And no truer proverb was ever spoken than this one: "Pride goeth before destruction" (Proverbs 16:18).

Trace Haman's proud path to destruction. It began with a genuine promotion (perhaps for faithful service) by King Ahasuerus (3:1); it moved to boastful arrogance over his advancement; and it culminated in self-exaltation. Three steps to the gallows!

Proverbs 29:23 cautions, "A man's pride shall bring him low: but honor shall uphold the humble in spirit." Where has a recent promotion or achievement in your life set the stage for possible boasting, self-exaltation, and demotion? Haman fell into the painful trap of pride. Look up 1 Peter 5:6-7 and let it guide your next step today.

Swallowing of pride seldom leads to indigestion.

🖌️ **Insight:** Epitaph for an Agagite
Etched into Haman's tombstone might well have been the words "He died of *I* trouble." An actual epitaph for Haman has been discovered in the collection of Jewish writings called the Talmud (Megillah 7b). It reads simply, "Cursed be Haman; blessed be Mordecai!"

16 *The Jews Receive a Reprieve / Esther 8–10*

Heart of the Passage: Esther 8:1-8; 9:1-2, 12-32

Overview: The final chapters of Esther's drama read like the ending of a fairy tale. Mordecai is promoted, the Jews' enemies are destroyed, and Esther secures letters from the king establishing the Feast of Purim as a perpetual reminder of God's great deliverance. In the epilogue (chapter 10), Mordecai receives historical recognition in the Persian annals. Such acclaim from pagan historians comes not because of arrogant claims or self-exaltation (as with Haman) but because Mordecai exemplifies servanthood in his speech and conduct.

Chapter 8	Chapter 9		Chapter 10
Reversing the Law	Repulsing the Enemy	Remembering Purim	Rewarding Mordecai
Fighting	Feasting		Favoring

Faith is as simple, and as difficult, as believing that God cares.

Your Daily Walk: If you have ever watched an Oscar or Emmy Awards presentation, you have probably heard many of the winners attribute a large portion of their success to the *director.* Can you suggest why?

Now that you have completed reading the book of Esther, a divine drama that unfolds on the real stage of history, to whom do you think Esther and Mordecai would attribute *their* success?

Think back over the characters you have met in the book; then briefly answer the following questions:

1. How many events in the book clearly demonstrate God's sovereign control? roll of the dice, king's insomnia?_____

2. What is one lesson you can learn from . . .
Esther's two banquets?_____
Mordecai's unrewarded kindness? _____
Haman's casting of lots?_____
Haman's hanging?_____

3. What is one way you can cooperate with the Director of *your* life to bring glory to Him?_____

Insight: The Feast of Dice
The Feast of Purim derives its name from the lots or dice (Hebrew, *purim*) which Haman cast (3:7; 9:24). Archaeological digs at Susa have uncovered numbered dice similar to those which Haman might have used in his superstitious choice of a date.

Placing the Books of Ezra, Nehemiah, Esther, & Job

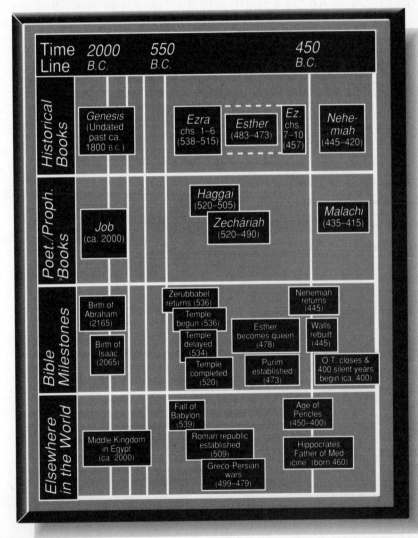

Time Line	2000 B.C.	550 B.C.			450 B.C.
Historical Books	Genesis (Undated past ca. 1800 B.C.)	Ezra chs. 1–6 (538–515)	Esther (483–473)	Ez. chs. 7–10 (457)	Nehe-miah (445–420)
Poet./Proph. Books	Job (ca. 2000)	Haggai (520–505) Zechariah (520–490)			Malachi (435–415)
Bible Milestones	Birth of Abraham (2165) Birth of Isaac (2065)	Zerubbabel returns (536) Temple begun (536) Temple delayed (534) Temple completed (520)	Esther becomes queen (478) Purim established (473)		Nehemiah returns (445) Walls rebuilt (445) O.T. closes & 400 silent years begin (ca. 400)
Elsewhere in the World	Middle Kingdom in Egypt (ca. 2000)	Fall of Babylon (539) Roman republic established (509) Greco-Persian wars (499–479)			Age of Pericles (450–400) Hippocrates Father of Medicine (born 460)

Job

The book of Job addresses the ancient question of man's suffering and so examines one of life's most perplexing questions. Overnight the patriarch for whom the book is named finds his blessings turned into heartaches as he loses his health, wealth, family, and status in a crushing series of tragedies. Seeking to know why, Job soon finds the wisdom of his four human counselors inadequate. Finally, Job questions God Himself and learns valuable lessons on the sovereignty of God and the need for complete trust in the Lord.

Focus	Conflict	Counsel		Confidence
Divisions	Job's Affliction and Lament	Job's Counselors and Controversy		Jehovah's Answer and Acquittal
	1 3	4 37		38 42
Topics	God's Works	Men's Misunderstandings		God's Words
	Satan Questions God	Friends Question Job		God Answers Job
Place	Land of Uz (North Arabia)			
Time	Patriarchal Period (About 2000 B.C.)			

Job's Affliction and Lament / Job 1–3

17

Overview: Job, a godly and wealthy resident of Uz, watches helplessly as his life of health, blessings, and prosperity collapses around him. Unknown to him (but known to the reader because of chapters 1 and 2), Job's problems do not begin on *earth*, but rather in *heaven*. With God's permission (and within divinely imposed limitations) Satan launches a series of devastating attacks in an attempt to force Job to renounce God. In the midst of each trial, Job's faith in God shines brightly, though personal turmoil tears at Job's heart as he asks repeatedly, "Why, God?"

Heart of the Passage: Job 1–2

Chapter 1	Chapter 2	Chapter 3
Job's First Trial: Arranged 12	13 Endured 22	Job's Second Trial: Arranged 6	7 Endured 13	Job's Heartbreak Expressed
Testing Commences		Turmoil Commences

Your Daily Walk: Three times in the New Testament, Satan is referred to as a wild animal. How many of the three can you recall before looking up the Bible passages? Why is each symbol appropriate?

1 Peter 5:8 _____
Revelation 12:9 _____
Revelation 20:2 _____

A smooth sea never made a skillful mariner.

Satan is alive and well, roaming far and wide on planet earth! If you doubt that, just ponder the story of Job, a man who was "perfect and upright, and one that feared God, and eschewed evil" (1:1). Job was a man of integrity, moral consistency, and submission to God. And the very attributes of godliness that made Job such a usable vessel for God's service also made him an inviting target for Satan's attacks. Paul wrote, "All that will live godly in Christ Jesus shall suffer persecution" (2 Timothy 3:12); and Job is clearly "Exhibit A."

Have you appropriated the protective armor which God intends for you to use in warding off the flaming missiles of Satan? Not sure? Before you go any further today, take a look at God's checklist of armor in Ephesians 6:11-17. Make sure each piece is firmly in place. (You might want to ask a friend or family member to double-check for you!)

Insight: A Name from Antiquity
The name of both the book and its hero, Job (Hebrew, *'iyyôb*) appears in extra-Biblical texts as early as 2000 B.C., indicating that Job is perhaps the oldest book of the Bible.

18 Cycle #1: Eliphaz and Job / Job 4–7

Overview: After a week of silently mourning his fate, Job's three human counselors begin to analyze his situation. Eliphaz, apparently the oldest, speaks first. He reasons that righteous conduct brings blessing, while sin brings suffering; therefore, Job must be guilty of transgression and needs to repent. Job responds by stressing that his despair is justifiable. He challenges Eliphaz to produce one shred of evidence against him. After silencing his accuser, Job directs his attention to God. He bombards God with questions about the painfulness of life and pleads with Him not to treat him like a marked man (7:20).

Heart of the Passage: Job 4, 6

Chapter 4	Chapter 5	Chapter 6	Chapter 7
"God Is Just"	"You Are Guilty"	"I Am Innocent"	"Leave Me Alone, God"
Eliphaz's Reasons		Job's Rebuttal	

Your Daily Walk: Are the following true or false?

T F 1. Suffering in your life is always due to personal sin or disobedience (Job 1:8).

T F 2. Suffering in your life is a sure sign that you are doing what God wants you to be doing (1 Peter 4:15-16).

T F 3. Sometimes there is no earthly reason (though there may be a heavenly one) why you are allowed to suffer physically or emotionally (Job 1:12; 2:6).

Prepare for the worst, expect the best, and gratefully receive whatever God sends.

Eliphaz was not the first (nor will he be the last) counselor or friend to reason along these lines: "Suffering is always a telltale sign of sin in the life of the sufferer." However, Jesus Himself laid that false conclusion to rest when He encountered a man blind from birth. In response to the disciples' question, "Master, who did sin, this man, or his parents, that he was born blind?" (John 9:2), Jesus responded, "Neither . . . but that the works of God should be made manifest in him." God sometimes permits suffering that He might demonstrate His perfect strength in the face of human weakness.

Are you being afflicted through loss of health, finances, or family? Check to be sure there is no earthly cause for your pain; then trust God that there may well be a heavenly reason.

Insight: Eliphaz, "Wise Man" from Teman

According to Jeremiah 49:7, Eliphaz's hometown of Teman was famous for its counselors and wise men—just what Job needed!

164

Cycle #1: Bildad and Job / Job 8–10

Overview: When Bildad speaks, he lays aside the normally courteous introductions (compare 4:1-6) to confront Job directly. His charge is the same as that of Eliphaz: "God is just; Job is guilty." Bildad seeks to bolster his argument from tradition and history. As in Job's previous rebuttal, he replies first to his human counselor (9:1-24), before directing his complaint toward God. Job recognizes the justice of God, but cannot reconcile that justice with his unexpected affliction. This leads Job even deeper into despair as he laments his very birth.

Heart of the Passage: Job 8–9

Chapter 8	Chapter 9	Chapter 10
"Only the Guilty Suffer"	"Both the Guilty and Innocent Suffer"	"Stillbirth Would Have Been Better"
Bildad's Theory	Job's Theology	

Your Daily Walk: Have you ever felt as if there was a communication gap between you and God? God seemed too big or too remote to be genuinely concerned about your little hurts. You sensed that you needed a go-between, an umpire, an advocate to carry your complaint personally to God and see that it was communicated accurately.

In the midst of his turmoil, Job lamented, "Neither is there any daysman [umpire] betwixt us, that might lay his hand upon us both" (9:33). But *you* have an Umpire! "There is one God, and one mediator between God and men, the man Christ Jesus" (1 Timothy 2:5). You have a distinct advantage over Job, for you have the Lord Jesus Christ ready to make intercession for you (Hebrews 7:25).

Open your spiritual closet and conduct a search for skeletons of hurt that you have never entrusted to God. List them in the margin, and commit each to your "Daysman." Remember, it is His job to go before the Father on your behalf. Then be prepared to enjoy the day, confident in the knowledge that your seeming communications gap with God has been bridged!

Sign on a counselor's door: "If you have troubles, come in and tell me about them. If you don't, come in and tell me how you do it."

Insight: More Than 99 and 44/100 Percent Pure
Job knew that the purest water and the strongest soap were powerless to remove the stains of sin. Only cleansing from God could accomplish that (Psalm 51:7; Isaiah 1:18). Have you allowed the Word of God to bring cleansing to your life today (John 15:3)? If not, take a "clean-up break" right now!

20 *Cycle #1: Zophar and Job / Job 11–14*

Overview: Zophar leaves courtesy even farther behind (11:2-6) as he multiplies the accusations against Job. He reminds

Heart of the Passage: Job 11, 13

Job that God is both awesome and all-knowing, therefore Job needs to repent. Only then will God restore him. Job begins his third defense on a note of sarcasm (12:2). He acknowledges God's awesome character, but still proclaims his own innocence. Again, Job turns his comments from his earthly counselors to his heavenly Father as he bemoans man's fragile estate. But in the midst of Job's despair, there arises a glimmer of hope as he contemplates life beyond the grave.

Chapter 11		Chapter 12	Chapter 13	Chapter 14
"God Is Great"	"You Are Guilty"	"God Is Great"	"You Are Groundless"	"I'm Still Grieved"
Zophar's Case		Job's Conclusions		

1 ... *12* | *13* ... *20*

Your Daily Walk: Criticism hurts, but slander pierces. Job's "friends" turned out to be little more than "forgers of lies"

Repay evil with good, and you deprive the evildoer of all the pleasure of his wicked- ness.

(13:4; literally, "falsehood plasterers"). The Bible has many references to accusers plastering untruths or half-truths on blameless believers. For example, the psalmist cried out, "The proud have forged a lie against me" (Psalm 119:69). But even in the face of such undeserved treatment, the psalmist restrained himself, saying, "But I will keep thy precepts with my whole heart." Even slander- ous attacks do not justify hurtful retaliation. For the believer, God has a better way!

He wants you to react scripturally to your accuser in a sanctified way: Kill him with kindness! In the words of the apostle Paul, "Be not overcome of evil, but overcome evil with good" (Romans 12:21). Is there someone who has hurt you deeply with words in recent days? You have a choice. You can either attempt to get even by retaliating, or you can overcome evil by responding in love. Map out a strategy today to turn one of your false accusers into a friend through the irresistible, overcoming love of God. Begin to put your plan into practice, then step back and give God time to work.

Insight: Malpractice . . . or Something Worse!
Job uses imagery similar to the revoking of a physician's license because of malpractice (13:4). By contrast, the ancient law code of Hammurabi provided that if a doctor operated on some- one's eye unsuccessfully, the doctor's eye was to be blinded as well.

Cycle #2: Eliphaz and Job / Job 15–17

21

📖 **Overview:** The second cycle of debates begins with Eliphaz driving straight to the heart of his accusation: "Why doth thine heart carry thee away? . . . That thou turnest thy spirit against God?" (15:12-13). Eliphaz graphically describes the anguish and ultimate end of the wicked, hoping that Job will make an application to his own situation. Job immediately reacts by proclaiming Eliphaz and his companions "miserable comforters" (16:2). After declaring that God alone has crushed him, he sinks deeper into despair until at last he hits bottom, seemingly hopeless and alone. And there he discovers that God has been there all along.

Heart of the Passage: Job 15–16

Chapter 15	Chapter 16	Chapter 17
"Job Is Hypocritical"	"God Is Harsh"	"All Is Hopeless"
Eliphaz's Charge	Job's Candor	

👣 **Your Daily Walk:** Job's argument in 16:7-17 could be summarized this way: "If God be against us, who can be for us?" He would, however, ultimately come to know a truth which would later be recorded for our comfort and encouragement: "If God be for us, who can be against us?" (Romans 8:31). The obvious answer to both questions is *nobody!* But is God *for* us or *against* us? How can we be sure in the face of discouraging circumstances?

On separate slips of paper, write down the difficulties you are facing now that would tend to make you conclude God is not on your side: prolonged illness, overdue bills, loss of a job, loss of a loved one. Then turn to Romans 8:35-39 to see how many of your problems can actually separate you from God's love. Death can't. Distress can't. Famine can't. In fact, nothing can!

Now take those slips of paper and burn them one by one. As you do, thank God that His love is stronger than any care you have written down or any problem you will encounter today.

The true measure of God's love is that He loves without measure.

✏️ **Insight:** Silence Is Golden

Do you know the difference between minor and major surgery? It's minor when somebody else has it. It's major when you have it—right? Just so, it is easy for Job's friends to talk when it's Job who bears the pain. Like many since, their silent sympathy (2:13) helped more than their well-meaning words. Often the best thing we can do is just sit in silence and share the hurt that is in our brother's heart.

22 Cycle #2: Bildad and Job / Job 18–19

Heart of the Passage: Job 18:1– 19:6

📖 **Overview:** In his second attempt at counseling Job, Bildad paints the darkest picture yet of the fate of the wicked: His light will be put out; his schemes will bring about his own doom; his strength will be devoured; and his every step will be accompanied by darkness, weakness, and terror. Estranged from his family and friends, Job turns once again to his heavenly Father for consolation. Rebounding from the depths of depression and desperation, Job's faith is rekindled in a majestic stanza of faith and trust: "I know that my Redeemer liveth and . . . in my flesh shall I see God" (19:25-26).

Chapter 18		Chapter 19	
"You Are Wrong"	"The Wicked Are Trapped"	"You Are Worthless"	"My Redeemer Lives"
1 4	5 21	1 20	21 29
Bildad's Cruelty		Job's Confidence	

Having got all wrinkled up with care and worry, it's time to get your faith lifted.

✔️ **Your Daily Walk:** Be careful what you lean on in time of need. If your source of strength proves inadequate, you will be left broken and disillusioned.

Job counted on his friends and family to understand his plight. After all, if you can't turn to your loved ones in time of need, where can you turn? Notice the outcome of Job's misplaced trust: "Mine acquaintance are verily estranged from me. My kinsfolk have failed . . . my familiar friends have forgotten me. . . . My maids count me for a stranger. . . . My inward friends abhorred me: and they whom I loved are turned against me" (19:13-15, 19). Mired in despair and disillusionment, Job lifts his eyes heavenward. From the valley of dark depression, Job soars to the mountain peak of God's consoling presence.

Find a hymnal that contains the gospel song, "Leaning on the Everlasting Arms." Thoughtfully read the stanzas, and then do what the songwriter recommends: Lean on Jesus.

📝 **Insight:** Climbing the Summit of Faith with Job
Notice Job's growing faith in a *heavenly* solution to his *earthly* woes.

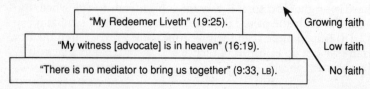

"My Redeemer Liveth" (19:25).	Growing faith
"My witness [advocate] is in heaven" (16:19).	Low faith
"There is no mediator to bring us together" (9:33, LB).	No faith

Cycle #2: Zophar and Job / Job 20–21 23

Overview: Zophar, not noted for his originality, continues to harp on the same theme as his two companions: the retribution of the wicked. He sidesteps Job's hope-filled defense to declare that the wicked's satisfaction will be short-lived and his doom certain—generalizations which Zophar expects Job to apply personally! Job's rebuttal employs many of the same terms, questions, and arguments his accusers have used. There are exceptions to the theory that only the righteous prosper and only the wicked suffer. God showers His blessings on the wicked as well as the righteous—a fact which undermines Zophar's argument but brings no comfort to Job.

Heart of the Passage: Job 20:1-11; 21:22-34

Chapter 20		Chapter 21		
"Your Argument Upsets Me"	"My Argument Should Upset You"	"Open Your Ears"	"Open Your Eyes"	"Open Your Heart"
1 3	4 29	1 6	7 26	27 34
Zophar's Repetition		Job's Retaliation		

Your Daily Walk: Optimism is akin to faith; pessimism is akin to doubt. To which are you akin?

The story is told of a man who went into a restaurant with no money, figuring on paying for his meal with the pearl he hoped to find in the oyster he planned to order. That's an *optimist!* Then there was the man who refused to get married because he was sure he could never find a girl who deserved to be as happy as he would make her. That's a *pessimist!*

Somewhere in between is the *Biblicist*, the person who, without denying the harsh realities of his present situation, can still focus all the promises and provisions of God on living above his circumstances. Zophar had only pat answers and pious cliches to offer Job. As a result, his counsel brought anguish instead of comfort.

How can you truly comfort a friend or family member who is hurting emotionally, physically, or spiritually today? Plan carefully what you will say . . . and won't say. Then pay that person a comforting visit.

A pessimist is a person who is seasick during the entire voyage of life.

Insight: Words with a Hollow (but Familiar) Ring

In his rebuttal, Job skillfully employs the words of his opponents. For example, in the space of a single verse (21:28), Job paraphrases (and parodies) the words of all three counselors: Bildad (8:22), Eliphaz (15:34), and Zophar (20:26).

24 Cycle #3: Eliphaz and Job / Job 22–24

**Heart
of the
Passage:
Job 22–
23**

Overview: Still refusing to admit the possibility of an innocent man having to suffer, Eliphaz begins round three of the
dialogue. However, this round does not go full cycle. Bildad's
contribution is very brief (chapter 25), and Zophar does not speak
at all. The arguments now become painfully pointed. Eliphaz
confronts Job with the question, "Is not thy wickedness great? and
thine iniquities infinite?" (22:5). In the face of Eliphaz's direct
accusations, Job does not retaliate.

Chapter 22	Chapter 23	Chapter 24
"You Are the Wicked Man"	"Where Is My Judge?"	"Where Is Justice?"
Eliphaz's Indictment	Job's Inquiry	

**One
grain of
faith is
more
precious
than a
pound of
knowl-
edge.**

Your Daily Walk: Hide-and-seek is an entertaining children's
game, the object being to find someone who is trying to
evade you.

Hide-and-seek in the spiritual realm is neither entertaining
nor enjoyable. In fact, it can be downright frustrating. The question, "Where are you, God?" is as old as the days of Job.

Job 23:8-12 contains a striking mixture of doubt and trust.
Job had kept God's ways, obeyed God's commands, and even
"esteemed the words of his mouth more than [his] necessary *food*"
(23:12). And yet, wherever Job turned in the midst of his crisis—
"forward . . . backward . . . on the left hand . . . on the right hand"
(23:8-9)—God seemingly was not there.

Although Job could not put the pieces of the puzzle together, he realized that God could. And therein lay the key, for
God wanted his unquestioning confidence. Trust, not knowledge,
was the issue.

A jigsaw puzzle makes a great family fun project after dinner.
If you don't have one around the house already, buy one on the
way home from work. And as you struggle together to make the
pieces fit, share with your children a lesson from Job's life about
what to do when the pieces of life don't seem to fit.

Insight: Do You Get the Point Yet, Job?
In each cycle of debates, the accusing tone of Job's counselors becomes more persistent and pointed. In cycle #1, they speak
about the wicked and good; in cycle #2, the wicked; and now in
cycle #3, the object of their verbal abuse is clearly Job himself.

Cycle #3: Bildad and Job / Job 25–28 **25**

📖 **Overview:** Bildad does not argue with Job, but rather offers two generalizations: God is great and man is a worm—conclusions which Job finds utterly comfortless. Job's rebuttal is in the form of a discourse on God's sovereignty, in which he reemphasizes his innocence, and reaffirms his confidence that God's scales of justice will ultimately balance. Job then ponders the magnitude of God's wisdom, concluding, "Behold, the fear of the Lord, that is wisdom; and to depart from evil is understanding" (28:28)—though that understanding still eludes him!

Heart of the Passage: Job 25, 28

Chapter 25	Chapter 26	Chapter 27	Chapter 28
"God Is Great"	"God Is Sovereign"	"God Is Just"	"God Is Wise"
Bildad's Summary	Job's Summary		

👣 **Your Daily Walk:** Do you understand the importance of understanding? Look up the following verses to see what each has to say about the importance of understanding in the life of a believer:

Proverbs 3:5 Don't lean on your own understanding.
Proverbs 4:7 Whatever else you get, get understanding!
Proverbs 9:10 _____
Proverbs 16:16 _____
Job 28:28 _____
Psalm 111:10 _____

A person becomes wise by watching what happens to him when he isn't.

The word for "understanding" in Job 28:28 signifies moral discernment. It involves taking an objective look at your circumstances, having a proper perspective of God's will in the matter, and finally proceeding down the correct path of action.

To understand God's will, therefore, means more than simply knowing what to do; it means doing what you know. It means being "doers of the word, and not hearers only" (James 1:22). Where in your walk with God do you know more than you are presently doing? How can you show God you truly understand His will?

✏️ **Insight:** Counselors Out of Counsel
As each cycle of debate progresses, Job's accusers find they have less and less to say. Notice the number of verses spoken by each accuser as he moves through the three cycles: Eliphaz (48, 35, 30); Bildad (22, 21, 6); Zophar (20, 29, 0)!

26 *Cycle #3: Zophar and Job / Job 29–31*

Heart of the Passage: Job 29:1-7; 30:1-8; 31:5-15

Overview: Zophar, realizing the debate has reached a stalemate, maintains his silence rather than giving a third rebuttal. But while Job's advisors have at last grown silent, the problem of his suffering lingers on, prompting Job to think back to the good old days. In the past God had blessed him with protection, prosperity, and the respect of his neighbors. But now all that has changed. Poverty has replaced prosperity; respect has given way to ridicule; disease has destroyed his health and vitality. Looking inward, Job concludes his punishment is unjustified. Looking upward, he can only plead, "Let me be weighed in an even balance, that God may know mine integrity" (31:6).

Chapter 29	Chapter 30	Chapter 31
"I Remember the Good Old Days"	"I Resent the Bad New Days"	"I Remain Perfectly Innocent"
Job's Past Glory	Job's Present Groaning	Job's Personal Piety

God still speaks to those who take the time to listen.

Your Daily Walk: A piece of bread grows stale when left in the wrong environment too long. A room becomes stale when fresh air fails to circulate through it. Even a Christian life can become "stale" without a fresh exposure to God's Word each day. If you don't believe it, just ask Job! His concluding statement in 31:40 is short but significant: "The words of Job are ended." There was nothing more to say. His friends had run out of arguments; Job had run out of explanations; in a word, the situation had grown "stale" . . . until God spoke.

Do you sense that your walk with God has been growing stale or stagnant? Then try what Job tried. Be still for a time and let God do the talking. Find a place free from distractions (phone, children, human voices), and spend an uninterrupted 15 minutes reflecting on God's Word and listening for God's voice. It's not easy . . . but it's worth it!

Insight: Past Blessings, Present Woes

In chapters 29–30 Job contrasts his lot in life ("in months past," 29:2) with his present state of despair ("But now," 30:1). Can you discover at least three of the contrasts Job mentions?

"In months past . . ."	"But now . . ."
_____	_____
_____	_____
_____	_____

Cycle #3: Elihu and Job (Part 1)
Job 32–34

27

Overview: Throughout the lengthy debates, three men have dialogued with Job. But standing in courteous silence is a fourth man, younger than the rest. At last, angry with Job for his self-proclaimed innocence and indignant with Job's three friends for their deficient answers, Elihu can remain silent no longer. In four lengthy monologues he declares his evaluation of Job's situation. The problem as Elihu diagnoses it is pride. Although Job has not brought on his trials by sinning, yet he does sin in the midst of his trials by proudly demanding an answer from God. Elihu reminds Job that a gracious God sometimes has to use affliction in order to gain our attention and save us from even more serious consequences.

Heart of the Passage: Job 32:1-9; 33:8-22; 34:10-15

Chapter 32	Chapter 33	Chapter 34
Elihu's Alternative Answer	God's Purpose in Pain	God's Justice with Mankind
Introduction	Instruction	Impartiality

Your Daily Walk: Pride is a curious, competitive thing. You are not proud because you are rich; you are proud because you are *richer*. You are not proud because you are good-looking; you are proud because you are *better-looking*.

In Job's case, he was not proud because he was righteous; he was proud because he saw himself as *more righteous* than other sufferers, and therefore felt he had the right to demand an explanation from God.

C. S. Lewis was right: "A proud man is always looking down on things and people; and, of course, as long as you're looking down, you can't see something that's above you"—even if that "something" is God! Here's a thought to copy down and carry with you throughout the day: "Pride" always demands that "I" be in the middle, but there's no place for "I" in "humble." Take it from Job, the quickest remedy for "I" trouble is looking up into the face of the great "I Am."

Always keep your head up, but be careful to keep your nose at a friendly level.

Insight: Who Is Elihu?
Elihu (the name literally means "my God is He") was a Buzite, living near Edom, for Buz (Genesis 22:21) was a brother of Uz (Job 1:1) and an Aramean (Genesis 10:22-23). Elihu acted as a moderator in the dialogue between Job and his friends, and his speeches thus served to prepare the way for the time when God Himself begins to speak in chapter 38.

28 *Suffering vs. Sovereignty*

Step Back

Scripture Reading: Philippians 1:12-30

One question has plagued mankind since the beginning of time: If God is just and almighty, how can there be evil and suffering in the world—especially in the case of the innocent?

If God is indeed almighty and just, then logic declares that one's suffering indicates the measure of his guilt in God's eyes. In other words, one's sin is being punished by suffering. And the greater the sin, the greater the suffering.

Job suffered at such depths that his friends virtually gave up hope for him. Through chapters 3–37, they debate whether God would allow such intense suffering to happen to an innocent man.

But Job's three friends are overly simplistic in their understanding of the nature of God. Elihu's later claim that God uses suffering to cleanse and purify the righteous is closer to the truth in Job's case, but still falls short.

The simple conclusion of the matter is that God is sovereign and worthy of obedience and worship . . . no matter what He chooses to bring into one's life. Job comes to the point at which he must learn to trust in God's goodness and power in the midst of adversity. And to do this he must enlarge his understanding of God.

You see, even a man as blameless as Job (see 1:1) must repent of pride and self-righteousness. He must come to the end of himself. He must humble himself before God, acknowledging His greatness and majesty.

That's the message we need to grasp today. God is the Lord of "things in heaven, and things in earth, and things under the earth" (Philippians 2:10). He is all-powerful and all-knowing. And His every act results in ultimate good.

Look Up

We can sometimes see more through a tear than through a telescope.

Because we are human and God is God, His ways may sometimes seem totally incomprehensible to us. And yet, we know as Job did that we can trust Him totally.

In light of this, perhaps you need to talk with the Lord about some tough circumstances of your life that are causing you to question God. Let the message of Job encourage you to refocus your eyes on your loving, sovereign Lord.

Move Ahead

The apostle Paul was one who could cope with outrageous circumstances positively because He could see God at work in them. Read Philippians 1:12-30. Let his example also inspire you to build your trust in God—and to thank Him that your circumstances are really as good as they are!

Cycle #3: Elihu and Job (Part 2)
Job 35–37

29

Overview: Job has observed: "It profiteth a man nothing that he should delight himself with God" (34:9). Elihu now attempts to prove there really is profit in serving God, regardless of the price of pain. Through suffering, people can learn much about God's justice, chastening, and holiness. Truly, "The Almighty . . . is excellent in power, and in judgment, and in plenty of justice" (37:23). Only in a clearer picture of God will Job find the answers to his questions.

Heart of the Passage: Job 35; 37:14-24

Chapter 35	Chapter 36	Chapter 37
"Man Is Not like God"	"God Is Not like Man"	"God Is Sovereign over Man"
Elihu's Contention		Elihu's Conclusion

Your Daily Walk: A young lad once approached his father to ask, "Dad, why does the wind blow?" To which the father responded, "I don't know, son."

The boy continued, "Dad, where do the clouds come from?"
"I'm not sure, son."
"Dad, what makes a rainbow?"
"No idea, son."
"Dad, do you mind me asking you all these questions?"
"Not at all, son. How else are you going to learn?"

The earthly father, unable to answer questions about nature, left his son with little hope that his father could handle the thornier questions about life. But there is a heavenly Father, the God of creation, the One who made the thunder and rain, wind and clouds (37:5-11), who also knows the answers to life's deepest riddles. Is He your heavenly Father? Are you a part of His family? You can't buy your way in or work your way in. You must be born into the family of God.

There is nothing round the corner that is beyond God's view.

Sound impossible? Then spend a few minutes reading John 3:1-18. Nicodemus learned directly from Jesus what it means to be "born again." You can, too!

Insight: God's Works—Mighty Yet Mysterious
Elihu draws on more than 30 images from the physical and natural world (36:26–37:24) to show the majesty and might of God's creative power. And yet, these wonders of nature that are a daily part of life are at the same time incomprehensible (36:26, 29; 37:5), for they perform God's bidding both as a curse and as a blessing (37:13). Even the elemental forces do not escape God's control.

30 *Jehovah's Answer for Job / Job 38–39*

Heart of the Passage: Job 38:1-18

Overview: God now speaks "out of the whirlwind" (38:1) and begins to direct probing questions at Job—questions designed to illustrate the greatness of God and the smallness of man. Obviously, this breaking of the heavenly silence is not exactly what Job had in mind in 31:35! He can only tremble in awe, silently answering, "No . . . No . . . No . . ." to God's divine interrogation. God invites Job to review the whole realm of creation from A to Z—astronomy to zoology. His questions do not answer Job's specific *why* but they do begin to answer the bigger and as yet unasked question, *who*.

Chapter 38	Chapter 39
"Do You Understand All About the Physical World?"	"Do You Understand All About the Animal World?"
Jehovah Interrogates Job	

One thing you can learn by watching the clock is that it passes the time by keeping its hands busy.

Your Daily Walk: Have you ever experienced the thrill of meeting an important dignitary or world leader—a queen, ambassador, prime minister, or president? Relatively few people have, but millions dream of such an event. Perhaps you have even rehearsed what you would say if such a meeting took place.

Because of the suffering he had endured, Job's deepest longing was for an audience with the Lord of the universe. However, when that dream came true, Job found himself powerless to voice his accusations or offer his excuses. God's awesome presence silenced him totally!

How many accusations or excuses have you offered to God recently for your actions (or inactions)? Would you feel comfortable offering those same excuses to God if you were to meet Him face to face? Or, would you, like Job, stand silently before Him? The exciting (yet sobering) truth is that someday you *will* stand before Him . . . and see Him as He is (1 John 3:2). That purifying truth is designed to help you be prepared (not paralyzed) for that long-awaited meeting. How can you prepare today to meet the Lord gladly face to face?

Insight: Job's Astronomy Lesson

In 38:31-33 God demonstrates His sovereignty over constellations of stars. Look up the names mentioned in verse 31 in a good encyclopedia. Try to locate the constellations in the sky some night when conditions are good. Remember, your God has "bound" them and can "loose" them all!

Job's Acquittal / Job 40–42

Overview: After Job's initial confession of God's sovereignty (40:1-5), the Lord continues His interrogation. Using illustrations drawn from the animal world, the Almighty shows Job his own frailty and finiteness until at last Job cries out in repentance, "Have I uttered [things] that I understood not; things too wonderful for me, which I knew not" (42:3). Understanding God's control, not asking God questions, meets the need of Job's heart. Job's story is nearly at an end. Having learned the lesson for which God allowed the suffering, Job now watches as his trials and turmoil turn into triumph. The divine Judge not only restores Job's prestige, but also the patriarch's possessions and family.

Heart of the Passage: Job 40:1-14; 42

Chapters 40–41	Chapter 42	
Job Sees God's Majesty	Job Sees God's Justice	Job Sees God's Grace
1	6 7	17
Jehovah Illuminates Job		

Your Daily Walk: The most unsavory meat you will ever be called upon to eat is the time you will have to "eat crow." If you don't believe it, ask Eliphaz, Bildad, and Zophar (42:7-9). Not only was their evaluation of Job's situation wrong (and as a result, their counsel was misguided), but in the end, their "patient" offered a prayer for their healing!

Think back over your study of the book of Job. How many times were you tempted to agree with the diagnosis of one of Job's three friends? Would you have had to "eat crow" along with them?

Two lessons emerge from the aftermath of Job's suffering: Be quick to bear another's burdens (Galatians 6:2), but be slow to judge another's actions (Matthew 7:1). At the end of the book of Job in your Bible (or on a separate sheet of paper), write a short postscript capturing some of the lessons and insights you will take with you from your study. God may never call upon you to suffer as Job did, but He expects you to learn from Job's experience of suffering.

Experience is what you get when you were expecting something else.

Insight: Measuring a Generation

How long is a "generation" in the Bible? Job 42:16 states, "After this lived Job a hundred and forty years, and saw his sons, and his sons' sons, even four generations." Divide 140 years by four generations, and it appears that a generation during the time of Job was approximately 35 years.

Psalms

O ver a period of 10 centuries, inspired hymns of worship were composed and compiled to form the anthology known as the book of Psalms (from a Greek word meaning "a song sung to the accompaniment of a plucked instrument"). Authored by David and six other writers and used as the temple hymnbook, these heart-stirring pleas and praises capture the essence of what it means to walk daily with God. Each of the five sections bears a topical likeness to a book of the Pentateuch, and each closes with a ringing doxology of praise.

Section	Book 1: Psalms 1–41	Book 2: Psalms 42–72	Book 3: Psalms 73–89	Book 4: Psalms 90–106	Book 5: Psalms 107–150
Main Author(s)	David	David & Korah	Asaph	Anonymous	David
Possible Compiler	David	Hezekiah		Ezra/Nehemiah	
Content	Laments	National Anthems		Praise Anthems	
Topical Likeness to Pentateuch	Genesis (Mankind)	Exodus (Redemption)	Leviticus (Worship)	Numbers (Wandering)	Deuteronomy (Word of God)
Benediction of Praise	41:13	72:18-19	89:52	106:48	150:1-6
Span of Authorship	About 1,000 Years				
Dates of Compilation	1020–970 B.C.	970–610 B.C.		Until 430 B.C.	

The Darkest Hour of the Day *Psalms 1–6*

1

📖 **Overview:** The first six psalms form a fitting introduction to the entire Psalter. In them you will learn the importance of meditating on God's Word (1), acknowledging the Lord as King (2), and constantly being devoted to prayer in good times and in bad (3–6).

Heart of the Passage: Psalm 3

Psalm	Author	Key Idea	(Verse) Referred to in N.T.
1	Unknown	Portrait of Two Lives	(2) Rom. 7:22
2	David*	The Lord and His Anointed	(1-2) Acts 4:25-26; (7) Acts 13:33
3	David	The Darkest Hour of the Day	(8) Rev. 7:10
4	David	A Bedtime Prayer	(4) Eph. 4:26
5	David	A Morning Prayer	(9) Rom. 3:13
6	David	A Tearful Prayer	(8) Matt. 7:23; 25:41

*See Acts 4:25

✍️ **Your Daily Walk:** Can you stand your ground when you are in the minority? How about when the minority is shrinking and the opposition is growing?

Psalm 3 is the first of 14 psalms that contain a hint in the title regarding the historical situation which prompted David to write them. The superscription reads: "A psalm of David, when he fled from Absalom his son" (see 2 Samuel 15:16-17). Those 11 words summarize the heartbreak of a father, the humiliation of a deposed monarch, and the overthrow of a great military leader. As David's favorite son, Absalom, usurps the throne, the king enters one of the darkest periods of his life.

But beginning with verse 3, David shifts his focus from his problem to his Problem Solver. He remembers that God is a shield to protect him, glory to adorn him, and a head lifter to encourage him (v. 3). God gives peace in the midst of distress (v. 5) and fearlessness in the face of opposition (v. 6). Truly, without God there is no victory; with God, every foe can be vanquished.

Sleeplessness in the face of mounting problems is a sure sign your focus is in the wrong place! Write out the words of verse 5 and place them where you will see them last thing tonight and first thing tomorrow morning. Remember, your Problem Solver never sleeps!

Standing your ground is easier when you're grounded in faith.

🖊️ **Insight:** And Speaking of the Darkest Hour of the Day . . .
The first half of Psalm 3:8 is quoted elsewhere in the Old Testament by someone who was also having a "dark day"—in fact, one of the darkest, loneliest, wettest days anyone has ever experienced. Do you remember who? (Check Jonah 2:9 for the answer.)

179

2 *Waiting for the Judge / Psalms 7–12*

Heart of the Passage: Psalm 7

 Overview: All but one of the psalms in today's reading begin with a cry of lament: "O Lord my God," "O Lord," "Lord." These short but potent songs express the psalmist's desire that justice prevail (7), the wicked be brought low (9–10), and God's holy name be exalted (8, 11–12).

Psalm	Author	Key Idea	(Verse) Referred to in N.T.
7	David	Waiting for the Judge	(9) Rev. 2:23
8	David	Crown of Creation	(2) Matt. 21:16; (4-6) Heb. 2:6-8
9	David	Peril of the Wicked	(8) Acts 17:31
10	Unknown	Peril of the Pilgrim	(7) Rom. 3:14
11	David	Trust from the Temple	
12	David	Truth from God's Mouth	

All things come to him who waits— even justice.

Insight: Cush, the Unknown Benjamite

The Cush referred to in the title of Psalm 7 remains a mystery, since no such contemporary of David's is mentioned in the Bible. Some commentators have suggested Cush might be another name for Shimei (2 Samuel 16:5; 19:16), the Benjamite who cursed David and threw rocks at him during David's hasty retreat from Jerusalem following Absalom's revolt. Now read Psalm 7 again . . . with feeling!

Your Daily Walk: Ponder each of the following statements for a few moments before placing a check (✓) next to the ones you agree with:

_____ 1. God is Judge of all the earth.
_____ 2. God's justice is perfect and impartial.
_____ 3. The path of the wicked leads to destruction.
_____ 4. A wicked response to a wicked man is sin.

What you have done if you checked all four statements is to give mental assent to the fact that God will settle all accounts justly and in His own perfect timing (Psalm 7:8-9). The wicked will be punished; the righteous will be rewarded—but not always as quickly as you might like!

Now take those same four statements and translate them into a real-life situation. For David, that meant saying: *"God is Judge of all the earth* . . . including this man Cush, who is hurling rocks and curses at me. *God's justice is perfect and impartial* . . . and He will vindicate me from Cush's slanderous accusations without my attempting to do so. *A wicked response to Cush would be sinful* . . . therefore, I will wait upon the Lord." Now do the same with a "Cush" in your own life! As you wait for the Judge to settle the injustices in your life, make Psalm 7:1 your patient prayer.

180

Past Conquests, Future Confidence
Psalms 13–18

3

Overview: In sharp contrast to the fate of the fool who denies God's existence (14), many blessings accrue to the one who serves God with a whole heart: joyfulness (13), fellowship with God (15), satisfaction (16), preservation (17), and confidence in facing the future (18).

Heart of the Passage: Psalm 18

Psalm	Author	Key Idea	(Verse) Referred to in N.T.
13	David	From Sighing to Singing	
14	David	From Folly to Faith	(1-3) Rom. 3:10-12
15	David	A Man After God's Heart	
16	David	Satisfaction from God	(8-11) Acts 2:25-28; 13:35
17	David	Protection from God	(15) 1 John 3:2
18	David	Past Conquests, Future Confidence	(2) Heb. 2:13; (49) Rom. 15:9

Your Daily Walk: Living in the glow of yesterday's victories can be (a) helpful, (b) harmful, (c) both helpful and harmful. (Pick one.)

You probably selected (c)—"both helpful and harmful." As David sits down to write Psalm 18, he has many memories of God's past deliverances in his life. God has been his "strength . . . rock . . . fortress . . . deliverer . . . buckler [shield] . . . high tower" (v. 2). David knows from firsthand experience that God is the One who hears, who avenges, who lifts up, who rescues, who rewards, who girds with strength those who put their trust in Him. And that knowledge gives David confidence to trust God in future days as well: "I *will* love thee. . . . I *will* call upon the LORD. . . . Therefore *will* I give thanks unto thee, O LORD" (vv. 1, 3, 49).

A complacent Christian is a contradiction in terms.

But there is a danger for those who bask in yesterday's victories: COMPLACENCY. Just because God has promised to fight for you does not mean you can sit idly by and do nothing! Look at David's action steps of obedience: "I have kept the ways of the Lord. . . . I did not put away his statutes from me. . . . I kept myself from mine iniquity" (vv. 21-23).

This evening, pull out something that reminds you of God's faithfulness thus far this year (a photo album, appointment calendar, or diary), and spend a few minutes reliving past victories. Now talk to God about what you intend to do during the rest of the year as you walk in confident obedience to Him.

Insight: Haven't I Sung That Somewhere Before?
If the words of Psalm 18 seem familiar, it's probably because you read them before . . . in 2 Samuel 22! (Do you recall the occasion that prompted David to compose those verses?)

181

4 My Guide and Protector / Psalms 19–24

Heart of the Passage: Psalm 23

Overview: The Lord can be seen in many different roles in these six psalms. He is the Creator (19), the Helper (20), the King (21), the Crucified One (22), the Shepherd (23), and the Glorious One (24). For each role there is a corresponding responsibility for the people who would follow Him as their God and King, Shepherd, and Sovereign.

Psalm	Author	Key Idea	(Verse) Referred to in N.T.
19	David	The Sky and the Scriptures	(4) Rom. 10:18; (9) Rev. 19:2
20	David	Trust in the Midst of Trouble	
21	David	Rejoicing After Rescue	
22	David	A Sob and a Song	(1, 7-8, 16, 18) Matt. 27:35, 39, 43, 46
23	David	My Guide and Protector	(1) John 10:11; Heb. 13:20
24	David	My Creator and King	(1) 1 Cor. 10:26, 28

God watches and weeds us, and continues His labor upon us, until He brings us to the end of His promise.

Insight: A Trinity of Shepherd Psalms

Psalms 22, 23, and 24 form a trio of songs about the Lord our Shepherd. In Psalm 22 He is the Good Shepherd who gives His life for the sheep (John 10:11); in Psalm 23 He is the Great Shepherd who guides and provides (Hebrews 13:20); and in Psalm 24 He is the Chief Shepherd, the sovereign Lord of the sheep (1 Peter 5:4). By the way, is He *your* Shepherd?

Your Daily Walk: Some of the most noted men in Scripture were shepherds. Can you think of three?_____. Joseph was a shepherd (Genesis 37:2). Along with his 11 brothers, he tended his father's flocks. Unknown to Joseph, God was preparing him for the day when he would "shepherd" the nation of Egypt through seven years of famine.

Moses was a shepherd. For 40 years he coped with balky sheep in Midian, not knowing that soon he would be putting his "pastoral education" to work leading a balky nation of Israelites.

David was a shepherd. As a young lad he nurtured his father's flocks, unaware that soon he would be anointed to "shepherd" God's people.

For David, likening God to a loving, caring shepherd in Psalm 23 was natural because David knew firsthand the role of a shepherd. Try paraphrasing Psalm 23 in your own words, using a metaphor of which you have firsthand knowledge. For example: "The Lord is my Boss . . . my Teacher . . . my Pastor . . . my Coach . . . my Father." Or do more than one and creatively explore several aspects of God's work in your life.

182

The Shepherd's Psalm

5

Step Back

When David the shepherd wrote the song that later was numbered the Twenty-third Psalm, he may not have realized how deeply it would touch humanity for generations to come. Why? Because, deep down, we all know we're sheep. And the comfort we can derive from its thoughts are as comforting as if our own Shepherd, Jesus Christ, were to carry us in His arms.

Scripture Reading: Hebrews 13:20-21

The Bible frequently refers to believers as sheep. So this psalm is about us. Consider some of the facts about sheep—and think how they may apply to us:

1. *Sheep have virtually no defenses.* Most of God's animal creations have some kind of effective defense mechanism, whether claws or teeth, special coloring or speed, strength or sharp senses. But sheep have none. They're weak, slow, and awkward. They can't even growl. Their only protection comes from their shepherd. And the same is true with the Christian.

2. *Sheep have difficulty finding food and water.* They must depend totally on their shepherd for sustenance. If they fail to get it, they'll eat poisonous weeds and die. We're just as dependent on the God who sustains us.

3. *Sheep can be easily frightened.* And fright can lead them to do things that can threaten their life. So their shepherd attempts to keep them calm, by singing and simply being with them. We can have the same kind of reassuring relationship with our Shepherd.

4. *Sheep have a poor sense of direction.* They get lost easily—even in their own territory. Believers can behave very similarly. We simply cannot be our own guide; we get in trouble every time we do. We must trust our Shepherd and listen to His voice implicitly.

5. *Sheep cannot clean themselves very well.* It falls on the shepherd to keep them clean. We too are by nature unclean. Only our Shepherd can cleanse us.

Look Up

Being likened to a sheep is not a flattering portrait for us. But let's be honest, it's a true one. We can choose to be proud and ignore the truth, or we can turn to our Shepherd in loving dependence, assured of His constant care and love. Thank Him for that as you meditate on Hebrews 13:20-21.

God does not comfort us to make us comfortable, but to make us comforters.

Move Ahead

Today, wear or carry a woolen item to remind you of the sheep and the shepherd. Share something you've learned today about being a sheep to a friend or acquaintance. Perhaps your conversation will encourage another sheep to enter the flock.

6 Praying Through the Alphabet
Psalms 25–30

Overview: As David penned the psalms you read today, he thought of the multifaceted character of the God he served. The Lord is "good and upright" (25:8), "my light" (27:1), "my strength" (28:7), "King for ever" (29:10), and "my God" (30:2, 12).

Heart of the Passage: Psalm 25

Psalm	Author	Key Idea	(Verse) Referred to in N.T.
25	David	Praying Through the Alphabet	
26	David	Judging the Accused	
27	David	Fear Swallowed Up by Faith	(1) John 12:46; (12) Matt. 26:60
28	David	Cry of the Downcast	(4) 2 Tim. 4:14; Rev. 22:12
29	David	Voice of the Lord	(3) Rev. 10:3
30	David	Confidence of the Uplifted	(5) John 16:20

Your Daily Walk: Psalm 25 is the first "alphabetic psalm" in the Psalter. Here's why that is an appropriate designation.

Prayer is the mightiest of all weapons that created natures can wield.

Write out the letters of the English alphabet vertically in the margin; A, B, C, etc. Now, can you think of one Bible verse that begins with each of those letters? For example, **A**—"**A**ll we like sheep have gone astray" (Isaiah 53:6); **B**—"**B**lessed are the poor in spirit" (Matthew 5:3). See how many of the 26 letters you can match with a Bible verse.

What you just attempted with the English alphabet, David does in Psalm 25 with the Hebrew alphabet. With only minor variations, David proceeds through the entire Hebrew alphabet, capturing his thoughts in alphabetical order. You might think of it as "praying through his problems from A to Z."

Because of the way David "packaged" his prayer requests, he was able to remember them long after the psalm was written. In that way he could check up and see how God had faithfully answered each request. You can do the same thing by beginning a Prayer Log. Write down your prayer requests, date them, pray daily and systematically for them, and watch God work! (And remember, God answers prayers three ways: "yes," "no," and "wait!") Then you, like David, can make your prayer time as memorable as A, B, C!

Insight: Other Alphabetic Psalms in the Psalter

The Hebrew alphabet has 22 letters. Knowing that fact, how do you suppose the psalmist has organized the following alphabetic psalms: Psalm 34? Psalm 145? (One letter is missing.) Psalm 119? (Hint: Divide 176 by 8.)

Praying for Your Persecutors
Psalms 31–36

7

Overview: A proper perspective can help you face any circumstance and can bring you from gloom to glory (31), from failure to forgiveness (32), from false security to confident trust (33), from affliction to adoration (34), from persecution to praise (35), and from darkness to light (36).

Heart of the Passage: Psalm 35

Psalm	Author	Key Idea	(Verse) Referred to in N.T.
31	David	From Gloom to Glory	(5) Luke 23:46
32	David	Praise for God's Pardon	(1-2) Rom. 4:7-8; (5) 1 John 1:9
33	Unknown	My Maker and Monarch	(3) Rev. 5:9; (6) Heb. 11:3
34	David	Looking at Life from the Cave	(12-16) 1 Pet. 3:10-12; (20) John 19:36
35	David	Praying for Persecutors	(19) John 15:25
36	David	Life and Light in the Lord	(1) Rom. 3:18; (9) John 12:46

Your Daily Walk: Loving someone who is lovely is easy. Loving someone who is unlovely is difficult. But loving someone who is unlovable? That's what the Christian is called to do! Think back to Christ's words to His disciples: "Love your enemies, bless them that curse you, do good to them that hate you, and pray for them which despitefully use you" (Matthew 5:44). How can you pray for people like that?

Psalm 35 will give you part of the answer. Notice how David prayed for those who were pursuing and persecuting him:

David did not condone their actions. While praying for God's deliverance in his own life, David also prayed that God would confound his oppressors to show them the result of their folly.

David did not return evil for evil. He could have attacked his attackers in an attempt to vindicate himself. Instead, David treated them as he would have wanted to be treated (vv. 13-14).

David sought to maintain a proper focus in the midst of his sufferings. The psalm moves through three stanzas, each beginning with David's plight (1-8, 11-17, 19-26), but ending with David's praise that God is still in control (9-10, 18, 27-28).

Are you in the midst of being accused unjustly in your home, office, or school? Using David's prayer as your model, how can you respond in a way that will bring praise out of your plight?

In prayer, while we seek in appearance to bend God's will to ours, we are in reality bringing our will to His.

Insight: Psalms 34 and 35—Companions in Misery
Whether or not Psalm 35 was written as a companion to Psalm 34, it is appropriately placed next to it, not only because of similar phrases (34:7; 35:5-6) but because it speaks out of the kind of darkness which has just been dispelled in Psalm 34.

8 *Wounded by a Friend / Psalms 37–41*

Heart of the Passage: Psalm 41

Overview: Psalms is not merely a book of praise; it is also a book of practical counsel. Today you will learn how to deal with fretfulness (37) and failing strength (38-39); how to rest in God's faithfulness (40) and respond to a friend's unfaithfulness (41).

Psalm	Author	Key Idea	(Verse) Referred to in N.T.
37	David	Well-Being and Well-Doing	(11, 22, 29) Matt. 5:5
38	David	Cry of a Suffering Saint	(11) Luke 23:49
39	David	Faith in the Midst of Frailty	(12) Heb. 11:13
40	David	From the Mire to the Choir	(6-8) Heb. 10:5-9
41	David	Wounded by a Friend	(9) John 13:18

Praise is more spontaneous when things go right; but it is more precious when things go wrong.

Your Daily Walk: Psalm 41 marks the end of Book 1 of the Psalter. It concludes the section in the same way Psalm 1 commences it: by talking about the blessed (happy) person who is rightly related to God.

Think of Psalm 41 as a pyramid of praise in the midst of anguish, a sort of "How to Bless the Lord While Bedridden."

"Mine enemies . . . come" (5-9)	
"Lord, be merciful" (4)	"Lord, be merciful" (10-12)
"Blessed is he" (1-3)	"Blessed be the Lord" (13)

The psalmist is suffering from some physical ailment or injury (v. 3). What begins as a third-person description of the man who takes pity on the poor and needy (vv. 1-3) soon becomes the plea of a discouraged, bedridden saint: "Be merciful unto *me:* heal *my soul*" (v. 4). The longer the psalmist meditates on the Lord, the more confident he becomes of God's strength in his hour of need.

If you are sick or bedridden today, you can experience God's blessing even in the midst of your recuperation. Instead of moping about your condition, use the time to meditate on the mercies of God. How has God delivered you . . . preserved you . . . strengthened you . . . upheld you in recent weeks? Share a few of those faith-stretching experiences with a family member or hospital roommate. It may be just the encouragement that person needs to help him praise the Lord with you.

Insight: Dos and Don'ts of Counting on God

Psalm 37 contains 8 *dos* and 4 *don'ts*. Can you find all 12 and give each a modern-day paraphrase? (Example: "Fret not" = Don't get steamed up! "Trust in" = Lean on totally.)

Here Comes the Bridegroom
Psalms 42–49

9

Overview: Today you read some of the psalms attributed to the sons of Korah, descendants of the man who died for his rebellion against Moses (Numbers 16:1-33; 26:10). One part of this family became the temple doorkeepers (1 Chronicles 9:19); another the singers and musicians in the temple (1 Chronicles 6:31-33, 37).

Heart of the Passage: Psalm 45

Psalm	Author	Key Idea	(Verse) Referred to in N.T.
42	Korah	Cast Down but Confident	
43	Unknown	Lonely but Never Alone	
44	Korah	Failure Turned to Success	(22) Rom. 8:36
45	Korah	Here Comes the Bridegroom	(2) Luke 4:22; (6-7) Heb. 1:8-9
46	Korah	A City Unshaken	(4) Rev. 22:1
47	Korah	A Conquering King	
48	Korah	The City of God	(2, 8) Matt. 5:35
49	Korah	The Vanity of Wealth	(16-19) Luke 12:13-21

Your Daily Walk: Find a newspaper and turn to the society page. Notice the amount of print, pictures, and fanfare devoted to weddings. Psalm 45 was penned by a poet, who, like a sort of heavenly journalist, was trying to capture in word pictures the glory and splendor of a bride and bridegroom on their wedding day. Only this was no mere earthly wedding. Notice how Hebrews 1:8-9 quotes verses 6 and 7 of this psalm and ascribes them to Jesus Christ Himself!

Jesus Christ is the condescension of divinity and the exaltation of humanity.

In ancient Near Eastern weddings the man was more important than the woman. All the guests gathered to view his apparel and his attendants! The wedding processional was for the bridegroom, not the bride! And truly the Groom is worthy of glory and honor. Notice the description of His virtues: "Thy throne . . . is for ever and ever: the scepter of thy kingdom is a right scepter" (v. 6). "Thou art fairer than the children of men: grace is poured into thy lips" (v. 2). With His sword in place to demonstrate strength and justice, and adorned with truth, meekness, and righteousness, the King is indeed majestic.

Close your devotional time today by thoughtfully reading verse 17. Then look for one way you can introduce the next "generation" by word or deed to your King of Kings. Here comes the Groom!

Insight: Treating the Psalms Royally
Other "royal psalms" (psalms that picture Christ as King) include Psalms 2, 18, 20, 21, 72, 89, 99, 110, and 145.

10 A King's Cry for Cleansing
Psalms 50–54

Heart of the Passage: Psalm 51

Overview: Sin and confession are prominent themes in the psalms you read today (50). David provides a model of confession after his sin with Bathsheba (51), and goes on to describe the treacherous nature of the tongue (52) and the folly of pursuing evil (53). Only with God as your constant source of help (54) can you counter the daily temptations and pitfalls of life.

Psalm	Author	Key Idea	(Verse) Referred to in N.T.
50	Asaph	The Judge Who Is Not Silent	(12) 1 Cor. 10:26, 28
51	David	A King's Cry for Cleansing	(4) Rom. 3:4
52	David	The Treacherous Tongue	
53	David	The Futility of Evil	(1-3) Rom. 3:10-12
54	David	God, My Helper and Upholder	

If our prayers do not change us, then we do not pray aright.

Your Daily Walk: New "miracle" products emerge all the time, loudly heralded for their ability to clean everything from "tough, ground-in dirt" to "ring-around-the-collar." But there is still one cleaning job they are powerless to accomplish: the cleansing of a dirty heart.

Psalm 51 was penned during the darkest hour of David's life. For perhaps 20 years, the shepherd-king had ruled in righteous grandeur. But overnight his sin with Bath-sheba changed all that. First adultery, then murder inflicted ugly scars on the king's life. Nathan the prophet was sent by God to confront David with the severity of his sin. And David responded with a heartfelt prayer for forgiveness: "Wash me . . . cleanse me. . . . Create in me a clean heart" (vv. 2, 10).

David knew that forgiveness involves two parties: the offender and the offended. Unless the offended party is willing to put away the wrong that's been done, fellowship cannot be restored. The price of pardon is never cheap, but David knew it must be paid. "The sacrifices of God are a broken spirit: a broken and a contrite heart, O God, thou wilt not despise" (v. 17).

Has your walk with God been interrupted by a dark stain of sin? Then get up right now and find a place where you can wash your hands. As you do, ask God to wash your heart as well. Confess your specific offenses against God, and experience His cleansing—the kind no soap can produce (1 John 1:9).

Insight: Seven Cries for Cleansing in the Psalms
In addition to Psalm 51, there are six other "psalms of a penitent heart" in the Psalter: Psalms 6, 32, 38, 102, 130, and 143.

Cataloging
the Psalter

Just as the nation of Israel was divided into many different tribes, so the Psalms can be divided into many different types. As you continue your journey through this book, you'll find it helpful to be able to classify each psalm you read. A majority of the psalms fall into one of three categories:

I *Lament Psalms.* These are petitions addressed directly to God by the individual or community in the context of distress. They usually include a description of the problems, a confession of trust, and a vow of praise to God, uttered with the confidence that God can and will deliver His people (examples: Psalms 3–7, 22, 42).

II *Thank Psalms.* These psalms, offered publicly by one or more worshipers, acknowledge God's faithful actions on behalf of His people in the past, or express confidence in His promise to act in the future (examples: Psalms 18, 27, 62).

III *Praise Psalms.* These hymns are based on the word "praise" or "hallelujah." They are joyful expressions of adoration for God's greatness, acknowledging Him as Creator, Sustainer, and Lover of His people (examples: Psalms 113, 117, 146–150).

In addition, you will encounter:

IV *Royal Psalms,* hymns describing the King, both earthly and heavenly, reigning over His kingdom (examples: Psalms 2, 95–96).

V *Woe Psalms,* poems expressing the psalmist's righteous indignation at God's enemies, and calling for God's swift retribution (examples: Psalms 49, 109, 137).

VI *Acrostic Psalms,* highly stylized poems in which each new section, verse, or line begins with a successive letter of the Hebrew alphabet (examples: Psalms 9–10, 25, 35, 119).

VII *Pilgrim Psalms,* songs sung by worshipers on the way up to Jerusalem for the yearly feasts (examples: Psalms 120–134).

VIII *Messianic Psalms,* prophetic songs describing the coming Messiah as King (Psalms 2, 24, 110), Servant (Psalms 22–23, 40, 60), and the Son of God (Psalm 118).

11 *Prayer While Being Pursued*
Psalms 55–59

Overview: Today's reading captures the emotions of King David during some of his most difficult days. Notice David's frank petitions and confident trust in God in the wake of being betrayed (55), brokenhearted (56), and pursued (57, 59). Through it all David knows "there is a reward for the righteous . . . [and] God . . . judgeth in the earth" (58:11).

Heart of the Passage: Psalm 59

Psalm	Author	Key Idea	(Verse) Referred to in N.T.
55	David	Betrayed by a Brother	(22) 1 Pet. 5:7
56	David	A Bottle Full of Tears	(4) Heb. 13:6; (9) Rom. 8:31
57	David	Faith of a Fugitive	
58	David	Weighing the Wicked	
59	David	Prayer While Being Pursued	

Your Daily Walk: Psalm 59 is the last in a series of three psalms (57–59) described as *Michtams* (songs of deliverance) sung to the tune of *Altaschith* ("Do Not Destroy"). Go back and refresh your memory about the situation behind Psalm 59 in 1 Samuel 19:11, "when Saul sent, and they watched the house to kill him" (title of Psalm 59). Everyone from time to time finds the need to eat on the run, and occasionally to ask directions on the run, but have you learned to praise on the run?

Praise is the best of all sacrifices and the true evidence of godliness.

Psalm 59 describes David as being on the run. Narrowly escaping Saul's murderous pursuit, David fled for his life. He was a fugitive . . . a pursued man . . . a man on the run. Perhaps finding a few minutes to stop and catch his breath, David took pen in hand and composed the words of Psalm 59, a song of confident praise in the midst of being pursued.

It is easy to complain about the "enemies" all around you—the circumstances that invade your life bringing anxiety and uncertainty. It is easy to pray for God to judge those enemies and remove those circumstances. But can you, like David, praise God for those circumstances and respond with a joyful attitude of praise while "on the run"? Reread the last two verses of Psalms 57, 58, and 59. Then complete this sentence: "Because God is my defense and refuge (59:16), today I will praise Him 'on the run' by

_____ ."

Insight: The Good Housekeeping "Selah" of Approval
The word *selah*, which occurs 71 times in the book of Psalms, may have marked a crescendo in the music, the end of a refrain, or a dramatic pause to highlight what had just been said.

Good News and Bad News
Psalms 60–66

12

Overview: Today you read five psalms of lament (60, 61, 63–65; watch for the cry, "O God") in which the psalmist stands upon the promises of God in the face of defeat, discouragement, and deceit. Through it all the psalmist finds that God is a praiseworthy refuge (62, 66).

Heart of the Passage: Psalm 60

Psalm	Author	Key Idea	(Verse) Referred to in N.T.
60	David	Good News and Bad News	
61	David	God, My High Rock	
62	David	God, My Immovable Defense	(12) Matt. 16:27; Rev. 2:23; 22:12
63	David	God, My Soul's Satisfaction	
64	David	Preserved from Panic	
65	David	God of Might	(7) Matt. 8:26
66	Unknown	God of Many	

Your Daily Walk: What was the best news you received in the last year? What was the worst news? Have you ever had someone come to you with the bittersweet statement, "I have good news and bad news . . ."? Which did you want to hear first?

The front page of any newspaper is adequate reason for the necessity of a saving God.

Psalm 60 was written in the aftermath of both good news and bad news for King David. At the peak of his power, David enjoyed victory over his foes near and far (2 Samuel 8:3-5). (That's the good news.) But David's sweeping success in battle caused his enemies to join forces through alliances. This psalm indicates that Edom attacked Judah from the south, bringing havoc on David's thinly defended homeland. (That's the bad news.) After hearing the bleak report, David sat down to capture his emotions in a Spirit-inspired song—Psalm 60.

David clearly recognized the sovereign hand of God in what had transpired. (Notice the pronoun *thou* repeated eight times in the first four verses.) Not only does God move in the affairs of men; He possesses the very nations (vv. 7-8)! Therefore, David could glory in God's mighty strength, knowing that "through God we shall do valiantly" (v. 12)—a confidence you can echo today.

Find a pencil and complete these two sentences:
1. "As I look at my circumstances, the *bad* news is . . ."
2. "As I look at the resources of God, the *good* news is . . ."

Insight: A Short Course in Israelite Geography (Psalm 60)
Verses 6 and 7 describe six points of significant Israelite geography in the time of King David. With the help of a good Bible map, see how many of the six you can locate.

13 *An Earth Full of Glory / Psalms 67–72*

Heart of the Passage: Psalm 72

📖 **Overview:** Just how praiseworthy is the great God of Israel? David and Solomon will show you as you read these psalms today. God is worthy of praise for His judgments (67), His compassion and provision (68), His attentiveness to the cry of His children (69–70), His strength on behalf of the weak (71), and His sovereignty over the nations (72).

Psalm	Author	Key Idea	(Verse) Referred to in N.T.
67	Unknown	A Missionary Psalm	
68	David	Majesty on High	(18) Eph. 4:8
69	David	Plea from a Sea of Troubles	(9) John 2:17; (21) Matt. 27:34; (22-23) Rom. 11:9-10; (25) Acts 1:20
70	David	Help in a Hurry	
71	Unknown	A Psalm for the Elderly	
72	Solomon	An Earth Full of Glory	

Prayer is a shield to the soul, a sacrifice to God, and a scourge to Satan.

🔖 **Your Daily Walk:** As you read Psalm 72, watch for the "Job Description of a Righteous Ruler." That will give you specific points to pray about as you uphold your national, local, and spiritual leaders in prayer. For example, a righteous ruler is to be concerned with:

. . . bringing peace to the people (vv. 3, 7).
. . . assisting the poor, needy, and oppressed (vv. 4, 12-14).
. . . generating a godly fear for the laws of the land (v. 5).
. . . refreshing the people through righteous reform (vv. 6-7).

Compare this psalm with Isaiah 11:1-5, and you will soon see who is prophetically pictured in this psalm: none other than Jesus Christ, the Messiah of Israel! But buried in the heart of the psalm is this statement: "Prayer also shall be made for him continually; and daily shall he be praised" (v. 15). Solomon, the author of Psalm 72, knew that God's representative in any generation needs and deserves the prayers and praises of his subjects.

Stop right now and thank God for those who serve in positions of authority over you. Pray that God will help them in their difficult roles as servants of the people. You might even want to write a short note to one or more of your elected officials, sharing what you have learned from Psalm 72.

📝 **Insight:** Modern Songs from an Ancient Psalm
At least two great hymns of the faith were spawned from the reading of Psalm 72: James Montgomery's "Hail to the Lord's Anointed," and Isaac Watts's well-known "Jesus Shall Reign."

God Our Rock

14

← Step Back

One of the beautifully illustrative pictures of God the Bible paints for us is that He is our Rock. In Psalm 62 David repeatedly describes God with that word-picture: "He only is my rock and my salvation; he is my defense; I shall not be moved. In God is my salvation and my glory: the rock of my strength, and my refuge, is in God" (vv. 6-7).

Scripture Reading: 2 Samuel 22; 1 Corinthians 10:4

It's a comforting thought: God is our immovable defense, our protective refuge, our absolute strength.

Beginning in Genesis 49:24, it's a picture of our God that can be gleaned throughout the Scriptures. Moses declares, "He is the Rock, his work is perfect: for all his ways are judgment: a God of truth and without iniquity, just and right is he" (Deuteronomy 32:4). Hannah—the mother of Samuel—alludes to God her Rock in 1 Samuel 2:2. David praises his Rock, his Fortress, his Deliverer in 2 Samuel 22. And God is referred to as a Rock about 20 times in the Psalms. In every case, God the Rock is strong to save. He is a place of safety and security.

In the New Testament, Christ becomes our Rock. He is a stumbling block, a "rock of offense" to the nation Israel (Romans 9:33). And in 1 Corinthians 10:4, Paul identifies the Rock of the exodus as Christ Himself.

God is our Rock. That means you can trust Him completely for His strength and protection.

↑ Look Up

When you're faced with a problem that seems to defy a solution, is your initial reaction to run to the Rock . . . or simply to run? If you can't do anything more when all your efforts have been tried and all other sources of help have come up short, then let God be your Refuge, your Strength, your Rock.

We may tremble on the Rock of Ages, but the Rock will never tremble under us.

That's not a sign of weakness on your part, but of strength. That was David's experience, as he relates it in Psalm 62. Nothing any other person could do to him would shake David's resolve in hiding in the stone fortress of God's loving protection. God was his sure strength. So David invites us to join him there.

Acknowledge God's strength in your life in prayer right now. And if you need to, run to the Rock yourself.

→ Move Ahead

Carve out some time today to trace the concept of God as our Rock through the Scriptures using a concordance. Then find a small stone to carry in your pocket or purse today to remind you of the protection and safety God promises to His obedient children.

15 *Thanks for the Memories / Psalms 73–77*

*Heart
of the
Passage:
Psalm 75*

Overview: Those who ignore God will find their path slippery and their prosperity short-lived (73, 75). By contrast, those who order their lives according to God's Word will discover hope in the midst of havoc (74) and resources to face every situation in life victoriously (76–77).

Psalm	Author	Key Idea	(Verse) Referred to in N.T.
73	Asaph	The Slippery Way of the Wicked	(28) James 4:8
74	Asaph	Hope in the Midst of Havoc	(17) Acts 17:26
75	Asaph	Thanks in the Midst of Memories	(8) Rev. 14:10
76	Asaph	Overthrowing the Mighty	(7) Rev. 6:17
77	Asaph	Battling the Blues	

*Praising
and
adoring
God is
the
noblest
part of
the
saint's
work on
earth, as
it will be
his chief
employ
in
heaven.*

Your Daily Walk: A famous comedian employs as his theme song, "Thanks for the Memories." It is difficult to hear the strains of that tune without reliving some of the memories spanning more than a half century that have made Leslie Townes Hope (aka Bob Hope) virtually a household word.

In the same way that a melody or favorite song can spark memories, the composer of Psalm 75 realizes that reliving the wondrous works of God can spark thanksgiving. Retelling the great deeds of God is an indispensable part of worshiping God. Thinking about His faithfulness and power in the past can only lead to one inescapable conclusion: He is worthy of praise! "I will declare for ever; I will sing praises to the God of Jacob" (v. 9). There are many ways to recall memories of God's past dealings in your life. As a family, or just by yourself, try one or more of the following Praise Projects this evening:

1. Look at some slides, home movies, or photo albums that remind you of God's faithfulness over the past year.

2. Swap memories with one other person about the most faith-stretching experience you have had so far this year.

3. Thumb back through your checkbook, and let it remind you of doctor's appointments (times of illness), repair bills (unexpected emergencies), and other times when God faithfully met your needs—physical, financial, and spiritual!

Insight: A Fitting Introduction to a New Group of Psalms
Psalm 73 introduces the third section in the book of Psalms, the "Leviticus Book." Leviticus is the book of worship. When Asaph needed help in sorting out life, he went to "the sanctuary of God," and there learned God's perspective.

What Might Have Been / Psalms 78–83 16

📖 **Overview:** The psalms of Asaph (50, 73–83) conclude with six testimonies to the greatness and faithfulness of the God of Israel. He has kept His promises in the past (78)—a comforting reminder in the face of an uncertain future (79–80). God is there (81) and He is not silent (82–83) when it comes to overthrowing idols and enemies.

Heart of the Passage: Psalm 81

Psalm	Author	Key Idea	(Verse) Referred to in N.T.
78	Asaph	Listen to the Past	(2) Matt. 13:35; (24) John 6:31
79	Asaph	Wait for God's Help	(2-3) Rev. 16:6
80	Asaph	Turn Back to God	
81	Asaph	What Might Have Been	
82	Asaph	The "Gods" on Trial	(5) 1 John 2:11; (6) John 10:34
83	Asaph	Doom for God's Enemies	

📝 **Your Daily Walk:** There is nothing quite so sad as recalling what might have been. Unfulfilled potential has a way of drawing you back to the scene of the failure and whispering in your ear, "If only you had . . ."

There were many "should haves" in Israel's long history. They should have waited patiently at the foot of Mount Sinai for Moses to return with the law of God . . . but they didn't. They should have believed the faith-inspired reports of Joshua and Caleb after spying out the Promised Land . . . but they didn't. They should have utterly destroyed the Canaanites and other pagan peoples in the land . . . but they didn't. And the Israelites' repeated failure to obey God caused them to forfeit many blessings which God wanted to give them . . . but couldn't.

Reread Psalm 81:13-16. Circle the words "should have" every time you find them. Then ask yourself this question: "Next year, when I look back on this year, what will I say I should have been doing that I am not currently doing? What can I do now to ensure that God's blessings are not just things that should have been or could have been in my life, but in fact have been."

The keenest pain comes from remembering what you should do—a day too late to do it.

📷 **Insight:** A Song to Be Sung When the Moon Is New

Psalm 81 was most likely sung at the annual Feast of Tabernacles (v. 3; compare Leviticus 23:24), a festive occasion commemorating God's faithfulness during the wilderness wandering. Every seventh year it culminated with the reading of the law of God (Deuteronomy 31:10-13), in order that the families might "hear, and . . . learn, and fear the LORD . . . and observe to do all the words of this law."

195

17 *Revive Us Again / Psalms 84–89*

Heart of the Passage: Psalm 85

Overview: Each psalm you read today contains a heartfelt petition to God: satisfy us again (84); revive us again (85); hear us again (86); gather us again (87); encourage us again (88); make us to sing again (89). And each psalm concludes with a benediction of confidence that God will do precisely that in response to the prayers of His people.

Psalm	Author	Key Idea	(Verse) Referred to in N.T.
84	Korah	Satisfy Us Again	
85	Korah	Revive Us Again	
86	David	Hear Us Again	(9) Rev. 15:4
87	Korah	Gather Us Again	
88	Heman	Encourage Us Again	(8) Luke 23:49
89	Ethan	Make Us to Sing Again	(9) Matt. 8:26; (20) Acts 13:22

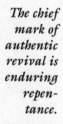

Your Daily Walk: One of the hardest things in the world to revive is a revival.

The chief mark of authentic revival is enduring repentance.

On Mount Carmel Elijah demonstrated to the entire nation that the Lord is God (1 Kings 18); but within a handful of years the people had returned to their worship of Baal. Jonah's preaching turned Nineveh upside down (Jonah 3:1-5). Only 150 years later, however, the city had returned to its pagan ways and was swept away like a flood by the Babylonians (Nahum 1:7-8).

Psalm 85 depicts a nation to which revival had come in the past. Verses 1-3 contain six statements of what God had done, but the revival was short-lived. Old patterns and practices had returned. Lukewarmness had replaced spiritual vitality. What the nation needed now was a *revived revival*. So the psalmist cries out on behalf of his countrymen, "Revive us again!" (v. 6).

Spiritual awakenings and national revivals are well documented in history . . . but what about today? Revival in your country can only come when first there is revival in its citizens . . . and that means it must begin with you and your family.

Tonight before you retire, kneel in a time of prayer for revival and spiritual awakening. Ask God to let it begin with you . . . and your family . . . and your church . . . and your business . . . and your neighborhood . . . and your nation.

Insight: Key to Revival—Tune In, Don't Turn Back
Revival can come when the prayer of your heart is this: "I will hear what God the LORD will speak; for he will speak peace unto his people, and to his saints: but let them not turn again to folly" (85:8).

196

A Reason for Singing / Psalms 90–97

18

Overview: Though the authors of most of the psalms you read today are unknown, the Object of their worship is well known: the God of eternity (90), the God of protection (91), the God of greatness (92), the God of majesty (93), the God of vengeance (94), the God of salvation (95), the God of glory (96), and the God of holiness (97).

Heart of the Passage: Psalm 95

Psalm	Author	Key Idea	(Verse) Referred to in N.T.
90	Moses	The Long and Short of Life	(4) 2 Pet. 3:8
91	Unknown	Under the Shadow of the Almighty	(11-12) Matt. 4:6
92	Unknown	How Great Thou Art	(5) Rom. 11:33; (15) Rom. 9:14
93	Unknown	The Lord Is King	
94	Unknown	Lord, How Long?	(11) 1 Cor. 3:20; (14) Rom. 11:1-2
95	David*	A Reason for Singing	(7-11) Heb. 3:7-11; 4:3, 5, 7
96	Unknown	A Psalm for All the Earth	(13) Acts 17:31
97	Unknown	Coronation of the King	(3) Rev. 11:5; (7) Heb. 1:6

*See Hebrews 4:7

Your Daily Walk: Would you describe your singing ability as . . . (a) fit for Carnegie Hall, (b) fit for the shower, or (c) something that gives other people fits?

Notice the two invitations in Psalm 95: "O come, let us sing" (v. 1), and "O come, let us worship and bow down" (v. 6). There is good reason for both, regardless of the quality of your voice. Why should you want to sing the praises of God? Because He is a great God and great King (v. 3); He is strong (v. 4); He is creative (v. 5). In a word, He is omnipotent!

The psalm has its own built-in application. What should be your response today in the light of that knowledge? "Today if ye will hear his voice [do you?], harden not your heart" (vv. 7-8). While God is omnipotent, He is not impassive. You can grieve Him (v. 10) by ignoring His commands; or you can honor Him by coming before His presence with singing!

Find a hymnbook and spend a few minutes paging through the many familiar songs of the faith, or look in the topical index under adoration or worship. Select one hymn to sing or read as a prayerful act of worship to your great God and King. Then lift up your voice, for He is worthy of your adoration!

After silence, that which comes closest to expressing the inexpressible is music.

Insight: A Psalm for All Ages

From ancient times the Christian church has widely used Psalm 95 (known as the *Venite,* from the Latin for "O come") as a call and guide to worship. Your church may want to do the same!

19 Joy in the Court of the King
Psalms 98–103

Heart of the Passage: Psalm 100

📖 **Overview:** In Psalm 103, the psalmist urges you to count your blessings. And Psalms 98–102 provide plenty of ideas to help you do just that by focusing on the many things for which you should be thankful: your salvation (98), answered prayer (99), God's mercy and truth (100), God's justice and holiness (101), God's care when you are downcast (102).

Psalm	Author	Key Idea	(Verse) Referred to in N.T.
98	Unknown	Celebration of the King	(3) Luke 1:54; (9) Acts 17:31
99	Unknown	Exaltation of the King	
100	Unknown	Joy in the Court of the King	
101	David	Living in Integrity	(4) Matt. 7:23
102	Unknown	Living with Adversity	(25-27) Heb. 1:10-12
103	David	How to Bless the Lord	(8) James 5:11; (17) Luke 1:50

Praise is simply letting off esteem.

🗒️ **Your Daily Walk:** When the president of the United States appears in public, he is often greeted by a rousing rendition of "Hail to the Chief." The title is appropriate, for the object of attention is none other than the commander-in-chief of the United States. But what do you play when the Lord God, the Commander-in-Chief of the universe, appears? How do you honor Him? What fitting song of tribute can you render Him?

You might want to start with Psalm 100! The opening line could well be translated, "Hail to the Chief," for that is the awesome stature of the Lord God: "For the LORD is good; his mercy is everlasting; and his truth endureth to all generations" (v. 5).

Isaac Watts captured the essence of verse 5 in this stanza of his hymn, "Before Jehovah's Awful Throne." Read the stanza twice, copy it onto a card or slip of paper, and make it your constant meditation throughout the day as you "serve the Lord with gladness":

> *Wide as the world is Thy command,*
> *Vast as eternity Thy love;*
> *Firm as a rock Thy truth shall stand,*
> *When rolling years shall cease to move.*

✍️ **Insight:** A Breath of Relief from Problems and Cares
Psalms 95–100 form a collection of "psalms of worship." In contrast to the lament and petition that characterize so much of the Psalter, these six psalms contain only worship and adoration as the psalmist fixes his gaze on God.

The God Who Keeps His Word
Psalms 104–106

20

📖 **Overview:** Today you see three snapshots of the great God you serve. He is big enough to create and rule the universe (104); He is small enough to rule in the hearts of His people (105); and He is loving enough to discipline His rebellious children (106).

Heart of the Passage: Psalm 105

Psalm	Author	Key Idea	(Verse) Referred to in N.T.
104	Unknown	The God Who Rules Creation	(4) Heb. 1:7
105	Unknown	The God Who Rules History	(8-9) Luke 1:72-73
106	Unknown	The God Who Remembers Iniquity	(10, 45, 48) Luke 1:68, 71-72

✔️ **Your Daily Walk:** Opinions may vary, but chances are good that the highest compliment you can pay any cook or chef is the request, "May I have a second helping?" There is something about asking for more of what you found so pleasing to the palate that warms the heart of any aspiring Betty (or Bobby) Crocker. If you've never done so, try it on your cook tonight!

Psalm 105 shows that what is true in the kitchen is also true in heaven. God loves to show His strength on behalf of His people. He wants you to sing about it, and to "make known his deeds among the people" (vv. 1-2). Even more, He wants you to show gratitude for past mercies by coming back for more (vv. 3-4)!

The psalmist illustrates his point by rehearsing the lives of Abraham and Moses—two men whose lives were dedicated to following hard after God. Over and over in their lives, God "remembered his holy promise" (v. 42) by bringing protection and provision, guidance and gladness to His faithful servants.

Pretend for a moment that the psalmist has reserved the last five verses of Psalm 105 to talk about your life. What could he add to what he has already said about the faithfulness of your promise-keeping God? Pen your own personalized "P.S." to the psalm. And if you have trouble thinking of something to write, ask God to make today a special chapter in your life as you walk with Him.

The thankfulness of the receiver ought to answer to the benefit of the bestower as the echo answers to the voice.

🗒️ **Insight:** Reliving the Plagues in Egypt
In Psalm 105:28-36 the psalmist mentions eight of the ten plagues God used to release the Israelites from Egyptian bondage. Can you recall the two he omitted? (If you need help, consult Exodus 7–12.)

1. _____
2. _____

21 *A Daily Walk Through Creation*

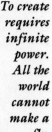

Step Back

Scripture Reading: Selected Psalms; Genesis 1:1–2:3

In Old Testament times, every morning a sacrifice of praise was offered to God, accompanied by the singing of a psalm from the Psalter—actually a collection of Hebrew hymns. According to the Jewish Talmud, specific psalms—selected to remind the worshiper of the seven days of God's creation—were sung on corresponding days of the week.

To enhance your worship of God this week (or expand your time with God today), why not follow this "daily walk" from the Psalms? For each day of creation, read the psalm listed below along with the corresponding passage in the creation account in Genesis. Which part of God's creation was the focus of each day?

Day 1: Read Psalm 24 and Genesis 1:1-5.
Day 2: Read Psalm 146 and Genesis 1:6-8.
Day 3: Read Psalm 95 and Genesis 1:9-13.
Day 4: Read Psalm 148 and Genesis 1:14-19.
Day 5: Read Psalm 8 and Genesis 1:20-23.
Day 6: Read Psalm 139 and Genesis 1:24-31.
Day 7: Read Psalm 92 and Genesis 2:1-3.

Look Up

To create requires infinite power. All the world cannot make a fly.

C. S. Lewis once wrote, "Because God created the Natural—invented it out of His love and artistry—it demands our reverence." Unfortunately, it's easy for us to take God's creation for granted. After all, we live in it every day!

Let this ancient exercise refresh your view of God's handiwork all around you. Take the opportunity to thank God for each facet of His creation day-by-day. And ask for His blessing and protection on them all. Remember—you play a role in that protection of creation through your actions as a steward of His resources.

Move Ahead

Make a date with God in the next few days to get away to a nearby national, state, or community park where you can sit with your Bible and spend a few moments meditating on His creation through His Word.

Use the readings above that relate to each day of creation as a springboard to worship Him for His magnificent workmanship in the world. Then take the opportunity to share with someone the importance of your conviction that the universe is a product of your God's creative hand.

The Lord Is Priest and King
Psalms 107–110

22

Overview: There is plenty to sing about in today's selection of psalms. First comes the song of the redeemed (107); then a song dedicated to the God of might and glory (108); and finally, a song of lament over the slanderous attacks of an enemy (109). But how can you sing when the godless are seemingly getting away with murder? Remember with the psalmist David that the Lord is King (110)!

Heart of the Passage: Psalm 110

Psalm	Author	Key Idea	(Verse) Referred to in N.T.
107	Unknown	A Song of the Redeemed	(9) Luke 1:53; (29) Matt. 8:26
108	David	A Song of Praise and Prayer	
109	David	A Song of the Slandered	(8) Acts 1:20; (25) Mark 15:29
110	David	The Lord Is Priest and King	(1) Matt. 22:44; Acts 2:34-35; (4) Heb. 5:6; 7:17, 21

Your Daily Walk: The opening verse of Psalm 110 is one of the most often-quoted verses in the New Testament. Using a good reference Bible or Bible concordance, see how many places you can find Psalm 110:1 quoted or alluded to in the New Testament (there are nearly a dozen!).

After reading the psalm, you'll understand why New Testament authors put such emphasis on this one verse. In it David, the king of Israel, spoke of yet another King as his "Lord." David, ruler of a nation, humbly acknowledged the lordship of the Ruler of all nations: "The LORD [God] said unto my Lord [Christ], Sit thou at my right hand, [a privilege which even angels do not enjoy, Hebrews 1:13] until I make thine enemies thy footstool." A final surrender is yet to take place in which "every knee [shall] bow . . . and . . . every tongue . . . confess that Jesus Christ is Lord" (Philippians 2:10-11).

David, for all his kingly might, learned there was Another in his life deserving of the title "Lord." To that sovereign Priest and King, David responded without hesitation. Is that true in your life as well? Have you enthroned Jesus Christ as King in your heart?

Carry a spare key in your pocket or purse today to remind you that the King of the universe wants to be the undisputed King of your castle. But only you can let Him in!

How divinely supreme is our Lord above all others!

Insight: In Case You Got Stymied in Your Search . . .
Quotations and allusions to Psalm 110:1 that you might want to mark in your Bible include Matthew 22:44; Mark 12:36; Luke 20:42; Acts 2:34-35; 1 Corinthians 15:25; Hebrews 1:13; 10:12-13.

23 *The Praiseworthy Name of God* *Psalms 111–118*

Overview: Praise permeates nearly every line of the psalms you read today! God is praiseworthy for His care (111), His

Heart of the Passage: Psalm 113

commandments (112), His name (113), His power (114), His uniqueness (115), His deliverance (116), His truth (117), and His mercy (118). What other response could there be than to "Praise the Lord!"

Psalm	Author	Key Idea	(Verse) Referred to in N.T.
111	Unknown	The Praiseworthy Works of God	(9) Luke 1:49, 68
112	Unknown	The Praiseworthy Man of God	(9) 2 Cor. 9:9; (10) Matt. 8:12
113	Unknown	The Praiseworthy Name of God	
114	Unknown	The Praiseworthy Power of God	
115	Unknown	The Only Praiseworthy God	(13) Rev. 11:18; 19:5
116	Unknown	Praise for God's Deliverance	(10) 2 Cor. 4:13; (11) Rom. 3:4
117	Unknown	Praise for God's Truth	(1) Rom. 15:11
118	Unknown	Praise for God's Mercy	(6) Heb. 13:6; (18) 2 Cor. 6:9; (22-23) Matt. 21:42; (26) Matt. 21:9

Your Daily Walk: Have you ever heard it said of an athlete, "He's so great at his event that no one can even touch him?"

Bless the Lord today; He blesses you every day.

What did the speaker mean by that? Why is greatness sometimes synonymous with remoteness?

Psalm 113 is a majestic proclamation of God's greatness: "The LORD is high above all nations, and his glory above the heavens. Who is like unto the LORD our God, who dwelleth on high" (vv. 4-5). Sounds pretty remote and untouchable, doesn't it?

But don't stop reading, for that exalted, glorious God "humbleth himself to behold the things that are . . . in the earth!" (v. 6). He is vitally concerned about such earthbound problems as poverty (v. 7), politics (v. 8), and families yearning for a child (v. 9). Little wonder the psalmist bursts forth in praise at both ends of the psalm!

God is almighty, but He is not aloof. When Hannah (1 Samuel 2), Mary (Luke 1:46-55), and Zechariah (Luke 1:67-79) got hold of that truth, they had no trouble praising God. Is there an unsaved friend with whom you could share the truth of Psalm 113 and introduce to the God who lives in human hearts?

Insight: A Package of Passover Psalms
Psalms 113–118 are sung yearly by devout Jews at the celebration of Passover, the first two (113–114) before and the last four (115–118) after the Passover meal. Thus it is possible that Psalm 113 was one of the last songs our Lord sang before His crucifixion (Mark 14:26).

God's Multifaceted Word / Psalm 119 24

 Overview: Psalm 119 is the longest psalm and the longest chapter of the longest book in the Bible. As such, it provides a natural spotlight for its subject which it describes: the multifaceted Word of God. Just as the psalm seems to go on endlessly as you read its 176 verses, so let your praise and love for God's Word be endless as you make it the focus of your devotional time today and every day.

Heart of the Passage: Psalm 119:1-16, 105-112

Psalm	Author	Key Idea	(Verse) Referred to in N.T.
119	Unknown	God's Multifaceted Word	(3) 1 John 3:9; 5:18; (62) Acts 16:25; (89) 1 Pet. 1:25; (137) Rev. 16:5, 7

Insight: 1 + 19 = 119

In Psalm 1, an anonymous psalmist declares that the blessed man is the one who meditates constantly on the law of the Lord. In Psalm 19, David describes the Word of the Lord in all its many facets. Today you will read Psalm 119 which expands upon Psalms 1 and 19 to produce a majestic testimonial to the power and perfection of God's Word.

The Bible is as broad as life, having indeed the same Author.

Your Daily Walk: A synonym is a word that means the same (or nearly the same) as another word, but is spelled differently. How many synonyms can you find for the following familiar Bible terms?

Salvation: _____

Psalm: _____

Word of God: _____

It is fitting that the longest psalm (and the longest chapter in the Bible) should have as its theme the Word of God. But how does a songwriter compose a psalm befitting the powerful, praiseworthy Word of the Lord? How do you do it justice? How do you declare its life-changing qualities without sounding trite or monotonous?

Answer: You write Psalm 119, an alphabetic psalm in which each of the 22 letters of the Hebrew alphabet is used eight times (eight being the number of "superabundance") to begin a two-line couplet describing some facet of the Word of God. It is law (to be obeyed), testimony (to be shared), precept (to be practiced), promise (to be claimed), way (to be followed). In all, 11 synonyms are employed in the psalm. As you find each synonym, use it to complete this sentence: "Since God's Word is _____, today I will respond by _____ ."

25 Peace Without and Within
Psalms 120–127

Heart of the Passage: Psalm 122

Overview: Psalms 120–134 deal with topics dear to the heart of travelers far from home: peace (120, 122); protection (121, 125, 127); and provision (123–124, 126). As you read these "hymns of the highway," imagine yourself on a long journey, with your destination now in view.

Psalm	Author	Key Idea	(Verse) Referred to in N.T.
120	Unknown	Searching for Peace	(3-4) James 3:6
121	Unknown	The Lord Our Keeper	
122	David	Peace Without and Within	
123	Unknown	Eyes on the Lord	
124	David	The Lord Our Helper	
125	Unknown	The Lord Our Protector	(5) Gal. 6:16
126	Unknown	The Lord Our Restorer	
127	Solomon	The Lord Our Security	

We sleep in peace in the arms of God when we yield ourselves up to His providence.

Your Daily Walk: World peace has always been an elusive commodity. Of the last 3,500 years of human history, fewer than 300 could be called "warless." More than 8,000 treaties have been made . . . and broken . . . during that time. Little wonder that one cynic has defined peace as "that brief glorious moment in history when everybody stands around reloading."

As David depicts the end of a long march to the Holy City of Jerusalem (Psalm 122), he contemplates the irony of the name: *Jerusalem, City of Peace,* though it has known so little peace. And so the psalmist exhorts, "Pray for the peace of Jerusalem" (vv. 6-8).

Just as the city of Jerusalem in David's day housed the very presence of the Lord, so your body today is the "temple [dwelling place] of the Holy Ghost" (1 Corinthians 6:19). You have the very source of peace residing in your life! Drawing upon that resource, how can you be a peacemaker in your world today? How can you work toward resolving conflicts (rather than starting new ones) in your home, office, school, and church? You might begin by praying, as David did, for "peace . . . for my brethren and companions' sakes" (vv. 7-8).

Insight: Hymns for the Hike to Jerusalem
Psalms 120–134 are identified in the titles as "songs of degrees" or "songs of ascents," anthems sung by pilgrims on their yearly trips to Jerusalem during the feast days. The psalms describe the progress of the pilgrim as he travels from a distant land (120) to within sight of the Holy City (121) and finally arrives (122) amid great joy (123–134).

Deep Water, Dark Nights
Psalms 128–134

26

📖 **Overview:** Blessing for the righteous (128) and judgment for the wicked (129) are waiting at the journey's end. And though there may be dark nights along the way (130), the quiet soul will find hope in the Lord (131). In the sanctuary of God (132, 134) and among the people of God (133) there is strength to face each new day.

Heart of the Passage: Psalm 130

Psalm	Author	Key Idea	(Verse) Referred to in N.T.
128	Unknown	Blessing for the God-Fearer	
129	Unknown	Vindication for the Righteous	
130	Unknown	Deep Water, Dark Nights	(8) Titus 2:14
131	David	Hope for the Quiet Soul	
132	Unknown	Finding a Place for the Lord	(5) Acts 7:46; (17) Luke 1:69
133	David	Getting Along in God's Family	
134	Unknown	Blessing God in His House	(1) Rev. 19:5; (2) 1 Tim. 2:8

👣 **Your Daily Walk:** Which of the following have you experienced during your lifetime? (1) You nearly drowned. (2) You lost a loved one through terminal illness. (3) You spent an entire night without sleep.

If you can identify with one or more of the above situations, you'll have no trouble identifying with the writer of Psalm 130, for all three images are contained in his eight-verse lament.

(1) *The psalmist is drowning in a sea of despair* (v. 1). The riptide of affliction has left him floundering in waters that are over his head! (2) *The psalmist feels like a marked man, in line for judgment* (v. 3). Unless the Lord forgives his iniquity, he knows his case is "terminal." Yet, in spite of his distress, (3) *the psalmist waits patiently for the morning* (vv. 5-6). The night of dark circumstances seems endless, but the psalmist knows the Lord will rescue him as surely as dawn follows night.

Relief from depression is only a praise away.

In the midst of deep water and dark nights, there is reason to be hopeful—as long as the hope is in the Lord! The psalmist's cure for depression is simple. It's not a pill but a Person, One who is as faithful in the 20th century A.D. as He was in the 10th century B.C.

✏️ **Insight:** Ascending Through a Psalm of Ascents
Here in Psalm 130, one of the psalms of degrees (ascents), the reader is transported with the psalmist from the depths of depression (v. 1) to the heights of hope and confidence (v. 8).

205

27 Wholehearted Praise / Psalms 135–139

Heart of the Passage: Psalm 138

📖 **Overview:** Sometimes it's easy to praise the Lord simply by recalling the past (135–136); at other times memories of the past produce more pain than praise (137). But even times of trouble and tears can be cause for praise (138) as you think about the infinite knowledge and unceasing presence of your omnipotent God (139).

Psalm	Author	Key Idea	(Verse) Referred to in N.T.
135	Unknown	Anthology of Praise	
136	Unknown	Antiphony of Praise	
137	Unknown	Tears Shed in Exile	(8) Rev. 18:6
138	David	Wholehearted Praise	(8) Phil. 1:6
139	David	The Everywhere, Everything God	(14) Rev. 15:3

The water of saints' praise is drawn out of a deep spring, the heart.

🗹 **Your Daily Walk:** When someone pursues a course of action with reckless abandon, we say that person "put his whole heart into it." List the goals you pursue wholeheartedly (academic excellence, athletic prowess, business success, a hobby or a vocation). Then ask yourself: "Why do I do the things I do with a whole heart?"

Psalm 138 introduces the last eight psalms attributed to King David. In it you will read of David's passion to praise God "with [his] whole heart" (v. 1). And the reasons are easy to find: (1) God answered David's repeated prayer for strength and protection in time of trouble (v. 3). (2) God magnified His Word by keeping His promises to David (v. 2; see 2 Samuel 7:8-16). (3) Though great and glorious in His character, God nonetheless took special note of David (vv. 5-6). Put it all together and you have David's motivation to praise God, even before the kings of the earth (v. 4)

Do you share David's enthusiasm to praise God today? Then why not organize a "Praise Potluck" with a few Christian friends? Have each person bring a favorite dish . . . and an account of something praiseworthy that God has done over the past month. As you eat and fellowship, praise God together with testimony and song. (Caution: This can be habit-forming! Proceed at your own risk.)

📖 **Insight:** The Lord Will, Because the Lord Is, and He Won't! Notice how the familiar truth of verse 8 ("thy mercy, O Lord, endureth for ever") is sandwiched between a statement of confidence ("The Lord will . . .") and a statement of commitment ("forsake not . . ."). All three are essential elements of praise.

A Life of Praise

28

⬅ Step Back

The book of Psalms—indeed the whole Bible—exhorts God's children to praise Him. Praise is simply joyfully expressing your adoration and appreciation for your worthy God. And the Psalms offer great guidance in praise.

Scripture Reading: Selected Psalms; 1 John 1:9

Who is to be praised? Read Psalm 145:1; 147:1.

Why is He to be praised? The reasons are innumerable, but start with Psalms 21:13; 89:5; 138:2; 145:4.

Who is to praise Him? Read Psalms 148 and 150:6.

When are we to praise Him? Read Psalms 35:28; 71:6; 72:15; 146:2.

How should we praise God? Here are some ideas to get you started:

Let your praise be:
Personal—your own deep feelings
Reverent—worshipful
Appreciative—full of thanks to God
Illuminating—teaching you about yourself and God
Sincere—honest and meaningful
Enthusiastic—refreshingly energetic

Demonstrate it in:
Poetry
Reciting a psalm
Artwork
Instrumental music
(see Psalm 150)
Singing
Expression in writing

⬆ Look Up

Dull. Dry. Boring. Weak. Lifeless.

Would you admit that those adjectives describe your Christian life?

Praise is a soul in flower.

The problem may stem from clogged communication lines between you and your loving God. Of course, God didn't clog them. So if you've let unconfessed sin pile up, consult 1 John 1:9 and Psalm 51:10 and talk about it to God. He delights to hear the sincere prayers of believers who desire His cleansing touch.

➡ Move Ahead

A life of praise can bring delight both to God and to yourself. Spend some time praising your Lord right now. To help put your feelings into words, pick one of these selected psalms: Psalms 8, 19, 29, 33, 36, 103–105, 111, 113, 117, 135–136, 139, 145–150.

But don't just tell God how you feel about Him. Tell someone you know who needs to hear the Good News about your praiseworthy Savior.

As Revelation 4:11 captures it, "Thou art worthy, O Lord, to receive glory and honour and power: for thou has created all things, and for thy pleasure they are and were created."

29 Finding Refuge on the Run
Psalms 140–145

Heart of the Passage: Psalm 142

Overview: Your enemies will either drive you *from* God or drive you *to* God. In David's hour of need he found a sure Refuge (140, 142), a trustworthy Friend (141), a listening Ear (143), a strong Arm (144), a merciful King (145)—and you can, too!

Psalm	Author	Key Idea	(Verse) Referred to in N.T.
140	David	Dwelling in God's Presence	(3) Rom. 3:13
141	David	An Evening Prayer for Purity	(2) Rev. 5:8; 8:3
142	David	Finding Refuge on the Run	
143	David	When All Else Fails	(2) Rom. 3:20; Gal. 2:16
144	David	From Darkness to Dawn	
145	David	An Alphabet of Praise	(3) Rom. 11:33; (17) Rev. 15:3

One live coal may set a whole stack on fire.

Your Daily Walk: For David, life had caved in . . . literally! Pursued by Saul's search-and-destroy party, David fled to the cave of Adullam. There he was joined by 400 rag-tag troops, every one of them "in distress . . . in debt, and . . . discontented" (1 Samuel 22:2). There David's emotions hit bottom. And there he penned Psalm 142—a prayer for those times when life caves in. A prayer, perhaps, that you need to pray today.

In the cave of Adullam, David felt hemmed in, emotionally drained, and without a friend in the world (vv. 3-4, 6). But rather than drifting *from* God, David's problems drove him *toward* God. Notice the object of his plea: "I cried unto the LORD . . . unto the LORD did I make my supplication. I poured out my complaint before him. . . . I cried unto thee, O LORD" (vv. 1-2, 5). Brought low by his pursuers, David found he had nowhere to look but up.

Where do you feel imprisoned today? By the emotional drain of family life? Pressure at work? Uncertain finances? A lingering illness? You, like David, have a choice. You can allow problems to drive a wedge between you and God. Or you can run to the only sure Refuge in time of trouble. David fled to a cave, but found a Fortress. Join your voice with his by making Psalm 142:7 your prayer: "Bring my soul out of prison, that I may praise thy name: the righteous shall compass me about; for thou shalt deal bountifully with me."

Insight: Songs for the Chief
The psalm title "To the chief musician" appears in 55 psalms as well as in the book of Habakkuk (3:19). Apparently the chief musician (choirmaster) of the temple had his own collection of psalms.

Praise for the Praiseworthy Lord
Psalms 146–150

30

Overview: Like the dramatic crescendo of a symphony, the book of Psalms builds to a climax of praise. Praise God from one generation to the next (146); praise God for His tender care (147); praise God for His creation (148); praise God for His justice (149); praise God for His greatness (150). Praise the praiseworthy Lord!

Heart of the Passage: Psalm 146

Psalm	Author	Key Idea	(Verse) Referred to in N.T.
146	Unknown	Praise for the Praiseworthy Lord	(6) Acts 4:24; 14:15; Rev. 14:7
147	Unknown	Praise for the God on High	(3) Luke 4:18; (9) Luke 12:24
148	Unknown	A Universal Symphony of Praise	
149	Unknown	Praise from God's People	
150	Unknown	A Fitting Benediction of Praise	

Your Daily Walk: There are at least two good reasons to praise the Lord, according to Psalm 146: (1) God wants you to do it often today ("While I live will I praise the Lord," v. 2); and (2) you will be doing it throughout eternity ("I will sing praises unto my God while I have any being," v. 2). With praise, as with any skill, practice makes perfect!

Act out a psalm in your Christian walk today!

Psalm 146 begins with a ringing call to praise: "Praise ye the Lord." And the logical question is: "Why? What has He done to warrant my praise?" Notice the psalmist's ready reply:

God is praiseworthy for what He has done in the past. He made "heaven, and earth, the sea, and all that therein is" (v. 6).

God is praiseworthy for what He is doing in the present. The psalmist uses 10 present-tense verbs in verses 6-9 to describe God's far-reaching activities today (can you find all 10?).

God is praiseworthy for what He will do in the future. "The Lord shall reign for ever . . . unto all generations" (v. 10).

Close your study of the book of Psalms by composing your own song of praise, patterned after Psalm 146. Begin with the phrase, "Praise the Lord!" Then praise Him for what He is doing in your life (past, present, and future). Conclude the same way the book of Psalms concludes: with a climactic shout to all within hearing distance, "Praise ye the Lord!"

Insight: Psalm 150, a Primer for Praise

Praise the Lord (where? v. 1) _____

(why? v. 2) _____

(how? vv. 3-5) _____

(who? v. 6) _____

Proverbs

Godly living in an ungodly world is no simple task. But the book of Proverbs—the Bible's primer of practical wisdom—teaches the skillful application of truth to everyday life. Contained in this unique collection of poetry, parables, questions, stories, and wise maxims are instructions regarding how to relate to parents and children, God and government, sin and self. In strikingly memorable form, Solomon—the principal author—gives his readers a "divine handle" on living to please God.

Focus	Prologue		Proverbs			Precepts	
Divisions	Purpose and Theme	A Father's Counsel	Words of Solomon (Part One)	Words of Wise Men	Words of Solomon (Part Two)	Words of Agur	Words About a Virtuous Wife
	1	2 9	10 21	22 24	25 29	30	31
Topics	Person of Wisdom		Principles of Wisdom			Practice of Wisdom	
	Solomon					Agur & Lemuel	
Place	Judah					Unknown	
Time	ca. 950-700 B.C.						

Fear of the Lord / Proverbs 1–4

1

Overview: Few books of the Bible open with a clear statement of the purpose for which they were written. But the author of Proverbs clearly states the book's purpose: "To know wisdom and instruction" (1:2-5). The Hebrew word for "wisdom" means more than human intelligence; it refers to skill or expertise. Just as the artisans and craftsmen who fashioned the tabernacle were described as "wise" (Exodus 31:1-11), so God wants His people to be "wise" (skillful) in the task of making moral and ethical choices. The first nine chapters of Proverbs take the form of a fatherly address to a young son—a divine primer for learning "the fear of the Lord."

Heart of the Passage: Proverbs 1:1–2:6

Chapter 1	Chapter 2	Chapter 3	Chapter 4
Beginning of Wisdom	Value of Wisdom	Rewards of Wisdom	Place of Discipline
Fatherly Concern: "Hear, ye children" (4:1).			

Your Daily Walk: Can you match each of these common fears (phobias) with its correct definition? (No fair peeking in the dictionary!)

_____ 1. acrophobia   a. fear of closed places
_____ 2. xenophobia   b. fear of heights
_____ 3. hydrophobia   c. fear of strangers
_____ 4. claustrophobia   d. fear of water

I fear God, yet am not afraid of Him.

While these phobias can be detrimental, there are other fears that can have a beneficial influence on your behavior (for example, fear of getting burned, fear of stumbling in the dark). Such fears do not terrorize or immobilize, but rather lead to constructive action (such as using a potholder or turning on a light).

The "fear of the LORD" is like that. Rather than sending you fleeing from God's presence in terror, it causes deep, abiding reverence and awe at the thought of God's power and glory. It stimulates you to pay attention when He speaks—and obey when He commands. Look up 2:1-5; 14:26-27; 23:17-18 to discover how and why you can live each day in the "fear of the LORD."

Insight: The Fool's Self-destruction
When people rebel against God, they end up destroying themselves. They fall by their own wickedness (11:5) and are snared by their own transgressions (29:6). Ponder the timelessness of God's wisdom as you consider the results of abortion, drug and alcohol abuse, broken homes, and homosexuality in our day.

2 *Pitfalls of Life / Proverbs 5–9*

Heart of the Passage: Proverbs 7–8

Overview: Beginning with chapter 5, Solomon turns from a general appeal to a more specific application of wisdom in the everyday situations of life. Pitfalls and snares abound, ready to entangle and destroy the unwary: immorality, indebtedness, laziness, falsehood, pride. Indulging in these sins is a sure invitation to poverty and disaster. Temptation, though alluring, can lead to deadly consequences. Don't listen to its call! Rather, respond to the call of wisdom, which among its many benefits is the "favour of the LORD" (8:35).

Chapters 5–6	Chapter 7	Chapter 8	Chapter 9
The Vices of the World		The Virtues of Wisdom	
Immorality	Adultery	Enduring	Inviting
Fatherly Admonition: "Attend unto my wisdom" (5:1).			

Temptation is not a sin, but playing with temptation invites sin.

Your Daily Walk: "I never have a problem with temptation," one man was heard to remark. "When it comes, I just give in to it!"

That's one way to deal with temptation—and you'll find it illustrated in the response of the young man in chapter 7. Confronted by the harlot's alluring charms, "He goeth after her straightway . . . as a fool" (7:22). Giving in to her temptation was easy . . . even momentarily pleasant. But the pain it produced was life shattering.

Are you exercising godly wisdom in your moral life? Or are you toying with immoral or adulterous thoughts—which can only lead to equally immoral and adulterous actions? Divorce courts are jammed today with well-intentioned couples who had insisted, "It could never happen to us." Solomon's advice to you: Wise up before it is too late. If you ignore God's commands, it *can* happen . . . and probably *will*.

Have a "Father and child" chat with your heavenly Father about your relationships with the opposite sex. Examine your thoughts and actions. Are confession and cleansing in order (1 John 1:9)?

Insight: How to Live Like a King

Solomon, author of more than 3,000 proverbs (about 900 of which are contained in the book of Proverbs; 1 Kings 4:32), was the richest, most influential king of his day. Yet he reports in chapter 8 that the key to happiness is not riches, or power, or other "kingly" possessions. Rather, it is wisdom—knowing God and obeying His Word. Think of it: The happiness of a king is within your reach!

Wise Words of Solomon / Proverbs 10–13 3

 Overview: One of the best ways to learn a wise action is to contrast it with a foolish one. Most of the proverbs you will read today are antithetical, using the conjunction *but* to contrast the path of folly with the path of faith. The curriculum is varied and intensely practical: how to use your mouth and your money; how to be a good neighbor; how to select your friends; how to conduct business; how to resolve conflicts. Think of today's reading as a training manual designed to teach you how to respond to life from God's perspective.

Heart of the Passage: Proverbs 10

Chapter 10	Chapter 11	Chapter 12	Chapter 13
Mouths and Money	Guidance and Generosity	Wickedness and Work	Laziness and Lying
How to Be Wise or Foolish			

Your Daily Walk: Try a change of pace today. Read today's portion with pen in hand, capturing the insights God gives into these practical areas:

1. What is the role of your tongue (10:19-21)? _____

2. How can your generosity add to your wealth (11:24-26)? _____

3. What can others tell about you by the way you respond to wise counsel (12:15)? _____

4. What are two kinds of "riches" (13:7-8), and which kind should you strive for? _____

5. Why does God set forth "laws" for you to keep (13:14)? _____

6. What happens if you do? What happens if you don't (13:13)? _____

7. Which proverb from today's section speaks most clearly to a need in your life? Write it out! _____
_____

A person can become wise by watching what happens when he isn't.

Insight: A Structural Summary of Proverbs

Chapters 1–9:   Fatherly Proverbs ("my son")
Chapters 10–15:   Antithetical Proverbs ("but")
Chapters 16–22:   Synthetic Proverbs ("and")
Chapters 23–31:   Extended Proverbs (more than one verse)

4 The Treasures of Wisdom

Scripture Reading: 1 Corinthians 1:30; Colossians 2:3; Proverbs 2

← Step Back

The key word in Proverbs, as you've no doubt discovered already, is *wisdom*. It's a word that seems to have little relevance in today's society, which puts so much emphasis on knowledge or even "savvy." To God, however, wisdom is a jewel He desires every child of His to possess.

Wisdom is defined as "the ability to live life skillfully." Living a godly life in an ungodly world, however, is no easy task. But Proverbs provides God's detailed instructions for His people to deal successfully with the practical affairs of everyday life, including how to relate to God, to your parents, to your children, to your neighbors, to your government.

Proverbs is one of the few books of the Bible that actually states its purpose (Proverbs 1:2-6). Through this book God desires to impart moral discernment and discretion and to help His children develop mental clarity and perception.

For New Testament believers, wisdom becomes an even richer gift. In 1 Corinthians 1:30, Paul refers to Christ as One whom God has "made unto us wisdom." In Christ, he adds, "are hid all the treasures of wisdom and knowledge" (Colossians 2:3).

↑ Look Up

If you realize that you aren't as wise today as you thought you were yesterday, you're wiser today.

Wisdom is not considered a profitable commodity in today's world. But to God, it is worth more than all the wealth of the world (Proverbs 3:13-14). Is that how you consider it? Are you seeking wisdom personally through your study of the Word and your fellowship with the Lord? Examine your heart in prayer before the Lord.

→ Move Ahead

God's wisdom is available to all. But it can be rejected if one chooses to do so (see Proverbs 1:24-25). The Bible calls those who reject God's wisdom scoffers and fools. Why? Because rejecting wisdom results in serious consequences (see 1:26-28, 31-32). When tragedy and trouble arise, the resources you need to survive and grow in it will not be available.

You've already read several chapters in God's book of wisdom. Are you taking the words you're reading seriously? Are you searching them diligently for the life-enhancing truths they hold for you?

God's wisdom is here for the taking. Read again through Proverbs chapter 2 and list the benefits of wisdom listed there. Then consider the alternative. It's really not even worth considering at all, is it?

214

Workable Wisdom / Proverbs 14–17 **5**

📖 **Overview:** Nowhere is wisdom more essential than in home and community relationships. A heart attitude controlled by the fear of the Lord is the key to proper responses toward others. Today's reading contains numerous proverbs designed to promote peace, prosperity, and justice in the interpersonal relationships of life. The structure of these proverbs is simple, but the range of topics is immense: temper and tongue, paths and pursuits, thoughts and motives. In each case, your commitment to godliness should be evident.

Heart of the Passage: Proverbs 16

Chapter 14	Chapter 15	Chapter 16	Chapter 17
Neighbors and Nations	Covetousness and Counsel	Law of the Lord	Friends and Foes
Wisdom That Works			

🐾 **Your Daily Walk:** Repetition has been called the mother of learning. It has also been called the mother of boredom! But when a statement is important enough for the author to repeat more than once, you can be sure it contains a message you can't afford to miss.

Reverent fear of God is the key to faithfulness in any situation.

One verse you'll find repeated in today's reading is this: "There is a way which seemeth right unto a man; but the end thereof are the ways of death." Can you find the two places where it is located? More importantly, can you find the application which the author wants you to discover?

Saving time or effort—and therefore shortening the path to success—is not a bad idea in any generation! But when the shortcut stems from an attitude of wanting to avoid advice (12:15) or hard work (15:19), the outcome can be disastrous. Check out the shortcuts you were planning to take today. Are they shortcuts to success, or shortcuts to disaster? The words of Proverbs 16:9, written on a 3 x 5 card and carried with you throughout the day, may be just what you need to keep yourself on "the way of righteousness" (16:31)!

📓 **Insight:** Accent on the LORD
Elohim (sometimes translated "God" in English versions, used only seven times in the book of Proverbs) was often applied to persons other than the true God. In contrast, *Jehovah* (often translated LORD in English, used eighty-seven times in Proverbs) is God's personal name, used of no one but God as He reveals Himself. How good it is to think of our LORD who cared enough to tell us about Himself, for He is the only true God.

215

6 *Wise Decisions in Life / Proverbs 18–21*

Heart of the Passage: Proverbs 19

📖 **Overview:** The varied statements of common sense in today's reading are descriptions of the perils facing the wise and the unwise, character sketches of the poor and mighty, and value judgments upon things which appear to be good and things which are good. Through it all, Solomon sees God at work in the hearts and affairs of people, helping them to avoid flattery and falsehood, and to display obedient behavior instead.

Chapter 18	Chapter 19	Chapter 20	Chapter 21
Words That Wound	Senseless Sons	Wicked Weights	Wicked Wealth
Wise Decisions in Life			

The yoke of the Lord Jesus will never fit on a stiff neck.

🐾 **Your Daily Walk:** What is it that keeps you from seeing yourself as you really are, others from seeing you as you wish you really were, and God from helping you become what you would really like to be?

As you ponder that riddle, take a look at the lesson contained in 18:12. (It's so important, you'll find it also in 16:18-19.)

Pride—in yourself, your possessions, your abilities—brings destruction. Humility—before God, before others, before yourself—brings honor. God delights in raising up the lowly (3:34), but He despises the proud (6:16-17; 16:5). A proud person fights himself (8:36), others (13:10), and God (16:5), and eventually his end is destruction. Just as pride caused Lucifer to want to be greater than God (Isaiah 14:12-14), resulting in condemnation (1 Timothy 3:6), so pride can ruin your life.

Look for opportunities today to exercise humility instead of pride. Nothing is as hard to do gracefully as getting down off your high horse—and nothing is as necessary! Look for one person whose needs and interests you can place above your own today. Go out of your way to express a word of sincere appreciation. Remember, all you have and are is given to you by God (1 Corinthians 4:7).

And if you had trouble with the riddle, remember that pride covers your own sins; pride obscures the view of others; and pride hinders service for God!

✏️ **Insight:** An Indian Proverb on Humility
One Indian word for *humility* literally means "dust," a fact which helps to explain the significance of this Indian proverb: "You can walk on the dust forever and it never answers back."

Wise Words for the King / Proverbs 22–24 7

Overview: The final 11 chapters of Proverbs contain sound counsel for those in positions of authority. The key to the section is hanging at the front door (21:1-2)—"The king's heart is in the hand of the LORD, as the rivers of water: he turneth it whithersoever he will. Every way of a man is right in his own eyes: but the LORD pondereth the hearts." Today's reading contains wise counsel for anyone in a position of responsibility: from parents to princes, pastors to potentates. Leaders need to know God's moral, ethical, and spiritual precepts if they are to direct their charges into God-honoring paths of conduct and character.

Heart of the Passage: Proverbs 24

Chapter 22	Chapter 23	Chapter 24
Right Actions	Right Associations	Right Expectations
Temptation and Temperance		

Your Daily Walk: It has been well said, "The things that count most in life are the things that cannot be counted." What do you value most? On a scale of 1 to 10 (with 1 being low and 10 being high), how much do you value . . .

_____ a good name?   _____ reverence?   _____ mercy?
_____ humility?   _____ generosity?   _____ honesty?

These qualities—and others—are indispensable for a godly leader. If you weren't totally satisfied with the numbers you assigned, spend some extra moments meditating on these potent proverbs:

If you're not afraid to face the music, you may someday lead the band.

- *A good name is rather to be chosen than great riches, and loving favor rather than silver and gold* (22:1).
- *By humility and the fear of the LORD are riches, and honour, and life* (22:4).
- *Be not a witness against thy neighbor without cause; and deceive not with thy lips* (24:28).

Insight: Proverbs—Handle with Care!
Learned world rulers once traveled to Jerusalem to hear the wisdom of Solomon (1 Kings 10). Later, Jesus would claim to be greater than Solomon (Luke 11:31). And Jesus warned that those who heard His teaching but failed to respond would one day be condemned by the rulers of Solomon's day. Today you are reading the same wisdom they responded to—and God expects you to handle it with the same care!

8 Wise Words from the King
Proverbs 25-29

Overview: Righteousness not only exalts a nation (14:34), it also stabilizes the nation's citizens! In his closing contribution to the book of Proverbs, Solomon records the riches of righteousness and the fatal danger of foolishness. Kings and peasants, false witnesses and friends, the righteous and the corrupt, the foolish and the wise, the slothful and the diligent, the deceitful and the dependable—Solomon has something to say to each! God's wisdom gives guidance in choosing the right response to life's situations, and a proper perspective on material possessions.

Heart of the Passage: Proverbs 25

Chapter 25	Chapter 26	Chapter 27	Chapter 28	Chapter 29
Kings and Subjects	Fools and Friends	Kisses and Curses	Poverty and Prosperity	Flattery and Favor
Right Responses			Proper Perspectives	

Your Daily Walk: At first glance you may be tempted to view these 138 proverbs as random, miscellaneous thoughts. But actually there is evidence of careful arrangement and grouping of proverbs that deal with similar topics. As you read, refer to these categories . . . and think of corresponding situations in your life that can profit from Solomon's counsel:

Wisdom is a divine endowment and not a human acquisition.

The Tongue (25:11-15)   Gossip (26:20-22)
Overindulgence (25:16-17)   Hypocrisy (26:23-28)
Unfaithfulness (25:18-19)   Stewardship (27:23-27)
Compassion (25:20-22)   Oppression (28:15-17)
Foolish Actions (26:1-12)   Poverty (29:13-14)
Laziness (26:13-16)   Correction (29:15-21)

Now circle the most troublesome area in your walk with God, and underline the area in which, with God's help, you are currently experiencing the greatest consistency. Thank Him for the latter; commit yourself this week to work on the former. You may even want to post this page in a prominent place as your "Assignment for the Week"!

Insight: Counsel by Comparison in Chapter 25
As you read Chapter 25, see if you can locate at least one helpful piece of counsel regarding these everyday situations.

Receiving honor: _____
Answering a contentious person: _____
Ministering to a depressed friend: _____
Eating sweets: _____
Staying with a friend: _____

Wise Words for Women / Proverbs 30–31 9

Overview: It's rare to hear anyone admit to ignorance, but Agur does exactly that! Yet with his questions about nature, he leads the reader to understand something of God's brilliance in contrast to the limits of human understanding. The capstone of the book of Proverbs is provided by Lemuel, who praises the virtues of a godly wife and mother. It is fitting that Proverbs, which begins in heaven (1:7), should end in the home (31:15) for if God's wisdom works, it had better work in the crucible of everyday life.

Heart of the Passage: Proverbs 31:10-31

Chapter 30				Chapter 31			
Words Godward		Warnings Manward		A Godly Mother		A Godly Wife	
1	6	7	33	1	9	10	31
An Odious Woman				A Virtuous Woman			

Your Daily Walk: Proverbs 31 devotes 22 verses to the virtuous woman, and not a single verse to the virtuous man! Anyone who thinks the Bible is not a "liberated" book has failed to read the book of Proverbs.

And what a woman of virtue this is! In the home she is a trusted companion (v. 11) who cares tirelessly for her household (vv. 12, 15, 18, 27). She is a skilled shopper (vv. 13-14) and seamstress (vv. 19, 22). Outside the home she is an astute businesswoman (vv. 11, 16, 18, 24). With strength and dignity adorning her conduct (v. 25), kindness and wisdom accompanying her speech (v. 26), and the fear of the Lord motivating her behavior (v. 30), she is indeed a priceless treasure (v. 10).

Women, take inventory right now of the virtues God wants your life to radiate. Can you identify areas that need to change? What strengths can you build upon? And men, don't miss the exhortation to you in verse 30: "She shall be praised!" Has it been too long since you gave your "Mrs. Far-Above-Rubies" the praise she deserves? Tonight, why not eat out . . . and make Proverbs 31:28 a reality in your life!

The most important thing a father can do for his children is to love their mother.

Insight: Proverbs in the Old, Parables in the New

Note the questions raised by Agur (30:4), and the answer supplied by Jesus Christ in John 3:13. Not only do many of Jesus' parables elaborate upon the proverbs you have read the past few days, but the best translation of the Old Testament Hebrew word for *proverb* is the New Testament Greek word for *parable!*

Ecclesiastes

A king of worldwide acclaim and legendary wealth, Solomon (traditionally understood to be the Preacher of Ecclesiastes) had every opportunity to examine life in all its complexities. Ecclesiastes is the inspired record of his intense search to find meaning and satisfaction on earth. His search yields the conclusion that, apart from God, all of life is "vanity"—hopeless futility. Power, prestige, pleasure—nothing can fill the God-shaped void in the human heart. Ultimate satisfaction comes only when we fear, honor, and obey God.

Focus	Life . . . Under the Sun			. . . Above the Sun
Divisions	The Emptiness of Life's Pursuits	The Emptiness of Life's Possessions	The Emptiness of Life's Passing	The Solution to Life's Emptiness
	1 2	3 6	7 10	11 12
Topics	"Hear God!"			"Fear God!"
	"Vanity of Vanities; All Is Vanity (1:2)			
Place	Inside the Human Heart			
Time	In the Days of King Solomon			

The Meaning of Life Explored
Ecclesiastes 1–6

10

Overview: Making sense out of life is not always easy. This is the problem facing the preacher of the book of Ecclesiastes as he thinks his way through what he has seen and experienced in life. Every enterprise he has undertaken—from acquiring wisdom to amassing wealth—has ended in emptiness. In a sudden burst of emotion the preacher realizes that God does indeed appoint the times and purposes of life. But his insight fades as he focuses on the futility of life under the sun, and he overlooks the One who alone can put life together into a meaningful whole.

Heart of the Passage: Eccl. 1–2

Chapters 1–2	Chapter 3	Chapters 4–6
Meaningless Endeavors	Meaningful Times	Meaningless Conditions
The Exploration of Life's Meaning		

Your Daily Walk: Think about the people in your school, office, or neighborhood, and select the three you would consider "Most Likely to Succeed." Now analyze what it is that caused you to select them over other possible candidates. Is it their money . . . intelligence . . . position . . . possessions?

If any Old Testament character was ever a candidate for success, Solomon was the one! Blessed with wisdom, wealth, status, power, and prestige, he had everything a man could want—or did he? Look at his evaluation of it all: "Pleasure . . . is vanity . . . laughter . . . is mad . . . silver and gold . . . wisdom . . . the labor that I had labored to do . . . all was vanity and vexation of spirit, and there was no profit under the sun" (2:1-11).

A depressing picture? Perhaps. But don't miss verse 24. As Solomon sees the events and endeavors of life from God's perspective and the good things of life as gifts "from the hand of God," his life takes on meaning and purpose. Make a list of the good things you are enjoying today that come from the hand of God: health, employment, family, education, etc.

The answer to the question, "What is the purpose of life?" is not a What but a Who.

Insight: Silver Threads Among the Gold
One of the most moving passages in Ecclesiastes is the figurative description of the aging process (12:1-7). Realizing that the afflictions of age will catch up with everyone, the writer of Ecclesiastes counsels his audience: "Remember now thy Creator in the days of thy youth, while the evil days come not" (12:1). There's no better advice for anyone at any age!

11 The Meaning of Life Explained
Ecclesiastes 7–12

Overview: Up to this point the preacher has concentrated mainly on the problems of life without seeking an explanation. But the deeper he probes life's patterns and perplexities, the more conclusive becomes the evidence that points him to the solution: Fear God. When wisdom turns to vanity, fear God (7:18). When God's ways seem unsearchable or uncertain, fear God (8:12-13). When all is said and done, fear God (12:13), for this is the whole duty of man.

Heart of the Passage: Eccl. 7, 9, 12

Chapter 7	Chapters 8–10	Chapters 11–12
Wisdom Amidst Wickedness	Purpose Amidst Perplexity	Worship from the Womb to the Tomb
The Explanation of Life's Meaning		

Your Daily Walk: If life to you seems meaningless, then you could be on the verge of the greatest discovery of your life. God has many unusual ways of drawing individuals to Him and of demonstrating His love and care. With Job, He used tragedy; with the psalmist David, He used the life of a fugitive; with the preacher of Ecclesiastes, He used the emptiness of existence on earth. What is He using in your life today to teach you the same important lessons?

Make sure the thing you are living for is worth dying for.

It is interesting to note that every time the word *God* appears in the book of Ecclesiastes, it is the Hebrew word meaning Creator. The personal name *Lord* never appears. The preacher is speaking not of a God he knows personally, but of a God who is far above—like many speak of God today. And this is why the discovery of life's meaninglessness apart from God can be so important. If an empty, unsatisfying life causes you to search for the personal God of the universe, then you are about to meet the most important Person in life!

The Bible says that meaningful life . . . eternal life . . . abundant life . . . only come through knowing God and His Son Jesus Christ (John 10:10; 17:3). Thoughtfully read those two verses several times. Then tell God the desire of your heart. He is there waiting to meet you—right now.

Insight: An Atheist's Testimony Concerning Ecclesiastes
An atheistic professor, after reading Ecclesiastes, commented that it was the only book in the Bible that made sense to him. Too bad he overlooked the last two verses of the book!

222

Song of Solomon

King Solomon is credited with writing over a thousand songs in his lifetime. However this is the one that he calls the "Song of Songs" or "the best of all possible songs." The king's words weave a tapestry of love and devotion toward his young bride, touching on both the joys and heartaches of marriage. Though interpreters disagree whether the book is simply a lyric love poem or the depiction of an actual event in Solomon's life, most see it as an allegory for the Savior's eternal love for His bride the church.

Focus	Fostering of Love		Faithfulness of Love	
Divisions	Adoration of Lover	Joined to Lover	Separated from Lover	Devoted to Lover
	1:1 3:5	3:6 5:1	5:2 7:10	7:11 8:14
Topics	Courtship	Consummation	Conflict	Cultivation
	Love Growing	Love Fufilled	Love Tried	Love Enduring
Place	Israel, in the country and the palace			
Time	Perhaps 1 Year			

12 *A Wedding Song of Love*
Song of Solomon 1–8

Heart of the Passage: Song of Solomon 1–3

Overview: Of the more than 1,000 songs that King Solomon wrote (1 Kings 4:32), the Song of Solomon is, by his own admission, the "song of songs" (1:1). Set in a rustic pastoral setting, it depicts the romance and marriage of Solomon to a Shulamite shepherdess, and the happiness and heartaches of their wedded life together. At least three interpretations have been suggested for the book: (1) It is an allegory of God's love for His nation Israel; (2) It is a picture of Christ's love for His bride, the church; (3) It is a functional drama depicting Solomon's many marriages (1 Kings 11:3).

Chapters 1–3	Chapter 4	Chapters 5–6	Chapters 7–8
Falling in Love	United in Love	Struggling in Love	Growing in Love
Courtship	Consummation	Conflict	Cultivation

A good marriage is the union of two forgivers.

Your Daily Walk: Few institutions have been criticized more than the institution of marriage. And yet, for all its detractors, marriage continues to enjoy amazing popularity. Each year, more than two million American couples go to the altar to say, "I do!"

It should not surprise you to learn that the Bible has much to say about marriage. After all, it was God's idea in the first place! He performed the first wedding (Genesis 2); His Son performed His first public miracle at a wedding (John 2); and the book of Revelation concludes with a wedding (Revelation 19). In fact, marriage is one of the chief ways God uses to explain Himself. Ephesians 5:22-23 is a sobering reminder to Christian couples that their marriage is to be the picture to the world of Christ's love for His bride, the church.

Song of Solomon has been described as God's marriage manual for those whose marriages are sending out an SOS. But whether your marriage is on smooth seas or in stormy waters, take time this evening to read at least part of the book together with your spouse. Then tell your mate, "I love you!" It just might be the start of renewed romance in your marriage.

Insight: Love from Hermon to Heshbon
In the Song of Solomon 15 geographical locations are mentioned. Locate as many as you can with the help of a Bible atlas or the maps in the back of your Bible.

Isaiah

I saiah's ministry spans four decades and the reigns of four kings in Judah. His book's 66 chapters, like a miniature Bible, parallel the 66 books of the Old and New Testaments. The first 39 chapters, like the 39 books of the Old Testament, stress the holiness and justice of God and pronounce woe and condemnation on Judah. The final 27 chapters focus on the future, calling forth the theme of the New Testament—Messiah is coming to bring comfort to His people and judgment for the nations.

Focus	Judgment			Transition	Hope		
Divisions	Judgment Is Coming for Judah	Judgment Is Coming for Judah's Neighbors	Judgment Is Coming on All the Earth	Interlude: Assyria at the Gates of Jerusalem	Comfort and Peace Are Coming	Prince of Peace Is Coming	Restoration of God's People Is Coming
	1 12	13 27	28 35	36 39	40 48	49 57	58 66
Topics	Condemnation (1:4)				Consolation (40:1)		
	Sinful Servant (Judah)				Suffering Servant (Christ)		
Place	Judah and Her Neighbors				Israel and the World		
Time	About 40 Years (722–681 B.C.)				Thousands of Years		

13 *Judah's Indictment / Isaiah 1–4*

Heart of the Passage: Isaiah 1

📖 **Overview:** A crisis exists in the nation of Judah. Wickedness has permeated every fiber of the social, political, and spiritual life of the country—a condition which God finds intolerable. Divine indictment falls from the lips of His prophet Isaiah. Unless repentance sweeps the nation, God will reduce His people to ruin. Famine and pestilence will replace feasting and pleasure to show that the Holy One of Israel still rules in Zion. King and commoner, priest and prophet—no one will be safe when the terrifying day of God's wrath descends upon His people.

Chapter 1	Chapter 2	Chapter 3	Chapter 4
Judah's Indictment	Jehovah's Mountain	Judah's Judgment	Jehovah's Branch
"Hear!"	House	Holocaust	Holiness

Just because you are "without honor in your own country," doesn't necessarily mean you are a prophet!

🗡 **Your Daily Walk:** What do these three cities all have in common: Pompeii, Hiroshima, and Sodom?

Answer: They are all sites of historic disasters. Pompeii was destroyed in the eruption of Mount Vesuvius; Hiroshima was destroyed by an atom bomb in World War II; and Sodom was destroyed by heavenly fire and brimstone in the days of Abraham.

Now add to that list the name of Judah. Up until the days of the prophet Isaiah, Sodom stood alone as the universal symbol of depravity and shameful disgrace. If your nation was compared to Sodom, you had sunk as low as you could go morally, spiritually, and socially (1:9). But now in God's eyes, Judah had replaced Sodom as the object of scorn and ridicule (1:10). And Judah's judgment would be even more severe because Judah's privilege had been even more significant.

Opportunity brings responsibility—in Judah's day and in yours. Make a list of the religious freedoms you enjoy today: freedom to pray, to memorize Scripture, to share your faith without fear of physical harm, to worship in the church of your choice. If judgment fell today in proportion to your use (or abuse) of those privileges, what might happen? And what can you be doing today to see that it does not?

✏ **Insight:** From the Tragic to the Trivial (1:21-23)

In Isaiah's funeral dirge over Jerusalem, the prophet shows that every aspect of city life has been affected by the nation's spiritual revolt: justice, morals, money, and even the quality of the wine!

226

Judah's Immanuel / Isaiah 5–7

14

📖 **Overview:** Isaiah's national call for repentance is so urgent that even his personal call and commission to the prophetic office must wait until chapter 6. Isaiah's "Woe" (I am sinful, v. 5) is met by God's "Lo" (I am holy, v. 7), resulting in Isaiah's "Here am I; send me" (I am available, v. 8) and God's "Go" (I want to use you, v. 9). The task set before Isaiah is an unenviable one, for God promises from the start that the people will be spiritually deaf and nearsighted. But armed with confidence in his Immanuel, Isaiah begins to declare harsh words from on high in the courts and palaces of Judah.

Heart of the, Passage: Isaiah 6–7

Chapter 5	Chapter 6	Chapter 7
Song of the Vineyard	Sending of Isaiah	Sign of Immanuel
Condemnation	Commission	Coming

✒️ **Your Daily Walk:** It is not so much what God can do *through* you as it is what you will allow God to do *to* you that determines the measure of your effectiveness for Him.

God had a message for Isaiah to deliver—a message of holiness and judgment, a message of hope in the midst of heartache. But before His prophet could carry the message, Isaiah had to first carry the burden. He had to come to grips with his own sinful condition—his own waywardness and spiritual lukewarmness—before he could confront an entire nation suffering from the same tragic conditions. Before Isaiah could stand toe to toe with the king of Judah, he had to first kneel before the King of the universe. After his vision of God, Isaiah had a rekindled sense of God's awesome holiness and grandeur, and had no trouble volunteering for the Lord's service.

Are you trying to serve God before you have seen Him? Take a tip from Isaiah: Make no *appeal* till first you *kneel*, for that's the way to serve with *zeal!* After you have walked with God today, share with at least one other person how he or she can walk with Him too.

God is not so much seeking those with the ability to do everything, as He is those with the willingness to do anything.

🖼️ **Insight:** An Object Lesson in the Palace (6:1)

Isaiah received his call "in the year that king Uzziah died." Thus, his call is linked with the king's death, a premature death by leprosy for flouting God's holiness—the very condition that would bring about the death of the nation as well.

15 *Holy, Holy, Holy*

 Step Back

Scripture Reading:
1 Peter 1:13-25

In Isaiah 6, the prophet captures in words his vision of God's holiness when he was commissed to be a prophet, and it's an awesome portrait. "Holy, holy, holy, is the LORD of hosts: the whole earth is full of his glory" (6:3).

And with that glimpse of the sublime holiness of God, Isaiah cried out, "Woe is me! for I am undone" (6:5). In the light of God's perfection, Isaiah saw himself for what he was: a sinful creature.

R. C. Sproul comments,

"If ever there was a man of integrity it was Isaiah ben Amoz. . . . He was considered by his contemporaries as the most righteous man in the nation. He was respected as a paragon of virtue. Then he caught one sudden glimpse of a Holy God. In that single moment all of his self-esteem was shattered. In a brief second he was exposed, made naked beneath the gaze of the absolute standard of holiness. As long as Isaiah could compare himself to other mortals, he was able to sustain a lofty opinion of his own character. The instant he measured himself by the ultimate standard, he was destroyed—morally and spiritually annihilated. He was undone. He came apart. His sense of integrity collapsed (The Holiness of God, *pp. 43–44).*

⬆ Look Up

The beauty of holiness needs no paint.

How would you compare your life to Isaiah's? We can be thankful for one thing: Isaiah's experience with God was not normative for the rest of us. If it were, who of us could survive it?

Generally, God points out areas of sin in our lives a little at a time. As He does, we can deal with those sins by confessing them and asking Him to direct us by His Spirit. But God revealed to Isaiah all his sin all at once. And it was a magnificently humbling experience from which he would never fully recover.

Isaiah had seen God's holiness with his own eyes. And that one glimpse not only revealed God for who He is, but it revealed Isaiah for who he was.

God cleansed Isaiah of his sin that day. Why not reread Isaiah 6 and ask Him to begin cleansing your life as well.

➡ Move Ahead

To say that God is holy is to say that He is completely separate from sin, that He is pure and clean. To say that something or someone is holy is to say it is set apart unto God for His glory.

Our holiness can never approach God's. Yet we can still strive to be holy. Read 1 Peter 1:13-25, and memorize verse 16. Make that verse more than a set of words in your mind; make it your goal today and every day.

Judah's Prince of Peace / Isaiah 8–12 **16**

Overview: Isaiah's family life becomes an eloquent testimony to the trustworthiness of his prophecies (8:18). His firstborn son Maher-shalal-hash-baz acts as a constant reminder of the Assyrian threat upon Jerusalem (8:1-4). But in the face of "trouble and darkness . . . [and] anguish" (8:22), Isaiah proclaims a note of hope. "The people that walked in darkness have seen a great light" (9:2). There is coming a Child whose very names instill hope and confidence: Wonderful Counselor, Mighty God, Everlasting Father, Prince of Peace. Though shadows of judgment darken the horizon, the redeemed ones can sing His praises, for the ultimate victory is already assured!

Heart of the Passage: Isaiah 8–9

Chapters 8–9	Chapter 10	Chapter 11	Chapter 12
A Coming Child	A Coming Calamity	A Coming Branch	A Cause for Praise
Prince of Peace	Army of Assyria	Righteous Rod	Holy One

Your Daily Walk: No more tragic summary of a general's life could ever be penned than this: He won the battle but lost the war. In war, as in the Christian life, the ultimate outcome depends not on who wins every battle but rather on who wins the final battle. One setback does not mean the war has been lost.

As Isaiah looked at the prophetic horizon, he saw defeat and destruction for his nation. The battle would be lost. Judah would fall because of her pride and wickedness. But the war would not be lost! Messiah, the Prince of Peace, the Righteous Branch of Jesse, would come to turn seeming defeat into victory.

Think about the prophetic future of your nation and then list the trends you observe spiritually, morally, and politically. Looks pretty bleak, doesn't it? Now across your list write the last half of 12:6: "Great is the Holy One of Israel in the midst of thee." As in Isaiah's day, the future is as bright as the promises of God.

Security is not the absence of danger, but the presence of God no matter what the danger.

Insight: The Open Road

In Bible times the most important international highway was the *Via Maris* ("the Way of the Sea"). Mentioned in Isaiah 9:1, the Way of the Sea originated in Egypt and followed the coastline of the Mediterranean Sea north; it turned inland across the Carmel Ridge at Megiddo, passed through the Valley of Jezreel, and continued to Damascus, giving both armies and caravans access to the great empires of the ancient world.

229

17 *Judgment on Babylon and Moab*
Isaiah 13–16

Heart of the Passage: Isaiah 13

Overview: God's kingdom is worldwide, and so is His judgment. Moving out from the borders of his nation, Isaiah aims his verbal missiles at Judah's pagan neighbors for their interference in God's program of righteousness. A hundred years before Babylon's rise to prominence, Isaiah predicts her role first as oppressor, then as oppressed. The same judgment awaits Assyria, Philistia, and Moab—enemies that would be broken in their apparent moments of victory.

Chapter 13	Chapter 14	Chapter 15	Chapter 16
The Fall of Babylon		The Fall of Moab	
Predicted	Celebrated	Celebrated	Predicted
Babylon's Gloom		Moab's Doom	

Truth is never cheap, but the righteous can always afford it.

Your Daily Walk: In baseball, if a batter connects for a hit only three times in ten, he is called a good hitter. How often did an Old Testament prophet have to "connect" with his prophecies in order to be called a good prophet (Deuteronomy 18:20-22)? _____

Isaiah devoted all of chapter 13 to the "Rise and Fall of the Babylonian Empire." How was his prophetic batting average?

• Isaiah predicted that Babylon's destruction would come from a far country, not a neighboring power (v. 5). Babylon fell in 539 B.C. to a warring people living 350 miles east of Babylon.

• Isaiah predicted the name of that conquering nation: Media (v. 17), a fact which history confirms.

• Isaiah predicted permanent extinction for Babylon (vv. 19-22). The site has been deserted since the fourth century B.C.

• Isaiah predicted even the nomadic Arabians would avoid once-mighty Babylon (v. 20). The desolate site has been regarded with superstitious dread by Arabian bedouins ever since.

If Isaiah's God-given prophecies are that trustworthy, what does that tell you about Isaiah's God? Take one of your burdens to the Lord right now and leave it there. You'll be glad you did!

Insight: Burdens, Burdens Everywhere

Chapters 13–23 contain a long list of burdens—oracles of divine judgment upon offending nations. As such they form a fitting interlude between Isaiah's predictions of Assyrian invasion (chapters 1–12) and the onset of that invasion (chapters 28–39).

Judgment on Ethiopia and Egypt *18*
Isaiah 17–20

 Overview: Damascus, Ethiopia, and Egypt next feel the chastening strokes from Isaiah's prophetic pen. The glory of Damascus would be removed, leaving behind leanness of body and soul. But a handful would repent and, like the last gleanings from an olive tree, provide hope for a future harvest. Ethiopia's people would be pruned away like branches and would fall in battle. But one day they would come to Zion and pay homage to God, acknowledging Him as their Sovereign. Egypt would experience civil war, economic ruin, and spiritual poverty, showing the bankruptcy of Egypt's false gods.

Heart of the Passage: Isaiah 17, 19

Chapter 17	Chapter 18	Chapters 19–20
Doom for Damascus	Threshing for Ethiopia	Infamy for Egypt
Judgment on Judah's Neighbors		

Your Daily Walk: With the help of an atlas or map of the world, answer the following questions:

1. Can you locate Babylon? Why not? (13:19-20)
2. Can you locate Moab? Why not? (15:1)
3. Can you locate Ethiopia? Why? (18:1, 5, 7)
4. Can you locate Egypt? Why? (19:1, 4, 16, 24)

God is not merely in the business of casting down nations; He also sustains them, chastens them, purifies them, and prepares them for the worldwide role He has for them to play.

To say that God chastens and purifies Ethiopia or Egypt or Australia or America is to say that God chastens and purifies Ethiopians, Egyptians, Australians, and Americans. The process is seldom pleasant, but it is always beneficial.

Think of your life as if it were a tree. Have you been drawing deeply from the nutrients of God's Word? Are you well watered or experiencing drought? Are there "branches" of your life that need pruning? If Isaiah began a chapter, "The burden of . . . you!" how would it read? Take the words of 17:7 and let them guide you to the response God desires from you right now.

Every wrathful judgment of God in the history of the world has been a holy act of preservation.

Insight: A Noisy Shadow (18:1)

Ethiopia, a land "shadowing with wings," is literally a land "whirring with wings." The Hebrew term is similar to the word *tsetse* imitating the sound of buzzing insects.

19 Judgment on Jerusalem and Tyre
Isaiah 21–23

Heart of the Passage: Isaiah 21

Overview: Even in the midst of declaring prophecies of doom and destruction, Isaiah's heart breaks for the guilty nations involved. Babylon, "the desert of the sea," will be mercilessly crushed by Media, causing the prophet both heartache and dismay. Doomed men are never a pretty picture, and for Isaiah Babylon has become more than simply a vision of death row. The same holds true for Jerusalem. Though her coming judgment is richly deserved, Isaiah finds it difficult to divorce himself from the grim fate of his countrymen. The prophet can draw meager comfort from God's promise that judgment will be stayed during Isaiah's lifetime (22:14).

Chapter 21	Chapter 22	Chapter 23
	Judgment Promised for the . . .	
Desert of the Sea	Valley of Vision	Inhabitants of the Isle
Babylon	Jerusalem	Tyre

More spiritual failure is due to laziness than to disbelief.

Your Daily Walk: For the next 60 seconds, go to the nearest window and count the number of people you see from your vantage point. Now ask yourself this question: "How many of those people do I really care about?"

The faceless crowd has become a common and accepted part of life on this planet. It is often so easy to become calloused, indifferent, and unmoved by the lost condition of those around you. Isaiah knew that one of the best ways to develop a passion for souls is to ponder the destiny of lost men and women. Where are they going? And what awaits them there if no one cares enough to confront them with God's love and their own lostness?

The thought of judgment coming upon his countrymen caused Isaiah to bow in prayer and then move into action. What about you? Go back to the window for another minute, this time to pray for those you count. You cannot reach them all, but can you reach one today? Ask God to give you boldness and a door of opportunity to do precisely that.

Insight: God's Plan and Purpose

At least four purposes were served by prophets such as Isaiah: They pointed out the people's immoral condition; they called the nation back to the Law of Moses; they warned of coming judgment; and they predicted the coming of the Messiah.

Judgment Turned to Jubilation *Isaiah 24–27* **20**

Overview: For the last 11 chapters, Isaiah has been looking at his world through a magnifying glass, targeting devastating judgments for specific nations. But in today's section, he steps back to survey the prophetic landscape with a telescope, and what he sees causes him to respond in jubilation. Earth and heaven alike experience God's sifting judgment. The redeemed ones, vindicated at last, break forth in spontaneous song, exalting the Lord of the universe. Though often downcast and downtrodden, the people of God now have something truly worth singing about: refuge, deliverance, and ultimate triumph in the Holy One of Israel. Is that the song of your lips today?

Heart of the Passage: Isaiah 26–27

Chapter 24	Chapters 25–26	Chapter 27
Punishment for the People	Praise for the Lord	Preservation for God's People
Day of the Lord	Devotion	Deliverance

Your Daily Walk: The dictionary defines *crisis* as "the turning point for better or worse in an acute disease or time of distress." Using that definition, find a newspaper or news magazine and circle the headlines of at least 10 crisis points in the world today.

Isaiah 24–27 has been called "Isaiah's Apocalypse," for in it you will read of the ultimate downfall of earthly enemies, angelic hosts (24:21), and even death itself (25:8). The theme of the section is judgment, but permeating nearly every paragraph is a note of joy: singing by the remnant of God's people (24:14-16), gladness for God's greatness (chapter 25), and praise for the praiseworthy God of Zion (chapter 26). Truly God's people are blessed, even in times of crisis.

Think of a crisis as the time when you discover all that C(h)ris(t) is.

What is your attitude as you face the crises of today? Is your countenance as glum as the news? Or can you smile and sing in the midst of the storm, knowing who allows the winds to blow? Place the words *"Smile! You have something to smile about"* in a prominent place. Let them remind you as you face each new challenge today that the victory is already assured.

Insight: What Do You Get at a Feast of Fat Things?
The "fat things" Isaiah refers to in 25:6 are choice dishes prepared with olive oil and bone marrow—the most desirable items of food to the ancient Near Eastern palate.

21 *The Prophet's Perspective*

Scripture Reading: 1 Peter 1:10-12

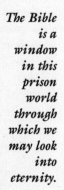

Step Back

Like many of the prophets, Isaiah communicated God's revelation concerning four prophetic eras:

1. *The contemporary time of Isaiah.* Isaiah addresses current events in light of God's judgment frequently through the book. This involved "forthtelling" rather than "foretelling," but both are aspects of God's prophetic message.

2. *The captivity of Judah.* Isaiah prophesied of the exile of Judah in Babylon. Only God knew exactly when this would occur, but Isaiah first mentioned this fate in 11:11. Later, when Hezekiah was king, the prophecies became even clearer (see 39:6).

3. *The coming of Christ.* Prophecies of this nature occur especially in the latter part of Isaiah, chapters 40–66. Insights regarding both the first and the second coming of Christ are revealed.

4. *The culmination of history.* Isaiah reveals events of the end times, such as the reign of Christ as the Prince of Peace (see 9:6), and the regathering of Israel after being dispersed throughout the world (see 27:12-13; 43:5-7; 65:8-10). On the farthest horizon, Isaiah foresees the new heavens and a new earth (see 65:17).

Look Up

Obviously the prophets, including Isaiah, did not fully understand all of the promises God revealed to them, but even so they faithfully recorded and preached those truths. They did so because they knew and trusted the God who revealed them.

As you read 1 Peter 1:10-12, put yourself into the prophets' shoes. Consider the awesomeness of their task. Think of the absolute trust in God they possessed. According to Peter, what was the purpose of their recording those truths?

In prayer, thank God for His prophets and for His Word recorded by them and captured for you in the Bible. Ask Him to give you diligence in your study of His Word.

The Bible is a window in this prison world through which we may look into eternity.

Move Ahead

You have a great advantage over the prophets, for in the Bible you possess the full counsel of God revealed. How much do you know of God's prophecies?

Ask your pastor or Sunday school teacher to recommend a study guide or book outlining the prophets' message. It's a fascinating and faith-building study that can revolutionize your walk with God.

Woe on Israel and Judah / Isaiah 28–30 **22**

Overview: Like lightning crackling in the distance, Isaiah's prophecies begin to focus on the ominous approach of the Assyrian armies. Ephraim (northern kingdom) reels like a drunkard, oblivious to the danger and falsely confident in the armies of Egypt to deliver her in time of trouble. But there shall be no such deliverance. Ariel (Jerusalem, symbol of the southern kingdom) stands next in line for judgment if her citizens follow Ephraim's sorry example by relying upon Egypt for protection.

Heart of the Passage: Isaiah 28

Chapter 28	Chapter 29	Chapter 30
Condemnation on Israel	Condemnation on Judah	Cause for Condemnation
"Woe to Ephraim!"	"Woe to Ariel!"	Woeful Rebellion

Your Daily Walk: Place a check (✓) next to each of the following calamities you have experienced in your lifetime:

_____ Sat in a chair that collapsed under your weight.

_____ Had a flat tire on a busy street.

_____ Loaned something of value and had it lost or damaged.

_____ Set the alarm clock for 6 A.M., and it rang at 8 A.M.!

What do these traumas in everyday life have in common? They are all examples of misplaced confidence. You put your trust in an object (such as a chair or a tire or an alarm clock) and it let you down. Or you relied on another person who failed you.

Isaiah warned both Ephraim and Ariel, "Don't put your trust in the armies of Egypt, for they will fail you. Put your trust in the Lord of hosts, for He will never fail you nor forsake you." Heedless of the prophet's warnings, the nations misplaced their trust—and felt the sting of God's discipline.

Are you in danger of doing the same? See if you can complete this sentence in 10 different ways: "Today, I am trusting God for . . ." If you have difficulty coming up with 10 endings to that sentence, perhaps a good deal of your trust is in untrustworthy objects and people. What needs to change in order to make God the One you lean upon?

The man caught up with this world is not ready for the next one.

Insight: Feeling the Full Force of Judgment (28:19-20)

The coming judgment upon Jerusalem would be so severe that beds and blankets would run out, and even the news of what God was doing would bring sheer terror to the listener's ears.

23 Wait for the Coming King / Isaiah 31–35

Heart of the Passage: Isaiah 33

Overview: As Isaiah continues to study the prophetic horizon, he sees more than coming calamity. True, the prospects are not pleasant for the rebellious people of God. But there is also a coming King who will bring peace like a river, freedom for the captives, justice for those suffering oppression, and judgment upon heaven and earth. In the light of His sure coming, the people of God are urged to watch and wait patiently, expectantly, and purposefully. Their redemption is nigh!

Chapter 31	Chapters 32–33	Chapter 34	Chapter 35
Watch Out for Egypt	Watch for the King	Wait for the Coming Judgment . . . Expectantly	Joyfully
Look Out!	Look Up!	Shape Up!	Sing Out!

Praise is not a vain compliment, but the uninhibited hug of a child for his father.

Your Daily Walk: Picture this scene. It is Sunday morning. You quietly enter your church and wait for the prelude to begin. But to your surprise, a brass band bursts through the doors playing "Stars and Stripes Forever."

The prelude sets the mood for what is to follow. A good prelude does not draw attention to itself (as does our humorous illustration), but rather prepares the listener for what is to come. In the same way, Isaiah's prelude of pain (chapters 31–35) prepares the people of God for the consolation that follows (chapters 40–66). The Lord is both Sovereign and Savior. Those who deny His strength will have difficulty accepting His salvation.

Can you think of a way that each of the following attributes of God acts as a prelude to what He wants to do in your life?

God's creative power (Psalm 19:1-3) prepares me to learn that _____.

God's infinite knowledge (Psalm 139:1-6) gives me the confidence that _____.

God's perfect holiness (Isaiah 1:18) warns me of the importance of _____.

Insight: Don't Bet on the Horses

In Bible times horses were owned only by the rich. The average Hebrew used the more sturdy donkey or ox for travel and plowing. In general, the horse was a "weapon" of war and represented military power. For this reason God repeatedly warned the Israelites not to place their confidence in nations with horses and chariots (Isaiah 31:1), but rather in Him alone.

Historical Interlude—Hezekiah
Isaiah 36–39

24

📖 **Overview:** Isaiah the prophet becomes Isaiah the historian during chapters 36–39. Two major historical events dominate the narrative: the attempted invasion of Judah by the Assyrian army in 701 B.C., and the critical illness that threatened King Hezekiah's life. The taunts of the Assyrian invaders are turned into cries of anguish and retreat as 185,000 die at the hand of the angel of the Lord—a direct answer to Hezekiah's specific prayer. God answers another of Hezekiah's prayers by extending his life 15 years. But by using those extra years for selfish pursuits rather than for God's purposes, Hezekiah seals the fate of his nation. The stage is set for Babylon to conquer and carry off the people of Judah, bringing down the curtain on God's judgment.

Heart of the Passage: Isaiah 36–37

Chapter 36	Chapter 37	Chapter 38	Chapter 39
Assyria's Invasion	Isaiah's Instruction	Hezekiah's Illness	Babylon's Introduction
Assyria's Influence Wanes		Babylon's Influence Begins	

✔️ **Your Daily Walk:** All those who like to be ridiculed, please stand up.

That is one invitation you would probably just as soon ignore! After all, no one likes to be mocked or ridiculed for taking a stand. But as Paul warned young Timothy, "All that will live godly in Christ Jesus shall suffer persecution" (2 Timothy 3:12). As a Christian called upon to stand for God in a godless world, you may find yourself asked to swallow the bitter pill of ridicule—and swallow it regularly.

Suffering for Christ's sake is to be viewed as a privilege.

It happened to Hezekiah and his countrymen. Jeered at by the Assyrian hordes and belittled for their faith in God, the people of Judah had the last laugh. Through it all they learned that ridicule means little when you know the great God of heaven!

Has the thought of ridicule or verbal abuse stopped you from taking a stand for God? Have you avoided suggesting an office Bible study or evangelistic house party in your neighborhood because of the fear of what others might say? Take a tip from Hezekiah: You're on the winning team!

📓 **Insight:** "Rats, Foiled Again!"

Herodotus, an ancient Greek historian, cites instances of mice infestations in Assyria. Perhaps the deadly plague brought by the angel of the Lord was bubonic . . . and thus ironic!

25 *Comfort for God's People / Isaiah 40–43*

Heart of the Passage: Isaiah 40, 42

Overview: The book of Isaiah has been likened to a miniature Bible, its 66 chapters paralleling the 66 books of the Old and New Testaments. The first 39 chapters of Isaiah, like the 39 books of the Old Testament, proclaim judgment upon sinful mankind. God's patience is great, but He will not allow persistent sin to go unpunished. Beginning with today's section, the final 27 chapters of Isaiah, like the 27 books of the New Testament, proclaim a message of comfort and hope. The Messiah is coming to be the Savior of sinful people. Therefore, " 'Comfort ye, comfort ye my people,' saith your God" (40:1).

Chapter 40	Chapter 41	Chapter 42	Chapter 43
Comfort for God's People	Case Against God's Rivals	Servant of God's People	Savior of God's People
Israel	Idols	Israel's Holy One	

I would rather work with God in the dark than go alone in the light.

Your Daily Walk: What would need to happen for you to feel totally comfortable? What would need to change about your finances, your job security, your relationships with other people, your health, your appearance, or your academic performance before you would be able to relax and feel totally at ease without a worry in the world?

"I'd have to have all my bills paid!" But what about the new ones that will certainly arrive tomorrow? "I'd have to have a fortune in the bank!" But what if the bank went bankrupt and you lost it all? "I'd have to enjoy perfect health!" But what if you were in an accident and lost your ability to work?

The measure of your comfort will always be the measure of your confidence in God. For Isaiah to declare "Comfort ye" after 39 chapters of judgment would seem ludicrous—unless you recall *who* is providing the comfort! Type or print the first five verses of chapter 40 on a notecard, and put it under your pillow tonight. When you wake up tomorrow, let it be the first comforting thought of your day. God will go before you all day—so relax and enjoy His presence!

Insight: The Thoroughly Comfortable Chapters (40–66)
Though the idea of comfort is found only twice in the first 39 chapters (12:1; 22:4), you will find it numerous times in the balance of the book (40:1-2; 49:13; 51:3, 12, 19; 52:9; 54:11; 57:6; 61:2; 66:13).

Impotent Idols and Omnipotent God **26**
Isaiah 44–48

Overview: In an amazing collection of specific prophecies, Isaiah foretells the agent of comfort God will use in delivering His people (Cyrus, king of Persia), and the means of comfort God will employ (destruction of idolatrous Babylon). Isaiah taunts those who would put their trust in mere images of stone or wood. From the same piece of wood a workman fashions gods to be worshiped and logs to be burned (chapter 44). By contrast, the God of Israel writes history in advance, predicting kings by name centuries before their birth! Is it any wonder God declares, "I am God, and there is none else; I am God, and there is none like me" (46:9)? Is it any wonder God calls forth judgment upon Babylon—or upon anyone who would dare to substitute trees and rocks for the omnipotent Lord of Hosts, the Holy One of Israel?

Heart of the Passage: Isaiah 44–45

Chapter 44	Chapter 45	Chapter 46	Chapter 47	Chapter 48
Folly of Idols	Greatness of God	Frailty of Idols	Babylon's Demise	Israel's Deliverance
Impotent Idols			Omnipotent God	

Your Daily Walk: Idolatry is such a harsh-sounding word. It's a good thing God's people today don't struggle with idolatry—or do they?

What really is idolatry? One commentator defines it this way: "Idolatry is anything that comes between you and God." Using that definition, an uncomfortably long list of things could potentially fall into the category of becoming idols:

Television	Your sweetheart	Eating
Clothes	Your spouse	Golfing
Your job	Your child	Skiing
Your car	Your ambition	_____ ing

If it's more precious to you than God, spell it I-D-O-L.

(You fill in the blank on the last one.)

Pick one item from the above list, and ask yourself the question: "Is this thing drawing me toward God or away from Him?" Then do what Isaiah 46:8-9, 12 suggests!

Insight: Would the Real Servant Please Stand Up?

When you find the word *servant* in Isaiah, pay close attention to the context. The word can refer to any of the following four, and you must carefully decide: Is it David (37:35), Isaiah (44:26), the nation Israel (41:8-9), or the Messiah (49:5-6)?

27 *Sufferer for God's People* / *Isaiah 49–51*

Overview: For the people of God, the path of restoration is the path of servanthood and suffering. There is coming One who will pardon iniquity and will restore righteousness to Zion. In contrast to the rebellion of Israel, this Servant will come willingly and humbly to offer Himself as a sacrifice for many (50:6). Therefore, the faithful ones are called upon to hearken to God's voice (51:9,17), for "righteousness is near" (51:5).

Heart of the Passage: Isaiah 51

Chapter 49	Chapter 50	Chapter 51
Judah's Restoration	Judah's Repentance	Judah's Righteousness
Help in Zion	Healing in Zion	Hearken in Zion

Your Daily Walk: Take a sheet of paper and divide it in half. Now pretend for a moment that you can afford to hire a servant to do all the tasks you normally perform but find unpleasant. On the left side of your paper, list those tasks. (Think of it as writing your personal servant's job description.) On the right side, list the tasks you presently do that you would want to keep for yourself, even if you had a servant.

Service can never become slavery to one who loves.

Chances are, the tasks you listed on the left side are menial and repetitive. They require fitting your schedule to someone else's; they demand time, money, and inconvenience.

The remarkable thing about Isaiah's depiction of the coming Messiah is this: Though Christ could have come with swords flashing and armies marching to impose His righteousness upon mankind, He chose instead to come as the Suffering Servant, allowing people to smite Him and shame Him (50:6), in order to show the full extent of His love. And the Supreme Servant calls all who would follow Him to a similar lifestyle of servanthood, demonstrating God's love in action.

It's easy to be served; it's difficult to serve. But with God's help, even the activities on the left side of your paper can become joy (rather than drudgery) in your life. Look around for creative ways to do those mundane tasks, and thank God for the opportunities He gives you each day to be a servant to others.

Insight: A Trilogy of Comforting Truths
The final 27 chapters of Isaiah form three 9-chapter "sections of solace": The Deliverance of God's People (40–48), The Deliverer of God's People (49–57), and The Glory of God's Delivered People (58–66).

Suffering on Behalf of God's People
Isaiah 52–57

28

📖 **Overview:** Nowhere in the pages of the Old Testament will you see a clearer picture of the horrible price of your redemption than in the section you will read today. Meditate upon the many verses that show the anguish your Savior endured in paying the awful price of sin.

"His visage was so marred more than any man" (52:14).

"He was wounded . . . he was bruised . . . the chastisement of our peace was upon him; and with his stripes we are healed" (53:5).

"The LORD hath laid on him the iniquity of us all" (53:6).

"He was cut off out of the land of the living" (53:8).

"It pleased the LORD to bruise him; he hath put him to grief. . . . He hath poured out his soul unto death: . . . he was numbered with the transgressors; and he bare the sin of many" (53:10, 12).

Heart of the Passage: Isaiah 52–53

Chapter 52	Chapter 53	Chapter 54	Chapters 55–56	Chapter 57
Exalted Servant	Suffering Servant	Faithful Servant	Redemption by the Servant	Rebuke from the Servant
Providing Redemption			Responding to Redemption	

✓ **Your Daily Walk:** The passage you will read today contains the single most important piece of good news you will ever hear! It can be summarized in just three words: *incarnation, redemption, invitation.*

Incarnation: Jesus Christ, the Son of God, came in the flesh (53:2-3), becoming all of God in a human body.

Redemption: He came to suffer and die, to "make his soul an offering for sin" (53:10), to bear "the sin of many" (53:12).

Invitation: He stands ready to provide mercy and forgiveness for all who will respond. "Ho, every one that thirsteth, come ye to the waters" (55:1).

What have you done with the invitation of the Suffering Servant? Have you ignored it, rejected it, or accepted it? If you have never done so, take Him at His word today. Say yes to the One who died that you might live eternally.

We cannot look at the cross and still think our lives are of no account to God.

📰 **Insight:** A Servant Song in Five Stanzas

Think of 52:13–53:12 as a 15-verse song with 5 stanzas of 3 verses each. (Mark them in your Bible.) The Servant Song begins and ends with exaltation (stanzas 1 and 5), moves through rejection (stanzas 2 and 4), and climaxes in agony (stanza 3).

29 *Portrait of the Messiah*

Scripture Reading: Philippians 2:5-11

← Step Back

Isaiah paints a portrait of the Messiah as the Suffering Servant in 52:13–53:12. And of this prophecy, commentator G. Campbell Morgan writes, "There is nothing, either in the Old or the New Testament, more arresting than this portrayal of the Servant of the Lord, in which we are conscious of an appalling gloom, which nevertheless burns and shines with ineffable glory."

The specific ways in which Jesus Christ fulfilled the prophecies of Isaiah contribute strong evidence for the trustworthiness and inspiration of Scripture. Consider how Isaiah's prophecies were quoted by various New Testament authors and applied to our Lord:

- Isaiah 52:15 quoted in Romans 15:21
- Isaiah 53:1 quoted in John 12:38; Romans 10:16
- Isaiah 53:4 quoted in Matthew 8:17
- Isaiah 53:5-6 quoted in 1 Peter 2:22-25
- Isaiah 53:7-8 quoted in Acts 8:32-33
- Isaiah 53:12 quoted in Mark 15:28; Luke 22:37

Isaiah pictures a Messiah who is exalted, yet despised. Wounded for our sins. A Lamb led to the slaughter for our atonement. It's a picture of One who humbly sacrificed Himself on our behalf. His suffering is horrifying to contemplate, yet was not without purpose. And because of that suffering, He is surely worthy of our heartfelt worship and devoted obedience.

Jesus Christ is God in the form of man; as completely God as if He were not man, as completely man as if He were not God.

↑ Look Up

Consider Philippians 2:5-11, the apostle Paul's moving description of the same Suffering Servant. Ask yourself how are your attitudes toward your own circumstances, and perhaps toward the calling of God on your life, different from the Savior's?

As you worship today, thank God for Christ's loving act of sacrifice on your behalf. And ask Him to build within you the character qualities that made Christ's life shine while He walked the earth.

→ Move Ahead

In Acts 8:26-38, you'll read a story in which this passage of Isaiah is instrumental in bringing a person to Christ. Be prepared today to share a word of testimony concerning your suffering Savior to someone. It may open the door for you to share further, just as it did to Philip nearly 2,000 years ago.

Judah's Groan and Glory / Isaiah 58–62 30

Overview: As Isaiah looks at his contemporary situation, there is little to commend it. Empty ritual, meaningless fasts, and broken fellowship mark the spiritual life of the nation. But like the first rays of sunlight after a summer storm, Isaiah catches a glimpse of the glorious future awaiting the people of God. A day is coming when darkness will be swept away, affliction will cease, "violence shall no more be heard" (60:18), and the glad tidings of salvation shall be proclaimed throughout Zion. The desolate land shall be inhabited and prosperous, prompting praise to the ends of the earth that God has not forsaken His people after all. Groaning has indeed given way to glory.

Heart of the Passage: Isaiah 59–60

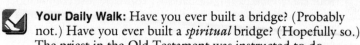

Chapter 58	Chapter 59	Chapter 60	Chapter 61	Chapter 62
Forgotten Fasts	Broken Fellowship	Rebuilt Nation	Rebuilt People	Renewed Fellowship
Judah's Groan		Judah's Glory		

Your Daily Walk: Have you ever built a bridge? (Probably not.) Have you ever built a *spiritual* bridge? (Hopefully so.)

The priest in the Old Testament was instructed to do precisely that: build a bridge between holy God and sinful mankind. He did it through the offering of endless sacrifices, the blood of animals to cover the sins of a nation.

The nation of Israel was selected by God to be a bridge-builder to surrounding nations, to show by her lifestyle of faith that God rewards those "that diligently seek him" (Hebrews 11:6).

And the same job description has been passed down to you! As a Christian, you are to be salt in a bland world, light in the midst of darkness, and a priest bringing people back to God (Matthew 5:13-14; 1 Peter 2:9).

Think of today as a unique opportunity to build a bridge between a lost sinner and his loving God. Perhaps you can't build an entire bridge in a single day, but you can begin that all-important process by your speech, conduct, and genuine concern in the life of another.

Bridge-building. It's time-consuming, costly—and worth whatever it takes!

Blessed is the influence of one true, loving soul on another.

Insight: Glory in the Old, Glory in the New

With one Bible open to Isaiah 60, and another to Revelation 21, see how many similarities you can find between those two glory-filled chapters. There are nearly a dozen!

31 *Judah's Glorious Future / Isaiah 63–66*

Overview: In the light of present calamity and coming glory, there can only be one fitting response from God's people: repentance for their pride and rebellion. "But now, O LORD, thou art our father; we are the clay, and thou our potter; and we all are the work of thy hand" (64:8). The twin themes that have dominated Isaiah's message—condemnation and consolation—appear again in the concluding verses: "The hand of the LORD shall be known toward his servants [consolation], and his indignation toward his enemies [condemnation]" (66:14). Therefore, "Let the LORD be glorified" (66:5).

Heart of the Passage: Isaiah 66

Chapter 63	Chapter 64	Chapter 65	Chapter 66
Recalling God's Mercies	Repenting of Pride	Remaking Heaven and Earth	Rejoicing in Jerusalem
Judah Speaks to Jehovah		Jehovah Speaks to Judah	

From the errors of others, a wise man corrects his own.

Your Daily Walk: Congratulations! You have just completed reading the 37,044 words of the book of Isaiah (if you read it in the KJV), making it the fifth longest book in the Bible. (Can you guess which books are longer?) As you conclude another month in God's Word, pause to consider what you have learned about the great God you worship and serve:

In *Proverbs* you learned that the fear of the Lord is the beginning of wisdom, giving you the skill to make decisions that please God and that can keep you on the path God wants you to follow. In *Ecclesiastes* you learned that life's possessions and pursuits will never fill the void that God alone can fill. In the *Song of Solomon* you learned that your marriage relationship is to be a picture to the world of God's selfless love for you. And in *Isaiah* you learned that God cannot allow sin to go unpunished. That's why He sent His Son as the Suffering Servant.

Write the above paragraph on a postcard and mail it to yourself. When it arrives, pray those thoughts back to God as your daily commitment to make your choices, pursuits, and relationships pleasing to the Holy One who bought you with His blood.

Insight: Every Nation and Tongue
Isaiah 66:18-19 depicts people streaming into a new Jerusalem from Tarshish (Spain), Pul and Lud (Africa), Tubal (Turkey), and Javan (Greece). This glorious conclusion to the book of Isaiah reminds us that God has a place in His new world for people of faith—from all nations.

Jeremiah

O n the time clock of history, Judah is only seconds away from destruction as God calls Jeremiah to the task of preaching repentance to an affluent, self-satisfied people. In the book bearing his name, Jeremiah challenges his countrymen to recognize their errors and repent. However, Judah's response is not repentance but rejection. For more than 40 years, the sinful nation remains deaf to Jeremiah's repeated warnings until at last it is too late. The Babylonian army arrives; vengeance falls; and God's justice and holiness are vindicated.

Focus	Prophecies to Jews					Prophecies to Gentiles	
Divisions	Call of Jeremiah	Condemnation of Judah	Conflicts of Jeremiah	Consolation from Jeremiah	Consistency of Jeremiah	Condemnation of Nine Countries	Consummation of Jerusalem's Judgment
	1	2　　25	26　29	30　33	34　45	46　　51	52
Topics	Ministry	Message	Misery			Vengeance	Vindication
	Jeremiah's Sermons				Jeremiah's Sorrows		
Place	Judah				Babylonia		
Time	About 40 Years						

1 *Call of Jeremiah / Jeremiah 1–3*

Heart of the Passage: Jeremiah 1; 2:13-19

Overview: For centuries prophets had come to God's people with the ultimatum, "Shape up or God will ship you out in judgment." But their message fell on deaf ears and stony hearts. At last it is time for God to show His words are no idle threat. He selects a messenger—Jeremiah, the tenderhearted son of a priest of Anathoth—to announce that Judah's condition is terminal. For their idolatry and indifference, the people will reel in judgment at the hands of the Babylonians.

Chapter 1	Chapter 2	Chapter 3
Jeremiah's Call	Judah's Condemnation	Jehovah's Challenge
"Get Ready!"	"Remember!"	"Return!"

To err is human, but when the eraser wears out ahead of the pencil, you're overdoing it.

Your Daily Walk: Have you ever watched a sand castle begin to crumble as the tide advances? It's a study in erosion. First the foundation is undermined. Then the walls begin to sag. Finally the entire structure comes crashing down.

Erosion is like that . . . even in the Christian life. A habit that you once considered unthinkable is grudgingly tolerated. And what you tolerate is all too soon condoned . . . then endorsed . . . then openly promoted as acceptable in God's eyes.

It's such a subtle thing, this erosion. Subtle . . . yet devastating. It happened in the nation of Judah. Perhaps it's happening in your life as well. In your personal life . . . your business ethics . . . your use of money . . . your relationship with your spouse or children. And while you are free to ignore the presence of erosion, you are not free to escape its consequences, for they are as sure as the Word of God.

Are you toying with defection or defilement in your Christian life, confident that God's patience will last? Then hear what God says by reading the penetrating reminder in Exodus 34:6-7.

Insight: The Span of Jeremiah's Ministry (1:1-3)

	JEREMIAH		
Josiah (good)		Jehoiakim (bad)	Zedekiah (bad)
640 630 620 610		600	590 586

(Jehoahaz and Jehoiachin have been omitted as each ruled only 3 months.)

246

Judah's Faithlessness / Jeremiah 4–6 2

Overview: Today's section paints a word picture of the coming Babylonian invasion. You can almost hear the hoofbeats of the horses, the war cries of the invading Chaldeans, the screams of anguish from God's people as they experience the deadly consequences of their rebellion. But the cure is no worse than the disease, for Judah has even forgotten how to blush (6:15) in her zeal to pursue every kind of loathsome activity and proud indulgence.

Heart of the Passage: Jeremiah 5

Chapter 4	Chapter 5	Chapter 6
Disaster from the North	Pollution from Within	Punishment from Without
Chaldea	Corruption	Calamity

Your Daily Walk: What would you think of a doctor who, upon discovering a tumor buried deep in your body, responded, "Take two aspirin and you'll be just fine"? How about a fireman who responded to a three-alarm fire by saying, "It will probably burn itself out soon enough"? Or a policeman who, upon arriving at the scene of a burglary, merely shook his head and said, "Boys will be boys"?

In each case, the response is inappropriate to the situation. Tumors demand surgery; fires need to be extinguished; lawbreakers must be punished for their lawless deeds.

And therein lies a parable. Ours is a day in which we have lost sight of the seriousness of sin. Character defect . . . error in judgment . . . slip of the tongue . . . moment of weakness—call it what you will, God's Word plays no such semantic games. Any transgression of God's law is sin (1 John 3:4), and the payment due for falling short of God's glory is death (Romans 3:23; 6:23).

God looked in vain for one person in the city of Jerusalem who stood for justice and godliness in Jeremiah's day (5:1). Will He find it any different in your city today? Confession and commitment—there is no better way to turn your world around! If God were to look in your town (and He is doing precisely that), what would He find?

It doesn't take such a great man to be a Christian; it just takes all there is of him.

Insight: "Now Hear This (Did You Hear Me?)"
If something is important, it bears repeating. And the fact that Babylonia was destined to become God's avalanche of judgment upon wicked Judah is repeated in Jeremiah's prophecy 164 times!

247

3 Worthless Worship / Jeremiah 7–10

Heart of the Passage: Jeremiah 8

Overview: Idolatry and hypocrisy have permeated every fiber of Judah's national life. People, prophets, and priests alike practice worthless worship in haughty indifference. But through Jeremiah, God delivers a ringing indictment. Their nation—with all its outward splendor—will be reduced to a heap of ruins because of the people's arrogance and idolatry. At the thought of Judah's imminent "divine surgery," Jeremiah weeps unashamedly for his hardhearted countrymen.

Chapter 7	Chapter 8	Chapter 9	Chapter 10
Dangerous "Safety"	Foolish "Wisdom"	Treacherous Tongues	Senseless Statues
Complacency	Folly	Perjury	Idolatry

Your Daily Walk: A bird flies thousands of miles over unfamiliar terrain to avoid winter's cold. A salmon swims vast distances to return to its place of birth. A hunting dog tracks and retrieves its prey, never having been taught those skills.

As long as your conscience is your friend, never mind about your enemies.

What do these phenomena have in common? They are all examples of instincts at work: those God-given aptitudes which cause creatures to respond in ways they were never taught.

Just as there are natural instincts which God has placed within you for your physical well-being, so too there are spiritual "instincts" to guard your spiritual health. You'll read about one in 8:4-9, the instinct that pricks your conscience when you sin, prompting you to respond, "What have I done?" Like the warning light on your dashboard, that instinct alerts you to the presence of a problem.

But you must take the next step. Judah responded by ignoring the warning. Are you in danger of doing the same? Even the swallows of Capistrano know better than to ignore their God-given instincts. Pick one of the divine nudges you are feeling right now and respond obediently to it.

Insight: The Valley of Slaughter (7:30-34)
Tophet literally means "altar" or "fireplace." It was where child sacrifices were offered to the heathen deity Molech—a practice outlawed by Josiah (2 Kings 23:10) and repudiated by God (Jeremiah 7:31). The valley of Hinnom later became the city dump where fire burned continuously to consume the rubbish. As such its name became a synonym for hell (Mark 9:47-48).

Broken Covenant / Jeremiah 11–15

4

📖 **Overview:** God instructs Jeremiah to take a linen girdle (a tight-fitting belt or sash) and bury it by the Euphrates River. Later he is told to dig it up again. The result is predictable: one ruined girdle, unfit to wear any longer. And the parallel is painfully clear. Selected by God for a place of intimate fellowship (just like the girdle), Judah would now be cast away in judgment for her corruption.

Heart of the Passage: Jeremiah 13

Chapter 11	Chapter 12	Chapter 13	Chapters 14–15
A Broken Promise	A Bitter Complaint	A Rotten Girdle	A Backslidden People
"Why Do the Righteous Suffer?"		"How Will the Unrighteous Suffer?"	

Your Daily Walk: Moses, the servant of God, and Samuel, the first prophet in Israel. What do these two great men of the Old Testament have in common?

The answer may shock and disturb you. God declared that their combined prayers would not be sufficient to avert the disaster soon to come upon rebellious Judah (15:1).

There is a time to pray . . . to repent . . . to come to God on your knees. But there is coming a day when it will be too late to pray—for yourself or another.

Today you have the freedom to seek God or to avoid Him, to acknowledge your need or to sidestep the issue. Today many people may be praying for you: your spouse, children, parents, friends, minister. And you may choose to scoff at those prayers. But the alternative to getting *right* with God is getting *left*—waking up to a day in which even Moses and Samuel could not move God in prayer on your behalf.

Isaiah 55:6 states, "Seek . . . the LORD while he may be found." And when you obey that command, you'll find a wonderful promise waiting for you in Hebrews 11:6!

Duties delayed are the devil's delight.

Insight: Jeremiah, the Audiovisual Expert
The rotten girdle (13:1-11) is just the first of 10 audiovisual tools Jeremiah uses to communicate his message. Can you identify the others found in these passages?

13:1-11 _____	19:1-13 _____
13:12-14 _____	24:1-10 _____
14:1-9 _____	27:1-11 _____
16:1-9 _____	32:6-15 _____
18:1-6 _____	43:8-13 _____

Penetrating
Sermons from the
Prophets' Pens

The dual themes of repentance and judgment ("Shape up or ship out") are common to all 17 prophetical books, Isaiah–Malachi. But each prophet spoke to a unique contemporary situation. Notice the theme and period of each prophet's message. Refer to this chart often as you read through the prophets.

Prophet	Message for His Day (and Yours)	Time Period
Jonah	God loves the Gentiles.	To Assyria before the Exile
Nahum	Doom of Nineveh for its brutality	
Obadiah	Doom of Edom for its treachery	To Edom before the Exile
Hosea	God's love for adulterous Israel	To Israel before the Exile
Amos	God's people are ripe for punishment.	
Isaiah	Messiah is coming.	To Judah before the Exile
Jeremiah/ Lamentations	Judgment now, glory to follow	
Joel	Judgment will fall like a plague.	
Micah	God's people on trial	
Habakkuk	The just shall live by faith.	
Zephaniah	God's day is coming.	
Ezekiel	God is not finished with His people.	To Judah during the Exile
Daniel	God's hand in world events	
Haggai	The danger of halfheartedness	To Judah after the Exile
Zechariah	The glory of the Messiah	
Malachi	The danger of hardheartedness	

Prophet and Potter / Jeremiah 16–20 **5**

📖 **Overview:** Jeremiah himself becomes an object lesson to his nation, for his very life models the reality of what is soon to befall Judah. The prophet is commanded to remain celibate and avoid funerals and feast days—a daily reminder to his countrymen that they will soon experience involuntarily what Jeremiah is called to experience voluntarily. Loss of family, comfort, and joy await God's rebellious people—a message that is finally heard . . . and results in beatings and imprisonment for the faithful prophet of God.

Heart of the Passage: Jeremiah 16; 18:1-10

Chapter 16	Chapter 17	Chapter 18	Chapter 19	Chapter 20
Celibate Servant	Shameless Sabbath	Patient Potter	Broken Bottle	Imprisoned Prophet
Rebuke				Rejection

🗝️ **Your Daily Walk:** *True or False:* Salvation is a free gift (before you answer, read Ephesians 2:8-9).

True or False: Discipleship is a costly pursuit (before you answer, read Luke 14:25-33).

For Jeremiah, following God and obeying His will involved paying an enormous price: the price of lost comfort, restricted freedom, and personal sacrifice (16:1-13). Jeremiah willingly endured some unusual restrictions in order to accomplish a unique mission in life.

It costs to follow Jesus Christ, but it costs more not to.

Similarly, Christ urged those who would follow Him as His disciples to sit down first and count the cost. Salvation is a free gift, but discipleship is a costly pursuit.

What might that cost involve for you? Perhaps it means giving up a lucrative business . . . a cherished ambition . . . the applause of the crowd. Whatever it is, you will discover it by asking and answering this question: "What is there in my life today that is complicating the possibility of my following in the footsteps of the Master?" Let God speak to you from Jeremiah's example. Then if spiritual surgery is necessary, give God the freedom to use the scalpel of His Word on your life. Discipleship is often painful, but it is always profitable.

📖 **Insight:** Searching the Heart, Trying the . . . Reins?
Funny how words change their meanings. The Hebrew word translated "reins" (17:10) literally means kidneys—a figure of speech for a person's innermost being or mind. When God tests the reins, He is looking at the deepest motives and thoughts.

6 *Last Chance for Judah's Leaders*
Jeremiah 21–25

Heart of the Passage: Jeremiah 21–22

📖 **Overview:** Time is running out for Judah. Already a growing sense of doom grips the nation. Popular opinion regarding the prophet of God stands at an all-time low. But even that cannot deter Jeremiah from his appointed task: declaring to leaders and lay persons alike God's displeasure with their conduct. Moving from the nation in general to the nation's leaders in particular, Jeremiah singles out three kings for judgment before turning his attention to the Messiah-King who will restore righteousness and justice on the earth. The nation will lie desolate for 70 long years when the wrath of God is finally poured out upon His wayward flock.

Chapters 21–22	Chapter 23	Chapter 24	Chapter 25
Bad News for Jerusalem	Righteous Branch for Judah	Two Baskets of Figs	A Bowl of God's Fury
Sermons		Signs	

Most every nation has the government it deserves.

🗒️ **Your Daily Walk:** Everyone knows the name of the president of the United States. But can you name three members of his cabinet? Do you know who your state governor is? Your mayor? Your state senators? Your congressional representative?

It is difficult to pray for someone you do not know by name. And it is difficult to pray fervently for someone you do not know personally. But those are your specific responsibilities: to offer "supplications, prayers, intercessions, and . . . thanks . . . for kings, and for all that are in authority" (1 Timothy 2:1-2).

Your refrigerator or kitchen cupboard would make a fine "prayer prompter" if you attached the names (and better yet, the faces) of several elected officials. Pray for one or more each time they come to mind.

If you are tired of reading about scandals involving politicians (and such scandals are as old as Jeremiah's day; see 22:11-30), there is no finer "preventive medicine" than the faithful prayers of godly citizens!

📓 **Insight:** The Worst-Kept Secret in Town
The duration of the Babylonian capitivity was a matter of public record. Jeremiah prophesied its length, not once but twice (25:11-12; 29:10). Later while Daniel was living in Babylon, he would read Jeremiah's prophecy, check his calendar, and conclude that God was going to restore His people to their own land after 70 years of captivity (Daniel 9:1-3).

Conflicts of Jeremiah / Jeremiah 26–29 7

Overview: Jeremiah's messages of judgment arouse strong opposition, especially in the palace. During Jehoiakim's reign, Jeremiah is threatened with a death sentence. While Zedekiah rules, Jeremiah dons a wooden yoke to portray the importance of Jerusalem surrendering to the yoke of Babylon—and thereby arouses the denunciation of the false prophet Hananiah. In the midst of this turmoil, Jeremiah sends the exiles in Babylon a letter of encouragement urging them to settle down for an extended (and predicted) period of captivity.

Heart of the Passage: Jeremiah 26–27

Chapter 26	Chapter 27	Chapter 28	Chapter 29
A Plot to Kill	A Picture to Warn	A Prophet to Refute	A People to Inform
Jehoiakim	Zedekiah	Jeremiah	Exiles

Your Daily Walk: Is your yoke on straight? Take a moment and read about it in Matthew 11:28-30. How does it compare with Jeremiah's experience?

Jeremiah's yoke was a heavy wooden implement made of straps and crossbars, representing the harsh domination of Babylon. Jesus' yoke symbolizes His relationship with His disciples, a fellowship of joy and rest. Jeremiah's was a heavy, lonely burden; Jesus promised to share the burden with His followers.

Both yokes stand for submission: one to a foreign conqueror, the other to a Savior's love. Jeremiah spoke to a rebellious nation about the need to yield to the enemy in order to survive. Jesus also spoke of yielding, not to an enemy but to a Friend—One who provides all that is necessary for life and godliness.

As you go about your routine today, picture yourself yoked to Jesus Christ. Take a piece of paper and make a list of things you would do differently if you knew He was yoked with you and literally walking along beside you. What problems would you turn over to Him? What worries would you forsake? What attitudes would you change? Would you talk to Him more often? Let His presence make a difference in your life today.

The man who lives by himself and for himself is liable to be corrupted by the company he keeps.

Insight: Did You Hear the Yoke About the King of Moab?

Jeremiah wore a yoke as a visual reminder to the nation of Judah of their approaching bondage. In addition he was instructed by God to send yokes to the kings of Edom, Moab, Ammon, Tyre, and Zidon, for all these nations would suffer a similar fate (27:2-7).

8 Consolation from Jeremiah
Jeremiah 30–33

Heart of the Passage: Jeremiah 32

Overview: God's promise of restoration begins a section describing both the worst of horrors (the time of Jacob's trouble) and the best of blessings (God's new covenant with Israel). God pledges to reestablish the nation after it has been purified by the discipline of exile. As a sign of His promise, He orders Jeremiah to purchase a field that would soon belong to the conquering Babylonians. As surely as day follows night, that land would one day become part of the restored nation to be ruled by the Righteous Branch, David's messianic descendant.

Chapter 30	Chapter 31	Chapter 32	Chapter 33
Reprimanding a Country	Renewing a Covenant	Purchasing a Land	Promising a Legacy
Punishment	Provision	Pledge	Prospect

As no place can be without God, so no place can encompass and contain Him.

Your Daily Walk: Your five-year-old has just popped the question, "Daddy, Mommy, what is God like?" Write down the first 10 words that come to mind. (Even if you don't have a five year old, the exercise will do you good!) _____

_____

If you had trouble describing God in simple terms even a child could understand, today's passage might help you. Few passages of Scripture present such a complete picture of God. Here you can find the God who hates sin and judges it (30:12-15), yet loves and forgives the sinner (30:18-22). You see the God of wrath (30:23-24) and the God of love (31:1-9). Above all you find portrayed the saving God who regathers His scattered flock (31:10-22) and establishes with them a new covenant (31:23-34)—a promise that rests on the sure guarantee of His sovereign power (31:35-37; 33:19-22).

Now go back and check your initial answer to the question, "What is God like?" Using Jeremiah's thoughts to help, can you express your answer in terms both simple and scriptural? Better still, find a five-year-old to try your answer on!

Insight: A Familiar King in a Foreign Context (30:9)

The reference to David reigning over the restored nation of Israel can be interpreted in at least two ways: (1) Figuratively, it may refer to the coming of Messiah. (2) Literally, it may refer to David himself being one day resurrected to reign as a regent under Messiah (compare Ezekiel 37:24-25 and Hosea 3:5).

Written on Their Hearts

9

Step Back

In your reading yesterday you caught a glimpse of the new covenant in Jeremiah 31:31-34—the high point of Jeremiah's prophecies. In those verses God reveals His heart for His people Israel. And there He makes three primary declarations about His new covenant with them:

Scripture Reading: Matthew 26:17-30

1. *He will put His law in His people's minds.* His law will be internal rather than external. Rather than on stones, He will write His law on their hearts so that it impacts their very lives from within. God's new covenant would give His people the inner ability to obey His standards of righteousness and thereby enjoy His blessings. The prophet Ezekiel explains that this would result from God's gift of the Holy Spirit in the lives of believers (Ezekiel 36:24-32). So, under the new covenant, God the Holy Spirit would actually dwell within each believer (see Joel 2:28-32).

2. *He said, I "will be their God, and they shall be my people."* That simply continues the relationship with them that He had already established. In other words, the new covenant wasn't meant to replace the old, but to fulfill it.

3. *He will forgive His people's sins.* Because Israel had sinned, they received God's curse. But as part of the new covenant, God will "forgive and forget." How can a holy God ignore sin? He can't. But it's not that the sin is overlooked, it's that it is paid for by a Substitute . . . whom we know to be Jesus Christ.

Look Up

As He shared a final meal with His disciples, Jesus took the cup and invited them to drink from it, saying, "This is my blood of the new [covenant], which is shed for many for the remission of sins." The cup represents the blood of Jesus, which in turn represents His atoning gift, His poured-out life, His substitutionary death.

God does not ask about our ability or our inability, but about our avail-ability.

As you read Matthew 26:17-30, thank God in prayer for His commitment to you through the new covenant, and for the atoning death of Christ which made it all possible for you to enjoy eternal life with Him.

Move Ahead

God has made an unshakable, unbreakable covenant with His people. What commitments have you made to Him?

Compose a list of life goals you want to accomplish in God's power—goals for spiritual disciplines, witnessing, Bible study, teaching, whatever they may be.

Remember, God deserves no less than your best. After all, that's what He gave you.

10 Countdown to Jerusalem's Fall
Jeremiah 34–39

Heart of the Passage: Jeremiah 36; 39:1-10

Overview: In many ways the book of Jeremiah deserves the title, "The Life and Ministry of a Man of God." Chapters 1–33 center around Jeremiah's prophetic sermons; chapters 34–52 deal primarily with Jeremiah's personal traumas and trials. Whether in the midst of broken covenants, burned scrolls, or brutal persecution, Jeremiah stands true to his prophetic mission. Pleading with his countrymen to go into exile voluntarily, Jeremiah "the traitor" watches instead as they resist Jerusalem's collapse and captivity to the end.

Chapters 34–36	Chapters 37–38	Chapter 39
Problems in the Palace	Problems in the Prison	Problems on the Battlefield
Jehoiakim's Fury	Jeremiah's Misery	Jerusalem's Fall

We make our decisions, and then our decisions turn around and make us.

Your Daily Walk: You are driving down the highway when you encounter a sign that reads "Dangerous Curve Ahead." Immediately you are confronted with a choice: (1) You can observe the warning and slow down. (2) You can ignore the warning and maintain your rate of speed. (3) You can oppose the warning and speed up. Whichever response you exercise, you will not change the truth of the sign. The curve remains dangerous regardless of whether you acknowledge the fact or not.

All three responses are illustrated in today's reading. Jeremiah *obeyed*, Judah *ignored*, and Jehoiakim *opposed* the Word of God. Each expected to "negotiate the curve." But two of the three ended up "on the rocks." This poses a painful question. If God's Word doesn't budge an inch, then what should your response be to such clear commands as these: "Be ye not unequally yoked. . . . Flee also youthful lusts. . . . Let not the sun go down upon your wrath" (2 Corinthians 6:14; 2 Timothy 2:22; Ephesians 4:26)? Pick one and respond to it . . . today!

Insight: Scripture in the Making

Chapter 36 is a glimpse into the process by which God's revelation to Jeremiah achieved written form. According to verse 4, what was revealed from God to Jeremiah was spoken by Jeremiah to Baruch, and written down by Baruch in the form of a scroll. The transfer of God's words from the prophet's mind to the finished scroll was accurate (v. 18), and once written down, the Lord stood by it as His revealed Word and will (vv. 29-32).

Calamity After Jerusalem's Fall
Jeremiah 40–45

11

Overview: Though God's people have marched into exile, God's Word continues to come through the mouth of His prophet. When Nebuchadnezzar establishes a puppet governor over the city of Jerusalem, Jeremiah chooses to remain in the city—and urges his countrymen to do the same. But after Gedaliah's brutal assassination, the surviving Jews disregard God's clear command and flee to Egypt for safety, taking the unwilling prophet with them. There Jeremiah predicts Egypt's destruction and Judah's discipline at the hands of Jehovah for knowing what to do—but refusing to do it.

Heart of the Passage: Jeremiah 42–43

Chapter 40	Chapter 41	Chapters 42–43	Chapters 44–45
Jeremiah's Release	Ishmael's Rebellion	Flight to Egypt	Forecast for Egypt
Safety	Slaughter	Disobedience	Disaster

Your Daily Walk: Think back over the last few years of your life: the joys, heartaches, traumas, and triumphs. If you knew back then what you know now, would you have been as eager to go through those years?

God is as wise in what He *conceals* as He is in what He *reveals* about the future. There is nothing that can sour your enjoyment of life *today* like a thorough knowledge of (and morbid preoccupation with) what life will bring *tomorrow*. That's one of the reasons why Jesus instructed His disciples, "Take therefore no thought for the morrow: for the morrow shall take thought for the things of itself. Sufficient unto the day is the evil thereof" (Matthew 6:34).

Jeremiah found divine strength to face ridicule, imprisonment, assassination, and even deportation—one day at a time. Look for and circle the words "Thus saith the LORD" every time you find them in chapters 40–45. Let that tenfold reminder encourage you that God has a word for you today and every day!

Worry is wasting today's time to clutter up tomorrow's opportunities with yesterday's troubles.

Insight: The Day Obelisks Became Obsolete (43:13)

Part of Jeremiah's prediction of Egypt's ruin at the hands of the Babylonians included the destruction of Egypt's places of worship. Beth-shemesh ("house of the sun") is the Hebrew name for ancient Heliopolis (modern-day Tell Husn), which is near Cairo. Re, the sun god, was worshiped there using images called "obelisks." One of the Heliopolis obelisks is now in Central Park in New York City.

12 The Fall of Jerusalem's Neighbors
Jeremiah 46–49

Heart of the Passage: Jeremiah 46

Overview: Like a majestic symphony building to a crescendo, Jeremiah closes his book with a mighty sweep of prophetic judgment. Moving from west to east, Jeremiah shows that the God of Israel rules in the affairs of people everywhere: from Egypt to Elam, Damascus to Edom. For their wicked idolatry and staunch refusal to acknowledge the one true God, Judah's neighbors would fall to enemy armies, showing that no nation is big enough to flaunt God's justice and get away with it.

Chapter 46	Chapter 47	Chapter 48	Chapter 49
The Fall of Jerusalem's Neighbors:			
Egypt	Philistia	Moab	Ammon and Edom
Shame	Sword	Salt	Sackcloth

Example is a language everybody can read.

Your Daily Walk: Chances are you have never visited Egypt. And it's for certain you will never travel to Philistia, Moab, Ammon, or Edom. (Why? Take a look at 47:4; 48:2; 49:2, 10. Then check a world map or globe.)

But you can still profit from their sad examples! Here is a sermon-in-a-sentence from three extinct nations. Which nation represents a problem you are currently wrestling with? Circle the name of the nation, along with its one-verse epitaph. You might even want to display the verse in a prominent place in your home or office. Let it remind you often that "Project Prevention" in the Christian life involves growing *wiser*, not merely *older*, in your relationship with God.

> **Moab:** *"Cursed be he that doeth the work of the LORD deceitfully [dishonestly]" (48:10).*
>
> **Ammon:** *"Wherefore gloriest thou in ... thy flowing valley ... that trusted in [thy] treasures?" (49:4).*
>
> **Edom:** *"Thy terribleness [prestige] hath deceived thee, and the pride of thine heart" (49:16).*

Have you learned a lesson they overlooked?

Insight: The Bottom Line
Question: What is the fundamental reason why Egypt, Philistia, Moab, Ammon, Edom, Damascus, Kedar, Hazor, Elam, Babylon, Israel, Judah, and many other nations in world history were destroyed? *Answer:* Because they magnified themselves against the Lord (48:42).

The Fall of Babylon and Jerusalem
Jeremiah 50–52

13

📖 **Overview:** Babylon, the last and greatest enemy of Judah, will suffer the same fate as the rest of Judah's ungodly neighbors. "And Chaldea shall be a spoil. . . . It shall be wholly desolate: every one that goeth by Babylon shall be astonished, and hiss at all her plagues" (50:10, 13). But Jeremiah concludes his prophetic masterpiece with a note of hope. Though Jerusalem has fallen as predicted, her king, Jehoiachin, is shown unexpected kindness in Babylon. In the restoration of this covenant-breaking king, Jeremiah pictures the future restoration of covenant-breaking Judah by her covenant-keeping God.

Heart of the Passage: Jeremiah 52

Chapter 50	Chapter 51	Chapter 52
Dirge of Babylon	Daughter of Babylon	Downfall of Jerusalem
Judah's Foe		Judah's Fall

🔖 **Your Daily Walk:** The tragic words of chapter 52 sound the death knell for God's people. Surely their end has come; the nation is finished; the curtain has closed on the checkered history of Judah. After all, only a handful survive the holocaust.

But suddenly, like a lighted match in a blackened room, the reader sees a flicker of hope. Jehoichin—wicked, corrupt, but the all-important link in God's promise of a perpetual dynasty for David—becomes the beneficiary of a "government pension" in Persia (52:31-34). God is not dead; Judah is not doomed; God's promises live on! And those promises become the faith-sustaining influence in the lives of two young deportees: Daniel and Ezekiel.

Time cannot erase the promises of God; circumstances cannot dim them; wicked kings cannot destroy them. But *you* can effectively nullify them if you don't claim them! A good promise to begin with would be Hebrews 13:5. And a good time to begin would be right now.

More people would learn from their mistakes if they weren't so busy denying them.

✏️ **Insight:** A Chill Wind Out of the North (50:9)
In 539 B.C. Babylon fell to Cyrus the Persian without a fight. But Cyrus did not destroy the city. Later, the city revolted and Darius Hystaspis captured it and destroyed its walls. From that time the city decayed and declined until, by the 3rd century B.C., it was little more than a desert. Not until the 19th century A.D., however, would archaeologists finally uncover its desolate ruins!

Lamentations

I t was final—God's warning had come
through the prophet Jeremiah, but the
people of Judah had refused to listen. In
586 B.C. as the Babylonian army attacked,
judgment was poured out on the city and
the people were carried into exile. Jerusalem
lay ruined and empty. For days Jeremiah
lamented over the city and its future. As
he cries out in the darkness of destruction,
Jeremiah is given a spark of hope. God
promises forgiveness and grace. The period of
judgment is limited, and in His mercy God
will restore the city and return the captives.

Focus	God's Chastening and Control				God's Character
Divisions	Destroyed City	Crushed Population	Lamenting Prophet	Lost Glory	Repentant Kingdom
	1:1　　1:22	2:1　　2:22	3:1　　3:66	4:1　　4:22	5:1　　5:22
Topics	The Sorrow	The Reason	The Hope	The Contrast	The Plea
Place	Jerusalem				
Time	Approximately 586 B.C.				

Weeping over a Wasteland **14**
Lamentations 1–5

Overview: In Lamentations the prophet Jeremiah turns to poetry to express his deepest feelings and emotions over the tragic fall of Jerusalem. The book consists of five exquisitely written poems, the first four in acrostic or alphabetic fashion. Each verse begins with a successive letter of the Hebrew alphabet, with the exception of chapter 3, where three verses are given to each letter. The prophet begins by weeping over Jerusalem in the midst of her desolation and destruction. But through his tears, Jeremiah turns his heart to view the sovereign God behind it all. As he considers God's control of human affairs, Jeremiah is able to shout victoriously, "Great is thy faithfulness" (3:23). After a final rehearsal of Jerusalem's siege, the prophet intercedes for the restoration of the nation after its punishment is complete.

Heart of the Passage: Lamentations 3

Chapters 1–2	Chapter 3	Chapter 4	Chapter 5
Jerusalem's Desolation	Jeremiah's Deliberation	Jerusalem's Defeat	Jeremiah's Desire
God's Chastening and Control			God's Character

Your Daily Walk: Congratulations! You have just completed one of the longest and least-read sections of Scripture— Jeremiah and its sequel Lamentations. Though often passed over, these portions contain some crucial principles for living. Take a moment to think through the material you have covered the past two weeks. What are some of the lessons you have learned from "the weeping prophet"? Here are some suggestions to help you get started:

1. God's judgment is sure, though not always immediate.
2. God doesn't promise freedom from difficulties, but He does promise strength to go through them.
3. God stands by His promises regardless of what people may do.

Pity weeps and runs away; compassion comes to help and stay.

Now it's your turn. Call up someone who is also reading through the Bible this year and share a principle from your study of Jeremiah's writings. Or if you know someone who needs encouragement, drop them a note and share your "gem"!

Insight: Poems That Cry
In addition to being in acrostic form, Lamentations chapters 1–4 were composed using the so-called limping meter—a cadence reserved for funeral dirges. How appropriate for Jerusalem and the weeping prophet, Jeremiah!

Ezekiel

B orn a priest, Ezekiel ministers as a
prophet during the last days of the
decline and fall of Judah. While Jeremiah
remains in Jerusalm, Ezekiel preaches to
the exiles in Babylon. Similar to Jeremiah
in pronouncing God's severe judgment on
the faithless nation, Ezekiel also adds a
blessed note of hope—God's promise of a
restored nation in the future. Emphasizing
the glory of the sovereign God, Ezekiel
portrays God's purpose through both
judgment and blessing "that all might
know that I am the LORD."

Focus	Judah's Fall				Judah's Foes		Judah's Future	
Divisions	Vision and Call	Signs and Sermons	Departing Glory	Parables of Judgment	Judgment on Enemies	Judgment on Egypt	New Life for Israel	New Temple for Israel
	1 3	4 6	7 11	12 24	25 28	29 32	33 39	40 48
Topics	Before the Siege (592–587 B.C.)				During the Siege (586)		After the Siege (586–570)	
	Condemnation					Consolation		
Place	Babylon							
Time	About 22 Years (592–570 B.C.)							

Signs and Sermons / Ezekiel 1–6

15

📖 **Overview:** While Jeremiah is preaching about the judgment of God on Judah and awaiting the final fall of Jerusalem, his contemporary Ezekiel is 600 miles away in Babylon interpreting God's judgment to those Jews already in captivity. Though Ezekiel's preaching is similar to Jeremiah's—proclaiming doom for the disobedient—it also contains large doses of hope and instruction. The 70-year exile will teach God's people "that I am the LORD" (a phrase repeated more than 50 times in the book), thus preparing them for their day of restoration.

Heart of the Passage: Ezekiel 1

Chapter 1	Chapter 2	Chapter 3	Chapter 4	Chapter 5	Chapter 6
Wheels in Wheels	Call and a Scroll	Watchman on the Wall	Brick and Bread	Shave and a Haircut	Saved and Scattered
Ezekiel's Preparation			Jerusalem's Condemnation		

👣 **Your Daily Walk:** Have you ever been a long way from home and—just when you needed it most—received a letter or a phone call from the folks back home? Do you remember how great it felt to hear familiar voices or to read about familiar people while you were in unfamiliar surroundings? That "close-to-home" feeling is life's best remedy for loneliness!

Loneliness is more than a circumstance; more self-inflicted than outwardly caused.

Ezekiel's book opens with the well-known "wheel-within-a-wheel" vision—a vision filled with significance for captives far from their beloved Jerusalem and accustomed to thinking of God as residing in the temple "back home." In his vision Ezekiel sees God sitting upon a throne with wheels—a mobile seat of glory and splendor capable of transporting God anywhere He desires . . . even to the heart of a heathen land. Thus, God offers "close-to-home" comfort for His people who are far away in their new surroundings in Babylon.

It's one thing to be miles from home physically; it's another to be far from home spiritually. Like the prodigal son of Luke 15, you may feel lonely, anxious, estranged—in a "spiritual exile" brought about by disobedience or neglect. If that's the case, why not "call home" right now? Your Father's line is never busy and He is waiting with open arms.

🛠 **Insight:** Before You Serve Him, Be Sure You See Him
Ezekiel's vision of God's glory uniquely prepared the prophet for his difficult assignment. Can you discover three other servants of God who experienced similar periods of long and intense preparation? (Hint: Check Exodus 3:1-10; Isaiah 6:1-10; Daniel 10:5-14.)

263

16 *The God Who Will Be Known*

*Scripture
Reading:
1 Corin-
thians
13:12*

 Step Back

Ezekiel opens with one of the more intriguing and exciting passages of Scripture: a vision of God that began with a storm and living creatures, followed by astounding wheels and finally the glory of God Himself in the form of brilliant light.

Remarkably, after centuries of being associated exclusively with the temple in Jerusalem, now God's glory was appearing to the exiled people in Babylon. Toward the end of his book, Ezekiel would see the restoration of God's glory to Jerusalem.

Ezekiel's visions—and his book as a whole—reveal a God who desires to be known by His people. In this single book, the clause "Then they will know that I am the LORD" appears 65 times—clearly demonstrating God's intention.

In the first 24 chapters, God is known through the fall of Jerusalem and in the temple's destruction. In chapters 25–34, God is known through His judgments on the nations. And in chapters 35–48, God is known through the restoration and renewal of His nation Israel.

God reveals Himself and every aspect of His character because He desires to be known. And He is thereby acknowledged to be God indeed.

 **Look Up**

*Study the
Bible to
be wise,
believe it
to be safe,
practice
it to be
holy.*

"For now we see through a glass, darkly; but then face to face: now I know in part; but then shall I know even as I am known" (1 Corinthians 13:12).

In the imperfect polished metal mirrors of Paul's day, one could see only a fuzzy reflection. The apostle notes that, in contrast to seeing God clearly in heaven, we can see Him only indirectly while we are on earth.

But the promise remains that someday, we will know the Lord as fully as a finite human can know an infinite Being. As you talk with Him in prayer today, thank Him for this glorious promise.

Move Ahead

How can you know God now? Primarily through His Word. By studying it individually and with fellow believers, you can come to understand who He is, how He works, what He wills.

Are you involved in a regular Bible study? Ask your pastor to recommend some Bible study resources. And if you're not already involved in an ongoing Bible study group, why not invite two or three friends to join you in the great adventure of getting to know God better? It's a glorious foretaste of the perfect knowledge you will have of Him in heaven.

Departing Glory / Ezekiel 7–11

17

Overview: In a colorful series of visions, Ezekiel next foresees the *what, why,* and *how* of God's judgment upon Judah. The *what:* total destruction of Jerusalem and the departure of God's glory from the temple. The *why:* generations of idolatry, wickedness, and spiritual indifference. The *how:* through the cruel Babylonians, God's handpicked agents of judgment. But the harshness of the sentence is tempered by a tender reminder: A remnant will survive, receive sanctuary in a foreign country, and return again to the Land of Promise.

Heart of the Passage: Ezekiel 7, 11

Chapter 7	Chapter 8	Chapter 9	Chapter 10	Chapter 11
Sentence Passed	Crimes Restated	Executioners Loosed	Judge Departed	Remnant Spared
"The end is come: it watcheth for thee" (7:6).				

Your Daily Walk: Even the world's finest mountain climber ascends the tallest precipice by the smallest of increments: step by step, yard by yard. Progress from bottom to top may appear gradual and slow. The climber may not even notice he is making headway. But the thrill of the climb comes when—standing at the top—he turns around and discovers how far he has ascended one step at a time.

Sin may open bright as the morning, but it will end dark as night.

Judah had ascended no mountain. In fact, the nation had been *descending* for generations. But their descent had been slow and gradual: one sin, one wicked king following another. The downward movement continued until the nation hit bottom, and the view wasn't pretty.

God's Word is described in James 1:23-24 as a mirror, reflecting a person's true spiritual condition. As you look into God's Word today, what do you see: a person like Paul, who made it his ambition to "press toward the mark [the summit] . . . of the high calling of God in Christ Jesus" (Philippians 3:14)? Or a person who is sliding downward by gradual increments of unrepented sin and sloppy spiritual habits? Find a hill near your home where you can take a vigorous walk—and have a vigorous talk with God about the direction of your life. It can make a mountain of difference!

Insight: Ezekiel's Hair-raising Revelation
In the temple vision of chapter 8, God's messenger grabs Ezekiel by a lock of his hair to transport him to the scene—a painful but effective way of ensuring that Ezekiel doesn't miss the point!

18 The Prophet's Preaching

Scripture Reading: Psalm 139

◀ Step Back

Ezekiel, "The Prophet of Visions," opens his book with this declaration: "The heavens were opened, and I saw visions of God."

A vision in prophetical terms was a visual revelation experienced by a man of God. Through visions, God revealed truths through pictures and words. Ezekiel's visions include the Vision of God (1:4-28); the Vision of the Roll (2:9–3:3); the Vision on the Plain (3:22-23); four Visions of Jerusalem (8:1-18; 9:1-11; 10:1-22; 11:1-25); the Vision of Dry Bones (37:1-10); and the Visions of the Apocalypse (40:1–48:35).

But while visions play a major role in Ezekiel's prophecy, he also uses other forms to reveal God's truth to the people of Judah.

Using *symbolic actions,* Ezekiel performed in such a way as to communicate a vivid truth—often to the scorn and contempt of his audience. These include drawing the city on a clay tablet, teaching of Jerusalem's imminent fall (4:1-3); lying down, picturing the discomforts of captivity (4:4-8); shaving his hair off then burning it, striking it with a sword, and scattering it, thus picturing the utter destruction of Jerusalem (5:1-17), and others.

Using *allegories,* Ezekiel told stories much like John Bunyan did in *Pilgrim's Progress.* His stories—mostly relating to Jerusalem's fall—include the vine (15:1-8); the faithless wife (16:1-63); the two women (23:1-49); and the boiling cauldron (24:1-14).

Using *apocalyptic language and images,* Ezekiel revealed much about the end times, in passages such as 6:1-14; 7:5-12; 20:33-44; 39:1-29; and 47:1-12.

Using *poems,* Ezekiel lamented the coming destruction in 19:1-14 and 27:1-36.

▲ Look Up

Pause right now to thank God that He is a God who communicates creatively, earnestly, and fully with His people, that they might know His will. Ask yourself if perhaps He is trying to send you a message toward which you've been hard-hearted.

How rare it is to find a person quiet enough to hear God speak.

Move Ahead

Each of the Old Testament prophets had a distinct personality that God used. For instance, Jeremiah tended to be strong and harsh in his denunciation, whereas Ezekiel was more consoling.

Are you enabling God to use your personality—whether strong and dynamic, humble and quiet, or something in between—to communicate His Word to others? God created you—and desires to use you—as a special instrument of His will. As you read Psalm 139, resolve to let Him do just that today.

Parables of Judgment / Ezekiel 12–15   19

Overview: Like Jeremiah before him, Ezekiel illustrates his messages with dramatized parables. In today's reading, Ezekiel "packs his bags" and exits the city through a hole dug in the wall to symbolize Judah's upcoming exile. He then attacks the sins that have led Judah to this sorry end: prophets who have whitewashed wrongs instead of preaching repentance, and elders who have led the nation into idolatry. Like a dried-up grapevine, Judah has become fruitless, fit only for judgment.

Heart of the Passage: Ezekiel 14

Chapter 12	Chapter 13	Chapter 14	Chapter 15
Baggage for Exiles	Prophets for Hire	Wayward Elders	Worthless Wood
Future Pain . . .	. . . for the Sins in the Past and Present		

Your Daily Walk: Remember the last time a prayer of yours went unanswered?

Why do you think that happened? (a) You didn't ask for the right thing. (b) You didn't ask often enough. (c) God didn't care about your problem. (d) You were too far away from God to hear His answer. (e) You need to wait a little longer.

Chapter 14 sheds some light on the question of unanswered prayer. The idolatrous elders of Israel sent representatives to Ezekiel to make inquiry of the Lord through the prophet. Though the exact nature of their request is not stated, God's response is enlightening: He wouldn't honor their request because they weren't honoring Him.

God will only answer when you come close enough to hear.

An idol in your life need not be a statue of stone or wood. It can be anything (or anyone) that steals your heart, causing you to become more committed to something or someone than you are to God. And unanswered prayers are sure to follow, for God speaks in a still, small voice that is difficult to hear at a distance (1 Kings 19:11-12). Cut out the margin quote as a reminder that if your prayer life is in "neutral," perhaps it's because your heart is "idoling." Fill your heart instead with the kind of faith described in Ezekiel 11:19-20.

Insight: Here a Sign, There a Sign, Everywhere a Sign
Throughout the book of Ezekiel you will find 10 dramatic actions that Ezekiel used to heighten the impact of his message. Today's section contains two such signs, both found in chapter 12. The others are located in chapters 4–5, 21, 24, and 37. Refer back to yesterday's reading for more information.

20 *More Parables of Judgment*
Ezekiel 16–19

Heart of the Passage: Ezekiel 18

Overview: Continuing his analysis of Judah's sins in strongly worded and vividly illustrated sermons, Ezekiel portrays the nation as the Lord's unfaithful wife who has wantonly gone after other gods. This spiritual adultery has led to unwise political alliances (the eagles of chapter 17), which can only end in disaster (the caged lions of chapter 19). But amid the imagery of doom and destruction, the prophet portrays a "twig of hope": The worthless dead vine will be replaced by a productive cedar of future righteousness, and God's people will be restored to proper relationship with Him!

Chapter 16	Chapter 17	Chapter 18	Chapter 19
Too Lewd to Pardon	Two Ominous Eagles	Two Fathers Two Sons	Two Lions in Cages
Bad Wife	Bad Politics	Bad Proverb	Bad News

We are morally responsible to God because we are made in the image of a moral Deity.

Your Daily Walk: Fill in the blank: "The person(s) most responsible for my mistakes and failures in life is/are

_____."

Did you write *my parents? my peer group? my teachers? God? the Devil? Dr. Spock?* According to the Bible, the only correct answer is the pronoun *myself.* You are responsible for your choices and actions, whether right or wrong.

Consider the testimony of chapter 18. "The soul that sinneth, it shall die" (18:4, 20). "The son shall not bear the iniquity of the father, neither shall the father bear the iniquity of the son" (18:20). "If the wicked will turn from all his sins that he hath committed . . . he shall surely live, he shall not die" (18:21). "I have no pleasure in the death of him that dieth, saith the Lord God: wherefore turn yourselves, and live ye" (18:32).

Write the word *ME* in large letters on a 3 x 5 card, and use it as a bookmark as you read the rest of Ezekiel. That way you won't forget who's responsible for your actions—and also who's loved and forgiven by God!

Insight: Who's Who Here?

To help you unravel the puzzle of chapter 17, use this guide: "great eagle" (v. 3) = Nebuchadnezzar; "highest branch of the cedar" (v. 3) = house of David; "the top of his young twigs" (v. 4) = Jehoiachin; "land of traffic" (v. 4) = Babylonia; "seed of the land" (v. 5) = Zedekiah; "another great eagle" (v. 7) = king of Egypt.

Pictures of Sin / Ezekiel 20–23

Overview: Turning from the present state of wayward Judah, Ezekiel now examines her past and catalogs her history of sinfulness. No commandment has been left unbroken: idol worship, dishonor of parents, extortion, mistreatment of widows and orphans, profaning the Sabbath, uncleanness, adultery, incest, dishonest business dealings, even child sacrifice (22:4-12; 23:37-39). Through it all, God has patiently held back His anger. But no more: "I . . . have drawn forth my sword," God declares, "[and] it shall not return any more" (21:5).

Heart of the Passage: Ezekiel 21:1-17

Chapter 20	Chapter 21	Chapter 22	Chapter 23
A Legacy of Sin	The Wages of Sin	A Summary of Sin	Two Sisters of Sin
Swords		Smelter	Sorrow

Your Daily Walk: If you've ever stepped on a bee while barefooted, you learned two things very quickly: (1) bees take a dim view of being stepped on; and (2) bees have an effective way of making that known.

Pain can be a wonderful teacher. It's just a pity that while we quickly learn to avoid bees, we tend to learn more slowly regarding sin. Yet the truths of the Bible, the testimony of the prophets, the teachings of Christ—all point to the same time-proven principle: *Sin hurts.* Yet how often we tend to repeat even the sins which cause us—or those we love—damage.

Looking back over the sinful history of Judah in today's passage, is it any wonder that God's patience at last ran out toward people who simply wouldn't learn, people who continually hurt themselves and damaged each other by indulging in the same sinful ways?

How many times so far this year have you been stung by the same sin? Perhaps it's a bad habit you can't seem to break, or an unhealthy attitude you haven't dealt with, or a strained relationship you have yet to mend. In your prayer time today, single out one such "bee" to avoid, and ask God to guide your footsteps.

The other person's sins, like the other car's head-lights, always seem more glaring than our own.

Insight: The Plans Are Man's, the Odds Are God's
Reread 21:18-23, and see if you notice anything unusual. On the average you can expect to predict correctly the toss of a coin 50% of the time. But God predetermined the casting of lots to perfection so that Nebuchadnezzar did precisely what God wanted!

22 *Judgment on Enemies / Ezekiel 24–28*

Heart of the Passage: Ezekiel 28:1-19

Overview: Even *personal tragedy* can become an opportunity for *prophetic testimony*. When Ezekiel's wife dies, God does not permit the prophet to exhibit any public display of mourning, which pictures the inexpressible grief soon to befall Judah. Next the prophet turns the verbal missiles of God's judgment upon Judah's neighbors, showing that no nation is exempt from God's discipline. Ammon, Moab, Edom, Philistia, Tyre—each will be powerless to escape the edge of His unsheathed sword.

Chapter 24	Chapter 25		Chapters 26–28
Death in the Family	Death in the Nations:		
	Ammon, Moab, Edom, Philistia		Tyre
At Home	East and West		North

Those who think too much of themselves don't think enough.

Your Daily Walk: Pride is not necessarily a bad thing. A certain amount of pride in God-given ability and talent is a needed component of the self-esteem and confidence needed for balanced mental health.

But pride can become the most serious of spiritual sins. Without the tempering influence of large doses of humility, pride tends to become arrogance, boastfulness, conceit, selfishness—a whole host of damaging traits abhorrent to God (and obnoxious to everyone else!). As the writer of Proverbs 16:5 points out, "Everyone that is proud in heart is an abomination to the LORD: . . . he shall not be unpunished." God's throne has only enough room for one!

"Self" sat on the throne in Tyre. And as a result, that entire nation earned the destruction of a wrathful God (28:17; 26:7-14). As you ponder its fate today, check the interior of your heart's "throne room."

Who's sitting there right now?

Insight: The High Price of Proud Living

According to Proverbs 6:16, "These six things doth the LORD hate: yea, seven are an abomination unto him." And heading the list is pride. To underscore the seriousness of a haughty heart, look up the biblical "epitaph" of these four men. What caused the downfall of . . .

. . . Ahithophel (2 Samuel 17:23)? _____

. . . Haman (Esther 3:5; 7:9)? _____

. . . Nebuchadnezzar (Daniel 4:30-33)? _____

. . . Herod (Acts 12:21-23)? _____

Judgment on Egypt / Ezekiel 29–32 **23**

Overview: As Ezekiel moves through the four points of the compass, he focuses at last on Egypt, the longtime enemy of God's people. In contrast to so many of Judah's neighbors, Egypt would not be totally destroyed, but would be reduced to a place of insignificance. Captivity would come and the glory of Pharaoh would fade. But God would not be finished with the people of Egypt. After scattering them, He would raise them up again, "and they shall know that I am the LORD" (30:26).

Heart of the Passage: Ezekiel 30–31

Chapter 29	Chapter 30	Chapter 31	Chapter 32
Captivity of Egypt	Calamity in Egypt	Pharaoh's Glory	Pharaoh's Groaning
Judgment on Egypt		Judgment on Egypt's Pharaoh	

Your Daily Walk: While today's reading may not do much to enhance your love for the book of Ezekiel, there is at least one persistent lesson which it teaches: *As the leadership of a nation goes, so goes the nation.* Fully half of Ezekiel's woe upon Egypt is directed not at the nation, but at the nation's leadership. Pharaoh's pride and false confidence in his army lead to the desolation of the once mighty Egypt.

As the leadership of a nation goes, so goes the nation.

That should alert you to the importance of the leadership in your own country, community, and church. Each election is an opportunity for you to exercise your God-given right to choose those of proven character who will guide you into God-honoring paths.

Take a few minutes today to write a short note of encouragement to a civic leader, church officer, or congressman. Assure them of your prayers and support as they struggle with the difficult issues before them. You might even want to share with them the principle you learned today from Ezekiel 29–32: As go the leaders, so go the people.

Insight: Charting the Future of Egypt

Vision	Begins	Date (B.C.)	Prophecy
1	29:1	January 586	Forty years of desolation (29:12)
2	29:17	April 570	No prince in Egypt (30:13)
3	30:20	April 586	Broken military strength (30:22)
4	31:1	June 586	No help from Assyria (31:3, 10-16)
5	32:1	March 584	Defeat by Babylon (32:11-12)
6	32:17	March 584	Death by the sword (32:20-21)

24 *New Life for Israel / Ezekiel 33–36*

Overview: Ezekiel's emphasis shifts from the failures of Judah's past to the promises of Judah's future. Jerusalem has fallen, and the prophet's tongue—silenced for three years—is loosened at last to declare that a new Shepherd is coming. As a Leader to the leaderless, He will tenderly care for the flock of Israel, rescue His people from their scattered homes of exile, and restore them to their covenant land.

Heart of the Passage: Ezekiel 33

Chapter 33	Chapter 34	Chapter 35	Chapter 36
A New Watchman	A New Shepherd	An Old Enemy	A New Flock
Ezekiel	David	Edom	Israel

Your Daily Walk: Imagine that you are a watchman assigned the "night shift" on the walls of Jerusalem, entrusted with protecting the inhabitants sleeping peacefully beneath you. Suddenly, you see the torches of an approaching army! You reach for your ram's horn to sound the alarm when a number of disturbing thoughts interrupt your motion:

A wise person will make more opportunities than he finds.

"I might be mistaken. . . . My friends might get mad if I wake them up. . . . I'm really not that good on the trumpet anyway . . . ." As doubts fill your mind, precious moments slip away . . . *until the enemy attacks the slumbering city—and it is eternally too late!*

Unthinkable? Then imagine this: During a conversation with an unsaved co-worker, you let numerous witnessing opportunities slip by because you're worried about how the words will sound. Or you allow an undisciplined son to go his rebellious way because you don't want to make him mad. Or you fail to admonish a Christian friend because you fear being misunderstood. In each case, you lifted the Lord's horn to your lips—but failed to blow!

Read again God's instructions to the watchman Ezekiel (33:7-9) and compare it to Paul's admonition in Galatians 6:10. Then make a list of the opportunities you might have this week to sound God's alarm to a sleeping world in grave danger.

Insight: Edom—A Blessing in Passing

You might wonder why the destruction of Edom (chapter 35) is included in today's passage. After all, Edom was included in the "Diary of Destruction" in chapters 25–32. The answer is that the demise of Edom is part of the future blessing of Judah, which is the major theme of chapters 33–36 (compare Lamentations 4:21-22).

Revived Bones / Ezekiel 37–39

25

 Overview: In a vision retold with such vivid detail that you can almost see the bones moving and can hear them rattling, Ezekiel announces Israel's future rebirth. Reassembled from afar and revived with God's own breath of life, the sun-bleached bones become a new Israel, more glorious and powerful than ever before. Then in a second vision, Ezekiel sees the revived nation utterly destroy its last foe—the mysterious and unidentified Magog—after which God is acknowledged by all nations as the mighty conqueror and undisputed Victor.

Heart of the Passage: Ezekiel 39:25-29

Chapter 37	Chapters 38–39
The Valley of Dry Bones	The Valley of Hamon Gog
Question	Answer

Your Daily Walk: Throughout the biblical account of the nation Israel, there is a remarkable ebb and flow to her success in world affairs.

When the people stray far from God, they suffer defeat in battle and ultimately are removed from their homeland. But when they cling to God and rely on Him alone, they are invincible: The valleys of their land are filled with the bones of their foes. Thus, the nation's success for God is linked to its dependence upon God.

Look back over the months or years of your own walk with God—the ups and downs, the highs and lows. Do you see the same principle in operation? *Closeness to God produces strength and victory; distance from God produces weakness and defeat.* Take time today to copy down the first verse of Psalm 46 and post it near your telephone. Then the next time someone calls to tell you about a struggle, share with that person your "very present" source of strength!

God wants us to be victors, not victims; to grow, not grovel; to soar, not sink; to overcome, not to be over- whelmed.

Insight: What's Going On Here?

By the time of the apostle John, the mysterious battle between Gog and God had become a byword for the cataclysmic final struggle of the end times. In Ezekiel, Gog is the prince of Meshech and Tubal, from the northlands of Magog. In Revelation, Magog is no longer pictured as a country, but a fellow culprit with Gog in the battle of Armageddon (Revelation 20:8). Beneath these two word pictures is a concrete truth: *When push comes to shove, evil is no match for the absolute power of God!*

26 *New Temple for Israel / Ezekiel 40–43*

Overview: Today's passage may contain some of the least inspirational reading in the entire Old Testament! And yet to the exiles in Babylon it must have been one of the most thrilling of all Ezekiel's visions. For in it, the prophet is given a preview of the new temple, built upon the site of the old one destroyed 14 years earlier. Ezekiel's "blueprint" of the temple includes exact—and at times tedious—measurements of the walls, gates, chambers, porches, posts, arches, and furnishings. But in the midst of all the cubits and courtyards, Ezekiel sees the glory of the Lord (absent from the temple since 11:23) returning to the new Holy of Holies where God intends to "dwell in the midst of the children of Israel forever" (43:7).

Heart of the Passage: Ezekiel 40:1-4; 43:1-5

Chapters 40–42	Chapter 43
Template for a New Temple	Residence for a Returning Lord
Cubits and Courtyards	Ordinances and Glory

Your Daily Walk: Fill in the following chart with your "vital statistics":

Height _____   Shoe size _____
Weight _____   Glove size _____
Waist _____   Coat size _____
Chest _____   Hat size _____

Now, what does your chart have in common with Ezekiel's vision in chapters 40–42?

Perhaps these words of Paul will give you a hint: "Know ye not that ye are the temple of God, and that the Spirit of God dwelleth in you?" (1 Corinthians 3:16). Both your chart and Ezekiel's chapters contain measurements of God's temple!

Your body, indeed your whole life, God claims as His temple. Knowing that, is there an area of your life that, like the ruined temple of Ezekiel's day, is in need of refurbishing? Enlist the aid of your spouse or friends in selecting an overdue self-improvement project that will help you "glorify God in your body, and in your spirit, which are God's" (1 Corinthians 6:20). He deserves it!

As the soul does not live idly in the body, so the Spirit of God cannot dwell in us without manifesting Himself by outward effects.

Insight: The True Measure of a Man (or Woman)

A cubit was the length of the forearm from the elbow to the tip of the middle finger—about 18 inches. How does your cubit compare?

Revived Worship / Ezekiel 44–48

27

📖 **Overview:** Ezekiel closes his mighty prophecy with the conclusion of the temple vision. In it he outlines new orders for worship, including procedures for priests, sacrifices, offerings, and feasts—much the same as worship in the glory days of Israel's religious past. Finally, Ezekiel describes the boundaries of the renewed nation, with divisions for tribes, priests, princes, and the people of Jerusalem. As a reminder of all that has taken place, the new city will be triumphantly named, "The LORD is there" (48:35).

Heart of the Passage: Ezekiel 44:4-7

Chapter 44	Chapter 45	Chapter 46	Chapter 47	Chapter 48
Priestly Orders for . . .			Population Orders for . . .	
Service	Supply	Sacrifice	The Nation	The Tribes
Reorganizing Worship			Rezoning the Land	

🔖 **Your Daily Walk:** To the exiled and homesick Jews, it must have been both comforting and convicting to hear Ezekiel talk about the new temple.

How the people must have loved to hear the details of the new worship they would enjoy in their restored homeland. And how they must have wept in shame and remorse at the thought of all they had forfeited through idolatry and indifference. Though they had given up on God, God had not given up on them. His attention to details shows His deep interest in the daily affairs of His chosen people.

God is powerful enough to move nations and direct world events—but He is also interested in where His people eat (44:3), what they wear (44:17-19), and whom they marry (44:22)! Indeed, your God is a God of detail—a God of *your* details. Take one of your hurts or disappointments and leave it with Him right now. He cares!

He who lives a life of love and charity is constantly at worship.

🗝 **Insight:** Metropolitan Jerusalem in Ezekiel's Vision (45:1-8)

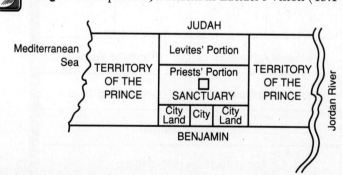

Daniel

Daniel presents a majestic sweep of prophetic history. World powers come and go, but God will establish His people forever. Nowhere is this theme more apparent than in the life of Daniel, a young Jew transplanted to Babylonia. His adventures in the palace and the lions' den show that even in exile God has not forgotten His chosen people. Daniel's dreams and interpretations of others' dreams convince Jew and Gentile alike that wisdom and power belong to God alone. God is in control, not only of the present, but of the future as well!

Focus	Nebuchadnezzar's Dreams		Daniel's Dreams	
Divisions	Nebuchadnezzar's Dream of the Statue	Daniel's Faith in the Lions' Den	Daniel's Vision of the Beasts	Daniel's Vision of the Man
	1 3	4 6	7 9	10 12
Topics	Personal Adventure		Prophetic Visions	
	Concerning Gentiles		Concerning Jews	
Place	Babylonia/Persia			
Time	About 70 Years (605–536 B.C.)			

Dream of the Statue / Daniel 1–3 *28*

Overview: Daniel, Ezekiel's contemporary during the period of Judah's exile in Babylonia, prophesies concerning the role of Gentile powers in God's program for His people. The first three chapters of the book describe the spiritual integrity of Daniel and his three friends. Selected for government service, they resist the pressure to conform to their pagan environment and instead take a clear-cut stand for the God of Israel. Whether in matters of diet, truthfulness, or spiritual discipline, the four young men live out their convictions—even at the risk of their lives.

Heart of the Passage: Daniel 1

Chapter 1	Chapter 2	Chapter 3
Dedication of Daniel	Dream of Nebuchadnezzar	Deliverance of Daniel's Friends
Desirable Diet	Splendid Statue	Fiery Furnace

Your Daily Walk: Some people are so indecisive, their favorite color is plaid! You ask them if they have trouble making decisions, and their response is, "Well, yes and no." Do you know someone like that?

Daniel and his friends would definitely not fit that category. Their commitments were crystal clear. Once they had "purposed in [their] hearts" to do something, they did it—fearlessly.

Not only did they make *decisive* decisions, they also made *discerning* decisions. When faced with a three-year "bachelor of Babylonia" training program, they accepted their new Babylonian names, but rejected their new (and highly attractive) diet. Why? Because it was the only part of the training program contrary to the law of God.

Divide a sheet of paper in half, labeling the left side "Things about my culture I can accept" and the right "Things about my culture I must reject." Then take a discerning look at the things your culture encourages. Like Daniel and his friends, dare to stand alone in matters where your convictions and culture clash.

It is better to die for a conviction than to live with a compromise.

Insight: What's in a (Babylonian) Name?
Hebrew Name . . . Changed to . . . Babylonian Name

Daniel ("God's Prince")	Belteshazzar ("Bel's Prince")
Hananiah ("Mercy of Jehovah")	Shadrach ("Command of Aku")
Mishael ("Who Is What God Is?")	Meshach ("Who Is What Aku Is?")
Azariah ("Jehovah Helps")	Abed-nego ("Servant of Nebo")

29 Daniel's Faith in the Lions' Den
Daniel 4–6

Overview: Perhaps when you think of Daniel, you think of a young man. But the book of Daniel covers at least 70 years in the life of this colorful prophet of God. Before beginning your reading today, note in the margin of your Bible that, according to the best estimates, Daniel was 76 years old in chapter 4 . . . 86 years old in chapter 5 . . . and an energetic 93 years old in chapter 6! Throughout his days, Daniel's faith shines brightly, whether interpreting a king's dream, reading the "handwriting on the wall," or taking a stand for his God.

Heart of the Passage: Daniel 6

Chapter 4	Chapter 5	Chapter 6
Nebuchadnezzar in the Pasture	Belshazzar in the Balance	Daniel in the Den of Lions
Downfall of the King	Downfall of the Kingdom	Downfall of a Plot

Your Daily Walk: Who is the most powerful human ruler in the world today? (Write your answer in the margin.) Can you think of three things that person is powerless to do, in spite of his or her power?

Faith is the daring of the soul to go farther than it can see.

Each of the three rulers you encounter in today's reading felt the hand of God in his life. For Belshazzar, it meant the end of his kingdom; for Darius and Nebuchadnezzar, the end of their self-worship as God's equals. When confronted by Daniel's God, all three quickly learned how puny they were by comparison.

There is perhaps no more potent power on earth than a Christian in the midst of a crisis. Both Nebuchadnezzar (4:37) and Darius (6:25-27) gave public praise to Daniel's God when they saw Daniel's stability in the midst of adversity. Do you want to bring honor to God like that too? The key is your reaction to situations where it's tough to be a Christian! The promotion you deserved (but didn't get), the speeding ticket you got (but didn't deserve), the time you did what was right (but it turned out all wrong)—those are the occasions when your faith is in the "fishbowl." Complete this sentence: "If God is to be praised in the midst of my problem, I need to respond (how?)—and with God's help, I will!"

Insight: How the Handwriting on the Wall May Have Looked

מנא מנא תקל ופרסין

The Prophet's Prayer Life

30

← Step Back

Daniel is one of the few individuals in Scripture about whom nothing negative is ever written. How did he live a life of such conviction and courage? What was the secret that enabled him to please and glorify God so consistently?

A number of answers could be given, but consider this. Time and again, Daniel is revealed to be a man who prayed faithfully. You'll find his key prayers in 2:17-23; 6:10-11; and 9:1-3.

No matter what circumstances he faced—and he faced some very treacherous ones—no matter how busy his schedule was, he found time to commune with God through prayer. As a matter of fact, the awesome revelations of chapters 10–12 were given to Daniel by God as a direct answer to his prayers (see 10:10-12).

We can gain much insight into living victoriously as Christians by modeling the lives of the prophets of God. Certainly, they were specially chosen by God for a unique task. And yet their lives were set apart for that purpose through their heartfelt devotion to God—a devotion that was fueled by fervent prayer.

Scripture Reading: Ephesians 6:18; a Psalm

↑ Look Up

Skim through some of the psalms until you find one you can identify with today. Let the words of that psalm usher you in to the presence of God, and spend extra moments with Him in prayer. Close your prayer by reading Ephesians 6:18—and practicing it.

A lot of kneeling keeps you in good standing with God.

→ Move Ahead

Having an informal outline for your prayer times with God may enable you to make the experience more focused and profitable for you. For instance, use the ACTS acrostic to balance your prayers:

A—Adoration: Spend several moments simply worshiping God for who He is and what He has done on your behalf.

C—Confession: In humility and honesty, bring before the Lord the sins you've committed through thought, word, or deed, and ask for His cleansing and restoration.

T—Thanksgiving: Praise God for the many aspects of your life that bring you joy—your family, your friends, physical provisions, etc.

S—Supplication: Bring before God the requests you may have, asking Him to intercede according to His will. Keep track of your requests in a journal, and note when and how God answers.

Prayer is an honest, sincere, and rejuvenating time of communicating with the Lord of the universe, the Lover of your soul. Nothing could be more delightful, for you or for Him.

31 *Visions of Israel's Future / Daniel 7–12*

Heart of the Passage: Daniel 9, 12

Overview: The first half of Daniel's book centers around the prophet's personal adventures; the second half focuses on his prophetic visions. God's people, a major political and military force among the Gentiles since the days of Joshua, now find themselves under Gentile domination. But even world powers do not rise or fall without the consent of almighty God. In a remarkable collection of prophetic glimpses, Daniel sets forth both the near and distant future of God's chosen people—a future filled with purifying judgment and blessing.

Chapters 7–8	Chapter 9	Chapters 10–11	Chapter 12
Prophecies Involving . . .			
Beasts	Weeks	Kings	Angels
Belshazzar	Darius	Cyrus	

People who admit they're wrong usually go farther in life than people who try to prove they're right.

Your Daily Walk: "Behold, the fear of the Lord, that is wisdom" (Job 28:28). When Job uttered those profound words, he had no idea that one day they would provide a fitting caption to place on the life of a prophet named Daniel! Reverential awe in the presence of the One who alone establishes kings and kingdoms is surely a wise place to begin planning your life. And it's not a bad place to return for periodic checkups to make sure your life stays on target.

Daniel soon realized that standing in the presence of God makes you keenly aware of your own sinfulness. Notice his emotional prayer of confession and intercession for his people: "O Lord, hear; O Lord, forgive; O Lord, hearken and do; defer not, for thine own sake, O my God: for thy city and thy people are called by thy name" (9:19).

Do you see God clearer as a result of your reading in the book of Daniel? If so, then you should also have a clearer picture of yourself. Make a list of the characteristics about yourself that have come into sharper focus. Now take that snapshot to the pages of Scripture and tackle one of the areas of weakness today!

Insight: The Chronology of Daniel in Capsule Form

Kingdom:	Babylonia		Persia	Babylonia	Persia	
King:	Nebuchad-nezzar	Bel-shazzar	Darius	Belshazzar	Darius	Cyrus
Chapter(s):	1–4	5	6	7–8	9	10–12

Major Prophets in Review

The five books which make up the "Major Prophets" (Isaiah–Daniel) span four centuries of time and the turbulent events of three world powers (Assyria, Babylonia, Persia) as they impacted the nation of Judah and the exiled people of God.

These books are indeed "major" in size (Isaiah, Jeremiah, and Ezekiel are three of the five longest books in the Bible), and "major" in importance. Dozens of Messianic prophecies are contained in their pages. Indeed, reading the Major Prophets is like seeing a prophetic panorama from here to eternity.

Here is a helpful chart to remind you of what you've read.

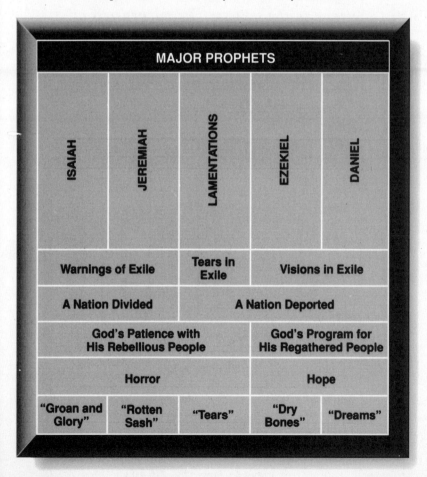

MAJOR PROPHETS				
ISAIAH	JEREMIAH	LAMENTATIONS	EZEKIEL	DANIEL
Warnings of Exile		Tears in Exile	Visions in Exile	
A Nation Divided		A Nation Deported		
God's Patience with His Rebellious People			God's Program for His Regathered People	
Horror			Hope	
"Groan and Glory"	"Rotten Sash"	"Tears"	"Dry Bones"	"Dreams"

Hosea

Hosea prophesies to a corrupt and idolatrous Israel from the pulpit of his own experience. Instructed by God to marry the harlot Gomer, Hosea finds mirrored in his domestic life an accurate portrayal of the unfaithfulness of God's people. Drawing a striking parallel from his marriage and his wife's defection, Hosea carries God's powerful message to the streets: The wickedness of Israel will bring swift tragedy and certain calamity. But though God's love must discipline, it will surely restore. His love desires the best for His beloved.

Focus	Hosea's Domestic Life		Israel's National Life		
Divisions	Harlotry in the Prophet's Family	Harlotry in the Prophet's Nation	Rebellion in Israel	Calamity in Israel	Coming Hope for Israel
	1　　　　　3	4　　　　6	7　　　　8	9　　　11	12　　　14
Topics	Loyal Love	Shameless Sin		Purifying Punishment	
	Adulterous Gomer and Faithful Hosea	Adulterous Israel and Faithful Jehovah			
Place	Northern Kingdom of Israel				
Time	About 45 Years (755-710 B.C.)				

Harlotry in the Prophet's Family
Hosea 1–3

1

📖 **Overview:** To the nation of Israel—a land steeped in idolatry—God sends the prophet Hosea, whose name means "salvation." Commanded to marry a woman named Gomer, Hosea is warned in advance of the future course of his family life: He would have "a wife of whoredoms and children of whoredoms" (1:2). Just as God foretold, Gomer deserts her prophet-husband for other lovers—a painful but graphic depiction of Israel's faithlessness in response to God's loyal love. When Gomer sinks to the level of a slave, Hosea is commanded to buy her back, for she is still his wife. In the same way the God of Israel pledges His continuing love for His people, even though their spiritual adultery will result in captivity and enslavement at the hands of the Assyrians.

Heart of the Passage: Hosea 1, 3

Chapter 1	Chapter 2		Chapter 3
Gomer's Faithlessness	Israel's Faithlessness	Israel's Restoration	Gomer's Restoration
Faithless Infidelity	Loyal Love		

✔️ **Your Daily Walk:** It's no accident that the first Bible verse you learned was probably John 3:16: "For God so loved the world, that he gave his only . . . Son." Or that the first song you learned was "Jesus loves me, this I know, for the Bible tells me so." Why? Because the love of God is foundational. It is a truth so simple even a child can grasp it, yet so profound even a theologian can spend a lifetime unraveling its implications.

Take a fresh look at the love of God today—this time through the tear-stained eyes of Hosea. God's love is unconditional (you don't have to earn it), unceasing (nothing can separate you from it, Romans 8:35-39), and active (God expresses it in tangible ways in your life). God has often told you in His Word, "I love you." When was the last time you told Him that? Turn to Psalm 116 and read it out loud. It's a beautiful—and biblical—way of telling God, "I love You!"

Love is the forgetting of oneself in the service of another.

📖 **Insight:** Some Things Never Change
Recent statistics show that a large percent of both married men and women have had or will have extramarital affairs. Divorce statistics indicate that reconciliation rarely occurs. Hosea's relationship with his unfaithful wife Gomer illustrates what the prophet Malachi declared: "For the LORD, the God of Israel, saith that he hateth putting away [divorce]" (Malachi 2:16).

2 *Harlotry in the Prophet's Nation*
Hosea 4–6

Heart
of the
Passage:
Hosea 4

Overview: What Hosea pictured with his life in chapters 1–3, he now prophesies with his lips in chapters 4–14. Israel's gross sin has not escaped the notice of her holy God. But God promises, "I will punish them for their ways, and reward them their doings" (4:9).

Chapter 4	Chapter 5	Chapter 6
Divine Debate	Divine Displeasure	Disobedient Deeds
Indictment	Injustice	Incomparable Mercy

What
this
country
needs is a
man who
knows
God
other
than by
hearsay.

Insight: " . . . 8 . . . 9 . . . 10 . . . You're Out!"

In chapters 4–6 Hosea demonstrates how the nation has broken each of the Ten Commandments. Can you find one statement corresponding to each broken command?

God's Command (Exodus 20)   Israel's Conduct (Hosea 4–6)

1. Have no other gods. _____
2. Make no graven images. _____
3. Do not misuse God's name. _____
4. Keep the Sabbath. _____
5. Honor your parents. _____
6. Do not kill. _____
7. Do not commit adultery. _____
8. Do not steal. _____
9. Do not lie. _____
10. Do not covet. _____

Your Daily Walk: Look at the list of Israel's offenses which you have just compiled. Keep in mind these were God's chosen people—recipients of the Old Testament Scriptures, the messages of the prophets, and a centuries-old heritage of His blessings. The judgment that Hosea now proclaims should never have had to come. But come it did, showing that no nation is exempt from the wrath of God when sin takes hold.

Next to the column labeled "Israel's Conduct," start a new one entitled, "My Nation's Conduct." Then don the robe of Hosea and evaluate what you find. Are conditions any better? Has your homeland responded to the preaching of God's Word any differently? God is waiting for you and your nation to respond with the words of Hosea 6:1, 3. Will you make that your sincere prayer right now?

Rebellion in Israel / Hosea 7–8 3

📖 **Overview:** Visual aids and interesting metaphors abound in the section you will read today. Hosea describes the nation as a dying man, a flaming fire, a half-baked cake, a silly dove, a deceitful bow, a pleasureless vessel, and a forgetful servant. With such overwhelming evidence there can be only one verdict: Guilty! For centuries the nation has sown seeds of wickedness; now it is time to reap the terrible harvest of judgment.

Heart of the Passage: Hosea 7

Chapter 7		Chapter 8	
Half-baked Commitment	Halfhearted Confession	Halfhearted Kings	Wholehearted Conquest
1 10	11 16	1 7	8 14
Israel's Problem		Israel's Punishment	

✓ **Your Daily Walk:** Try this personal preference survey:
How do you like your eggs cooked?
How do you like your meat cooked (rare, medium, etc.)?
How do you like your favorite beverage served?

Now suppose someone invited you over for breakfast and served you overcooked (or undercooked) bacon, runny (or hardboiled) eggs, and lukewarm coffee, tea, or milk. How would you respond to their "hospitality"? Would you want to come back for more?

Fire is the test of gold; adversity of strong men.

Back in the early days of the nation of Israel, the people promised to follow God in wholehearted obedience (Exodus 19:8). But now as Hosea surveys the scene, the nation resembles a half-baked cake (7:8). Impure motives, incomplete obedience, and spiritual indifference characterize the people. Little wonder God's heart is grieved over the condition of His covenant nation.

Think of your Christian life today as a cake, and the difficult circumstances you are facing as the heat God is using to prepare you. Where are you tempted to "hop out of the oven" before the transformation is complete? Why not bake a special (and hopefully, edible) cake today, or surprise the family by bringing one home tonight. As you enjoy it together, share with each other areas in your life that are still "in the oven," becoming what He wants them to be.

📝 **Insight:** The Sowing and Reaping Principle
Hosea 8:7 is one of the best-known verses in the book, and contains a principle found at least two other places in the Bible: 2 Corinthians 9:6 and Galatians 6:7-8. Can you state what it is?

4 *The Bridegroom and the Bride*

Step Back

Scripture Reading: 2 Corinthians 11:1-2; Revelation 19:6-10

God calls Hosea to be His prophet to Israel during her last days. Hosea's personal tragedy is used by God as an intense illustration of the national tragedy of Israel.

It's the story of one-sided love and faithfulness between a prophet and his faithless wife (Hosea and Gomer). And that story mirrors God's relationship with His faithless people, His "bride." For just as Gomer is married to Hosea, so Israel is married to God.

In both cases the bride becomes a harlot, running after other lovers. Even so, on both Hosea's and God's part, unconditional love keeps pursuing, seeking, even though it is rejected.

Interestingly, the prophet's love for his wife drives him to buy back his wife from the slave market. God's love for His people would in a future day entail buying them back through an act of sacrificial love, the payment of His Son's death on the cross.

Look Up

Divine love is no abstract theory, it is a living Person.

The imagery of marriage for the relationship of God with His people is rich with meaning. It signifies God's utter, eternal love and devotion.

In our age, the church is called the bride of Christ. The apostle Paul beseeches the Corinthian believers to be faithful to the Bridegroom, Jesus Christ (2 Corinthians 11:1-2). And one of the most thrilling insights that John shares with us in Revelation is of the Marriage Feast of the Lamb (Revelation 19:6-10).

As you read those two passages, consider what it means to be part of the bride of Christ. Then thank your Bridegroom in prayer for His eternal loving devotion.

Move Ahead

When the Bible refers to the bride of Christ, it's usually in connection with God's desire that she be pure, spotless, and set apart for her Bridegroom.

God does not take those characteristics lightly. In His perfection and holiness, He cannot abide sin. Does your life bear a stronger resemblance to Gomer's, or to the spotless bride of the Lamb?

The first step toward a holy life is turning to God wholeheartedly in humble repentance. It's the first step along the path to victorious living.

Calamity in Israel / Hosea 9–11   5

📖 **Overview:** After repeated postponements of Israel's day of reckoning, the time to settle accounts has come at last. Barrenness and bondage will replace prosperity and peace in the nation. Because of unchecked sin and worthless worship, Israel will be removed from the land in a tragic blast of judgment and death. Destruction, famine, and forced labor will befall God's people in these terrible "days of recompense" (9:7). And yet, though the nation deserves to be utterly destroyed, God will keep His promises. Blessing will come when God's judgment is completed.

Heart of the Passage: Hosea 9

Chapter 9	Chapter 10	Chapter 11
Day of Visitation	Day of Vexation	Day of Restoration
Recompense	Removal	Return

✍️ **Your Daily Walk:** Which of the following situations have you experienced?

1. You thought you were going the right way on a one-way street, only to discover you were wrong.

2. You were told a cup was full of hot liquid, but you burned your mouth on it anyway.

3. The light on your dashboard told you something was wrong with your car and you ignored it.

Habit is the easiest way to be wrong again.

In each case you were experiencing a rebuke. The oncoming traffic on the one-way street, the burned tongue, the blinking light, each in its own way was telling you that you were doing something wrong, and would face serious consequences if you didn't heed the warning.

How do you respond to God's rebukes in your life? Do you know how to rebuke another person so that the result is therapeutic, not simply threatening? Remember, part of your responsibility as a Christian is to ". . . reprove, rebuke, exhort with all longsuffering and doctrine" (2 Timothy 4:2). Every time you see a one-way sign today, let it remind you of the importance of responding to—and issuing—a rebuke the way God desires.

🖌️ **Insight:** You Can Learn a Lot from a Prophet's Pen

Hosea's book is rich with truth about God's love . . . God's justice . . . God's impatience . . . God's discipline. Use each of those words to complete this sentence: "This past week I have learned that God's _____ is . . ." Try it!

6 *Coming Hope for Israel / Hosea 12–14*

Heart of the Passage: Hosea 14

📖 **Overview:** God is holy and just, but He is also loving and gracious. God must discipline, but because of His endless love He will ultimately save and restore His wayward people. "I will heal their backsliding, I will love them freely: for mine anger is turned away from him" (14:4). Hosea, whose heart has already been broken once by the harlotry and shameful behavior of his wife Gomer, now pleads one last time for his countrymen to repent: "O Israel, return unto the LORD thy God" (14:1).

Chapter 12	Chapter 13	Chapter 14
Israel's Disobedient Past	Israel's Desolate People	Hosea's Desperate Plea
Looking Backward	Looking Forward	Looking Inward

Every man must do his own growing, no matter how tall his parents are.

✓ **Your Daily Walk:** When it comes to growing a garden, there are usually two kinds of people: those with green thumbs who grow everything, and those who are all thumbs and grow nothing. To which group do you belong?

There is nothing quite like the sight of a majestic tree towering over the landscape . . . unless, of course, it is the sight of a forest of trees blanketing the hillside. Perhaps you never stopped to realize that all those trees began exactly the same way as the plants in your humble garden: with a seed. Small . . . seemingly insignificant . . . virtually ignored by those who walk by it. Yet that seed contains the awesome potential for growth and reproduction that will one day transform it into a majestic tree.

It is not surprising, therefore, that when Hosea searches for a suitable illustration to describe the potential of God's restored people, he finds it in a picture drawn from nature: "the lily . . . roots . . . branches . . . olive tree . . . corn . . . vine . . . green fir tree . . . fruit" (14:5-8).

Nature silently but eloquently testifies to the fact that God is in the business of transforming seeds into trees if you will but entrust them to His loving hands. A little talent . . . a little money . . . a little time—each can become something great in God's economy. Copy this motto onto a 3 x 5 card, put it on your dashboard or desk, and make it your order for the day: "Little is much when God is in it."

📖 **Insight:** In the Way of the Lord, Watch Your Step! (14:9)
It is ironic but true that the very paths which cause the righteous to stand will cause the wicked to stumble . . . every time.

Joel

Addressing hearts that have grown cold to the things of God, Joel confronts the people of Judah. He reminds them of the recent destruction brought by a plague of locusts. Yet that disaster, a judgment in itself, will seem pale beside the catastrophe still to come. Unless the nation repents, it will be destroyed by an army from the north. The only hope of escape is for the people to repent. If they do, then God will divert judgment and will deliver an unparalleled blessing—judgment on all Judah's enemies and the matchless gift of peace to Zion!

Focus	Past Judgment of God's People	Future Judgment and Restoration of God's People	
Divisions	Devastation of the Locusts	Day of the Lord	Doom of the Nations
	1:1 1:20	2:1 2:30	3:1 3:21
Topics	Israel's Review	Israel's Future	Gentile's Future
	Historical Invasion	Prophetic Invasions	
Place	Southern Kingdom of Judah		
Time	Approximately 835 B.C.		

7 The Lord's Locust Lesson / Joel 1–3

Heart of the Passage: Joel 1; 2:12-29

Overview: A plague of locusts hits Judah with the fury of an invading army, destroying vegetation and turning the usually verdant countryside into a lifeless desert. Fields of grain disappear, grapevines are stripped bare, fruit trees and gardens are wiped clean. The prophet Joel seizes the occasion to preach God's message to Judah: The present calamity is only a warning. An even greater devastation awaits those who continue to live in sin and rebellion. The day of judgment is coming, and only those who sincerely repent and return to God will be sheltered from the terrible force of His righteous wrath.

Chapter 1	Chapter 2	Chapter 3	
Day of the Locust	Day of the Lord	Judgment of the Nations	Blessing of God's Nation
Plague	Punishment		Prosperity

(Chapter 3 columns marked: 1 ... 17 | 18 ... 21)

Your Daily Walk: *Question:* What do these three activities have in common: skydiving without a parachute, walking blindfolded across the freeway, and disregarding God's laws?

A swarm of locusts, like "little sins," can do more damage to a field than a full-grown cow.

Answer: They are all activities that, while perhaps momentarily exhilarating, lead to inescapable—and deadly—consequences.

Though he knew nothing about skydiving or freeways, Joel knew full well the danger of disregarding God's commandments. The terrible scourge of locusts became the perfect illustration of wrathful judgment to come—and the perfect occasion for Joel to warn his countrymen. Although it was too late to escape the bite of the locust, there was still time to escape the "bite" of God's chastening hand.

Learn a lesson from the locusts! Do your days pass without prayerful contact with God? Have your "little sins" ceased to bother you? Have you slipped away from daily study and regular weekly worship? (Can you hear the buzzing locusts?) The danger is real, but shelter is as near as your Father's "everlasting arms" (Deuteronomy 33:27). Wouldn't that be a good place to rest . . . right now?

Insight: A Day Like No Other

For some helpful research on "the day of the LORD" (mentioned 9 times in Joel and 25 other times in Scripture), look up Isaiah 2:12; 13:6-9; Zephaniah 1:14; and 2 Peter 3:10-14. Then share the insights you gain with one other person.

Amos

Externally, the northern kingdom was marked by flourishing business, solid economy, stable government. But internally the diagnosis of the nation's condition was grim. Idolatry, injustice, greed, hypocrisy, oppression, and arrogance indicated a growing malignancy of deep-seated sin. Amos, a farmer by trade, dons the mantle of a prophet to make God's message crystal clear to those who had grown soft and lax in luxurious living: "Repent, or perish." The storm clouds of judgment are soon to break over God's people.

Focus	"Prepare to meet thy God, O Israel" (4:12).			
Divisions	Pronouncements of Judgment on Israel	Promptings of Judgment by God	Pictures of Judgment for Amos	Promises After Judgment for God's People
	1 2	3 5	6 7	8 9
Topics	Sermons		Signs	
	Indictment		Encouragement	
Place	Neighboring Nations	Northern Nation of Israel		
Time	About 10 Years (760–750 B.C.)			

8 Pronouncements of Judgment / Amos 1–2

Heart of the Passage: Amos 2:6-16

Overview: Amos, a herdsman and farmer from the rural regions of Judah, emerges as God's prophetic spokesman to Israel. In the midst of a period of prosperity and peace, the northern 10 tribes have become indifferent to their God. Their complacency, immorality, and idolatry will be tolerated no longer. First to Israel's neighbors, then to Israel herself, Amos forcefully delivers God's stern warning, "I will send a fire . . ." (1:4, 7, 10, 12, 14; 2:2, 5).

Chapter 1						Chapter 2		
Judgment Pronounced on . . .								
Damascus	Gaza	Tyre	Edom	Ammon	Moab	Judah	Israel	
1 5	6 8	9 10	11 12	13 15	1 3	4 5	6 16	
Gentiles						Jews		

It would tire the hands of an angel to write down all the pardons God bestows upon true penitent believers.

Your Daily Walk: In *The Chronicles of Narnia*, C. S. Lewis portrays the Son of God as Aslan, a great and powerful lion. Over 2,000 years before, the prophet Amos used the same imagery, describing God as a roaring lion ready to leap on His prey in judgment (1:2).

If you had to choose another animal to which God might be likened in today's section, perhaps it would be the elephant, the proverbial "animal that never forgets." Nation by nation, God carefully recounts the transgressions which have accumulated, showing that each nation is ripe for judgment. God never overlooks a sin.

But for His children, God has made a special provision—a gracious "lapse of memory." Both Isaiah (43:25) and Jeremiah (31:34) promise the repentant sinner that God erases from His memory all trace of past sins. Sadly, many Christians still live under the shadow of past sins which God has long ago forgiven and forgotten. Does that describe you? Then try this exercise. Using a red pen, write out the sins from your past which God could seemingly never forget. Then look at what you have written through a piece of red cellophane or red-stained glass (the way God looks at your sins through the blood of Jesus Christ). What you see is what God remembers!

Insight: Seven, the Painfully Perfect Number

Eight times in two chapters Amos uses the expression, "For three transgressions . . . and for four." Add them up and you have seven—the prophet's way of signifying a full and complete multiplying of sin, thereby deserving the fullness of God's wrath.

Promptings of Judgment / Amos 3–5

9

Overview: Amos now moves from the general to the specific in his description of Israel's injustice and God's indictment. Violence, oppression, rebellion, and drunkenness characterize the nation's lifestyle. Through famine, pestilence, drought, mildew, death, and defeat, God has patiently called the nation back to Himself. "Yet have ye not returned unto Me, saith the LORD." As a result, there is but one recourse for the nation: "Prepare to meet thy God" (4:12).

Heart of the Passage: Amos 4

Chapter 3	Chapter 4	Chapter 5
Israel's Sin of Presumption	God's Plea to Return	Amos's Call for Repentance
No Fear of God	No Love for God	No Hope but God

Your Daily Walk: In the margin, make a list of as many activities as you can think of that regularly take place at your church (you'll probably be able to think of at least 20). Then look up Amos 5:21-25 and draw a line through each item on your list that Amos mentions. Are you surprised at the result?

You will often hear messages preached on the love of God, but when was the last time you heard a message on "The Things God Hates"? And yet, in the space of only five verses, Amos outlines at least seven activities which God despises. The Israelites were giving offerings, holding feasts, praying prayers, and singing songs . . . but all were only empty religious motions. Though the people's actions were correct, their attitudes were corrupt—a condition which God found to be detestable.

Here's one sure way to help you avoid Israel's mistake. Take your list of religious activities and turn it into a prayer list today: "Father, may my worship be acceptable to You; may my singing in the choir bring praise to Your name; may my gifts and offerings be an expression of gratitude for all You have given to me; may my service to others be genuine and wholehearted!"

Though Amos had a tongue like a whip for the oppressor, it spoke out of a heart of love for the oppressed.

Insight: Where Do You Get Your Sermons, Amos?
Amos shows a striking familiarity with the Pentateuch, the first five books of the Old Testament. For example, compare . . .

Amos	Pentateuch	Amos	Pentateuch
4:1	Deuteronomy 15:7-9	4:6-7	Deuteronomy 28:23, 48
4:4	Deuteronomy 14:28; 26:12	5:7, 10	Exodus 23:6-8
4:5	Leviticus 2:11; 7:13	5:21	Numbers 29:35

10 *Pictures of Judgment / Amos 6–7*

Heart of the Passage: Amos 7

📖 **Overview:** Continuing his reprimand of Israel, Amos challenges those who have developed a false sense of security in their money, homes, beds of ivory, and lives of leisure. But possessions alone can never bring security. To picture this, the prophet visualizes a locust swarm, a devastating fire, and a plumbline. Though the first two judgments are stayed by God, there is no escaping the fact that the nation has drifted far from God's righteous standards. God's long-postponed punishment can be delayed no longer.

Chapter 6	Chapter 7		
Prophecies of Israel's Punishment	Pictures of Israel's Punishment:		
	Grasshoppers	Fire	Plumbline
	1 3	4 6	7 17
Judgment Is Close	Judgment Is Clear		

🔖 **Your Daily Walk:** *Thought for the day:* Before you set your heart on something, look around to see how happy it has made those who have it.

The real value of a thing is the price it will bring in eternity.

If you want a quick barometer of your relationship to God, look at your attitude toward things. Do you possess them, or do they possess you? Do you find yourself content with what you have, or covetous of what others have? Do you love people and use things, or vice versa?

The Israelites enjoyed many material blessings from God. But rather than putting their trust in the One who owned them, the people looked for security in the things they owned. Because of the nation's misplaced affections, God declared He would remove both His people and their possessions.

What three material possessions do you prize above all others? 1. _____ 2. _____ 3. _____ Which of the three comes closest to possessing you? (Circle one.) Thank God for the blessings He has entrusted to you. Then in an act of prayerful commitment, transfer the ownership of each one back to Him. You'll be saying by your life, as well as your lips, that you are finding your security in Him alone.

📓 **Insight:** Playing "Follow the Leaders"

The tragedy of those leaders who were at "ease in Zion" (6:1) was that they continued in their self-centered, extravagant lifestyles, totally insulated from the ruin that was overtaking their country. Amos warns that those same leaders would later lead the pitiful columns of exiles going off into captivity (6:7).

Minor Prophets
in Perspective

T he twelve short books which make up the "Minor
Prophets" (so called because of their length, not
their importance), were originally grouped together
on one scroll in the Hebrew Bible, and simply called "The
Twelve." Together, they cover a time span of about 400
years (ca. 800–400 B.C.). Theologically, the Minor Prophets
focus on warnings of impending judgment, teachings on
righteous living, encouragement to the faithful and oppressed, and predictions of God's future plans.

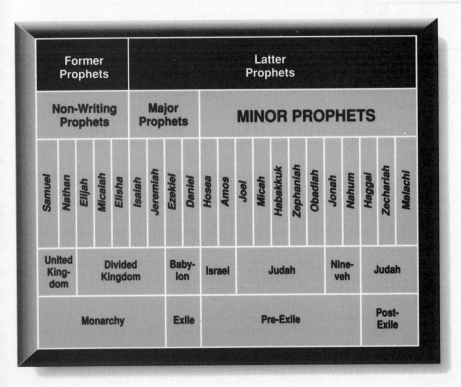

Former Prophets		Latter Prophets																			
Non-Writing Prophets		Major Prophets		MINOR PROPHETS																	
Samuel	Nathan	Elijah	Micaiah	Elisha	Isaiah	Jeremiah	Ezekiel	Daniel	Hosea	Amos	Joel	Micah	Habakkuk	Zephaniah	Obadiah	Jonah	Nahum	Haggai	Zechariah	Malachi
United Kingdom		Divided Kingdom					Baby-lon		Israel		Judah					Nine-veh		Judah		
Monarchy						Exile			Pre-Exile									Post-Exile		

11 Promises After Judgment / Amos 8–9

Overview: If "a picture is worth a thousand words," then today's section provides one of Amos's most eloquent descriptions of judgment. He pictures the nation as a basket of summer fruit—fully ripened and ready for destruction. Next, the prophet shows God standing beside the altar in an ominous forecast of coming calamity upon the nation's worthless worship. Divine discipline must come, but in its wake will follow restoration and renewal. God will raise up the people again, restore them as a nation, and root them in the land.

Heart of the Passage: Amos 9

Chapter 8	Chapter 9	
Israel, Ripe for Judgment	God's Reasons for Judgment	Israel's Restoration After Judgment
	1 10 11	15
In the Basket	At the Altar	In the Land

Your Daily Walk: Perhaps you have seen the popular slogan, "With God all things are possible." But more accurately, even with God some things are impossible! After reading the last chapters of Amos, see how many ways you can complete this sentence: "It is impossible to _____ ."

It is impossible for God to do that which is contrary to His nature.

One thing you will discover in today's section is the truth that it is impossible to hide from God. Amos chapter 9 sounds remarkably similar to Psalm 139 in its description of God's inescapable knowledge and judgment. Since today's reading is short, why not read Psalm 139 as well, particularly verses 7-12. Which locations does the psalmist consider and then rule out in his attempt to hide from God? (You should be able to discover at least five.) And what does he conclude about the likelihood of hiding from God in the dark (v. 12)?

God's presence will either comfort you (if you are walking with Him in obedience) or convict you (if you are walking in disobedience). Which of those two words (*comfort, conviction*) best characterizes your relationship with God today? If your answer disturbs you, don't fail to get alone with God and take a hard look at your life. Remember, those who try to play hide-and-seek with God always lose.

Insight: The Get-Rich-Quick Scheme That Failed
Amos 6:4-7 answers the what and who of Israel's luxurious living; 8:5-6 describes the how: long hours, lax ethics, and abuse of the poor and needy. It's a reminder that money can only buy things that are for sale—and happiness is not one of them.

Obadiah

O ne of the worst things that can happen is to have your enemies line up to destroy you. However, defeat takes on a different meaning when close friends and brothers also join the opposition. When Judah called out to her Edomite "cousins" for help against the advancing Babylonian troops, Edom stood aloof and behaved like one of Judah's foes. God's displeasure with Edom as it comes through the prophet Obadiah is clear, "As you have done, it will be done to you." Edom will be destroyed. Judah will live in peace.

Focus	Destruction of Edom		Success of Israel	
Divisions	Destruction Predicted	Destruction Explained	Judgment on Nations	Restoration of Israel
	1:1 1:9	1:10 1:14	1:15 1:16	1:17 1:21
Topics	Edom's Arrogance	Edom's Antagonism	Edom's Annihilation	
	Defeat of Israel		Victory of Israel	
Place	Edom and Israel			
Time	Approximately 840 B.C.			

12 Edom's Fate / Obadiah

Overview: Obadiah is given the unenviable task of confronting two members of a feuding family. The Jews in Judah (descendants of Jacob) and the Edomites in Edom (descendants of Esau) were blood brothers but with little visible love between them. When the enemies of Judah attacked the capital city of Jerusalem, the Edomites rushed in to help the enemy! As a result, God sends Obadiah to predict doom for the nation for refusing to be its "brother's keeper."

Heart of the Passage: Obadiah 8-14

Verses 1-9	Verses 10-14	Verses 15-21
Certainty of Edom's Doom	Causes of Edom's Doom	Consequences of Edom's Doom
"As thou hast done, it shall be done unto thee" (v. 15).		

Insight: Brotherly Feuding Through the Centuries

Trace the animosity between the two lines of Esau and Jacob as described in the following verses:

Humility learned now helps us avoid humiliation later.

Reference	History of a Feud
Genesis 25:20-23	Struggle begins in the womb.
Genesis 25:24-26	Characters revealed at birth.
Genesis 25:27-34	"Stewing" over a birthright.
Genesis 36:1-9	Esau moves to the land of Edom.
Numbers 20:14-21	Edom refuses Israel passage.
1 Samuel 14:47	Saul fights against Edom.
2 Samuel 8:14	David makes Edomites his servants.
2 Chronicles 20:1-23	Edom joins Ammon and Moab.
2 Chronicles 28:17	Edom fights against Judah.
(Secular Sources)	Edomites destroyed in A.D. 70.

Your Daily Walk: Pride was at the root of Edom's problem. The Edomites had built themselves up until at last God tore them down, "for God resisteth the proud, [but] giveth grace to the humble" (1 Peter 5:5).

What kinds of "building programs" are you involved in today in your own life? your family? your church? Are they the kind God will resist or reward?

Carry a nail wrapped in a paper towel in your pocket or purse today to remind you that building for God (the nail) demands humility (the servant's towel) if what you build is to last for eternity. Share that object lesson from Obadiah with one other person today!

Jonah

G od calls Jonah to warn the Assyrian city of Nineveh of impending destruction. However, the brutal Assyrians are Israel's bitter enemies, and Jonah both fears and despises them. Instead of heading to Nineveh, Jonah sets sail in the opposite direction. A storm ensues, Jonah is tossed overboard and is swallowed by a great fish. After three days the fish deposits Jonah on dry land. Jonah then goes to Nineveh and preaches as God had instructed. When the people repent, Jonah's resentment grows until God must teach him a lesson in compassion.

Focus	Revival for a Prophet				Revival for a Pagan City			
Divisions	Prophet's Disobedience	Prophet's Danger	Prophet's Prayer	Prophet's Deliverance	Prophet's Obedience	Pagans' Repentance	Prophet's Complaint	Prophet's Rebuke
	1:1　　1:3	1:4　　1:17	2:1　　2:9	2:10	3:1　　3:4	3:5　　3:10	4:1　　4:5	4:6　　4:11
Topics	Mercy on Jonah				Mercy on Nineveh			
	Jonah in the Ship		Jonah in the Fish		Jonah in the City		Jonah in the Suburbs	
Place	The Sea				The City			
Time	Approximately 760 B.C.							

13 *The Greatest Fish Story / Jonah 1–4*

Heart of the Passage: Jonah 3–4

Overview: Running from God is not something reserved for thieves and murderers. Sometimes preachers get into the act as well! Consider the story of Jonah, a prophet commissioned by God to preach an ultimatum ("Shape up or ship out!") to Israel's archenemy, Assyria. Jonah quickly goes A.W.O.L. (Absent Without Leave) and finds a ship headed in the opposite direction. Destination: Tarshish. God sends first a storm, then a hungry fish to turn Jonah around and head him back toward Nineveh. After delivering his one-sentence sermon, Jonah watches helplessly as the entire city of Nineveh—right down to the cattle—repents in sackcloth and ashes. When God spares Israel's enemies, it takes a hot wind, a shade-giving vine, and a hungry grub to teach Jonah a lesson about the mercy of God for sinful mankind.

Chapter 1	Chapter 2	Chapter 3	Chapter 4
Jonah in the Ship	Jonah in the Fish	Jonah in the City	Jonah in the Suburbs
Protesting	Praying	Preaching	Pouting

In the chess game of life, never forget that the first move is God's; and so also is the last.

Your Daily Walk: One of the most interesting discoveries about the book of Jonah is that everyone obeyed God except the preacher! The storm . . . the dice . . . the sailors . . . the fish . . . the Ninevites . . . the east wind . . . the gourd . . . the worm . . . everyone and everything obeyed God's command except the one who claimed to be a follower of God.

Check up on yourself. Do your actions support or deny your claims of being a Christian? God often gives a second chance for obedience (as with Jonah), but wouldn't it be much simpler and less painful to obey Him the first time around?

Put yourself in Jonah's sandals and write a short, first-person account of how you would have reacted in one of these situations: on the ship, in the fish, in the city, or on the hillside. Can you identify the "Nineveh assignment" that God is asking you to tackle today?

Insight: A Fishy Story—Could It Happen? Did It Happen?
In answer to the question, "Could it happen?" read Baxter's *Explore the Book* (iv, 151-154) for two documented cases of men who were swallowed by sharks or whales—and then lived to tell about it. To answer the question, "Did it happen?" check Matthew 12:39-40 for confirmation of the story from an irrefutable source!

Micah

*S*in had infiltrated every segment of society. False prophets preached for money, immoral princes oppressed the poor, corrupt judges allowed injustice to rule the land. Such were the days of Micah, country preacher turned prophet of God. Micah pleads with his countrymen to turn away from sin and back to God. But the message falls on deaf ears—ears that will soon instead hear the clamor of invading armies. But within the hardness lies hope. When justice is accomplished, God will restore His people to their covenant land.

Focus	Retribution	Restoration	Repentance
Divisions	Calamity and Its Causes	Condemnation and Consolation	Controversy and Covenant
	1 2	3 5	6 7
Topics	Day of Calamity	Day of Comfort	Day in Court
	Punishment	Promise	Pardon
Place	Judah and Israel		
Time	About 25 Years (735–710 B.C.)		

14 *Calamity and Its Causes / Micah 1-2*

Heart of the Passage: Micah 1:1–2:2

Overview: The nation is immoral and corrupt; the time to repent has come and gone; the earlier prophets have been unheard and unheeded. Such is the state of Judah as Micah emerges during the reigns of Jotham, Ahaz, and Hezekiah. His task: to indict the unrepentant people of God and to announce the irreversible edict of God: "Behold, the LORD cometh forth out of his place . . . and the mountains shall be molten under him . . . for the trangressions of Jacob . . . and for the sins of the house of Israel" (1:3-5).

Chapter 1	Chapter 2	
Reproof of Judah's Sin	Wrath for Judah's Rebels	Reward for Judah's Remnant
1	11 12	13
Judah's Punishment	God's Promise	

Busyness in the King's business is no excuse for neglecting the King.

Your Daily Walk: It's late at night. You're driving home—exhausted—after a long day of working, shopping, and errand running. As you make a mental checklist of the activities you've completed, you have that sinking feeling that you've forgotten something. Suddenly, the engine sputters and stops—and you remember what you had overlooked. You failed to fill the gas tank!

How often in your hurry to get things done do you lose sight of what's really important? How often in your daily prayers do you find yourself doing all the talking and then "hanging up" with a quick "amen" before God has a chance to talk to you? How often do you return from church exhausted from teaching, leading, singing—having been to the "pump" but forgetting to "fill up"?

Micah opens his prophecy with the admonition: "Hear, all ye people; hearken, O earth, and all that therein is" (1:2). All the world is commanded to halt its activities and pay attention to God's Word. "Be still," the Lord says, "and know that I am God" (Psalm 46:10).

Today when you pray, slow down! Pause and be still for a long minute before you say "amen"; give God a chance to speak to you and fellowship with you. Remember, you're a person He created to love and enjoy eternally, so relax and rest in His presence!

Insight: Micah's Priorities in Matthew's Pages
What's on your personal list of things to do today? Check Matthew 6:33 to see what should be right up there at the top!

Condemnation and Consolation **15**
Micah 3–5

Overview: Micah might well have summarized his prophecy this way: "I have good news and bad news!" The bad news? Destruction of Judah's oppressive princes and greedy priests will be swift and terrible; Jerusalem, for her iniquity, will be "plowed [under] as a field, and . . . become heaps" (3:12). And the good news? Though destruction will be fierce, a remnant will be spared to inherit blessings of peace and safety once again. From the obscurity of a village called Bethlehem will arise a Messiah who will be "ruler in Israel" (5:2) and will usher in a new day of righteous living and unparalleled glory!

Heart of the Passage: Micah 3, 5

Chapter 3	Chapter 4	Chapter 5
Rebuking False Prophets	Restoring True Religion	Ruling Jacob's Remnant
False Peace	Kingdom of Peace	Prince of Peace

Your Daily Walk: *"He did it—why shouldn't I?"*

No doubt you've heard that statement many times—and perhaps even used it a few times yourself in reference to the behavior of a public figure. The judge indicted for bribery, the politician cited for tax evasion, the preacher caught in adultery—almost any edition of your local newspaper will supply ample evidence of leaders "leading" in the wrong direction, thus making it easier for others to rush into the same sins, arguing, *"He did it—why shouldn't I?"*

But look at the example of Christ, and those same words form a fitting question: *"He did it—why shouldn't I . . . visit the sick . . . care for the poor . . . put the needs of others above my own?"* Just as you ask the above question in relation to Christ, others will ask it of you, for "he that saith he abideth in [Christ] ought himself also so to walk, even as [Christ] walked" (1 John 2:6, see memory verse below).

Write the first line of today's Daily Walk on a slip of paper or a 3 x 5 card. Post it on the dashboard of your car or carry it in your wallet or purse. That way you'll be frequently reminded to follow—and become—a good leader!

Man is a creature that is led more by patterns than by precepts.

Insight: Walk the Way Your Savior Walked

On the reverse side of your card, copy this verse as a reminder of whom you're walking with: "He that saith he abideth in [Christ] ought himself also so to walk, even as he walked" (1 John 2:6).

303

16 Controversy in the Courtroom
Micah 6–7

Heart of the Passage: Micah 7:18

Overview: Controversy erupts in the courtroom as Micah describes God's people on trial. Heaven and earth comprise the jury as the charges are leveled against Israel: halfhearted worship, empty ritual, persistent rebellion, deception, hypocrisy, greed, idolatry. The verdict can only be "guilty as charged." The sentence: a generation of exile in Babylon. Yet the message of Micah is not complete until he preaches the richness of God's forgiveness and grace. "Who is a God like unto thee, that pardoneth iniquity, and passeth by the transgression of the remnant of his heritage? he retaineth not his anger for ever, because he delighteth in mercy" (7:18). Micah knows that God's discipline only comes within the context of His everlasting love. The aftermath of His wrath brings mercy and forgiveness.

Chapter 6	Chapter 7	
The Charges Against Israel	A Verdict of Guilty	An Aftermath of Grace
1	6 7	20
God's Justice	God's Mercy	

Your Daily Walk: In one verse (6:8), Micah succinctly sums up God's three "minimum daily requirements" for His people: "What doth the LORD require of thee, but to *do justly*, and to *love mercy*, and to *walk humbly* with thy God?" Can you think of one way in which you can fulfill each of these requirements in your walk with God today?

The only part of the Bible you truly believe is the part you obey.

Here are some sentence completions to get you started. Don't be satisfied until you've made Micah's words your marching orders!

"In order to *do justly* with my employer/employees today, I will be careful to_____."

"Because God's love is reflected when I *love mercy*, today in my family relationships I will _____."

"Because God is exalted when I *walk humbly* with Him, the next time I go to church I will_____."

Insight: Wicked Balances, Wobbly Scales

Merchants in Micah's day were so dishonest that many of them carried two sets of balance weights for their business transactions: a heavier set to be sure they got more than they paid for, and a lighter set to ensure that their customers received less than they expected. Read about God's response to this "double standard" in 6:10-16.

The Weight of Sin

17

← Step Back

Sin. It's a simple word, yet it carries the weight of humanity with it. Those three letters carry the concept of iniquity, wickedness, rebellion, ungodliness, lawlessness, wandering, disobedience, falling away. It's missing the mark God has established for us. It's rejecting God's righteous standards.

Sin may be considered to be anything that does not express, or is contrary to, God's character. All sin, even sins against oneself or others, is ultimately against God.

The prophets continually addressed the sin of God's people. God had established a covenant with them—an agreement that they would abide by His laws of holiness and obedience, and that He would protect, lead, and bless them. He kept His part of the covenant; His people rebelled against theirs.

Through His teachings, Christ pointed out specific sins, including sacrilege (showing irreverence toward holy things, Mark 11:15-18); hypocrisy (failing to practice what one preaches, Matthew 23:1-36); covetousness (Luke 12:15); blasphemy (Matthew 12:22-37); transgressing the Law (Matthew 15:3-6); pride (Matthew 20:20-28); fruitlessness (John 15:1-6); and prayerlessness (Luke 18:1-8).

And yet, the Bible not only denounces sin. It also offers the remedy to it.

Scripture Reading: Matthew 18:21-35; 20:28; 26:28

↑ Look Up

Forgiveness is one of the most beautiful words of human language. All the sins we commit can be forgiven.

How? On the basis of Christ's death. When John the Baptist announced the coming of Christ, he called Jesus the "Lamb of God" who takes away the sin of the world (John 1:29). And Christ Himself explained that His death provided the basis for God's forgiveness of all our sin (Matthew 20:28; 26:28).

It's easy to read the prophets and become overwhelmed by the sinfulness of humanity. And each of us should come to grips with the sin that separates us from God. But don't get stuck under the pile. As a child of God, you have been forgiven in Christ.

Only one petition in the Lord's Prayer has any condition attached to it; it is the petition for forgiveness.

→ Move Ahead

Forgiven people should be forgiving people. Christ taught that truth in the parable of the unmerciful servant. Read that story carefully in Matthew 18:21-35. Then search your heart for any unforgiving spirit you may be holding against someone you know. Put Christ's words into action today by seeking out that person and sincerely offering your forgiveness.

305

Nahum

By the time Nahum comes on the scene Nineveh is even more wicked than it had been during the time of Jonah about 100 years earlier. The repentant spirit of the people and the revival that stemmed from Jonah's visit is gone. Now a terror to the entire world, the fortress city of Nineveh seems impenetrable. But God will no longer overlook the city's horrible sins, and He sends Nahum to deliver the message of impending destruction. The entire Assyrian empire will be destroyed and the mighty city of Nineveh will be gutted by a raging fire.

Focus	God's Displeasure Proclaimed		Nineveh's Doom Predicted		Nineveh's Downfall Portrayed	
Divisions	Praise for God's Justice	Joy for Nineveh's Destruction	Destruction of Nineveh	Contrast with Former Glory	Sins of Nineveh	Inevitability of Destruction
	1:1 1:7	1:8 1:15	2:1 2:10	2:11 2:13	3:1 3:4	3:5 3:19
Topics	Sentence of Judgment		Sight of Judgment		Sense of Judgment	
	Psalm of Justice		Description of Justice		Reason for Justice	
Place	In Judah Against Nineveh, capital of Assyria					
Time	Approximately 660 B.C.					

No More Time for Nineveh / Nahum 1–3 **18**

Overview: "To whom much is given, much is required." Nineveh had been given the privilege of knowing the one true God. Under Jonah's preaching this great Gentile city had repented, and God had graciously stayed His judgment. But now, about 150 years later, Nahum proclaims the downfall of once-mighty Nineveh. The Assyrians had forgotten their revival and had returned to their habits of violence, idolatry, and arrogance. As a result, Babylon would so destroy the city that no trace of it would remain—a prophecy fulfilled in painful detail.

Heart of the Passage: Nahum 1

Chapter 1	Chapter 2	Chapter 3
God's Displeasure Proclaimed	Nineveh's Doom Predicted	Nineveh's Downfall Portrayed
God's Worthiness	Mankind's Worthlessness and Pride	

Your Daily Walk: One Nineveh, and yet really two—both pagan and idolatrous, both under God's sentence of judgment. One repented after Jonah's preaching and received a "stay of execution." The other felt Nahum's stinging condemnation. One was allowed to live; the other was annihilated. What made the difference?

An important spiritual truth can be found in Nineveh's sorry end: the principle of communication to the next generation. Nineveh's revival was short-lived, not because the people involved were insincere in their repentance, but because they failed to pass on their newfound knowledge of God to the succeeding generation. As the years rolled along, Jonah, the "prophet from the sea," and the great God he represented, were largely forgotten. Revival dwindled and died, and in its place returned all the old pagan practices.

Do you see the importance of teaching the truths of God to your offspring? Without that knowledge they are likely to fail when confronted with the same kinds of crisis situations which you, in God's strength, have learned to conquer. Share with your children a spiritual truth God is teaching you. Remember, their knowledge of God will depend in part upon your faithfulness in passing on the truth.

Nahum's message rumbles and rolls, leaps and flashes, like the horsemen and chariots he describes.

Insight: How Missing Is Missing (3:11)?
When Nahum proclaimed to Nineveh, "Thou shalt be hid," he meant what he said! After Nineveh's destruction in 612 B.C., the site lay obliterated and undiscovered for nearly 2,500 years!

Habakkuk

Habakkuk prophesies in Judah before its final overthrow by Babylonia. Honestly concerned with how God could chasten Judah by means of a nation even more sinful than itself, Habakkuk deals with some perplexing questions: Why is a just God silent? Why do the pleas of the faithful seem to go unheard? The reply comes in the statement of a timeless principle of God's sovereignty: God will deal with the wicked in His way and in His time. Meanwhile righteous people must continue to trust God (2:4).

Focus	Habakkuk's Perplexity				Habakkuk's Prayer
Divisions	First Question: Israel's Sin	First Response: Babylonian Invasion	Second Question: Babylon's Sin	Second Response: Babylon's Destruction	Prayer and Praise
	1:1 1:4	1:5 1:11	1:12 2:1	2:2 2:20	3:1 3:19
Topics	Sweeping a Dirty Nation Clean . . .		. . . Using an Even Dirtier Broom . . .		. . . As Only God Can Do!
	Questions and Answers				Wonder and Worship
Place	Judah				
Time	Approximately 607 B.C.				

Behind the Scenes / Habakkuk 1–3

19

Overview: The book of Habakkuk is not so much the sermons of a prophet as it is the saga of a prophet plagued with a problem. Looking around his native Judah, Habakkuk observes violence and injustice on every hand. What he sees causes him to cry out to God with his perplexing questions: "Why are the wicked prospering in Your nation, Lord? Why are the righteous beaten down? Why don't You do something to right the wrongs of society?" God's reply is even more shocking than the blighted conditions in Judah. "I am doing something, Habakkuk. I am about to use a nation even more corrupt than Judah—the Chaldeans—to cleanse My people of their wicked ways." In stunned disbelief, Habakkuk responds, "How in the name of holiness can you do that, God?" And when God patiently answers the prophet's question, Habakkuk responds in prayer and praise with faith that has resounded through the centuries.

Heart of the Passage: Habakkuk 1, 3

Chapter 1	Chapter 2	Chapter 3
Sweeping a Dirty Nation Clean . . .	. . . Using an Even Dirtier Broom . . .	. . . As Only God Can Do!
"The just shall live by . . . faith" (2:4).		

Your Daily Walk: Don't be afraid to bring your hard questions to God. But be prepared for a shock when He answers them . . . and the possibility that He may not answer them at all.

From a human point of view, God's heavenly ways don't always seem to make earthly sense. If Habakkuk had had his way, judgment would have rolled through Judah like a thunderstorm—now! But in God's timing the unjust conditions would continue (and worsen) before Babylon finally conquered Jerusalem. God was not asking Habakkuk to understand all the "whys" behind His timing; He simply wanted His servant to trust restfully in His control and walk by faith.

Habakkuk begins with a sob, and ends with a song.

Select a Habakkuk-like situation you are facing and list all the "why" questions you would like to ask God. Now at the bottom of the page write the words of 2:4b and 3:19 as fresh expressions of your confidence in the God who has all the answers!

Insight: A Quotable Quote from Habakkuk
The last half of 2:4 is so significant that it is quoted three times in the New Testament (Romans 1:17; Galatians 3:11; Hebrews 10:38). Don't you agree it's a thought worth repeating?

20 *His Story*

Scripture Reading: Acts 15:18; Ephesians 1:11, 14; Psalm 135

 Step Back

If there's one truth the prophets continually preach, it's that God is sovereignly in control of human history. Time and again they reveal details about the history of the nation Israel, the coming of the Messiah, the end times. And the prophets can reveal those details in advance because they are the messengers of the God who ordains them and carries them out.

Concerning history, Frederick Buechner writes:

Unlike Buddhism or Hinduism, biblical faith takes history very seriously because God takes it very seriously. He took it seriously enough to begin it and to enter it and to promise that one day he will bring it to a serious close. The biblical view is that history is not an absurdity to be endured or an illusion to be dispelled or an endlessly repeating cycle to be escaped. Instead, it is for each of us a series of crucial, precious, and unrepeatable moments that are seeking to lead us somewhere (from Wishful Thinking: A Theological ABC, *p. 38).*

God knows all things from the beginning of the world—it's His plan (Acts 15:18). That plan involves everything that happens (Ephesians 1:11). But more than just knowing the plan, God controls it (Psalm 135:6). And the end purpose is for His glory (Ephesians 1:14).

He is our sovereign God, working through human history to fulfill His purposes, revealing Himself to us through His Word, seeking to draw us to Himself in love, mercy, and grace.

Look Up

Our sovereign God, ruler of history, is worthy of your worship today. Let Psalm 135 guide you in praising God for His mastery of history . . . and of your life.

God's plan will continue on God's schedule.

Move Ahead

Sometimes it's difficult to see how the times we live in are in God's hands. Obviously, much that happens in our world is the result of the depravity of man and the work of Satan's forces. Even so, God knows all about it, and somehow will ultimately bring everything together into His glorious plan.

Today, as you read through your newspaper or watch the television news, try to look at it through the grid of God's Word. Let the news stories prompt you to pray for God's will in every circumstance. And thank Him that one day His glory will be completely revealed, and His will totally fulfilled.

Zephaniah

B ut I will also leave in the midst of thee an afflicted and poor people, and they shall trust in the name of the LORD" (3:12). Writing at one of the lowest points in the spiritual life of Judah, Zephaniah's primary concern is the impending Day of the Lord. That day signifies the final judgment of God on earth and the ensuing time of blessing and peace. However, Zephaniah knows that when judgment is over God will once again look with favor on His people, restore their fortunes, rejoice over them, and dwell among them (3:14-18).

Focus	The Judgment Day of the Lord			The Salvation Day of the Lord		
Divisions	Judgment of Whole Earth	Judgment of Judah	Judgment of Nations	Need of Salvation	Promise of Salvation	Promise of Restoration
	1:1 1:3	1:4 2:3	2:4 2:15	3:1 3:8	3:9 3:13	3:14 3:20
Topics	God's Wrath on Judah		God's Woes on the Nations	God's Will for the Remnant		
	Retribution and Judgment			Restoration and Joy		
Place	Judah and the Nations					
Time	Approximately 630 B.C.					

21 *The Days of the Lord's Wrath*
Zephaniah 1–3

Heart of the Passage: Zeph. 1

Overview: Zephaniah's pungent pen records only 53 verses, but in the process sets forth some of the strongest statements of judgment in the Old Testament. Looking out over the nation of Judah in particular and the world in general, Zephaniah fashions his fiery verbal assault. The day of the Lord will come with fury, ferocity, and finality, and God will have the last word. Retribution and judgment will give way to restoration and joy "in that day."

Chapter 1	Chapter 2	Chapter 3
Retribution for Judah	Retribution for Judah's Neighbors	Restoration for Judah
Picture of Judgment		Picture of Joy

Truth is violated by falsehood, but it is outraged by silence.

Your Daily Walk: Complacency has been called "the curse of Christendom." Complacency paralyzes (1:12) and produces lukewarmness. In fact, God finds complacency worse than outright rebellion (Revelation 3:14-16).

Try your hand at a personal investigation of complacency:

1. To me, complacency means _____ .

2. I see complacency in the Christian church today in the areas of _____ .

3. In my opinion, complacency among Christians today is a contributing cause of _____ .

4. Complacency rears its ugly head in my life most frequently in the area of _____ .

5. To attack this disease, I will begin today with God's help to _____ .

Complacency is like a malignancy. When ignored, it can be lethal; when confronted, it can be conquered. With God's help you can avoid having the tragic epitaph, "He/she was neither hot nor cold," applied to your Christian life. Sip a glass of lukewarm water as you talk to God about what you intend to do about the areas of lukewarmness in your spiritual life. You might want to enlist the help of a Christian friend whose heart for the Lord is anything but lukewarm.

Insight: "Now Hear This, Now Hear This. . . ."
In three short chapters Zephaniah uses words like "the day of the LORD," "the great day," "that day," "the day of the LORD's wrath," "the day," more than 20 times altogether. How many of these phrases can you find?

Haggai

"Consider your ways" and "finish what you have begun" are the resounding calls of the prophet Haggai as he tries to awaken the people spiritually. They have just returned from exile in Babylonia and are discouraged by the destruction in the city. But Haggai's message brings encouragement, particularly to the governor, Zerubbabel, who must inspire the people. "I am with you," declares the Lord as the people are called to rebuild and fight against future oppression. There is hope and future blessing for their obedience!

Focus	Finishing God's House		Finding God's Blessing	
Divisions	A Call to Build	A Promise of Glory	A Problem with Defilement	A Promise to a Servant
	1:1 1:15	2:1 2:9	2:10 2:19	2:20 2:23
Topics	Wrong Priorities	Wrong Perspectives	Incomplete Purity	Encouraging Promises
	"Build the house; and I will take pleasure in it" (1:8)			
Place	Jerusalem			
Time	September 1, 520 B.C.	October 21, 520 B.C.	December 24, 520 B.C.	

22 *A House Half Built / Haggai 1–2*

Heart of the Passage: Haggai 2:1-11

📖 **Overview:** The last three books of the Old Testament (Haggai, Zechariah, and Malachi) are the so-called "Postexilic Prophets" because each was addressed to the returnees from the Babylonian Exile. Under the leadership of Zerubbabel, the people began the task of rebuilding the temple (Ezra 1–6). But 14 years later, the temple foundation is covered with weeds rather than walls. Instead of completing the house of God, the people are busy building their own homes and careers. Into this sorry scene of misguided priorities steps Haggai to exhort the people to put first things first. Halfhearted obedience, Haggai reminds them, will never result in God's wholehearted blessing!

Chapter 1		Chapter 2			
A Call to Build		A Promise of Glory	A Problem with Defilement	A Promise to a Servant	
	1	9	10 19	20	23
Finishing God's House		Finding God's Blessing			

Do not have your concert first and tune your instruments afterward. Begin the day with God.

🖊 **Your Daily Walk:** Think a minute about the following sentence, then jot down your responses: "The five most difficult problems I wrestle with in my Christian life are . . ."

Chances are good that your list included the problem of priorities . . . maintaining balance in your walk with God. How much do you pray, and when? How much do you give, and to whom? When do you study God's Word, meet with God's people? And how do you fit all that around your responsibilities at work, at home, in the dorm, in the community?

The returning exiles allowed good things to replace God's best in their lives. It didn't happen overnight. But gradually, their time and energy were diverted into building something good (their own homes) instead of building God's best (the temple). Read the challenging words of Matthew 6:33. Then examine the good, better, and best priorities in your own life. What needs to change about the five priorities you've listed in the margin?

✒ **Insight:** Putting First Things First

Haggai assesses the nation's stagnant condition and summarizes it in 1:7-11: "Ye looked for much, and, lo, it came to little; . . . Why? . . . Because of mine house that is waste and ye run every man unto his own house." This eternal principle of making the Lord and His work your first priority is echoed by Jesus in Matthew 6:33: "Seek ye first the kingdom of God, and his righteousness; and all these things shall be added unto you."

Zechariah

U sing colorful visions and consoling sermons to portray God's glorious future plans for His covenant people, Zechariah encourages the workers engaged in rebuilding the temple. Although early enthusiasm has waned, the task is an important one, for the temple will be the focal point of the ministry of Israel's coming Messiah. God will keep His promises to His people, and fasting will turn to feasting when Messiah arrives. So put away sin, finish the temple, and await the Messiah with eager excitement.

Focus	Corrections			Directions	
Divisions	Visions of Horses and Horns	Visions of Scrolls and Chariots	To Fast or Not to Fast	Israel's Coming King and Shepherd	Israel's Coming Consolation
	1　　　　2	3　　　　6	7　　　　8	9　　　　11	12　　　　14
Topics	Eight Visions		Four Sermons	Two Burdens	
	Present Problems			Future Promises	
Place	Jerusalem				
Time	While Rebuilding the Temple (520–518 B.C.)			After Rebuilding the Temple (480–410 B.C.)	

23 Visions of Horses and Horns
Zechariah 1–2

Heart of the Passage: Zechariah 1:1-17

Overview: Zechariah is the longest of the Minor Prophets (the books of Hosea–Malachi) and contains more messianic prophecies than perhaps any other Old Testament book. Zechariah and Haggai ministered to the same audience, but their lives and books bear many striking contrasts. Haggai was old; Zechariah was young. Haggai exhorted; Zechariah encouraged. Haggai preached sermons; Zechariah shared signs. Haggai was an activist; Zechariah was a visionary.

Chapter 1		Chapter 2	
A Call to Repentance	A Man Among the Myrtles	A Man with a Measure	The Lord of All Mankind
1 6	7 21	1 5	6 13
Israel's Fate		Israel's Future	

What a father says to his children is not heard by the world, but it will be heard by posterity.

Your Daily Walk: How would you evaluate the contribution your father made to your spiritual life? (a) negligible; (b) sizable; (c) enormous.

Four times in his opening verses, Zechariah mentions the sorry state of Judah's fathers (1:2, 4-6) who, by ignoring God and pursuing evil, brought divine judgment upon themselves and their children.

Fathers, yours is an awesome assignment: to assist your children in becoming men and women of God. And the eloquent, yet painful testimony of Scripture is this: Children will seldom rise to a higher spiritual plane than that of their parents. Read the first six verses of Zechariah as if it were a manual entitled *How to Succeed as a Father* because that is just what those verses will help you do!

Insight: Eight Visions of Comfort and Woe

During the next three days, you will read Zechariah's eight night visions—five full of comfort and three full of condemnation. Can you give each a short title after you have read it?

Zechariah's Vision	My Title
1:7-17	"The Horseman Among the Myrtles"
1:18-21	_____
2:1-13	_____
3:1-10	_____
4:1-14	_____
5:1-4	_____
5:5-11	_____
6:1-8	_____

Visions of Clothes and Candlesticks
Zechariah 3–4

24

 Overview: The opening six verses of Zechariah's book give the reader valuable insight into how the visions that Zechariah relates should be interpreted. God is calling His people back to a fresh commitment to Him—a commitment demonstrated in rearranged priorities and rekindled worship. God desires to cleanse and use His nation. Like a candlestick and lamps, Israel can bear light to a darkened world "not by might, nor by power, but by my spirit, saith the LORD of hosts" (4:6).

Heart of the Passage: Zechariah 3

Chapter 3	Chapter 4	
Clean Clothes for Joshua	Seven Golden Lamps	Two Anointed Olive Trees
1	7 8	14
Visions of Judgment on Israel		

Your Daily Walk: *Question:* What do a light bulb covered with mud, a window covered with soot, and a life spotted with sin have in common?

Answer: They are all incapable of allowing light to shine through them for the benefit of others. Regardless of how bright and pure the light, the net result will be darkness until the dirt is dealt with. The problem is not with the source of light, but rather with the vessel through which the light is shining.

Jesus told His disciples, "Ye are the light of the world," and urged them, "Let your light so shine before men, that they may see your good works, and glorify your Father which is in heaven" (Matthew 5:14, 16). But He also warned them of the danger of dirtiness: "If therefore the light that is in thee be [turned to] darkness, how great is that darkness!" (Matthew 6:23). A life clouded with unconfessed sin is as frustrating as a mud-caked light bulb.

Take a "spot check" of your life right now. Do you have the Light within you (John 1:1-12)? If so, are there "dirt spots" that are obscuring that fact in the eyes of others? You'll find God's divine "glass cleaner" of forgiveness as near as 1 John 1:9.

You are only young once, but immaturity can last a lifetime.

Insight: The Prophet from the Temple Precincts

Zechariah, descendant of Iddo (1:1-7), was more than a prophet; he was also a priest (compare Nehemiah 12:1-16, noting especially verses 4 and 16). This helps to explain his frequent reference to the temple in his visions and sermons. Watch for two such "temple flashbacks" in today's section, and others in the rest of the book.

25 Visions of Scrolls and Chariots
Zechariah 5–6

Heart of the Passage: Zechariah 5

Overview: So far, Zechariah's night visions have revolved around the nation of Israel: her temple, her future, her Messiah. But now Zechariah shifts his focus to the world as a whole, for God's program is not restricted to His chosen people alone. He is the Sovereign of all nations. Just as mankind's wickedness is worldwide, so God's justice and mercy will extend to the four winds.

	Chapter 5		Chapter 6	
	Vision of the Flying Roll	Vision of the Lead-filled Ephah	Vision of the Four Chariots	Parable of the Crowns
1	4	5	11	1	8	9	15
		Visions of Judgment Over All the Earth		

Before you speak, listen. Before you write, think. Before you pray, forgive. Before you quit, try.

Insight: Eight Visions in Review

Now that you have wrestled with Zechariah's colorful (and at times mystifying) visions, here is a suggested interpretation for each picture: (1) The horseman among the myrtles (God will rebuild His people, 1:7-17). (2) The four horns and craftsmen (Israel's oppressors will be judged, 1:18-21). (3) The man with a measuring line (God will protect and glorify Jerusalem, 2:1-13). (4) Joshua's clean clothes (Israel will be cleansed by the coming Branch, 3:1-10). (5) The golden lampstand (God's Spirit is empowering God's appointed leaders, 4:1-14). (6) The flying scroll (individual sin will be judged, 5:1-4). (7) The woman in the ephah (national sin will be removed, 5:5-11). (8) The four chariots (God's judgment will descend on the nations, 6:1-8).

Your Daily Walk: God is as concerned about the worker as He is about the work. In fact, He often spends more time preparing the worker than He does using the worker to perform His work. Moses spent 80 years preparing for a 40-year assignment; Jesus spent three decades preparing for a ministry that would last only about three years. In God's estimation, the servant of God is as important as the service of God.

Zechariah's night visions were designed to encourage God's people who were sagging in their fervor for God's work. Before you tackle your next Sunday school lesson or other ministry preparation, fall in love with God all over again. Read some of your favorite passages from His Word; unburden your heart to Him in prayer; sing some of your favorite hymns and choruses. Then you, like Zechariah's countrymen, will have no trouble serving Him with zeal.

318

Fasting Turned to Feasting
Zechariah 7–8

26

Overview: Two years after his series of night visions, Zechariah addresses a question that has arisen during his ministry: "Should the returned remnant continue to observe days of fasting to commemorate the events of the deportation to Babylon?" God's answer: Justice, mercy, and compassion are more important than insincere fasts. With that principle in view, Zechariah presents a glorious picture of God's future blessings for the nation when there will be feasting instead of fasting—a promise designed to encourage the remnant to live righteously in the present day as well.

Heart of the Passage: Zechariah 7

Chapter 7		Chapter 8	
Empty Ritual	Empty Homeland	Restoration for the Remnant	Rejoicing by the Remnant
1 7	8 14	1 17	18 23
Fasting		Feasting	

Your Daily Walk: A recent appeal for a worthy charity began with this challenge: "Do something special for God." But is that really possible?

The Jews of Zechariah's day had set up a whole series of fasts to commemorate the tragic events of the Exile. No doubt as their stomachs growled on those occasions, they felt doubly religious. Surely God was taking notice of their self-denial. But look at God's response through His prophet: "When ye fasted and mourned . . . did ye at all fast unto me, even to me?" (7:5). The implied answer is "No!" They were really fasting (and later feasting) for themselves.

Paul continues this same thought in Colossians 3:17 when he says, "And whatsoever ye do in word or deed, do all in the name of the Lord Jesus." Whatever you do—on Sunday or Friday, whether fasting or feasting—should be to God's glory. On a slip of paper write or type these words: "Do all in the name of the Lord Jesus." Place the note on your refrigerator, bathroom mirror, or desk where you will see it often today. Then allow its message to help you make everything you do be something special for God.

Man sees your actions, but God sees your motives.

Insight: A City with a Sordid History
The question of fasting was raised by the people of Bethel ("house of God," 7:2), the site where King Jeroboam led the people in calf worship before the Exile (1 Kings 12:26-30). Zechariah's careful response helped ensure that an idolatrous form of worship would not spring up there again.

319

27 A Look at Israel's Military Future
Zechariah 9–11

Overview: Though horrible judgment would fall on Israel's neighbors, Israel would be preserved for the long-awaited day of her Messiah's arrival. The King of Zion would come riding upon the colt of a donkey to defend His people and defeat His enemies, just as He promised. Yet in spite of His offer of redemption, the King would be rejected and betrayed for 30 pieces of silver.

Heart of the Passage: Zechariah 9

Chapter 9		Chapter 10	Chapter 11
Zion's Fallen Neighbors	Zion's Future King	Messiah's Reign	Messiah's Rejection
1 8	9 17		
Judgment and Justice		Salvation and Suffering	

Your Daily Walk: Think back over your times of prayer this past week and compile a list of things you prayed for. You may want to arrange them by category: prayers for yourself, for others, for your nation, etc. Now take a mental inventory of all the worries and anxieties you are currently entertaining: pressing deadlines at work, a lingering illness, a broken relationship, a car that refuses to work properly, too much month and not enough money, a discipline problem in the home, a long dry spell without rain, the high price of almost everything.

A day without prayer is a boast against God.

As you catalog your anxieties, place a check next to those items you've already thought to pray about. Does the small number of checks surprise you? James 4:2 diagnoses the problem this way: "Ye have not, because ye ask not." It was true in the days of Zechariah. The God of creation, the God of all goodness, the God who made the clouds and the rain, nonetheless commanded His people, "Ask ye of the LORD rain . . . so the LORD shall make bright clouds, and give them showers of rain" (10:1). Though God is the giver of every good and perfect gift, He delights to have His children bring their petitions to Him.

Today, talk to God about the "un-prayer requests" in your life. Remember, God cannot answer petitions which you have not asked, though He knows what you need before you even pray.

Insight: A Prophetic Bull's-Eye from Five Centuries Away
Zechariah's prophetic marksmanship was incredible. Compare 11:12-13 with Matthew 27:1-9 and notice how both the purchase (a potter's field) and the purchase price (30 pieces of silver) were prophesied a full 500 years in advance.

A Look at Israel's Spiritual Future **28**
Zechariah 12–14

📖 **Overview:** Zechariah closes his prophecy with a breathtaking panorama of events in store for Israel "in that day." Topographically, the Mount of Olives would split in half (14:4). Spiritually, idols and false prophets would be removed from the land (13:2-3) and Jerusalem would become the focus of worship, with cooking pots as sacred as the bowls beside the altar (14:20). Militarily, God would destroy all nations that come against Jerusalem (12:9). Politically, the Lord would be King over all the earth (14:9). In short, every aspect of Israel's national life would reflect God's authority—an exciting prospect indeed!

Heart of the Passage: Zechariah 14

Chapter 12	Chapter 13	Chapter 14
Conquering Israel's Enemies	Cleansing Israel's Impurities	Coming as Israel's Sovereign
"And the LORD shall be king over all the earth" (14:9).		

✔️ **Your Daily Walk:** It is one thing to anticipate a future event; it is something else to act in response to that anticipation. As you read the final chapters of Zechariah, consider this: The prophet's predictions regarding Jesus' first coming were unerringly accurate. What does that suggest about Zechariah's foretelling of events surrounding Jesus' second coming?

Anticipation says there is coming a day of great mourning for those who looked upon the crucified Savior but never received Him personally (12:10-11). Action says, "Don't be numbered with them."

Anticipation says there is coming a day when every knee will bow before the Lord (14:9). Action inquires, "Have you bowed before Him voluntarily, or will you only worship Him when you have no other choice?"

Anticipation says there is coming a day when holiness will be the hallmark of God's people (14:20-21). Action demands, "Are you moving toward that goal in the public and private details of your life?" What are you anticipating about the future because you are a Christian? And what action does that suggest in your life . . . today?

If a man takes no thought about what is distant, he will find sorrow close at hand.

🔲 **Insight:** Plentiful Portraits of Messiah
Zechariah anticipates the first and second comings of Jesus Christ by portraying Him in more than a dozen prophetic pictures and roles. How many can you discover in the following verses? 3:1, 8-9; 6:12-13; 9:9; 10:3-4; 11:4-13; 12:10; 13:1, 7; 14:3, 9.

321

29 *The Day of the Lord*

Scripture Reading: Psalm 24; Isaiah 33:14-16

Step Back

The Day of the Lord is a common theme of the prophets. Yet it's a concept that is so huge, so overwhelming, so powerful, that it may be difficult for us to grasp.

That day signifies the final judgment of God on the earth and the eventual time of blessing and peace. It's not a literal 24-hour day, but a period of culmination of God's plan—including the return of Christ, the final judgments, and the end of history as we know it.

Both aspects—judgment and salvation, punishment and peace—are contained in the Day of the Lord.

The glimpses the prophets give us of that time are both harrowing and hopeful. For Judah, the message was one of impending doom; the nation would indeed by punished.

But beyond that cloud, brightness blazes. God will purify His people, the prophets announce. He will restore their fortunes. He will rejoice over them with shouts of joy. He will make them great. He will be in their midst. In short, beyond judgment, there is joy.

Look Up

The Bible says that those who desire the Lord's coming must know that He requires clean hands and a pure heart (see Psalm 24:3-4; Isaiah 33:14-16).

Nothing God has yet done for us can compare with all that is written in the sure word of prophecy.

The Day of the Lord may be frightening to consider, but for the sincere child of God who seeks His glory, there is comfort.

God's prophecies still stand. Are you ready for the Day of the Lord? Search your heart before the Lord; seek His cleansing and purifying touch.

Move Ahead

God revealed a wide array of truths through the prophets. Much of their revelation has come to pass; much remains to be fulfilled. But you can be assured, it will be fulfilled.

If you'd like to build a better understanding of the Day of the Lord and how it will unfold in relation to what is happening in the world today, ask your pastor or Bible teacher for resources you can use in your study. The better you know your Bible, the better you can understand current events.

Meanwhile, let your heart rejoice in these promises: "They shall not hurt or destroy in all my holy mountain: for the earth shall be full of the knowledge of the LORD, as the waters cover the sea" (Isaiah 11:9); "And he that sat upon the throne said, Behold, I make all things new" (Revelation 21:5). Come, Lord Jesus.

Malachi

Years after the restoration from exile, the spiritual condition of God's people has deteriorated. Again they have lapsed into the same sins that brought about captivity. They tithe sporadically, ignore the Sabbath, and intermarry with unbelievers. Their hearts have grown hard and their love for God has grown cold, yet Malachi comes to remind the people of God's love for them. Malachi's final warning about the purifying Day of the Lord marks the close of the Old Testament period which is followed by 400 years of silence in the biblical record.

Focus	God's Love		God's Rebuke		God's Promise		
Divisions	God's Love for the People		Rebuke of the Priests	Rebuke of the People	Righteous Remembered	Wicked Destroyed	Elijah Coming
	1:1 ——— 1:5		1:6 ——— 2:9	2:10 ——— 3:15	3:16 — 3:18	4:1 — 4:3	4:4 — 4:6
Topics	Past		Present		Future		
	Questions and Answers				Invitation and Warning		
Place	Jerusalem						
Time	Approximately 432–425 B.C.						

30 *Hearts of Stone / Malachi 1–4*

**Heart
of the
Passage:
Malachi
1–4**

Overview: Malachi brings down the curtain on Old Testament prophecy. Malachi the prophet and Nehemiah the builder were contemporaries, and the problems Nehemiah faced became the basis for the sermons Malachi preached. Corrupt priests, mixed marriages, calloused consciences—these were the conditions under which Malachi wrote. Using a question-and-answer style, Malachi highlights the arrogance and insensitivity of God's people. His convicting words of judgment usher in 400 years of silence during which God's prophetic voice is no longer heard. But the last book of the Old Testament anticipates the first book of the New, where John the Baptist breaks the silence by declaring, "Prepare ye the way of the Lord" (Matthew 3:3).

Chapter 1	Chapter 2	Chapter 3	Chapter 4
Sins of the Priests	Sins of the People	Payday for the People	Day of the Lord
Hard Hearts			Tender Hearts

**The
gospel is
neither a
discussion
nor a
debate;
it is an
announce-
ment.**

Your Daily Walk: Today you will read the last of the 929 chapters, 23,214 verses, 592,439 words, and approximately 2,728,100 letters in the Old Testament (if you are using a King James Version of the Bible). Congratulations! You've reached a significant milestone in your goal of mastering God's Word . . . and allowing it to master you.

Malachi concludes the Old Testament with a final reminder that sin must be dealt with. Tomorrow as you begin reading through the New Testament, you'll discover God's provision for mankind's sin-sickness—Christ the Messiah. Perhaps you've already heard and responded to that Good News for yourself. If not, what better time than right now to put your trust in the Savior. Then invite an unsaved friend to join you as you take a daily walk through the New Testament. It's a wonderful way to introduce others to your Savior as well.

Insight: And Now a Word from Our Creator
Of the 55 verses in Malachi, 47 are spoken by God—the highest proportion of any prophetical book. Malachi is also the only prophet who ends his book on a note of judgment rather than hope (note the final word of the book)—a fitting conclusion to the Old Testament because it underscores mankind's sinful condition and sets the stage for God's solution in the person of Messiah.

Matthew

M atthew records Jesus' preparation and proclamation as God's Messiah (Anointed One) to the people of Israel. Opposition to His ministry grows as religious leaders deny His claims and disavow His miracles, prompting Jesus to turn increasingly to His disciples. Through miracles, parables, and sermons, He prepares them for the climax of His earthly ministry—His sacrificial death, burial, and resurrection. Prior to His ascension, Jesus commissions His disciples to continue the work He had begun.

Focus	Preparation				Proclamation			
Divisions	Arrival of the Messiah	Teaching by the Messiah	Healing by the Messiah	Reactions to the Messiah	Sermons by the Messiah	Parables of the Messiah	Prophecies by the Messiah	Finished Work of the Messiah
	1 4	5 7	8 11	12 15	16 19	20 23	24 25	26 28
Topics	Teaching All Men			Teaching 12 Men				
	Increasing Acceptance		Increasing Antagonism					
Place	Bethlehem/ Nazareth		Galilee			Jerusalem		
Time	4 B.C.–A.D. 33							

1 Arrival of the Messiah / Matthew 1–4

Heart of the Passage: Matthew 1:18-25; 3:13– 4:11

Overview: Matthew begins his gospel with a record of genealogy of Jesus Christ. But this beginning is more than merely a tabulation of names, for the word *genealogy* can also mean "genesis." The Old Testament book of Genesis traces the creation of the universe and man; now Matthew shows that the advent of Jesus inaugurates a "new creation." From the call of Abraham, God has been moving to accomplish His great redemptive plan. Jesus, the prophesied Messiah, fulfills the Old Testament promises in every facet of His life: annunciation, birth, boyhood, baptism, and upbringing.

Chapter 1	Chapter 2	Chapter 3	Chapter 4
Jesus' Background	Jesus' Birth	John's Teaching	Jesus' Temptation
Coming of the Messiah		Character of the Messiah	

Faith is the starting point of obedience.

Your Daily Walk: How well do you obey divine directives? On an obedience scale of 1 to 10 (with 1 being "consistently disobedient," 10 being "consistently obedient"), how would you rate yourself?

Today's reading abounds with examples of the importance of obedience. The genealogy of chapter 1 sparkles with the names of those who obeyed God in times of spiritual decadence: Abraham, Ruth, David, Hezekiah, Josiah, Joseph. Chapter 3 describes the ministry of John the Baptist as he preached a message of repentance and fruit-bearing—a message demanding uncompromising obedience. In chapter 4, Jesus was obedient to God's will and Word, rather than agree to Satan's subtle temptations.

In what area of your life is God speaking to you about obedience? It is one thing to *know* what God wants you to do; it is something else to make *obedience* a commitment in your daily schedule. In the margin or on a piece of paper, write the acts of obedience performed by three different people in the genealogy (for example, Abraham obeyed God by leaving Ur). Now add your name to the list, together with an act of obedience you will undertake by faith today.

Insight: The Worldwide Impact of Messiah's Appearing
Christ's coming held significance not merely for the Jews, but for Gentiles as well. Note the four alien women listed in the genealogy of chapter 1, the Magi from the East, and Christ's Gentile following in 4:25.

Introduction to the
New Testament Historical Books

<table>
<tr><td colspan="6" align="center">Pauline Epistles: Individuals</td></tr>
<tr><td></td><td>1 Timothy</td><td>2 Timothy</td><td>Titus</td><td>Philemon</td><td></td></tr>
<tr><td rowspan="9">Pauline Epistles: Church</td><td>2 Thessalonians</td><td colspan="2" rowspan="9">"It seemed good to me . . . to write unto thee . . . that thou mightest know the certainty of those things . . ." (Luke 1:3-4).</td><td>Hebrews</td><td rowspan="9">Non-Pauline Epistles and Revelation</td></tr>
<tr><td>1 Thessalonians</td><td>James</td></tr>
<tr><td>Colossians</td><td>1 Peter</td></tr>
<tr><td>Philippians</td><td>2 Peter</td></tr>
<tr><td>Ephesians</td><td>1 John</td></tr>
<tr><td>Galatians</td><td>2 John</td></tr>
<tr><td>2 Corinthians</td><td>3 John</td></tr>
<tr><td>1 Corinthians</td><td>Jude</td></tr>
<tr><td>Romans</td><td>Revelation</td></tr>
<tr><td colspan="6" align="center">Acts</td></tr>
<tr><td></td><td>Matthew</td><td>Mark</td><td>Luke</td><td>John</td><td></td></tr>
<tr><td colspan="6" align="center">Historical Books</td></tr>
</table>

F ive Historical Books comprise the foundation of the New Testament. The first four, collectively known as the Gospels, present a four-dimensional glimpse of Jesus the Christ.

Matthew, a Jew, aims his words at a Jewish audience, showing them from the Old Testament prophecies that Jesus is their promised King and Messiah. Marks seeks to reach a Roman audience with the Good News of Jesus the Perfect Servant, come to minister to the spiritual and physical needs of mankind. Luke the physician portrays Jesus as the Perfect Man who seeks and saves the lost. John beams his message to all mankind, showing from Jesus' miracles and messages that He is clearly the Son of God.

The fifth historical book is the Acts of the Apostles which shows what happens when Spirit-empowered men and women take seriously their commission to be witnesses of the resurrected Savior.

2 *Teaching by the Messiah / Matthew 5–7*

Heart of the Passage: Matthew 5:1-20; 7:1-20

Overview: All candidates for public office must present a platform upon which to base their campaign. Jesus claimed to be the Messiah, the King of the Jews. The section you will read today, traditionally called the Sermon on the Mount, presents His "platform"—His statement of heaven (5:3, 10). Relationship to God (not simply adherence to ritual) and inward attitude (not merely outward action) become the focus of Christ's message. Only by building upon the sure foundation which God has provided (7:24-27) can we live a lifestyle of righteousness that exceeds that of the scribes and Pharisees (5:20).

Chapter 5	Chapter 6	Chapter 7
Righteous Requirements	Reassuring Relationships	Right Responses
How to Walk	How to Worship	How to Do God's Will

Your Daily Walk: *"Judge not, that ye be not judged" (7:1). "Wherefore by their fruits ye shall know them" (7:20).* How can you put these seemingly contradictory statements together? What is the point Jesus is trying to make?

Whatever other philosophers may have been, Jesus alone absolutely practiced what He preached.

Judging (7:1) has in mind the attaching of motives to another person's actions. You may conclude your neighbors are thrifty or cheap . . . friendly or nosy . . . attentive to detail or picky . . . depending on the motives you ascribe to them. Snap judgments and misunderstood motives only lead to the same kind of treatment in return.

By contrast, you have a Christian responsibility to be a *"fruit inspector,"* to evaluate your actions (and the actions of others) by the objective standards of God's inspired Word (7:20), and to adjust your behavior accordingly. Find a piece of fruit to nibble on as you read Matthew 7:1-5, 15-20. And as you do, if you find evidence of fruit that doesn't belong in your life, ask God to help you do some overdue pruning of your attitudes and actions.

Insight: The "Eyes" Have It

In the Bible the eye is often a symbol for moral qualities. The eye not only has sight, but it is also "bountiful" or generous (Proverbs 22:9); proud (Isaiah 5:15); "full of adultery" or lustful (2 Peter 2:14); and capable of pity (Deuteronomy 7:16). The good eye of Matthew 6:22 is fixed on God, while the person with bad eyes tries to look at God and the world at the same time and sees neither with clarity.

The Savior's Sermon

3

← Step Back

In Matthew's gospel we find six sections of the teachings of Jesus Christ: the Sermon on the Mount (chapters 5–7); the charge to the Twelve (chapter 10); the kingdom parables (chapter 13); the teaching on greatness (chapter 18); the woes to the Pharisees (chapter 23); and the Olivet discourse (chapters 24–25).

Scripture Reading: Matthew 6:9-13

Each one offers rich insights into the life-giving message He brought. And yet the message that most extensively describes authentic kingdom living is the first one—the one we call the Sermon on the Mount.

This sermon—which you read yesterday—is a picture of the lifestyle of a true subject of the King, a lifestyle that demonstrates through word and deed the ways of the Lord in the life of His disciple.

In this section, Christ shows the path of true happiness we should follow and the path of destruction we should avoid. He describes the right way and wrong way to pray, fast, give, and live.

Even though Christ's sermon stretches over three chapters in Matthew, it's actually only 107 verses. Jesus offers powerful truths on happiness, adultery, murder, forgiveness, divorce, oaths, retribution, hypocrisy, prayer, fasting, and much more.

In fact, if the Sermon on the Mount were the only portion of Scripture available to you, you could spend the rest of the year—if not the rest of your life—working out its applications in your daily living.

↑ Look Up

Take the time today to read again Matthew 6:9-13—the Lord's Prayer. But this time, don't read through it quickly as part of your daily reading; and don't let its familiarity drain the meaning from the words.

Before passing judgment on a sermon, be sure to try it out in practice.

Focus on each sentence, each word, and consider again what Christ is saying through that prayer. Then let it springboard you into a time of personal communion with your Master.

→ Move Ahead

On a note card, jot down a verse from the Sermon on the Mount that really gripped your heart when you read it.

On the other side of your card, complete this sentence: "On the basis of this verse, Christ is calling on me today to [what?], and with His help, I will!" That's one good way to translate a spoken sermon into a living one.

4 *Healing by the Messiah / Matthew 8–11*

Heart of the Passage: Matthew 8, 10

📖 **Overview:** Matthew concentrates on 10 miracles in chapters 8 and 9 that demonstrate Jesus' power over disease, the forces of nature, and the spirit world. Christ then bestows that same power and authority on His chosen apostles and sends them out as ambassadors of the kingdom. He first instructs them how to act, then warns them of the dangers they will face, as He calls them to committed discipleship. When news of John's imprisonment reaches Jesus, He publicly honors John as God's messenger and prophet. The One to whom John pointed now invites all who are burdened with cares to find rest and refreshment in Him.

Chapters 8–9	Chapter 10	Chapter 11
Divine Power Demonstrated	Divine Authority Delegated	Divine Authority Disregarded
Miracles	Messengers	Coming Miseries

It costs to follow Jesus Christ, but it costs more not to.

✔️ **Your Daily Walk:** Think back to your childhood days and try to recall one personality from the world of sports or entertainment that you wanted to be like when you grew up. Write that name in the margin. Then below it, list some of the things you did to pattern your life after that "childhood idol" in matters of dress, walk, and speech.

Without even knowing it, you had become a "disciple" of that great personality, a follower and a learner of everything he or she did and said. Every TV appearance, every word, every mannerism became an object of intense interest to you because of your commitment to be like that person . . . to model your life after another.

Does that help to clarify what it means to be a disciple of Jesus Christ? Look up the following verses to see what else Matthew has to say about the commitment and devotion that Christ demands of all who would follow Him and learn from Him today: 8:19-22; 10:35-38. Then complete this job description of your responsibilities as a disciple: "My role as Jesus' disciple is . . ."

🔖 **Insight:** The "Move" Every Christian Should Make
Repeatedly Matthew mentions that Jesus "was moved with compassion" (9:36; 14:14; 15:32; 20:34). Biblical compassion is seeing the need of someone around you, and then doing something about it. It is realizing that, though you cannot do everything, you can do something—and with God's help you will do what you can. What *will* you do?

Reactions to the Messiah / Matthew 12–15   5

Overview: A turning point in Matthew's gospel occurs in chapter 12. Mounting antagonism by the Jewish religious leaders erupts into open denunciation of Jesus. Attributing His miracles to the power of Satan, they demand yet another sign to substantiate Jesus' messianic claims. Because of their hardhearted rejection, Jesus begins to speak to them in parables—stories from everyday life whose deeper spiritual significance is explained only to the disciples. After a rude reception in His home town of Nazareth, Jesus withdraws across the Sea of Galilee to the regions of Tyre and Sidon in order to escape growing opposition.

Heart of the Passage: Matthew 12, 14

Chapter 12	Chapter 13	Chapters 14–15
Rejection by the Leaders	Instruction to the Disciples	Multiplied Loaves for the Multitudes
Pharisees	Parables	Provisions

Your Daily Walk: When someone gets particularly excited about an activity or achievement, you'll often hear the expression, "He lost his head over it!" Have you ever wondered where that phrase originated?

A pricked con- science should cry out in pain.

One suggestion is Matthew 14! There you will read the tragic ending of the life of John the Baptist, who "lost his head" over a king's immoral conduct in the palace. John, the uncompromising declarer of God's righteousness, stood fearlessly before Herod Antipas, pointed an accusing finger at the adulterous tetrarch, and declared, "It is not lawful [under Roman or divine law] for you to [marry your brother's wife]" (14:4). Herod was terrified (14:5); his wife was infuriated; and for John's unflinching stance, the prophet of God was beheaded.

All that is necessary for evil to prosper is for good men to do nothing. Moral issues command front-page attention: abortion, pornography, homosexuality. The Bible is not silent about these; are you?

First, do your homework in the pages of God's Word. (A concordance will help!) Then let your voice be heard for good and for God this week.

Insight: Matthew—A Lot of Old in the New
Repeatedly in Matthew you will find the phrase, "that it might be fulfilled which was spoken by the prophet" or its equivalent. Can you find such statements in today's section?

6 *Sermons by the Messiah / Matthew 16–19*

📖 **Overview:** Matthew records many crucial incidents from Jesus' life in these four chapters. Though Christ takes time to heal an epileptic boy, pay His temple tax, and confront the increasingly hostile Pharisees, it is clear that His primary concern is for His disciples—those He would soon leave behind to continue the work He had begun. Healings and discourses, miracles and parables—all focus on Jesus' faithful followers to prepare them for the difficult days just ahead.

Heart of the Passage: Matthew 16

	Chapter 16	Chapter 17	Chapter 18	Chapter 19
	Preaching of the King Concerning . . .			
	His Church	His Death	His Glory	The Lost	The Family
1	20	21	28		
	Unveiling Christ's Identity		Unveiling Christ's Priorities	

👣 **Your Daily Walk:** Imagine for a moment that you are Jesus of Nazareth. In one year's time your earthly life and ministry will be over. Your followers—an unlikely assortment of fishermen, politicians, and professional people—will be all you leave behind to continue the work you have begun. People like . . . Peter (who usually needed three reminders before he learned his lesson) . . . James and John (the hot-tempered "sons of thunder") . . . Thomas (the skeptic of the group).

By a Carpenter mankind was made, and only by the Carpenter can mankind be remade.

Question: How optimistic would you be that the task of taking the Good News of the gospel to a waiting world would ever be accomplished? And yet, today you will read some of the most significant words ever uttered by our Lord: *"I will build my church; and the gates of hell shall not prevail against it"* (16:18). Down through the centuries, in spite of persecution and dispersion, satanic attack and human failure, the church of Jesus Christ has continued. Why? Because it is God's vehicle to take the message of life to a dying world.

Now how optimistic are *you* that what God has begun, He fully intends to complete? God has all the resources you need to do the task for which He has left you here on planet earth. There is just one thing He lacks: your availability. And only you can provide that.

✏️ **Insight:** The Way of the Cross—Groan and Glory
Following Peter's insightful confession that Jesus is the Christ (16:16), notice how Jesus carefully blends the two strands of suffering and glory in the sections to follow. True of His own life, they would be true of the lives of His followers as well.

Parables of the Messiah / Matthew 20–23 7

Overview: Peter's dramatic confession of Jesus as "the Christ, the Son of the living God" (16:16) is followed by a statement with ominous overtones: "From that time forth began Jesus to shew unto his disciples, how that he must go unto Jerusalem, and suffer many things of the elders and chief priests and scribes, and be killed, and be raised again the third day" (16:21). After preparing His disciples for the unexpected events which would soon take place, Jesus begins His final journey to Jerusalem. Arriving to a hero's welcome, He is hailed as King while making His humble entrance into the city. It is now the final week of Christ's earthly life—a week the world would never forget.

Heart of the Passage: Matthew 20:17-28; 21:1-17

Chapter 20	Chapter 21	Chapter 22	Chapter 23
Position Before the King	Presentation of the King	Parables of the King	Pronouncements of the King
Haughty Disciples	Humble Lord	Helpless Pharisees	

Your Daily Walk: As you read through today's section, notice the three different reactions to Christ's words: inattention, irritation, and instant obedience. (Which would characterize you?)

The disciples were *inattentive*. Three times Christ described for them what would befall Him when they arrived in Jerusalem (16:21; 17:22-23; 20:17-19). But they failed to heed His words.

The Pharisees were *irritated*. Being the focus of someone's sermon is never very comfortable (21:45-46), especially when the preacher calls you "blind guides," "hypocrites," and "whited sepulchres" (23:24, 27). Rather than change their ways, they tried to silence the preacher.

The blind men were instantly *obedient*. They listened to Christ, acknowledged His authority, admitted their need, and responded to His call. As a result, they received their sight.

Select a verse from today's section which you have ignored, or which you find irritatingly convicting. How would the two blind men have responded to it? How will *you*? *When* will you?

Insight: Truly Quotable Quotes

Today's section contains at least nine quotations from the Old Testament (how many can you find?). All totaled, the gospel of Matthew contains nearly 130 allusions and quotations from Old Testament passages—more than any other New Testament book.

A man may go to heaven without health, riches, honor, learning, or friends; but he can never go there without Christ.

8 Prophecies by the Messiah
Matthew 24–25

Heart of the Passage: Matthew 24:36-51; 25:14-30

📖 **Overview:** Herod's magnificent temple captured the attention of all who passed by. Commenting on its beauty and splendor, the disciples set the stage for Jesus' Olivet Discourse, a prophetic look at future events. His followers are urged to watchful expectation coupled with faithful service because, despite the signs of His coming, the return of Christ will be unannounced. His coming will bring vengeance on His enemies, judgment on the nations, and rewards for His watchful followers.

Chapter 24		Chapter 25	
Coming Woes 1　　31	Coming Warnings 32　　51	Parables of Judgment 1　　30	Preparations to Avoid Judgment 31　　36
Events	Expectations	Examples	Exhortations

The return of our Lord is the Bible's greatest argument for a devoted life of service.

🚶 **Your Daily Walk:** Have you ever watched a young child at an airport or depot awaiting the arrival of grandparents or the return of his father from a business trip? How did that child express his eager expectation? Perhaps he stood on tiptoes . . . craned his neck for a better look . . . jostled for position among the other bystanders. Every fiber of his being shouted the message, "Someone very special is coming, and I want to be ready when he gets here!"

Christians should be people walking on tiptoes, anticipating the return of the Lord (2 Timothy 4:8). In addition to watchful expectation, you have been commanded to "occupy till I come" (Luke 19:13). Anticipating His coming is no excuse for neglecting the physical or spiritual needs of the world around you. Your task in the meantime is to be the "salt of the earth" and the "light of the world"—making others thirsty for God (salt) and then guiding them to Him (light). Think of one person in whose life you can "shake and shine" to God's glory today. Remember, a little salt goes a long way, but only when you spread it around!

🔨 **Insight:** The Stones That Stood Alone

Christ's prediction that "there shall not be left here one stone upon another" of Herod's breathtaking temple (24:2) was fulfilled to the letter. In A.D. 70, Roman soldiers, in their eagerness to recover the gold that had melted between the stones of the temple during its burning, literally tore the temple apart stone by stone and threw them into the valley below . . . exactly as Jesus had foretold.

Finished Work of the Messiah
Matthew 26–28

9

📖 **Overview:** The events during the final two days of Jesus' earthly life carry the shadow of the cross. Everything He says and does foreshadows that symbol of shame, sacrifice, and salvation: the anointing in Bethany, the Passover observance and Lord's Supper, the prayer in Gethsemane. Jesus is arrested and tried, first by the Jews, then by the Romans; He is condemned, executed, and placed in a tomb. But the story does not end there. In glorious triumph, Jesus comes forth from the grave in resurrection power. Indeed, the King of the Jews lives again, a message of Good News which His followers are commissioned to share.

Heart of the Passage: Matthew 27:15–28:20

Chapter 26	Chapter 27	Chapter 28
The Christ Arrested	The Christ Executed	The Christ Resurrected
Sacrificial Lamb		Glorified Lord

✍️ **Your Daily Walk:** The cross of Jesus Christ has been called "the fulcrum of cosmic history." The eternal destiny of every human being hinges on a person's relationship to Jesus and His work on the cross.

As you read today's section, think deeply about the crucifixion of Jesus and its significance. Can you say with Paul, "God forbid that I should glory, save in the cross of our Lord Jesus Christ, by whom the world is crucified unto me, and I unto the world" (Galatians 6:14)?

From Christ's death flow all our hopes.

Then think of what the cross means to your neighbors . . . friends . . . family members . . . fellow employees. Are you sure each of them has come to the foot of the cross in faith and received the salvation which only Jesus can provide? If not, how can you be instrumental in leading one person to Calvary today?

It may involve a phone call, a letter, a luncheon invitation, an evening get-together. Ask God for a prepared heart . . . a door to opportunity . . . and a boldness as you share the life-changing message of the gospel. That's your privilege!

📋 **Insight:** The Fragrance of Gratitude
Throughout Bible lands, oil to anoint and soothe the skin was common for all levels of society. However, wealthy people had expensive perfumes and ointments. The woman of Matthew 26:7 anointed Jesus with a precious perfumed oil that was worth almost a year's wages—a lavish gesture of love by anyone's standard.

335

Mark

M ark's gospel captures the twofold purpose of Christ's coming to earth: "to minister, and to give his life a ransom for many" (10:45). Mark describes Jesus as the Perfect Servant, emphasizing more the actions of Jesus (look for the oft-repeated term *straightway*), and gives briefer treatment to His teachings. Mark is a book of action, not words, directed to a Roman audience. Jewish customs are explained as the story moves briskly to the completion of Jesus' earthly life and ministry.

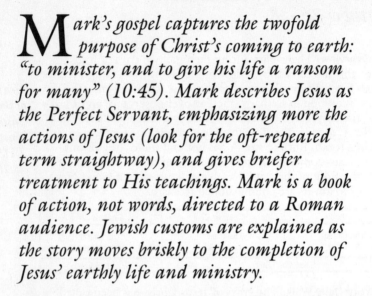

Focus	Servant			Sacrifice	
Divisions	Servants of the Servant	Service of the Servant	Sayings of the Servant	Sermons of the Servant	Suffering of the Servant
	1 3	4 7	8 10	11 13	14 16
Topics	The Son of Man on the Move			The Son of Man on the Cross	
	A Living Example			A Dying Savior	
Place	Galilee and Perea			Judea and Jerusalem	
Time	A.D. 29–33				

The Coming of the Servant / Mark 1–3 **10**

Overview: Mark begins his gospel without genealogy, birth narrative, or prologue. Plunging straight to the heart of his message, he begins with the ministry of John the Baptist, the forerunner who would prepare the way for Jesus' ministry of servanthood. Mark's emphasis throughout is on Christ's *works* rather than His *words,* as befitting a Servant. Numerous miracles of healing and exorcism precede the personal calls of five disciples— Andrew, Peter, James, John, and Matthew—and His choosing of the seven other disciples.

Heart of the Passage: Mark 1:1–2:17

Chapter 1	Chapter 2	Chapter 3
The Servant Introduced	The Servant in Action	The Servant Assisted
"Follow Me!"	"Believe in Me!"	"Be with Me!"

Your Daily Walk: Artists down through the centuries have tried to capture on paper or canvas what Jesus Christ might have looked like when He walked the face of the earth. Do you have a favorite artist's representation? Why do you like that one? Can you think of a Scripture verse that might give you a hint as to what Jesus Christ looked like?

If today's reading from Mark's gospel is any indication, Jesus was a man of incredible strength and stamina. He maintained an active schedule of service for God. And yet He was subject to all the human limitations with which you struggle: hunger (Matthew 4:2), thirst (John 19:28), fatigue (John 4:6). How was He able to maintain such an active pace? What was His "secret for successful service"?

First, *He was energized by the Holy Spirit* (Mark 1:10, 12)— the same Holy Spirit who empowers you as a child of God today (1 Corinthians 6:19-20; Acts 1:8). Second, *He was fortified daily by prayer* (Mark 1:35). He knew that the busier the schedule in God's service, the greater the need for prayer. Take a peek at your appointment calendar for today. Is it too busy for prayer? Then it's busier than God intended it to be. Start today and every day on your knees.

To attempt any work for God without prayer is as futile as trying to launch a space probe with a peashooter.

Insight: The Language of Urgency

Mark's account has been called the "action gospel" because of the way he uses the language of immediacy. In the three chapters you read today, Mark uses words such as *straightway, immediately, forthwith,* and *as soon as* a total of 15 times. Can you find them all?

11 *Mission of the Servant / Mark 4–7*

Heart of the Passage: Mark 4:1–5:20

📖 **Overview:** It's one thing to make great claims for yourself; it's something else again to back up those claims with convincing proofs. Through both His words (parables) and works (miracles), Christ proclaims His true identity to the disciples and the multitudes. At first even His closest companions are perplexed by His power and authority, wondering, "What manner of man is this, that even the wind and the sea obey him?" (4:41). But patiently—through the miracles of exorcism, healing, and even raising the dead—the Master Servant works to convince His followers of the nature of His person and mission.

Chapter 4	Chapter 5	Chapter 6	Chapter 7
Calming a Storm	Casting Out Demons	Sending Out the Disciples	Reaching Out to the Gentiles
"Be Still!"	"Go Home!"	"Go Forth!"	"Go Thy Way!"

If Christ is in your house, your neighbors will soon know it.

🛠 **Insight:** The Miracle That Transformed Ten Towns
The demon-possessed man from the region of the Gadarenes was naked and raging before his encounter with Christ. But afterward, he was "sitting, . . . clothed, and in his right mind" (5:15)—a transformation that did not escape the notice of his countrymen (5:19-20).

📘 **Your Daily Walk:** Last week you read about the rich young ruler (Matthew 19:16-22), a wealthy Godseeker who came to Jesus and asked to become one of His disciples. Jesus told him first to go and count the cost. The young man did . . . and was unwilling to pay the price. His gold had become his God.

Today you will meet another man who asked to become one of Jesus' traveling companions. He was willing to leave all to follow Jesus, but this time Jesus said no (5:18-20)! It was not a case of "Do you have what it takes to be My disciple?" (he did!) but rather, "Are you willing to go where I want to send you?" (he was!). For the former demon-possessed man, God's call to *go* was a call to *stay home*—"to publish in Decapolis how great things Jesus had done for him" (5:20). And by his willingness to be a witness right where he lived, 10 cities were impacted with the gospel of Jesus Christ.

Has your life been transformed by the miracle-working Jesus? If so, are you willing to go home . . . and tell family and friends "how great things the Lord hath done for thee" (5:19)? Where and in what situations can you be a witness today?

Four Gospel
Glimpses of Christ

	MATTHEW	MARK	LUKE	JOHN
Christ Portrayed as	Prophesied King	Obedient Servant	Perfect Man	Son of God
Original Audience	Jews	Romans	Greeks	All People
Key Word(s)	"fulfilled"	"straightway"	"Son of Man"	"believe"
Key Verse	21:5	10:45	19:10	20:31
Outstanding Feature	Sermons	Miracles	Parables	Teachings
Arrangement of Material	Topical	Chronological	Chronological	Topical
Tone	Prophetic	Practical	Historical	Spiritual
Percent Spoken by Christ	60%	42%	50%	50%
Quotations from Old Testament	53	36	25	20
Allusions to Old Testament	76	27	42	105
Unique Material	42%	59%	7%	93%
Broad Division	Synoptic Gospels (Humanity of Christ)			Supplemental Gospel (Deity of Christ)

12 *Magnificence of the Servant / Mark 8–10*

Overview: As opposition to Jesus' ministry increases, it is no longer safe to move openly in Galilee. So Jesus traverses the regions of the Decapolis, Caesarea Philippi, and Perea, thereby avoiding both the crowds and the deadly plots of the religious leaders. In the concluding days of His earthly ministry, Jesus begins to prepare His disciples for the fateful journey to Jerusalem that will mark the end of His life—and the beginning of their role as bearers of glad tidings.

Heart of the Passage: Mark 9

Chapter 8	Chapter 9	Chapter 10
Lessons from the Loaves	Preview of Power	Preaching in Perea
"Thou Art the Christ"	"This Is My Son"	"Jesus, Son of David"

Your Daily Walk: *"Now see here—I have my rights!"*

That's right! To be a servant doesn't mean you *have* no rights, but that you have freely *given up* the rights you possess in order to benefit another. True servanthood is based on love, not coercion.

Service is a gift of love to people given in gratitude for God's gift of love to you.

Think of the rights Jesus possessed: He was the Son of God, Creator of the world; "equal with God" (Philippians 2:6); "in the beginning with God" (John 1:2). And yet He chose to be born in a stable—to spend His life not lording it over kings, but reaching out to society's outcasts.

Though by rights He could have enjoyed the privileges of royalty, He "made himself of no reputation and took upon him the form of a servant, and . . . humbled himself and became obedient unto death, even the death of the cross" (Philippians 2:7-8). And in doing so, He was modeling His own instruction to the disciples, "If any man desire to be first, the same shall be last of all, and servant of all" (Mark 9:35).

Is there a job in your home or office, church or community, for which you would rather someone else take the responsibility—a job you think is beneath you? Instead of waiting to be served by another, take the initiative in serving as unto the Lord. After all, service is a gift of love to *people* given in gratitude for God's gift of love to *you!*

Insight: I Say . . . and I Say . . . and I Say Again!

If a statement is important, chances are good it will be repeated. With that in mind, glance at 8:31; 9:31; 10:33. What would you say is the focus of Jesus' life as revealed in those verses?

Final Week of the Servant / Mark 11–13 **13**

Overview: The final week of Jesus' earthly life dawns—that period of time which occupies more space in the Gospels than any other stage of Jesus' ministry. His arrival in Jerusalem coincides with the preparations for the Feast of Passover. Though events move quickly, Jesus is never hurried. There is time to clean out the temple, watch the widow contribute her two mites, and give final instructions to the disciples.

Heart of the Passage: Mark 11

Chapter 11	Chapter 12	Chapter 13
Triumphant Entry	Troublesome Encounters	Tribulation Envisioned
"Hosanna!"	Herodians	Horror

Insight: Eight Days Under a Microscope
Highlights of Passion Week include:
Sunday: Triumphant entry; Jesus weeps over Jerusalem
Monday: Fig tree cursed; temple cleansed
Tuesday: Fig tree withered; Jesus' authority challenged
Wednesday: (No biblical record)
Thursday: Last Supper; Gethsemane prayer; Judas' betrayal
Friday: Tried; denied; crucified; buried
Saturday: Tomb guarded
Sunday: Resurrection; appearance to the disciples

All God's giants have been weak people who did great things for God because they knew He was with them.

Your Daily Walk: Are you a "Poinsettia Churchgoer"— conspicuous by your *presence* at Christmas and Easter and by your *absence* the rest of the year?

The crowd following Jesus on Palm Sunday was an impressive sight—to everyone but Jesus! He knew it was easy to take up a palm frond, but difficult to take up a cross. Think of the servants who have been faithful in their ministry to you. Why not minister to at least one of them today by taking time to write a note of gratitude and encouragement!

Finally, solidify your own commitment to ministry and servanthood by memorizing this pivotal teaching of Jesus' life. It is found in capsule form in today's reading:

"And thou shalt love the Lord thy God with all thy heart, and with all thy soul, and with all thy mind, and with all thy strength: this is the first commandment. And the second is like, namely this, Thou shalt love thy neighbour as thyself. There is none other commandment greater than these" (Mark 12:30-31).

14 *Finished Work of the Servant*
Mark 14–16

Heart of the Passage: Mark 15:24– 16:20

Overview: The time has come for Jesus to demonstrate the full extent of His servanthood. For the Passover Lamb of God, the long-awaited hour has arrived. Conspired against by His enemies—betrayed by one close follower and denied by another— tried and finally executed, Jesus' life of service seems to be finished. But in the greatest of all miracles, Easter dawn reveals an empty tomb, setting the stage for Jesus to commission His followers to bear the glad tidings worldwide.

Chapter 14	Chapter 15	Chapter 16
Teaching in the Garden	Tragedy on the Cross	Triumph at the Tomb
Arrest	Agony	Ascension

The Christian's task is to make the Lord Jesus visible, intelligible, and desirable.

Your Daily Walk: Judas the betrayer, Peter the denier. And 10 other men who "forsook him, and fled" (14:50). Together they comprised the Twelve—not exactly an "All-Star" team for taking the gospel message to a dying world. Or was it?

An ancient legend suggests that Jesus, after His resurrection and ascension, was met at the portals of heaven by the angelic host who inquired of Him, "Lord, where is Your army?"

Pointing down to the Mount of Olives from which He had ascended, Jesus replied, "There—do you see them? *That's* My army."

Surprised and a bit skeptical, the angels asked, "That is Your army? But Lord, what if they fail You?"

Jesus replied, "If they fail Me, then everything I have done— My miracles, My messages, My earthly life, My sacrificial death— will have been in vain. But they won't fail Me, because I am with them."

The Lord who commanded His followers, "Go ye into all the world, and preach the gospel to every creature" (Mark 16:15) is the same One who said, "Lo, I am with you alway, even unto the end of the world" (Matthew 28:20). Are any of you out of work? The Carpenter is still looking for willing co-workers. Apply in prayer right now!

Insight: Life of a Servant, Death of a Servant
Christ was sold for 30 pieces of silver—the price of a common slave. He was executed by crucifixion, as only slaves and common criminals were. Even in death He modeled servanthood for all who would follow Him in life.

Luke

L uke presents Jesus as the perfect Man who came to save sinful people. A physician by occupation, Luke builds his narrative on a chronological presentation of Jesus' life, tracing the twin themes of growing belief and growing opposition. While Jesus' followers are challenged to count the cost of discipleship, those who oppose Him are plotting His undeserved death. But His death and resurrection validate His claims, thwart His enemies, and empower His disciples to continue His ministry to a lost world.

Focus	Advent	Activities		Antagonism			Authentication
Divisions	Arrival of the Son of Man	Authority of the Son of Man	Ministry of the Son of Man	Admonitions of the Son of Man	Illustrations of the Son of Man	Teaching of the Son of Man	Triumph of the Son of Man
	1 2	3 6	7 9	10 12	13 18	19 21	22 24
Topics	Seeking the Lord					Saving the Lost	
	Presentation		Preaching			Passion	
Place	Nazareth and Galilee			Jerusalem			
Time	5 B.C.–A.D. 33						

15 *Arrival of the Son of Man / Luke 1–2*

Heart of the Passage: Luke 1:26-56; 2:1-20

Overview: Dr. Luke—physician, historian, and writer of the longest gospel account (1,151 verses)—clearly states his purpose for writing in the opening verses of his book: "That thou mightest know the certainty of those things, wherein thou hast been instructed" (1:4). He begins with the details surrounding the miraculous births of two remarkable boys: John the forerunner, and Jesus the Messiah.

Chapter 1			Chapter 2
Announcement of John	Announcement of Jesus	Birth of John	Birth of Jesus
1 25	26 56	57 80	
John the Forerunner			Jesus the Messiah

"The object of all music should be the glory of God and pleasant recreation." —Bach

Your Daily Walk: Have you ever noticed how saints and songs seem to go together? It's hard for people of God to congregate without spontaneously enjoying the atmosphere of praise, thanks, and worship that music provides. One mark of a Spirit-filled believer is "speaking . . . in psalms and hymns and spiritual songs, singing and making melody in your heart to the Lord" (Ephesians 5:19). Even if you can't sing, you can still speak forth the majestic praises of God that are in your heart!

When Mary shared with Elizabeth the good news about a Savior to be born through her, the result was a song (1:46-55). When Zechariah's voice returned after his faith-inspired declaration of his son's name, he couldn't help but sing (1:67-79). When Jesus was born in Bethlehem, the heavenly hosts of heaven declared the news in a song (2:13-14).

Do you feel like singing (or speaking forth) the praises of your Lord right now? Then read out loud those songs of Mary, Zechariah, and the angels in today's reading. Better yet, compose one of your own. Praising God in song is never out of date—even if you can't carry a tune!

Insight: The Opening Chapters from a Prolific Pen
Who wrote the most books in the New Testament? Who wrote the most material in the New Testament? If you guessed Paul as the answer to the first question, you're right! If you guessed Paul as the answer to the second question, you're wrong! Luke's two books—the gospel that bears his name and the Acts of the Apostles—contain more verses than the 13 books attributed to Paul combined!

The Son of Man

16

← Step Back

The title Jesus used most often about Himself was "Son of Man," and it linked Him to a number of crucial concepts with which the Jews were familiar:

1. It identified Jesus with a conception of majesty that had been associated with the term since it was first used in Daniel 7:13.

2. It linked Him to the earth and to His mission on earth.

3. It focused on His lowliness and humanity (Matthew 8:20); on His suffering and death (Luke 19:10); and on His future reign as King (Matthew 24:27).

4. It pointed to His transcendence as a heavenly figure, the One who will be enthroned as ruler over the whole earth; His kingdom will never be destroyed (Daniel 7:14).

Therefore, within that one simple term can be found the fullness of both Christ's deity and humanity.

The title "Son of Man" also alludes to Adam, the first man. In fact, the apostle Paul uses the title "Last Adam" in 1 Corinthians 15:45 in contrast to the first Adam. Both Adam and Christ came into the world through a special act of God. Both entered the world free of sin; both acted on behalf of others as their representatives. But Adam's sin contrasts sharply with Christ's obedience.

Scripture Reading: Hebrews 2:14-18

↑ Look Up

The concept of Christ as being perfectly divine and completely human in one Person is one of the most difficult to grasp. After all, none of us has seen God, except as the Scriptures reveal Him. And none of us has seen a perfect human, except as Scriptures reveal Adam before the Fall and Jesus Himself. So how can we possibly comprehend Christ's nature?

No doubt we never fully will, this side of heaven. Even so, the concept is true. As human, Christ faced everything that we will ever face, and won. As God, He was able to become our representative on the cross, so that His death paid for our own sins.

As you read Hebrews 2:14-18 and ponder these rich truths today, thank God in prayer for the provision He made for you by sending His Son to walk the earth in human form.

Jesus was like a king who temporarily puts on the garments of a peasant while at the same time remaining a king.

→ Move Ahead

The gospel of Jesus Christ is so complex that thousands of scholars could write thousands of books each, and never fully mine its riches. And yet it's so simple, even a child can grasp it. Today, make yourself available to be used by God to share a word of testimony about Jesus Christ, the Son of Man, the Last Adam, your loving Savior.

17 *Authority of the Son of Man / Luke 3–6*

Heart of the Passage: Luke 3:1-22; 4:1-30

 Overview: Luke introduces the ministry of Jesus with three preparatory events: (1) the ministry of His forerunner, John the Baptist; (2) His baptism by John; and (3) His temptation by Satan. Christ's genealogy ties Him unmistakably to David the king, Abraham the patriarch, and Adam the first man. Rejection in His hometown of Nazareth causes Him to shift His headquarters to Capernaum, where He ministers for two full years. There Christ calls 12 men to be His closest traveling companions. And there by the shores of Galilee He begins to prepare them for the ministry He will soon entrust to them.

Chapter 3	Chapter 4	Chapters 5–6
Forerunner of the Son of Man	Spirit-filled Son of Man	First Disciples of the Son of Man
John	Jesus	Peter, James, and John

Weak doctrines will not be a match for powerful temptations.

Your Daily Walk: Can you name the fifth book of the Old Testament? _____

Can you quote one verse from that Old Testament book? _____

Satan's attacks are infinitely subtle. Sometimes he approaches in a direct frontal attack, providing an invitation to sin at a moment of weakness (as with David and Bathsheba, 2 Samuel 11:2). Other times he uses crafty deception in order to trick you into a sinful act (as with Eve in the garden, Genesis 3:1-6). But for each temptation there is available a ready defense: the Word of God (Psalm 119:11). Christ knew that. Three times He responded to Satan's *attacks* with a scriptural *counterattack* from the book of Deuteronomy. Do you know your Bible well enough to do the same? Do you, like Christ, have a verse in your "arsenal" to use against each of Satan's temptations?

Think through the areas of your life where you find yourself most vulnerable to temptation: lustful thoughts, outbursts of temper, worry, gossip, undependability. Then locate and memorize one verse that specifically speaks to that need. When Satan attacks, be ready!

Insight: The King Without the Curse

Jesus was indeed the Son of David and legal heir to the throne of Israel, as seen in the genealogy of chapter 3. However, in order to avoid "the curse of Coniah" (Jeremiah 22:28-30), Jesus' right to rule could not come through David's son Solomon. Look at Luke 3:31 to see how Christ avoided that curse!

Ministry of the Son of Man / Luke 7–9 **18**

Overview: Preaching; healing; discipling. In capsule form, that summarizes the daily activities of the Son of Man. Luke records the healings with careful attention to detail, as befitting a physician. And those documented miracles become the proof of Jesus' claims to a doubting John the Baptist (7:18-35), and a "faithless and perverse generation" (9:41). As He preaches and heals, Jesus patiently prepares His disciples to carry on in His absence. The stakes are high; the cost is steep. But the goal of saving lives eternally makes it all worthwhile!

Heart of the Passage: Luke 7:36-50; 8:41-56

Chapter 7	Chapter 8	Chapter 9
A Ministry of Mercy	A Ministry of Preaching	A Ministry of Multiplication
Centurion	Illustration	Transfiguration

Your Daily Walk: What was the longest period of time you ever prayed for the same request? Perhaps you were asking for physical healing, or the salvation of a loved one, or the sale of a house. Did you pray for that need every day for a month . . . six months . . . a year . . . two years . . . five years . . . ten years? Are you still praying for it?

In today's reading you will encounter a woman who carried the same burden for 12 long years (8:43-48). She had consulted physicians and spent her life's savings in a vain search for a cure to her problem. Perhaps as a last resort, she brought that burden to the Savior. And there, after 12 years of searching, her need was met. But without the search, she might never have found the solution.

Prayer is simply taking *a need you cannot supply* and committing it by faith to the God who is able to *"supply all your need according to his riches in glory by Christ Jesus"* (Philippians 4:19), then in confident trust leaving the results with Him.

Make these words your marching orders for the day: "I will trust while I wait, for my God is never late."

Prayer is committing a need you cannot supply to the God who can "supply all your need."

Insight: Tons to Eat and Bushels to Spare
Including women and children, the crowd fed by Jesus probably numbered around 15,000. If each consumed only five ounces of food, the total eaten would still have been more than two tons. And afterwards, the disciples picked up 12 bushel baskets of leftovers. He is just as able to meet your overwhelming needs!

19 Admonitions of the Son of Man
Luke 10–12

Heart of the Passage: Luke 10:1-37

Overview: Seventy disciples are sent out two-by-two with instructions to "heal the sick and say . . . The kingdom of God is come nigh unto you" (10:9). Their enthusiastic return prompts Jesus to rejoice in spontaneous praise to God (10:21). But the clouds of confrontation are already gathering. Some attribute His miracles to Satan rather than God. Others clamor for more miraculous signs. Pharisees attack His seeming disregard for their traditions. Jesus responds by denouncing the religious leaders for their hypocrisy, and by warning the disciples to be watchful as they work.

Chapter 10	Chapter 11	Chapter 12
Acceptance of the Son of Man	Antagonism Toward the Son of Man	Admonitions from the Son of Man
Sending Out the Seventy		Training the Twelve

Evangelism is the perpetual task of the whole church and not the peculiar hobby of certain of its members.

Your Daily Walk: Assume for the next few minutes that the population of the world is almost five billion (it is) and that you are the only Christian on earth (you aren't). If you led one other person to the Lord during the next 12 months, and the two of you led two other people to the Lord the following year, etc., how many years would it take (statistically, at least) before everyone in the world would be a Christian?

The startling fact of multiplication is this: If everyone approached the Great Commission with the attitude, "Each one win one," the task might well be completed in about 32 years!

Jesus sent out His disciples two-by-two but the job of spreading the gospel occurred one-by-one: one individual with Christ sharing the Good News with one individual without Christ. Does that help you see how important one witness—your witness—can be in accomplishing the goal? Write down the name of an unsaved acquaintance in the margin, and make that person the focus of your praying . . . and sharing. That's how the Good News gets around!

Insight: Something's Fishy About This Sign (11:29-30)
Luke records Jesus' words comparing Himself with the prophet Jonah and speaking of the "sign of Jonah." But what is the "sign of Jonah"? Luke doesn't say. Check Matthew 12:38-41. Could you explain it to a non-Christian friend? Try it.

Illustrations of the Son of Man (Part 1)
Luke 13–15

20

Overview: Teaching that is plain and to the point is bound to produce a response—sometimes positive, but more often negative! Christ's sermons are no exception. Never attempting to make God's truth merely palatable or comfortable, Jesus is not afraid to call for repentance (13:3, 5) or to call a fox a "fox" (13:32)! But there is a tender side to His teaching as well. The love of the Savior for lost sinners permeates chapter 15, where three times He states that the heavens rejoice over one lost sinner who repents (15:7, 10, 32).

Heart of the Passage: Luke 15

Chapter 13	Chapter 14	Chapter 15
Parables of the Danger	Parables of the Cost	Parables of the Lost
"Repent!"	"Consider!"	"Seek!"

Insight: The Bible's "Lost and Found" Department (Luke 15) The word *sinners* (15:1) designates the people of the street whom the Pharisees looked down upon with contempt because they did not know the Law (John 7:49) or keep the traditions of the elders. The Pharisees grumbled because they did not share Jesus' heart for reclaiming lost individuals. In response Jesus tells them three parables about a lost *sheep*, a lost piece of *silver*, and a lost *son* to show that God rejoices over the recovery of even one lost *sinner*.

God loves each of us as if there was only one of us to love.

Your Daily Walk: There is no sadder place than a *lost and found* department. Sad because so many items of value have become separated from their owners. Sad because useful items are sitting uselessly on the shelf. Sad because so many owners have forgotten they lost something. It's bad enough to be an unclaimed object; it's worse yet to be unwanted and unmissed.

Luke 15 provides a threefold reminder that God is not a forgetful owner whose lost possession is unwanted. Rather, He is a seeking, searching heavenly Father. Like a tender shepherd . . . a meticulous housewife . . . a yearning dad, He scans high and low for lost sinners as lost objects of His love and concern. In the words of an old hymn, *"Softly and tenderly Jesus is calling, Calling for you and for me; See, on the portals He's waiting and watching, watching for you and for me."*

What is your answer to the invitation of your Savior? The angels in heaven are waiting for another reason to rejoice!

21 *Illustrations of the Son of Man (Part 2) Luke 16–18*

Overview: With His gaze fixed on Jerusalem and in anticipation of the events marking the consummation of His earthly ministry, Jesus intensifies His final training of the disciples. Today's reading consists of material found only in Luke's gospel. The subject of stewardship is a central theme, for the disciples will soon be entrusted with the precious message of the gospel. Jesus outlines the duties of a servant, then illustrates His teaching from the lives of 10 lepers. Finally, He underscores the importance of prayer that is persistent and humble, as seen in the parables of the mistreated widow (18:1-8), and the repentant publican (18:9-14).

Heart of the Passage: Luke 16:1-17

Chapter 16	Chapter 17	Chapter 18
Exhortations for Stewards	Exhortations for Servants	Exhortations for the Self-righteous
Faithfulness	Forgiveness	Meekness

Your Daily Walk: If it is true that "prayer is the barometer of a Christian's spiritual condition," how does your barometer read today?

Prayer is the gymnasium of the soul.

Tucked away in today's reading is this significant verse: "And he [Jesus] spake a parable unto them [the disciples] to this end, that men ought always to pray, and not to faint" (18:1). What follows is the parable of the persistent widow, a parable aimed at fainting disciples! Does that include you? Are you passing out in the midst of your prayers? Or are you praying without fainting?

Praying is hard work, no doubt about it. That is one reason why maintaining an effective prayer life is so difficult. It takes consistent, daily effort. Prayer is also difficult because it is one of the activities Satan would most like to see you avoid. Through prayer you receive guidance and provision from God; through prayer God makes you a channel of His power. If *Jesus* needed to pray, and if Jesus told His disciples *they* ought always to pray, how about *you*? Call up a praying friend right now and ask that person to pray that you will be a more committed and consistent pray-er yourself.

Insight: Heavy, Heavy Hangs Around Your Neck (17:2)
The millstone of Jesus' day weighed several hundred pounds and could be turned only with the aid of a donkey—a definite handicap if you were tossed into the sea with one tied around your neck!

Teaching of the Son of Man / Luke 19–21 22

Overview: It is now the final week of Jesus' earthly life. In the city of Jerusalem—a city astir with the excitement of the feast days—some are prepared to welcome a King, while others prepare for an execution. Jesus Himself draws the battle lines by driving the moneychangers from the temple. From then on, the religious leaders double their efforts to trap Him in a treasonous statement. Though His hour of anguish draws near, Jesus continues the activities that have characterized His earthly ministry: teaching, healing, confronting, consoling.

Heart of the Passage: Luke 19

Chapter 19	Chapter 20	Chapter 21
The Temple Cleansed	The Temple Leaders Rebuked	The Temple's End Foreseen
Triumph	Testing	Tribulation

Your Daily Walk: A "little thing" is great or small, depending upon whose yardstick it is measured by.

What often seems insignificant to us has great significance to God. Zacchaeus was a little man who had climbed to a position of prominence by trampling others underfoot. He was a notorious sinner (19:7) and a despised tax collector, but he was curious enough to climb a tree in order to see Jesus. As the Savior passed by, He called Zacchaeus to commitment and Zaccheus responded.

A nameless widow came to the temple to give her seemingly insignificant offering to God—a mere pittance compared to the enormous sums being contributed by others. And yet Jesus declared that she gave more than all the others combined.

What is a seemingly insignificant feature in your life? Your income? Your stature? Your personality? Your family background? Use it to complete this sentence: "Lord, I realize that in the eyes of the world my _____ means very little. But faithfulness in a little thing is a great thing with You, and so I give it back to You right now, asking that You use my 'two mites' in a mighty way to Your glory!"

Let us at least give according to our income, lest God make our incomes match our gifts.

Insight: The Five-Hundred-Year Foal (19:30)
It was no accident Jesus rode into Jerusalem on a young donkey. Though the colt had been tied up by its owner only hours before (19:29-35), prophetically the animal had been "saddled and ready" for more than 500 years—since the days of Zechariah (9:9)!

351

23 *Triumph of the Son of Man / Luke 22–24*

Heart of the Passage: Luke 24

Overview: With his typical attention to detail, Luke provides a full account of the arrest, trial, and crucifixion of the Son of Man. In graphic word pictures Luke describes the diabolical plot of Judas, the warm fellowship of the Last Supper, the mental anguish at Gethsemane, the tragic denial by Peter, the miscarriage of justice at the trials, and the brutal agony of the Roman execution. But the dark days in Jerusalem give way to the brilliant dawning of that first Easter morning when angels announce, "He is not here, but is risen" (24:6)!

Chapter 22	Chapter 23	Chapter 24
Passover Lamb	King of the Jews	Risen Redeemer
Affliction	Execution	Exaltation

Praise God even when you don't understand what He is doing.

Your Daily Walk: If you have difficulty praising God on a daily basis, chances are it's not because you lack something to praise Him for, but simply because you have a short memory!

Consider this scene from Luke 24. It is Easter Sunday morning. Standing near the now-empty tomb is a group of women who are "perplexed" and "afraid" (24:4-5). Soon they are joined by Peter who is "wondering in himself" (24:12). The scene shifts to two men walking along the road leading to Emmaus. As they discuss current events in Jerusalem, they feel "sad" (24:17). *Question:* What could possibly be the source of so much sadness and perplexity?

Answer: The very event that Jesus had predicted *at least five times*—His resurrection! And yet, Instead of bringing joy and gladness to His followers, it brought heartache and grief—not because the news was bad, but because the disciples' memories were so short!

Is a short memory robbing you of the joy God intends for you today? Make a list of God's merciful dealings in your life so far this month. Remember them? Of course! Now smile.

Insight: A Finished Task Unfinished (24:44-49)

In one sense, Jesus' mission was finished because it was based on accomplished facts (His death and resurrection). But in another sense it was just beginning, for the world had yet to hear the Good News which only a handful of people knew firsthand. Luke's second volume, the Acts of the Apostles, will continue the exciting story!

John

T he gospel of John is a gospel apart. Matthew, Mark, and Luke, despite their different viewpoints, describe many of the same events in Jesus' life. But John presents unique material to prove to his readers that Jesus is God in the flesh, born to die as the sacrifice for human sin. Seven miraculous signs and seven "I am" declarations are cited to show that "Jesus is the Christ, the Son of God" (20:31). No finer evangelistic work has even been penned than John's gospel.

Focus	Presentation			Rejection		Resurrection
Divisions	Coming of the Son of God	Compassion of the Son of God	Claims by the Son of God	Conflict with the Son of God	Comfort from the Son of God	Crucifixion of the Son of God
	1 2	3 5	6 8	9 12	13 17	18 21
Topics	Seven Miracles				Upper Room	Supreme Miracle
	Demonstration				Instruction	Glorification
Place	Palestine			Judea and Galilee		
Time	A Few Years			A Few Hours		A Few Weeks

24 *The Coming of the Son of Man / John 1–2*

Heart of the Passage: John 1:1-18; 2:1-11

Overview: Matthew, Mark, and Luke are called the *synoptic gospels* (from the Greek word meaning "to see together") because they contain much of the same material. By contrast John, the supplemental gospel, provides a fourth dimension of Jesus' life and ministry. Fully 92 percent of John's material is not found in any other gospel account. John writes to convince his readers who Jesus is (the Son of God) and how new life can be found in Him (20:30-31). He begins in eternity past, showing how the Word who was one with God (1:1) became flesh in order to take His message of life to mankind.

Chapter 1		Chapter 2	
Identity of the Son of God:		Authority of the Son of God:	
The Word	The Lamb	Over Nature	Over the Temple
1 18	19 51	1 11	12 25
Word Became Flesh		Water to Wine	

Your Daily Walk: Today's chapters present Jesus in many different contexts: baptized in the Jordan, calling His disciples, performing His first miracle. These events were private, not public. Jesus came to the Jordan River without fanfare or media attention; only His close friends knew what He was doing.

It's not what we take up, but what we give up, that makes us rich.

In these days of the "electronic church" with radio and television carrying the gospel around the world, it is easy to focus on the medium and miss the message, and so the public proclamation has little personal impact.

But Jesus doesn't see us as members of a faceless mass audience; He is lovingly and intimately concerned about each of us as individuals. Read John 1:43 carefully, substituting your own town for *Galilee* and your own name for *Philip*. The message of our Lord remains the same. It's not intended for the masses but for each individual.

Carry a small mirror with you today, and (when nobody's looking) look at yourself from time to time. You're seeing the person Jesus is asking to "Follow Me." What will your answer be today?

Insight: Searching for Seven Signs in John's Gospel

John constructs his gospel around seven convincing miracles, building a case for Jesus' deity that is hard to refute. You'll find the first in chapter 2 (see 2:11) and the others in chapters 4–6, 9, and 11. Can you discover all seven?

The Riches of Salvation

← Step Back

Tomorrow you'll read a verse you probably already know by heart: "For God so loved the world, that he gave his only begotten Son, that whosoever believeth in him should not perish, but have everlasting life" (John 3:16).

That verse, in a few short words, captures the essence of salvation. True salvation is provided only by God Himself through the sacrificial death of His Son, Jesus Christ. By putting our faith in Christ, accepting for ourselves His death on our behalf, we are "born again" as John puts it (John 3:3).

The benefits of salvation are innumerable, but here are a few of the major ones:

1. *We are justified.* When we accept Christ's work on our behalf, we are accepted before God. In a word, we are "justified." That's a judicial term referring to a verdict of "not guilty." But more than that, it means all possibility of condemnation is removed (see Romans 5:16; 8:33-34). Because we are "in Christ," all of God's demands upon us are fulfilled.

2. *We are adopted.* We become children of God through the new birth. But more than that, we are actually adopted into the family of God as well. In adoption, a child is taken into a family and regarded as a true son or daughter, with all the privileges and responsibilities that belong to such a family member. Adoption brings a new status to one who receives Christ (see Galatians 4:1-5).

3. *We are sanctified.* The word *sanctify* means to set apart. For the believer, that refers to being set apart as a member of God's family—positionally. It also means we should strive to live a life that pleases God—experientially. And it also refers to being pefectly holy when we become just as Christ is—ultimately (see Hebrews 10:10).

Scripture Reading: Romans 5:16; 8:33-34; Galatians 4:1-5; Hebrews 10:10

↑ Look Up

Take a few moments today to consider the riches of Christ that are yours now that you are His. Eternal life, prayer, redemption, reconciliation, forgiveness, deliverance, glorification in the future, the list is virtually endless. Write down as many as you can, then turn that list into a praise list, and worship the Lord for His gracious benevolences toward you.

Salvation is moving from living death to deathless life.

→ Move Ahead

Using a concordance or study Bible, see if you can find Bible verses that relate to each item you've written. Together you may discover a wealth of benefits you may never have realized you possessed!

26 *Compassion of the Son of God / John 3–5*

Heart of the Passage: John 3:1-21; 5:31-40

📖 **Overview:** Jesus' ministry is not reserved for the temple or synagogue. At any time and in all places He is ready with a word and a healing touch. Nicodemus comes by night seeking answers . . . and finds the miracle of the second birth. The Samaritan woman comes seeking water at the well . . . and leaves to tell her city about a source of living water that will never run dry. The paralytic at the pool finds that even 38 years of lameness is no obstacle to the miracle-working Son of God. Jew or Samaritan, religious leader or religious outcast . . . Jesus' compassion knows no bounds.

Chapter 3	Chapter 4	Chapter 5
Nicodemus by Night	Woman at the Well	Paralytic at the Pool
Second Birth	Satisfied Thirst	Strengthened Limbs

The recognition of sin is the beginning of salvation.

✍️ **Your Daily Walk:** When the first seven astronauts were selected for the American space program, an important part of the screening process involved their answers to the simple statement, "I am . . ." Each was asked to complete that sentence 50 different ways. After using up the obvious answers—"I am a man, I am a test pilot, I am from Florida"—they quickly discovered how penetrating that question can become.

In John 5:31-40, Jesus highlights five testimonies that confirm His true identity: John the Baptist (v. 33), Jesus' miracles (v. 36), the Father (v. 37), the Scriptures (v. 39), and Jesus' own witness concerning Himself (v. 31). That witness is introduced, beginning with chapter 6, in the form of seven "I am" statements. (You'll find them in chapters 6, 8, 10–11, and 14–15.) But before you discover the seven ways Jesus completed that sentence, see how many ways you can complete it for Him. Can you finish the statement "Jesus is . . ." seven different ways? How about 50 different ways? (Hint: Start with the names of Jesus. According to *Meredith's Book of Bible Lists,* there are 39 of those!) When you're finished, you'll be refreshed by who He is and what He wants to do in your life each day.

📖 **Insight:** Finding the Gospel in the Gospel of John
The gospel (Good News) of Jesus Christ is stated nowhere more compactly than in John 3:16, whose very words ("God . . . only . . . son . . . perish . . . everlasting life") spell the acrostic **GOSPEL!** If you've never memorized that verse, do so today.

Claims by the Son of God / John 6–8 27

Overview: Early in His ministry Christ issues a challenge: "Search the scriptures; for in them ye think ye have eternal life: and they are they which testify of me" (5:39). Now His public declarations and miraculous demonstrations serve to confirm what the Old Testament said would be true of Him. Using the Jewish feast days as public forums, Jesus declares Himself to be the Bread of Life (6:35), the Sent One of God (7:28), the Forgiver of Sins (8:11), and the Light of the World (8:12).

Heart of the Passage: John 6:1-40; 8:1-12

Chapter 6	Chapter 7	Chapter 8
Five Thousand Fed	Jesus the Christ	Adulteress Forgiven
"I Am the Bread"	"I Am Messiah"	"I Am Before Abraham"

Your Daily Walk: When God is about to do something good, He starts with a difficulty. When He is about to do something great, He starts with an impossibility. And that means, regardless of your circumstances, you are a candidate for a miracle today!

The disciples were faced with an impossibility. On a moment's notice they were asked to feed 5,000 hungry men plus their families . . . with only the equivalent of five tuna fish sandwiches! To test His men, Jesus asked the obvious question: "Whence shall we buy bread that these may eat?" (6:5). And the disciples gave the obvious answer: "Nowhere!" But once they admitted that, from a human point of view, the situation was hopeless, Christ stepped in to prove His adequacy once again.

Others see only a hopeless end, but the Christian rejoices in an endless hope.

Are you facing a hopeless situation in your home, your marriage, your job, your friendships? The first step toward appropriating God's strength is to admit your own inadequacy. Have a tuna fish sandwich for lunch today, and as you munch, tell God about your "five barley loaves, and two small fishes" (6:9). That's more than enough for Him to produce a banquet of blessing . . . if you'll only give it to Him! As the little boy learned, little is much when God is in it!

Insight: The Unbelievably Believable Gospel

John's purpose in underscoring Jesus' miracles in his gospel account is "that ye might believe . . ." (20:31), and he will remind you often of that purpose. You'll find the word "believe" used 18 times in today's section, and more than 90 times in the book as a whole.

28 *"I Am"*

Scripture
Reading:
Exodus
3:14;
Selected
Verses in
John

← Step Back

When God said to Moses, "I am that I am" (Exodus 3:14), He was announcing the name by which He wished to be known and worshiped in Israel. It was a name that fully expressed who He was—the dependable and faithful God who deserves and desires the full worship and trust of His people.

That's why, when Jesus used the expression of Himself, the Jews were astonished. By saying, "Verily, verily, I say unto you, Before Abraham was, I am" (John 8:58), He was identifying Himself with the God of Israel.

The Jews considered it blasphemy. We know it to be simply honesty. The Jews sought to stone Him for daring to say He was God. We ought to worship Him for being God.

By saying, "I am" rather than "I was," Jesus expresses the eternity of His existence and His oneness with the Father.

But Jesus explained even further who He was throughout John's gospel:

- I am the Bread of Life (6:35).
- I am the Light of the World (8:12).
- I am the Gate for the sheep (10:7).
- I am the Good Shepherd (10:11, 14).
- I am the Resurrection and the Life (11:25).
- I am the Way and the Truth and the Life (14:6).
- I am the true Vine (15:1).

↑ Look Up

Jesus
Christ is
God's
every-
thing for
man's
total
need.

Jesus Christ was clear enough about His identity. One could consider Him to be a liar or insane, or else take Him at His word. But you know that Jesus was truly God's Son, and that His word is trustworthy indeed.

In light of that, let the descriptions that Christ gave Himself lead you into a time of praise, thanking Him for what every description means to you.

Get started this way:

"Lord, I praise You for being the Bread of Life, because to me that means . . ."

"Jesus, thank You for being the Light of the World, because that means I can . . ."

→ Move Ahead

Spend a few extra moments today looking up each of those verses in John, and read the verses just before and after them to get an idea of the context. Then do a little digging as to what each description means by using a study Bible or commentary.

Conflict with the Son of God / John 9–12 29

Overview: Christ's claims draw the attention of more than the hungry and sick. The scribes and Pharisees, religious leaders concerned about maintaining the status quo, respond with angry resistance. But how do you refute a Man who preaches that He is the Light of the World, then proves it by giving sight to the blind? . . . who claims He is "the resurrection, and the life" (11:25), then validates that claim by raising a man from the dead? The choice is clear: Either believe Him or seek to silence Him once and for all.

Heart of the Passage: John 9; 10:1-21; 11:1-44

Chapter 9	Chapter 10	Chapter 11	Chapter 12
Sight for the Blind	Shepherd for the Sheep	New Life for Lazarus	Coronation for the Christ
"I Am the Light"	"I Am the Door"	"I Am the Resurrection"	

Your Daily Walk: Suppose you were a roving reporter walking the streets of your city and asking people, "Who in your estimation is Jesus Christ?" What kind of answers would you expect to get?

In John 9 the man born blind was asked that very question . . . not once but several times. And each time he responded, the man had a clearer picture of who Jesus Christ was. In verse 17 "he is a prophet"; in verse 33 a "man . . . of God"; and in verse 38 the man fell at Jesus' feet and worshiped Him as Lord.

Jesus Christ is not a crutch; He is the ground to walk on.

Perhaps when you were first introduced to Jesus, you thought of Him as a great teacher . . . preacher . . . or example. But that's not how John presents Him. He wants to convince you that Jesus is nothing less than the Son of God, and that only through Him can you discover what life is all about (20:30-31).

Are you, like the man born blind, ready to change your opinion regarding Christ? He patiently waits for you to worship Him as Lord . . . nothing less will do. Will you acknowledge Him as your Sovereign right now?

Insight: Thinking on the Same Wavelength

Many of John's metaphors and themes were first used by the Old Testament prophet Isaiah. Here's a list of some:

	Isaiah	John
Freedom for the bound	61:1	8:36
Sight for the blind	35:5; 42:7	9:39
The shepherd and the sheep	40:11	10:1-21
Worldwide salvation	43:19; 45:22; 49:12; 60:3	10:16

30 *Comfort from the Son of God / John 13–17*

Heart of the Passage: John 14:1-6; 15:1-8; 17

Overview: The Upper Room Discourse contains Jesus' final words of instruction and encouragement to His disciples before His death. Only John records these intimate moments between Jesus and His men as He models true humility (chapter 13), describes the coming Holy Spirit who will comfort and empower them (chapters 14–16), and intercedes for the unity and protection of His disciples worldwide (chapter 17).

Chapter 13	Chapter 14	Chapter 15	Chapter 16	Chapter 17
	Last Words for the Disciples:			Last Prayer for
Serve	Trust	Abide	Overcome	the Disciples
Instruction				Intercession

A day without prayer is a day without blessing, and a life without prayer is a life without power.

Your Daily Walk: Five minutes. That's all the time it will take you to read through the 26 verses of Jesus' prayer in chapter 17. But those five short minutes may revolutionize your prayer life.

In those few verses Jesus prays for Himself (that God would be glorified in the death of His Son as He has been in His life, 17:1-5), for the 11 disciples (that they would be united, protected, and set apart in their service for Him, 17:6-19), and for His future followers (that they might know God and show God in their daily lives, 17:20-26). Like three concentric circles, Jesus moves from His "personal" needs to His "family" needs, and finally to the "worldwide" needs of His church.

What better model for a powerful prayer life than that of Jesus Christ Himself. Brief prayers . . . personal prayers . . . specific prayers . . . for yourself . . . your family . . . and God's worldwide program. As you close your devotional time today, "take five" in prayer. Unburden your heart to your heavenly Father, and intercede on behalf of others you know. (By the way, just five minutes of prayer daily adds up to more than 30 hours of talking to God each year!)

Insight: Comforting Answers to Perplexing Questions
Jesus begins His final address by responding to the questions of three of His disciples. Can you discover the three questions in chapter 14? (When you find them, notice how they set the stage for what Christ shares in chapters 15–17.)

Thomas: _____
Philip: _____
Judas: _____

Crucifixion of the Son of God
John 18–21

31

 Overview: In his account of Jesus' trials, John focuses on the appearances before Pilate and the governor's futile efforts to release Jesus. Yielding at last to political expediency and mob pressure, Pilate sentences Jesus to be crucified. Many of the details John includes are unique to his account: the Roman soldiers casting dice for Jesus' robe; the assignment of Jesus' mother to John's care; the spear thrust into Jesus' side; the post-resurrection appearances to Mary Magdalene, Thomas, and the seven disciples by the Sea of Tiberias. Through it all, John's purpose shines forth clearly: to present Jesus as "the Christ, the Son of God" in His life, death, and resurrection.

Heart of the Passage: John 20–21

Chapter 18	Chapter 19	Chapter 20			Chapter 21
Betrayal and Arrest	Trial and Death	Appearances to the Disciples			
		at the Tomb	in the Room		at the Lake
		1 18	19 31		
Before the Cross	On the Cross	After the Cross			

Your Daily Walk: A man was asked, "What is your occupation?" to which he replied, "I'm a Christian."

"No, you don't understand," continued the questioner. "I mean, what is your line of work?" "I'm a Christian," he responded.

"No, no, I'm trying to find out what you do for a living."

"Well, I sell insurance to pay the bills, but my full-time vocation 24 hours a day is being a Christian!"

In chapter 21 Peter (who caught fish to "pay the bills") learned that his full-time vocation was to be a Christian . . . a disciple . . . a shepherd of the flock. Noticing the tools of Peter's trade around him (the boat, the net, the catch of fish), Jesus asked, "Simon, son of Jonah, lovest thou me more than these?" This penetrating question was posed three times in all (21:15-17) as if to say: "Christian, who do you work for . . . really?" Once that issue is settled in your mind, you will have no trouble with the command: "Feed my sheep!"

God's work done in God's way for God's glory will never lack God's supply.

Insight: The Unnamed Author of the Gospel of John

Nowhere in his entire 21-chapter gospel account does the author state his name, though he calls himself "the disciple whom Jesus loved" (21:20, 23-24). Notice other possible (and perhaps intentionally veiled) references to this same anonymous author (who traditionally has been identified as John, the son of Zebedee) in 1:35-37, 40; 21:2.

Acts

B eginning with a frightened band of disciples in an upper room, Acts traces the outpouring of the Holy Spirit in Jerusalem following the ascension of Christ, and the subsequent spread and growth of Christianity throughout the Roman Empire. Written by Luke, Acts records the fulfillment of Jesus' Great Commission as Spirit-transformed disciples carry the gospel to "Jerusalem . . . Judea, and [to] Samaria, and unto the uttermost part of the earth" (1:8). The unstoppable message is just beginning.

Focus	Foundation of the Church				Founder of Churches					
Divisions	Spirit of the Church	Growth of the Church	Persecution of the Church	Expansion of the Church	First Journey of Paul	Second Journey of Paul	Third Journey of Paul	Arrest of Paul	Trials of Paul	Imprisonment of Paul
	1 4	5 7	8 9 10	12	13 15	16 18	19 20	21 23	24 26	27 28
Topics	Peter		Philip		Paul					
	To the Jews		To the Samaritans		To the Gentiles					
Place	Jerusalem		Judea & Samaria		Uttermost Part					
Time	2 Years (A.D. 33–35)		13 Years (A.D. 35–48)		14 Years (A.D. 48–62)					

The Church Empowered / Acts 1–4 1

Overview: Luke chapter 24 presents only a brief glimpse of Christ's ascension. Now in the book of Acts, Luke resumes his narrative by filling in the details he omitted from his gospel account. With Jesus' last words of instruction still ringing in their ears, the disciples go forth speaking words of eternal life, first to the Jews and then to the Jewish officials. Visited by their resurrected Lord and empowered by the promised Comforter, they fearlessly follow their "marching orders" in spite of mocking, threats, and physical abuse.

Heart of the Passage: Acts 1:8– 2:47

Chapter 1	Chapter 2	Chapter 3	Chapter 4
A Ministry of Patience	A Ministry of Preaching	A Ministry of Power	A Ministry of Perseverance
Jesus Ascends	Spirit Descends		

Your Daily Walk: Imagine that you are about to sit down to dinner when the cook informs you this will be your last meal for an entire week. Would that change your eating habits? How would you feel right after the meal?

Hopefully, no one really eats that way intentionally. The stuffed feeling on Tuesday night, followed by the headache on Wednesday and the hunger pangs on Thursday through Monday, would make such food-stuffing almost unbearable. Besides, it's quite unnecessary.

The Christian is bred by the Word and he must be fed by it.

Did you ever stop to think that what you would never tolerate in the physical realm is often the "standard fare" in the spiritual realm? A Sunday "feast" of Bible study, prayer, and worship . . . followed by six days of "famine."

The church in Jerusalem knew that a proper spiritual diet was essential. That's why "they continued *steadfastly* in the apostles' doctrine and fellowship, and in breaking of bread, and in prayers" (2:42).

Check up on your own spiritual diet. Is it well balanced with proper amounts of Bible study, fellowship, worship, and prayer? Take a few moments now to plan your spiritual diet for the rest of the week.

Insight: A Short Hike on a Sabbath Day
When the disciples returned to Jerusalem after Christ's ascension, Luke describes it as "a sabbath day's journey" (1:12). That may sound long, but it really wasn't—only about 3,000 feet, the distance one was permitted to walk outside the city limits on the Sabbath.

2 *The Church Enlarged / Acts 5–7*

 Overview: The advance of the gospel is all too soon opposed by the adversaries of the gospel. Attacks from without *and*

Heart within threaten to fracture the body of believers in Jerusalem.
of the Selfish lies (chapter 5), ethnic squabbles (chapter 6), and brutal
Passage: martyrdom (chapter 7)—each falls like a hammer blow upon the
Acts 5:1- young, struggling congregation. But prompt discipline, wise
16; 6; leadership, and unflinching commitment only serve to enlarge the
7:54-60 church as "the number of the disciples [multiplies] in Jerusalem
greatly" (6:7).

Chapter 5		Chapter 6	Chapter 7
Purging from Within	Persecution from Without	Designated Deacons	A Model Martyr
1 11	12 42		
Chastening the Church		Stoning of Stephen	

 Your Daily Walk: Complete this sentence—if you can: "The last time I was persecuted for my faith was when I _____

Persecut- _____ ."
ing the Religious tolerance is a treasure rarely prized until it is lost.
church is And yet, for more than a third of the world's population, freedom
like of religion is only a dream, not a reality.
smashing In America, Australia, Canada, England, and other parts of
the the free world, you rarely hear of people going to jail for their faith
atom; (as the apostles did), or being murdered for their faith (as Stephen
divine was). But even today there are still countries and areas in the world
energy is where taking a stand for Jesus Christ can cost a person his life.
released You may not live where persecution is the norm for Chris-
in huge tians, but you *can* get involved by interceding for countries where
quan- the gospel is suppressed and Christians are mistreated. A map of
tities the world mounted in a prominent place to act as your "prayer
and with prompter" is an ideal way to help you pray for your persecuted
miracu- brethren. Your minister or Sunday school teacher can supply the
lous name of a mission board that has information about the needy
effect. nations of the world. It's one way to "let brotherly love continue"
(Hebrews 13:1)—even half a world away.

Insight: Stephen's Four Appointments
1. He was appointed by *God* (6:1-7).
2. He had an appointment with the *people* (6:8-15).
3. He had an appointment before the *Sanhedrin* (7:1-53).
4. He had an appointment in *heaven* (7:54-60).

The Church Opposed / Acts 8–9

3

Overview: Jesus had made it clear before His ascension that the gospel was for both the Jew and the Gentile (1:8). But two years after delivering that commission, only Jerusalem had heard the glad tidings. In chapter 8, persecution hits—scattering all but the apostles into Judea and Samaria. Philip—one of the deacons chosen in chapter 6—extends his witness to Africa through the conversion of a visiting dignitary. Saul of Tarsus—archenemy of the infant faith—experiences a confrontation with the risen Lord on the Damascus road which transforms him from "Saul the Antagonist" into "Paul, Missionary to the Gentiles."

Heart of the Passage: Acts 8:26–9:31

Chapter 8		Chapter 9		
Mass Evangelism	Individual Evangelism	One Man's Conversion	One Man's Converts	One Man's Ministry
1 25	26 40	1 19	20 31	32 43
Philip		Saul		Peter

Your Daily Walk: Can you match the nicknames on the right with the given names on the left? No fair peeking till you've given it a try!

1. Joses (Joseph)   a. Cephas (John 1:42)
2. Simon   b. Niger (Acts 13:1)
3. James   c. Barnabas (Acts 4:36)
4. Simeon   d. The Less (Mark 15:40)

Nicknames can be revealing, for they often act as a mirror reflecting back to you the way others view your life. In today's reading you met a man named Joses (Joseph). But chances are good you didn't recognize him by that name. Why? Because his life was so marked by an encouraging spirit that he came to be known as *Barnabas*—"son of encouragement." And with good reason (9:26-27; 11:25; 15:37-39)!

What is *your* life so marked by that it would form a fitting nickname for *you*? "Son of Complaining," "Daughter of Criticism," "Son of Faith," "Daughter of Compassion"? Pick one and make it the basis of a personal "Project Barnabas" today. That's the name of the game!

Kindness is a language that the deaf can hear and the blind can see.

Insight: Why "Down" Is "Up" in Palestine
We read in 8:5 that "Philip went down to the city of Samaria," even though Samaria is north of Jerusalem. This makes sense when we realize that Israel's capital city is located atop a hill, and Samaria lies in a low plain. Moreover, we draw our maps with the top facing north, but the Palestinians drew them with the top facing east, looking inland from the Mediterranean.

4 The Church in Transition / Acts 10–12

Heart of the Passage: Acts 12

Overview: "Jerusalem . . . Judea . . . Samaria" (1:8). Now God sets the stage for the gospel advance to the "uttermost part of the earth." With the conversion of Cornelius, the outreach of the church is enlarged to include Gentiles as well. But it takes an unusual vision, a stubborn vessel (Peter), and a well-timed visit to break down centuries of deep-seated prejudice. The enemies of the gospel are also on the march, as seen in the martyrdom of James and the imprisonment of Peter—a futile attempt to stem the growth of the church.

Chapter 10		Chapter 11	Chapter 12
Peter Corrected	Peter Convinced	Peter Confronted	Peter Captive
1 22	23 48		
Deliverance from Predjudice			Deliverance from Prison

The world may doubt the power of prayer; the saints know better.

Your Daily Walk: Chapter 12 might well be titled, "The Answered Prayer and the Unanswered Door." As the disciples learned, without the latter there can be no enjoyment of the former.

Peter was in prison, in danger of experiencing the same cruel fate as did the apostle James. The *disciples* responded, as you might expect, with fervent prayer for Peter's safety (12:5). *God* responded, as you might expect, with answered prayer! But notice how the *disciples* responded to *God's* response!

• They explained away Rhoda's announcement by doubting first her sincerity, then her sanity (12:15).

• They explained away Peter's presence at the door by saying it was his angel (12:15).

• They failed to enjoy God's answer to their prayers because they failed to believe God would really do what they asked!

What are *you* praying for today? A healed relationship . . . a new job . . . victory over a bad habit? Would it surprise you if God answered your prayer? Get up from where you're sitting right now, walk across the room, and open a door. Let it be an expression of your faith that says, "When God's answer knocks, I won't be surprised!"

Insight: Postscript on Peter

So far you've encountered Peter's name 56 times in Acts. But now Luke's emphasis will shift—as seen in the fact that Peter's name appears in 15:7 and *nowhere else in the rest of Acts!*

Paul's First Journey / Acts 13–15   5

 Overview: Just as Jerusalem has been the center for Jewish evangelism, so Syrian Antioch now becomes the center for Gentile evangelism. Peter—who has played the leadership role in the first 12 chapters—now gives up the spotlight to Paul, whose travels and trials will dominate the last 16 chapters of the book. Chapter 13 also marks the beginning of Paul's missionary career—a career not initiated by personal choice so much as by divine calling. Returning to Antioch at the end of their first missionary journey, Paul and his traveling companion Barnabas report to their home church and seek to resolve the issue of including Gentiles in the previously all-Jewish church.

Heart of the Passage: Acts 15

Chapter 13	Chapter 14	Chapter 15
Calling Two Missionaries	Commencing the Mission	Convening a Council
Paul and Barnabas		Apostles and Elders

Your Daily Walk: Do you agree or disagree with this author's thought?

"Agreement makes us soft and complacent; disagreement brings out our strength. Our real enemies are the people who make us feel so good that we are slowly, but inexorably, pulled down into the quicksand of smugness and self-satisfaction."

Chapter 15 describes two sharp disagreements in the church. In fact, the chapter begins and ends with a disagreement.

The first was theological; the second was personal. The first was between acquaintances; the second between close friends and colleagues. The first was over essentials; the second over non-essentials. The first could not be resolved by "agreeing to disagree"; the second could. And God was honored in the way each was handled.

There is an agreeable—and a disagreeable—way to settle disagreements. Is there a brother or sister in Christ you need to approach in order to resolve a dispute? Is there a relationship in your immediate family that needs to be restored? Use Acts 15 as your guide; make today the "someday" you've been putting off.

Lord make my words gracious and tender, for tomorrow I may have to eat them!

Insight: The Backlash of Encouragement

The very thing that brought Barnabas and Paul together was the thing that eventually drove them apart: Barnabas's gift of encouragement. He was willing to give John Mark another chance (15:36-41)—a risk that Paul, for the sake of the work, was not willing to take.

6 *Our Mission*

◀ Step Back

Scripture Reading: Psalm 96

Acts 1:8 captures the flow of the work of God in the early church as believers witness of the risen Lord to *Jerusalem* (chapters 1–7), to *Judea and Samaria* (chapters 8–12), and to the *uttermost part of the earth* (chapters 13–28).

In his study guide, *Acts*, Vol. 1, Chuck Swindoll has labeled these segments Establishment, Scattering, and Broadening. And he applies them to our lives:

1. *The Establishment Stage.* This begins with our new birth—a time of great excitement, of receiving a great deal of nurturing and care, as Christ brings us closer to Himself. This time in our life is like the initial growth phase for the New Testament church.

2. *The Scattering Stage.* Here, pain, testing, disappointment and even persecution may begin to affect us. God uses circumstances and events to stretch us and deepen our roots. Our relationship with God takes on new depth as we begin to grow, mature, and focus on others' needs.

3. *The Broadening Stage.* In this final stage, life is seasoned, mature. The tested saint is extended and broadened, reaching out even further to a broader circle of people. The pains and scars of the past have made the believer even more useful and effective in ministering to others.

▲ Look Up

Many of us cannot reach the mission fields on our feet, but we can reach them on our knees.

As you think of those three stages, ask yourself which stage you might be in as an individual. If you're still in stage one, how does it feel to face the prospect of stages two and three? If you're in the final stage, what thoughts come to your mind as you look back on your life with the Lord?

▶ Move Ahead

The three stages of Acts can also be applied to missions. Your *Jerusalem*, for instance, refers to your own neighborhood or town. Your *Judea and Samaria* is your own nation. And the "uttermost parts" refers to the broader international scene.

How actively involved are you in missions? Is your involvement personal through your witness to others, active as you reach out evangelistically through your church or Christian organization, generous as you give to missionaries who depend on the support of believers back home? Remember, every believer should be involved in missions—both locally and globally, personally and corporately. It's not just a responsibility, it's a privilege.

Consider these truths as you read and ponder Psalm 96.

Paul's Second Journey / Acts 16–18

7

Overview: Paul's second missionary journey begins with a new companion—Silas. But the team soon doubles in size as Timothy is added at Lystra and Luke at Troas. Initially given a warm reception in Philippi, Paul and Silas soon experience flogging and imprisonment for disrupting the profitable soothsaying business. But God uses even this to bring a jailer and his family to salvation.

Heart of the Passage: Acts 16

Chapter 16	Chapter 17	Chapter 18
Preaching in Philippi	Trouble in Thessalonica	Continuing in Corinth
Heathen Hospitality	Jewish Jealousy	

Your Daily Walk: Do you have a Timothy? Is there someone you know who is relatively new in the Christian faith—someone you can encourage, instruct, assist—someone you can *disciple*?

Paul had a Timothy—a spiritual understudy, a son in the faith. Paul knew it is not enough merely to lead men and women to a saving knowledge of Christ. They need to be nurtured and assisted in their spiritual growth.

Read Acts 15:36; 16:4-5; and 2 Timothy 2:2. These verses reflect Paul's emphasis on discipling new Christians and establishing them in the Christian faith. In this way they could continue and expand the gospel's impact long after Paul had stepped off the scene.

If the chain of witness and discipleship had stopped with those early believers, where would *you* be today? What are you doing to forge *new* links in that chain? Take a few minutes to think of two people you know—non-Christians or young believers who need mature guidance in the faith. Write their names in the margin or on a card to slip in your Bible; begin to pray for them daily; and make an appointment to meet with them on a regular basis. You'll find you'll all grow in the faith!

Disciple-ship is more than getting to know what th teacher knows; it's getting to be what he is.

Insight: Paul and Silas—Practicing What They Preached

If anyone ever had reason to complain about their circumstances, certainly Paul and Silas would rank near the top of the list! They were flogged and thrown into prison unjustly. Though Roman citizens, they were denied their "civil rights." Yet in spite of abusive treatment you find no hint of anger in their attitude toward their captors. Rather than *seething,* they spent their time *singing* hymns!

369

8 *Paul's Third Journey / Acts 19–20*

Heart of the Passage: Acts 20:13-38

Overview: A short time after Paul returns from his second journey, it is time to leave on the third! (Go back to 18:22-23 to pick up the conclusion of one trip, the brief period of reporting at Antioch, and the commencement of the next.) At Ephesus Paul's gospel message produces some of the greatest response—and sharpest opposition—of any of the places he visits. Leaving the city in an uproar, Paul later returns to deliver a tearful farewell at Miletus. From this point on, he is determined to visit Jerusalem . . . knowing full well the reception awaiting him there.

Chapter 19	Chapter 20	
Riot in Ephesus	Raising of Eutychus	Farewell to Ephesus
1	16 | 17	38
Turmoil	Travel	Testimonial

Charity gives itself rich; coveteousness hoards itself poor.

Your Daily Walk: When was the last time you gave someone a special gift for an unspecial occasion? And when you did, how did it make you feel? Who was happier: the giver (you) or the recipient?

In today's reading Paul quotes his Master's words, "It is more blessed to give than to receive" (20:35). There's no better way to enjoy an instant blessing than by taking that verse to heart!

And you needn't have money in your pocket to do so, either. Giving a piece of yourself may mean sharing a talent God has given you (for sewing a seam, tuning a car, baby-sitting a youngster, giving relief to someone who cares for an elderly relative). Or it may involve simply being there—spending time with someone who needs to hear a friendly voice or feel a reassuring embrace.

Of course, if God has blessed you materially, there are many ways of sharing that with others as well. An extra bag of groceries delivered to a family out of work . . . a greeting card with a small check enclosed that says, "You have a friend who is thinking of you". . . a recreational outing for a single parent who is struggling on a bare bones budget—the creative possibilities are endless!

Insight: Artemis, the Universal Goddess
The magnificent temple of Artemis, goddess of fertility, was one of the wonders of the ancient world, truly befitting the goddess worshiped by "all Asia and the world" (19:27). Archaeologists have discovered more than 30 places around the world where Artemis was worshiped.

Paul's Arrest in Jerusalem / Acts 21–23 9

Overview: Though Paul has taken his last missionary journey, his missionary career is far from over. God now promotes him from being a missionary to the *people* to being a missionary to the *palace*. Paul travels to Jerusalem, prepared for imprisonment and even martyrdom. Once before the crowd and again before the council, Paul attempts to defend himself by relating his personal testimony. Narrowly averting an assassination plot, he awaits his opportunity to stand trial for "the hope and resurrection of the dead" (23:6).

Heart of the Passage: Acts 21

Chapter 21	Chapter 22	Chapter 23	
Paul's Arrest	Paul's Apology	Paul's Argument	Paul's Ambush
Jerusalem	Jews	Jeopardy	

Your Daily Walk: A gunman sneaks up behind the unsuspecting victim and loudly announces, "You'd better get ready to *live!*"

Oops! Something's wrong here—isn't the victim supposed to get ready to *die?* But stop and think: Which would be tougher to do in this challenging last quarter of the 20th century?

The apostle Paul was ready for both. He believed that a faith worth living for was also a faith worth dying for. As he proceeded to Jerusalem from Caesarea, Paul was well aware of the dangers he faced. But even the prophets of death did not deter him. His parting words were a ringing declaration that he was ready to live *or* die (21:13).

For you, the most difficult decision you will ever face may not come at the point of a gun. You may never be threatened by a jail sentence. More likely, you will face situations where you wish you could "die" but can't. Situations that wound your emotions so deeply you think it is impossible to recover. Situations involving confrontation, discipline, repentance, and forgiveness. But that's where your living faith in Christ can shine most brightly! When tempted to run from your problem today, run instead to your heavenly Father and ask Him for a living victory—the kind He specializes in giving!

If you haven't got problems, perhaps you should get on your knees and ask, "Lord, don't you trust me?"

Insight: When in Jerusalem, Do as the Romans Do. . . .
Paul's affirmative reply to the chief captain's question, "Art thou a Roman?" (22:27) saved him from a scourging, and frightened the captain, who could have been whipped or executed himself for beating a fellow Roman citizen—a direct violation of Roman law!

371

10 Paul's Three Trials in Caesarea
Acts 24–26

Heart of the Passage: Acts 26

📖 **Overview:** Though Paul is no longer free to take the gospel to others, God uses his imprisonment to bring the gospel to three Roman rulers: Felix, Festus, and Agrippa. Felix delays a verdict on Paul's case for two full years in hope of receiving a bribe. His successor, Festus, tries to shift the responsibility to the Sanhedrin in order to gain favor with the Jews. At last, Paul exercises his right as a Roman citizen by appealing his case to Caesar. Once again, before the visiting King Agrippa, it becomes clear that the corruption and indecision surrounding Paul's case can only be resolved in Rome.

Chapter 24	Chapter 25	Chapter 26
Expedient Felix	Erratic Festus	Embarrassed Agrippa
Looking for a Bribe	Looking for a Favor	Looking for an Excuse

The whole world is ordered and arranged to match and meet the needs of the people of God.

✒️ **Your Daily Walk:** Across the top of a sheet of paper, write the words "If only." Then complete that sentence with the first 10 things that come to mind. *("If only freckles were removable. If only I hadn't failed calculus. If only I didn't say 'if only' so often.")*

More than once, Paul may have found himself tempted to play the "If only" game: "If only I hadn't appealed to Caesar. If only Agrippa had come a few days earlier. If only Festus would quit procrastinating. If only I hadn't upset the crowd." But fortified by God's promise in 23:11 ("As thou hast testified of me in Jerusalem, so must thou bear witness also at Rome"), Paul saw each *disappointment* as a divine *appointment* for sharing the gospel. Rather than lamenting over the injustice of it all, Paul viewed his chains as God's way of penetrating the highest offices of the land with the Good News.

Write the words "My disappointment = His appointment" across your 10 "If only" statements. As Paul explained to the Romans (in this week's memory verse), that's the key to seeing God's control in every seemingly out-of-control circumstance of your day!

🔍 **Insight:** "The Power of a King with the Mind of a Slave"
The historian Tacitus made the above statement about Felix, and Felix's treatment of Paul seems to bear out this character analysis (24:24-27). He often met with Paul, not to wrestle with the issues that Paul raised, but to give Paul an opportunity to bribe him. Paul did not oblige and thus had to sit in prison for two years.

Paul's Trip to Rome / Acts 27–28

Overview: Paul's great ambition to reach Rome with the gospel is at last realized—but not without storm, shipwreck, and snakebite! Typical of Paul, he begins his ministry in Rome by preaching to the Jews (28:17-29). And (sadly) typical of Paul's listeners, they reject his message of salvation, prompting him to turn to the Gentiles. Luke ends his two-volume history of the New Testament church by describing Paul's two-year ministry in Rome —the apostle in chains, but the gospel very much "on the loose"!

Heart of the Passage: Acts 27:9– 28:10

Chapter 27		Chapter 28	
Paul in the Ship	Paul in the Storm	Paul on Malta	Paul in Rome
1 13	14 44	1 15	16 31
Bound for Rome		Bound in Rome	

Your Daily Walk: Are you in the habit of dreaming big dreams for God?

Hezekiah had a dream (2 Chronicles 29). He dreamed of turning his spiritually needy nation back to God, of uprooting pagan influences and guiding the hearts of his people back to a fervent worship of Jehovah. And though young, he saw his dream come true.

David had a dream (2 Samuel 7). He dreamed of building a magnificent house for God. And though he did not see his dream come true in his own lifetime, he was able to prepare the way for his son Solomon to make the dream a reality.

Paul had a dream. He dreamed of declaring the Savior's story before emperors in Rome. And his dream also came true.

What is *your* dream? What impact do you want to make for God during your lifetime? What legacy do you want to leave for your children?

Spend a few minutes right now dreaming a big dream for God. If you feel free to do so, share it with your spouse or a close Christian friend. Commit it to God. Pray for it. Work toward it. And in God's strength and timing, realize it to His glory!

Some men dream of worthy accomplishments, while others stay awake and do them.

Insight: The Endless Book of Acts

Each of the four gospel accounts has a conclusion, for Christ's work on earth was completed ("It is *finished*," John 19:30). But the book of Acts has no conclusion, for the Spirit-empowered work of sharing the gospel is not completed ("all that Jesus *began* both to do and teach," Acts 1:1).

A lthough Paul had not founded the church in Rome, he had heard of the exemplary faith and service of the Roman believers, and intended to visit them. Thus, the letter to the Romans serves to introduce both Paul and his message. As such, it has been called "the gospel according to Paul." Writing perhaps from Corinth on his third missionary journey, Paul sets forth some of the central doctrines of the Christian faith: justification by faith, life in the Spirit, unity in the body, and God's redemptive program for Jew and Gentile alike.

Focus	Doctrinal				Practical
Divisions	Problem of Unrighteousness	Provision of Righteousness	Pursuit of Righteousness	Program of Righteousness	Practice of Righteousness
	1 3	4 5	6 8	9 11	12 16
Topics	Sin	Salvation	Sanctification	Selection	Service
	Understanding the Gospel				Living the Gospel
Place	Probably in Corinth				
Time	About A.D. 57				

Problem of Unrighteousness
Romans 1–3

12

Overview: In his introductory greeting to the believers in Rome, the apostle Paul states the theme of his letter: the gospel of God in Jesus Christ (1:1, 3, 9, 16). Writing like an attorney, Paul begins his legal brief by describing the helpless condition of humanity. A rebellious nature has led to rejection of the Creator and worship of the creation. God in turn has permitted the sinful nature of human beings to express the fullness of its corruption. Civilized or savage, Jew or Gentile, the whole human race stands helpless before God. Truly, "All have sinned, and come short of the glory of God" (3:23).

Heart of the Passage: Romans 1; 3:21-31

Chapter 1	Chapter 2	Chapter 3
Humanity's Rejection of God	Humanity's Judgment from God	Humanity's Helplessness Before God
"There is none righteous, no, not one" (3:10).		

Your Daily Walk: Two Christians were talking about the president of a corporation who had died recently. The executive had been a moral man and a philanthropist, but an avowed atheist who had made no pretense of believing in Jesus Christ as his Savior. One friend mused, "It's hard to believe he won't be in heaven. He was such a good man, so thoughtful of his employees, so generous." To which the other gently responded with the words of John 3:18, "He that believeth on him is not condemned: but he that believeth not is condemned already, because he hath not believed in the name of the only begotten Son of God."

We never break God's laws; we only break ourselves upon them.

Perhaps you, too, have difficulty coming to grips with the lost condition of sinful people . . . or with your own lostness apart from Christ. Read Romans 3 again, thoughtfully, until the solemn truth of human *depravity* sinks in. Humanity's only hope—and yours—is faith in Christ's finished work. It's as simple as accepting God's offer of "salvation to every one that believeth" (1:16). Will you in believing faith come to Jesus Christ right now?

Insight: God Has No Favorites (2:11)
Jew and Gentile stand on an equal footing before God. Paul points out that if the Jew's ancient priority of privilege counted for anything, it meant priority of responsibility. Jesus reminded His followers that much is required of those who receive much (Luke 12:48).

Introduction to the
Pauline Epistles

Pauline Epistles: Individuals			
1 Timothy	2 Timothy	Titus	Philemon
2 Thessalonians			Hebrews
1 Thessalonians			James
Colossians			1 Peter
Philippians			2 Peter
Ephesians			1 John
Galatians			2 John
2 Corinthians			3 John
1 Corinthians			Jude
Romans			Revelation
Acts			
Matthew	Mark	Luke	John
Historical Books			

(left side label: Pauline Epistles: Church)
(right side label: Non-Pauline Epistles and Revelation)

"Grace be to you and peace from God the Father, and our Lord Jesus Christ"
—Paul

The 13 letters beginning with Romans and ending with Philemon all flow from the pen of Paul to various New Testament churches and pastors. The first nine were to churches Paul had founded or taken a personal interest in during his missionary journeys. The last four were written to encourage pastors in their difficult and demanding duties as shepherds of the flock of God.

Romans is foundational because of its theme of justification by faith alone. Unfortunately, the Corinthians were not living that way, and the Galatians were adding works as a basis for their confidence before God. All justified believers form one Body (Ephesians) which is called to unity (Philippians) and doctrinal purity (Colossians). And even as that Body lives and serves today, it looks to the future (Thessalonians).

Provision of Righteousness / Romans 4–5 13

📖 **Overview:** After painting humanity's sorry condition, the apostle Paul turns to God's merciful solution. Jesus Christ's death on the cross has paid sin's penalty and has satisfied God's righteous demands. To the one who in faith accepts Jesus' full payment, God stamps across the debt of sin, "Paid in Full." That is justification. Its basis is the work of Christ; its means is the grace of God; its requirement is faith in God and His promise. Abraham and David are illustrations from the past and examples for the present, showing how justification brings peace and access, hope and forgiveness, to the one who has faith in God.

Heart of the Passage: Romans 5

Chapter 4	Chapter 5	
How Justification Comes	What Justification Accomplishes	Why Justification Is Needed
1	11 12	21
Grace from God	Peace with God	Alienation from God

✍️ **Your Daily Walk:** It's only natural to be friends with those who are friendly . . . to like those who are likable . . . to love those who are lovely. Outgoing, attractive, pleasant people have a magnetic quality about them that draws the attention and affection of others. Human love is a response to favorable qualities in the object of one's affection.

Not so with God's love! He expressed His love for sinful humanity while we were "without strength" (5:6), "ungodly" (5:6), "sinners" (5:8), and "enemies" (5:10). God's love is not a response at all. It is a decisive act of His will toward the object of His affection. God loves you, not *because of* . . . but *in spite of* you!

Do you love as God loves, reaching out with concern and compassion to the needy and unlovely and even repulsive? If not, admit your lack of love to God (He knows already); meditate upon His unconditional love for you; then with God's help, allow the "love of God [to be] shed abroad" (5:5) from your heart to the heart of one other person who desperately needs to experience it today.

Those who deserve love the least are the ones who need it the most.

📓 **Insight:** A Big Word for a Big Truth
Justification means that, on the basis of the individual's faith in the finished work of Jesus Christ, God places to his account the spotless merits of Christ, and declares the sinner "righteous." Or as one commentator has described it, justification means that, in Christ, God sees me "just as if I'd never sinned."

14 *Putting the Word to Work*

Step Back

Scripture Reading: 2 Timothy 3:16-17

One of the interesting patterns you'll note in Scripture as you continue through the Epistles involves content and application.

You see, God gave us the Bible not merely for our information, but for our transformation. As the New Testament clearly teaches us, *knowing* and *not doing* is really not *knowing* at all. That's why Jesus frequently ended His talks with the words, "He who has ears to hear, let him hear."

This crucial movement from content to application underlies all the New Testament letters. For instance, in Romans, the apostle Paul outlines the basic truths of the Christian faith in chapters 1–11, then applies it in chapters 12–15. Ephesians 1–3 reveals doctrine, then moves to duty in chapters 4–6.

Paul is not the only author who consistently takes the profound truths of the faith into the realm of everyday life. John, James, even Jesus in His recorded sermons consistently spend at least half their time applying the content they have taught.

The lesson here is obvious: Knowledge must always lead to something even more important—obedience.

That may not be easy, but it's what God calls us to do. As Mark Twain once said, "Most people are bothered by those passages of Scripture they do not understand; but the passages that bother me the most are those I do understand."

Look Up

Knowledge is the eye that must direct the foot of obedience.

Are you letting your Bible reading become just an intellectual exercise, a means of gaining more information? Or are you letting its truths sift through your own life, so that you wrestle with the will of God in your own life every day?

The biblical pattern is clear: In God's eyes, knowledge requires obedience. Take some time to examine your own life in light of that pattern, and talk it over with God.

Move Ahead

In 2 Timothy 3:16-17, Paul lists the main purposes for which the Scriptures were given to us by God. As you read those two verses, note the four main goals of Scripture. Ask yourself how each of those goals can be realized in your own life.

If you're a teacher in your church, school, or even in your family, evaluate your own teaching style. Are you perhaps overemphasizing content to the neglect of application? To apply the truth of God with full integrity and transparency in your own life first and to your students next is to experience the joy of the teacher who fulfills his highest calling.

Pursuit of Righteousness / Romans 6–8 15

Overview: Paul anticipates the questions that will naturally arise as the result of hearing about a gospel of grace. "If God's grace is free, then am I free to sin?" "If I am free from the law, then can I ignore the ethical demands of the law?" "What is the relationship of the believer to the law?" "How can I enjoy freedom from the law and the flesh in my daily life?" Paul sounds painfully realistic in today's section! He has no illusions that becoming a Christian means the end of your troubles. Rather, it may be only the beginning! But the life-giving Spirit provides confidence, leadership, and intercession for victorious Christian living in the storms and complexities of everyday life.

Heart of the Passage: Romans 7:13–8:39

Chapter 6		Chapter 7		Chapter 8
Charge of License	Charge of Lawlessness	The Law Highlights Sin	The Law Condemns Sin	The Spirit Conquers Sin
1 14	15 23	1 12	13 25	
Problems with Grace		Problems with the Law		

Your Daily Walk: A do-it-yourselfer went into a hardware store and asked for a saw. The salesman pulled a chain saw from the shelf and commented, "This is our finest saw. Guaranteed to cut ten cords of lumber a day."

"I'll take it!" responded the customer jubilantly.

Next day he came back, haggard and exhausted, to return the chain saw. "Something must be wrong," he moaned. "I could only cut three cords of lumber a day with that thing."

"Let me try it," urged the salesman, pulling on the cord to start the motor. "Vvvrooommm," went the chain saw.

"What's that noise?" exclaimed the customer.

Chapters 7 and 8 may remind you of the plight of that do-it-yourselfer: wanting to do the right thing (chapter 7), but failing to apply the power for victorious living that God has supplied in the person of the Holy Spirit (chapter 8). See if you can find five promises in chapter 8 regarding the Holy Spirit's role in your daily life. Then select one and draw upon it today. That's why they're there!

If the burden God has given you seems too heavy to carry, be assured God never expects you to carry it alone.

Insight: Formidable Obstacles, Faithful Love

Take the 17 items mentioned in 8:35, 38-39 and give each a modern-day paraphrase. For example, "nakedness" could mean "an empty closet"; "distress" might become "too much month and not enough paycheck." Now read the passage—with feeling!

16 *Program of Righteousness / Romans 9–11*

Heart of the Passage: Romans 11

📖 **Overview:** If God's grace is freely provided for both Jew and Gentile, then several questions arise: "Why has God seemingly rejected His nation? And why are so few Jews responding to the gospel invitation?" The key lies in the history of God's dealings with Israel. Israel's past has been marked by God's sovereign selection—of Isaac (not Ishmael), of Jacob (not Esau), of Moses (not Pharaoh)—for His merciful purposes. Israel's present involves rejection by God because of refusal to respond to His invitation. "All day long I have stretched forth my hands unto a disobedient and gainsaying people" (10:21). But Israel's future holds the promise of consolation. God's rejection is neither complete nor final, as seen in the case of Paul.

Chapter 9	Chapter 10	Chapter 11
Consideration of Israel's Rejection	Clarification of Israel's Rejection	Consolation of Israel's Rejection
God's Righteousness in His Relationship with Israel		

The best teacher is the one whose life is the textbook.

✍️ **Your Daily Walk:** Does history *embalm* you or *enthuse* you?

After surveying the pages of Israel's history and seeing God's fingerprints on every page, Paul bursts forth in a spontaneous expression of praise and worship: "O the depth of the riches both of the wisdom and knowledge of God! How unsearchable are his judgments, and his ways past finding out!" (11:33).

For Paul, it is like thumbing through old scrapbooks of the history of his people and recalling the faithfulness of God in the midst of unbelief. Who would hesitate to entrust the future to a God like that?

Pull out some old photograph or scrapbook albums and spend a few minutes reviewing God's faithfulness to you and your family. Where did He meet the unexpected needs? provide safety? heal illness? give blessings you never dreamed of? Now express your confidence in Him for future needs, and close your time of prayer by reading out loud 11:36.

📝 **Insight:** God Is Never Without a Remnant (11:1-5)

Elijah worried in his day that he was the "Lone Ranger" for the Lord, when in fact 7,000 others had not bowed the knee to Baal. Can you find evidence of similar remnants during the Babylonian captivity (Daniel 3:14)? The return from Exile (Ezra 3:8; 7:10)? Jesus' day (Luke 2:25, 36-37)? Your day?

Practice of Righteousness / Romans 12–16 **17**

Overview: Doctrine is dynamic. What you believe will always affect how you behave. For 11 chapters Paul has set forth the foundations of the Christian faith. Now the balance of his letter moves into the practical outworking of that faith in the lives of believers. For every assignment in the Christian life, there is a corresponding enablement from God: Serve one another using the gifts God has given you; be subject to the higher authorities, using the Savior's attitude of love and submission; be sensitive to the needs of weaker brothers in matters of conscience; be united in purpose, having the mind of Christ.

Heart of the Passage: Romans 12–13

Chapter 12	Chapter 13	Chapters 14–15	Chapter 16
Love One Another	Be Subject to One Another	Accept One Another	Greet One Another
Practical Guidelines			Personal Greetings

Your Daily Walk: When someone strikes you on the cheek and you strike them back, that's expected—the *natural* reaction. When someone strikes you on the other cheek and you still don't retaliate even after running out of cheeks, that's remarkable—the *supernatural* reaction!

We are not merely to serve Christ, we are to be like Him.

The final chapters of Romans deal with *supernatural* responses to everyday situations—the kind possible only when Christ is in control. Can you think of a 20th-century example from your life that illustrates the kind of reaction Paul is calling for with each of the following exhortations?

Prefer one another (12:10) _____

_____

Be patient in tribulation (12:12) _____

_____

Give no man evil for evil (12:17) _____

_____

Avenge not yourself (12:19) _____

_____

Remember, anyone can *act* like a Christian, but it takes a true Christian to *react* like one!

Insight: The Epistle According to . . . Whom?
It may surprise you to learn that Paul did not write the book of Romans. Apparently a personal secretary wrote as the apostle dictated. In the case of Romans, who "wrote" this book? _____ (16:22).

381

1 Corinthians

I n New Testament times, Corinth was famous as the commercial hub of southern Greece. But it was also infamous as a center of immorality. Despite that, Paul established a church there near the end of his second missionary journey (Acts 18:1-17). Though the church was in Corinth, Corinth was also in the church, infecting its fellowship and witness. Paul recognizes the gifts and strengths of the church, but he also deals decisively with the problems plaguing it. His goal is that "all things be done decently and in order" (14:40).

Focus	Four Problems	Four Perspectives		
Divisions	Problems of Factions and Lawsuits 1 — 6	Perspectives on Marriage and Liberty 7 — 10	Perspectives on Worship 11 — 14	Perspectives on the Resurrection 15 — 16
Topics	Division	Discussion	Disorder	Disbelief
	Corporate	Private	Public	
Place	Written in Ephesus			
Time	A.D. 56			

Problems of Factions and Lawsuits 18
1 Corinthians 1–6

Overview: Churches aren't perfect because churches are full of imperfect people. Paul writes to the believers at Corinth to correct errors in their public and private behavior which are detracting from their gospel witness. In an orderly fashion Paul moves from point to point, setting forth godly guidelines for conduct consistent with "the grace of God which is given you by Jesus Christ" (1:4). Factions, immorality, lawsuits between believers—the list of offenses is lengthy. But Paul wastes no words in delivering comments that are potent and practical!

Heart of the Passage: 1 Cor. 2–3

Chapter 1	Chapter 2	Chapters 3–4	Chapter 5	Chapter 6
Fact of Divisions	Cause of Divisions	Cure for Divisions	Moral Abuses	Legal Abuses
Jealous Factions			Improper Actions	

Your Daily Walk: Two pastors were discussing the growing criticism aimed at the church of Jesus Christ. The conversation ended with a hearty laugh when one suggested to the other, "If all the critics of the church were laid end to end . . . maybe it would be a good idea to leave them there!"

It has always been easier to criticize than to confront, to comment from the sidelines rather than get involved in the process of implementing creative change. Paul's stern letter to the Corinthians was no mere 16–chapter list of criticisms and complaints. Rather, he cared enough to confront, to suggest new courses of action, and even to visit in person in order to motivate the church to implement necessary discipline.

Criticism from a wise man is more to be desired than the approval of a fool.

Think of individuals for whom you share a godly concern. Perhaps they have been dabbling in the occult or with morally compromising situations. And given the chance, they may continue in their deadly course—unless someone cares enough to confront them . . . someone like you. But before you approach them, be sure you are "prayed up" and blameless in conduct yourself. Confrontation is never easy, but God has promised to provide the strength to do what honors Him.

Insight: New Testament Las Vegas

Merchants and sailors from all over the Mediterranean would flock to Corinth to gamble, find prostitutes, and enjoy various adventures. The Temple of Aphrodite (goddess of love) overlooked the city from atop a hill named Acrocorinth. With its 1,000 prostitutes, it epitomized the ambiance of Corinth.

19 Perspectives on Marriage and Liberty
1 Corinthians 7–10

*Heart
of the
Passage:
1 Cor.
7–8*

Overview: Beginning with chapter 7, Paul answers a series of questions raised by the believers in Corinth:
- Is celibacy better than marriage?
- Is it permissible for Christians to eat meat offered to idols?
- Is it proper for a minister of the gospel to derive his living from that ministry?
- If an action is lawful, is it therefore permissible?

Building on Old Testament quotations and Christ's teachings, Paul sets forth God's perspective on marriage and Christian liberty.

Chapter 7	Chapter 8	Chapter 9	Chapter 10
Problems with Marriage	Problems with Meat	Counsel to Ministers	Caution About Murmuring
Be Careful	Be Considerate	Be Consistent	Be Content

*The
world is
far more
ready to
receive
the
gospel
than
Chris-
tians are
to hand
it out.*

Insight: Key Facts About Corrupt Corinth

Because of its strategic location on the narrow isthmus between the Aegean and Adriatic seas, Corinth attracted worldwide commerce—and with it, worldwide religious influences. The city became filled with shrines and temples, the most prominent being the Temple of Aphrodite atop the 1,800-foot prominence overlooking the city. This cosmopolitan center thrived on entertainment, vice, and corruption. Eventually, the city became so notorious for its immorality that the term "to act like a Corinthian" became a synonym for debauchery.

Your Daily Walk: Would you want to have been a charter member of the first-century "Church of Corinth"? Why or why not?

It was no accident that Paul aimed for the city of Corinth on his second missionary journey. The stakes were high; the location was strategic; the pressures were enormous. But Paul knew that a clear, convincing gospel witness in that cosmopolitan crossroads could potentially change the city, the province, and indeed the world!

God is still in the business of placing His children in strategic locations—locations where the purity of your marriage and the zeal of your walk with God can make a difference. Your town, like Corinth of old, may be notorious for its wickedness. Begin to pray today that it will become "notorious" rather for its gospel witness. And ask God to let that witness begin with you!

384

AN INTEGRATION OF THE NEW TESTAMENT

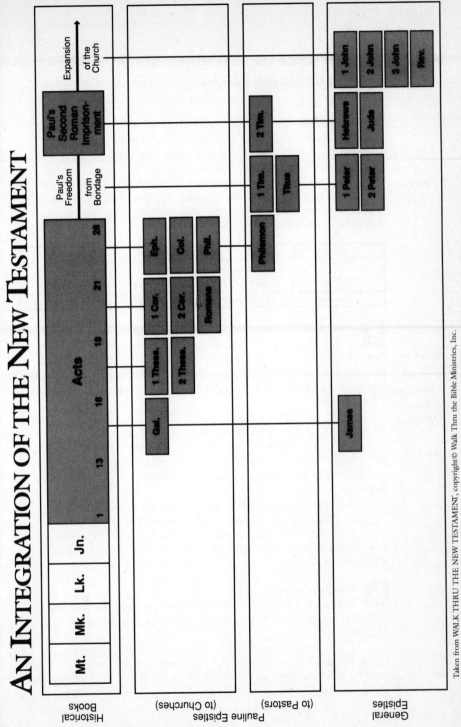

Taken from WALK THRU THE NEW TESTAMENT, copyright© Walk Thru the Bible Ministries, Inc.

20 *Perspectives on Worship*
1 Corinthians 11–14

Overview: Paul's letter so far has dealt with problems of a personal nature. But now he addresses public issues in the Corinthian church: the veiling of women, the importance of the Lord's Supper, and the use and abuse of spiritual gifts. Worship must be characterized by propriety and orderliness. Spiritual gifts must be exercised in love, for the edifying (building up) of the whole body of Christ. Only then is the church of God properly worshiping the God of the church.

Heart of the Passage: 1 Cor. 12–13

Chapter 11	Chapter 12	Chapter 13	Chapter 14
Settling Disorders Involving . . .			
Lord's Supper	Lack of Unity	Lack of Love	Lax Worship
Moderation	Manifestation	Examination	Edification

Your Daily Walk: Have you ever taken an aptitude or vocational interest test? If you have, you know these tests often measure dexterity, vocabulary, and problem-solving ability. Their purpose is to identify skills you have as a guide for future education and training. That way you might avoid becoming a square peg in a round hole.

Ministry is our love for Christ dressed in working clothes.

Here's a three-question "aptitude test" to help you discover your spiritual gift or gifts for use in your local church:

1. As you examine your church's ministry, where do you think improvement could be made? (This is probably an area which would involve your gift, as revealed by your sensitivity to need in that area.)

2. What type of ministry do you eagerly anticipate doing?

3. What type of ministry do others compliment you on?

Now take your answers to your minister or church leader, and discuss how you can get more actively involved in the life of your church.

Insight: Anatomy of a Church

Using each of the following statements from the physical world, see if you can state a corresponding principle regarding the church:

1. No single part of the body, regardless of its importance, can perform all the functions the body requires for survival.

2. The hidden parts of the body (such as the liver and lungs) are as essential as the visible parts.

3. The eye, though physically located "above" the hand or the foot, has great difficulty getting along without either.

Perspectives on the Resurrection
1 Corinthians 15–16

Overview: False teachers had been confusing the Corinthians by denying the doctrine of physical resurrection. Their attacks struck at the very heart of the Christian faith, for without the Resurrection, the Good News of the gospel is made null and void. Paul defends the Resurrection as a historical fact confirmed by more than 500 eyewitnesses (15:6). The Resurrection provides hope for the believer's body as well as his soul, and motivates the believer to be "steadfast, unmoveable, always abounding in the work of the Lord, forasmuch as ye know that your labor is not in vain the Lord" (15:58).

Heart of the Passage: 1 Cor. 15:1-22, 51-58

Chapter 15		Chapter 16	
Proof of Christ's Resurrection	Plan for Future Resurrections	Provision for the Poor	Personal Plans for Paul
Instruction in the Faith		Instructions for the Future	

Your Daily Walk: The human body is a truly remarkable machine. Car makers are pleased if their product lasts "5 years or 50,000 miles." But your body may well last you 5 . . . 10 . . . 15 . . . even 20 times that long!

That's not to say it won't require "periodic maintenance." And parts of it may wear out sooner than others. Some things will be gained that you don't want (like wrinkles and extra pounds); others will be lost that you do want (like hair and teeth).

For the Christian, however, there's an even more exciting prospect than the thought that his body might last 70 . . . 80 . . . 90 years. One day he will get a body that will last for all eternity! A body that won't wrinkle with age or fall apart with use. A body that will be incorruptible . . . immortal . . . sinless. As you minister for Christ today under the limitations of a handicap, poor health, arthritis, or just plain fatigue, ponder often and long over this warming truth from 1 Corinthians 15:35-44: "I've got some body waiting for me!"

Lift your voices in triumph on high, for Jesus is risen and man cannot die.

Insight: The Best-Attested Fact in Ancient History
Pretend for the next few minutes that you have been given the assignment of confirming (or denying) the rumor that Jesus rose from the dead. From Matthew 28, Mark 16, Luke 24, John 20–21, Acts 1, and 1 Corinthians 15, see if you can gather at least 10 pieces of evidence to prove that Jesus' claim of bodily resurrection is a fact of history, not a figment of someone's imagination.

P aul's troubles with the Corinthians
continued. After his first letter, Paul's
teaching, character, and motives were
brought under attack by some. Paul writes
to set forth his credentials and vindicate
his conduct, thanking those who support him
and appealing to the rebellious minority.
The book is heavily autobiographical,
offering glimpses into the life of Paul found
nowhere else in Scripture: his preconversion
background, his visions from God, his thorn
in the flesh, and his persecution for the cause
of Christ.

Focus	Consolation	Exhortation	Vindication
Divisions	Paul's Minister of the Gospel 1 ... 5	Paul's Motivation in the Gospel 6 ... 9	Paul's Authority as a Gospel Minister 10 ... 13
Topics	Character	Collection	Credentials
	The Repentant Majority		The Rebellious Minority
Place	Written in Macedonia		
Time	About A.D. 56		

Paul, Minister of the Gospel
2 Corinthians 1–5

Overview: Paul opens his second epistle to the Corinthians the same way he began his first one: by establishing his authority and documenting the source of his revelation. Whereas his first letter expressed thanksgiving for what God had done among the Corinthians, Paul's second one praises God for what He has done for Paul and Timothy. In contrast to the inferior glory of the old covenant (Moses' law) which killed and condemned, the glorious new covenant, sealed in Jesus' own blood, makes God's ministers bold and effective in calling people to repentance.

*Heart
of the
Passage:
2 Cor.
1–2*

Chapter 1	Chapter 2	Chapter 3	Chapter 4	Chapter 5
Paul the Comforter	Paul the Minister	Paul the Apostle	Paul the Sufferer	Paul the Reconciler
Apostleship Defined		Apostleship Defended		

Your Daily Walk: What is your favorite smell: the fragrance of rose blossoms? the aroma of chocolate chip cookies baking in the oven? a certain perfume? a barnyard full of animals?

Smell is an individual matter. One person's perfume may be another's pollution! In 2 Corinthians 2:14-16 Paul says that Christians should be giving off an inviting fragrance to those around them. And there's more to that than regular hygiene or using the right cologne, for Paul is speaking of the quality of your life. Perfume attracts; pollution repels. Will others sense the fragrance of Christ radiating from your life? Or is your Christian life so bland that others have trouble finding anything attractive about your conversation or conduct? Or worse, is there an unpleasant odor that is turning people away?

Check up on your I.Q. (Incense Quotient) right now! Then why not purchase a small bottle of cologne or perfume—a fragrance you don't normally buy—to remind you each time you use it of the importance of letting the fragrance of Christ radiate to those around you!

*It is for
us to use
every
moment
of today
as if our
very
eternity
were
dependent
on its
words
and
deeds.*

Insight: They Didn't Even Like His Looks!

Paul's need to write 2 Corinthians becomes clear when you note the severity of the charges against him: fickleness (1:17-23), pride (3:1), weakness (10:10), rude speech (11:6), meanness (7:8-10), dishonesty (12:16-19), and mental instability (5:13).

23 Paul's Motivation in the Gospel
2 Corinthians 6–9

Heart of the Passage: 2 Cor. 6, 9

Overview: Paul has defended his ministry as an ambassador for Christ by showing how individuals can be reconciled to a loving God. This leads Paul to plead with the Corinthians to be reconciled to *him* as their spiritual father (6:13), and to love him in the same way he loves them. In chapters 8 and 9 Paul gives the most comprehensive treatment of Christian stewardship found anywhere in the New Testament. He appeals to the Corinthians to follow the example set by the churches of Macedonia in generous, sacrificial giving—a reasonable response to God's indescribable gift in the person of His Son.

Chapter 6	Chapter 7	Chapter 8	Chapter 9
A Ministry of Purity	A Message of Praise	A Ministry of Giving	A Method of Giving
Separation		Stewardship	

Insight: What's in a Name (6:15)?

If you are "in" with God, you are "out" with the unbelieving world.

Of all the names for Satan (and there are nearly 20 in the pages of Scripture), perhaps *Belial* is the most appropriate, for it comes from a Hebrew derivation which means "worthless"!

Your Daily Walk: Find a jar with a tight-fitting cap, fill it half with cooking oil and half with water, screw on the cap, shake the jar vigorously for a few seconds, and set it aside as you read on.

To show the Corinthians just how senseless it is to enter into a binding arrangement with unbelievers, Paul gives five pairs of contrasts that mix like oil and water.

"Be ye not unequally yoked" (6:14-16)	
Righteousness	Lawlessness
Light	Darkness
Christ	Belial (Satan)
Faith	Unbelief
Temple of God	Idols

Notice there is an extra pair of lines for you to write in a "yoked" agreement you are contemplating. Is it as inconsistent as the five listed above it? Then take the apostle's advice: *Don't get into it!* If you do, the yoke's on you—and that's no joke.

Paul's Authority as a Gospel Minister
2 Corinthians 10–13

24

 Overview: Paul's final words to the Corinthians are sprinkled with the personal pronoun *I* as he speaks about his distinguished ancestry and dedicated service. He draws repeatedly upon his authority as an apostle in order to deal effectively with the problems in Corinth. In strong terms Paul exhorts the rebellious to repent so that his approaching visit can be a time of *rejoicing* rather than *rebuke*. The letter closes with the typical Pauline benediction and greetings.

Heart of the Passage: 2 Cor. 10, 12

Chapter 10	Chapter 11	Chapter 12	Chapter 13
Paul's Defense	Paul's Endurance	Paul's Vision	Paul's Plans
Authority	Apostleship		Admonition

Your Daily Walk:
An elephant and a flea, they say,
Crossed over a bridge one day.
To the elephant said the flea:
"We shook that one didn't we!"

Ridiculous? Of course. But no more ridiculous than when you boast of things you have done—and leave God out of the picture.

The Bible abounds with imagery of the believer's dependence upon God's strength and faithfulness:

- You are clay in the Potter's hands (Jeremiah 18:6).
- You are a branch abiding in the Vine (John 15:5).
- You are a member of Christ's body, of which He is the Head (Romans 12:4-5; Ephesians 1:22-23).

That's not to say boasting is inappropriate in the Christian life. In 2 Corinthians, perhaps Paul's most personal letter, he uses the word *boast* a total of 13 times. But notice *who* and *what* Paul was boasting about! "He that glorieth, let him glory *in the Lord*" (10:17).

Take Paul's advice right now! In a note, phone call, or visit, share with one other person today the greatness of your God. It might be just the encouragement that person needs to trust in Him also!

You will never need more than God can supply.

Insight: The Irony of the Church's Mission
Question: Is the church's role to build up or tear down?
Answer: Both! To build up Christians (Ephesians 4:16), and to tear down Satan's spiritual strongholds (2 Corinthians 10:4-5).

Galatians

P aul's letter to the Galatians doesn't open with his usual greeting of praise and prayer for the saints. There is an emergency at hand! The Galatians have listened to false teachers who have come into the church teaching that salvation is a mixture of works and grace. Paul warns the believers about the bondage this type of deception brings and exhorts them to return to the freedom that is theirs in Jesus Christ. He goes on to show that it is in the Spirit, not the flesh, that the Christian life is successfully lived.

Focus	Defending the Gospel Minister		Defending the Gospel's Message		Demonstrating the Gospel's Might	
Divisions	Perverters' Renunciation	Paul's Apostleship	Law Cannot Set Free	Grace Sets Free	Peril to Freedom	Practice in Freedom
	1:1 1:10	1:11 2:21	3:1 4:20	4:21 4:31	5:1 5:12	5:13 6:18
Topics	Autobiography		Argument		Application	
	Authority, Not Opinion		Freedom, Not Bondage		Spirit, Not Flesh	
Place	South Galatian Theory: Syrian Antioch North Galatian Theory: Ephesus or Macedonia					
Time	South Galatian Theory: A.D. 49 North Galatian Theory: A.D. 53–56					

Unshackled in Christ / Galatians 1-6

25

Overview: The epistle to the Galatians has been called "the charter of Christian liberty." It is Paul's manifesto of justification by faith and the liberty that produces. Paul directs this great charter of Christian freedom to people who are about to forsake the priceless liberty they possess in Christ. Certain Jewish legalists are influencing the believers in Galatia to trade their freedom in Christ for bondage to the law. Paul writes to refute their false gospel of works and to demonstrate the superiority of justification by faith.

Heart of the Passage: Galatians 3, 5

Chapter 1–2	Chapters 3–4	Chapters 5–6
Authority, Not Opinion	Freedom, Not Bondage	Spirit, Not Flesh
Labor	Liberty	Life

Insight: How Many Fruits of the Spirit Are There (5:22-23)? *Answer:* One! It's no accident that Paul chooses the singular word "fruit" over the plural "fruits" to show the unity of these nine Christian virtues as a cluster of characteristics originating in Christ and manifested in the power of the Spirit.

Abiding lives always bear the most abundant fruit.

Your Daily Walk: Find a piece of fruit (an apple will do nicely) and a sheet of paper. Then in the next five minutes, see if you can make 25 observations about that "fruity" object. Describe it in terms of its shape, size, color, weight, texture, smell, and taste.

Now suppose someone asked you, "What does a Christian look like? Describe one for me." What would you say? A good place to start would be the fruit of the Spirit. Nine characteristics of that fruit are given in 5:22-23, and they are qualities that only a Christian can exhibit consistently. Why? Because only a Christian who has the supernatural Holy Spirit within can produce a supernatural life without—a life characterized by joy, peace, patience, and more!

Pick one of the nine Spirit-given "fruit flavors" in 5:22-23. Write it on a 3 x 5 card and tape it to your dashboard, desk, refrigerator, or mirror. Then ask God to exhibit that quality in your life today. Some are inward attitudes (love, joy, peace); others are outward actions (long-suffering, gentleness, goodness); and still others are Godward responses (faith, meekness, temperance). But all are unmistakable marks of the Christian!

Ephesians

T he Ephesians had unlimited spiritual
wealth at their disposal, yet they lived
as spiritual paupers. So Paul wrote to
encourage them to understand and claim
their heavenly resources. Only then could
they draw on them for their earthly walk. In
the first half of his letter, the apostle outlines
the heavenly wealth—adoption, redemption,
inheritance, and power. In the second half
he shows the practical applications of those
doctrines. Paul made it clear—believers are
not to have merely an earthly viewpoint.
God has given to us His riches.

Focus	The Christian's Wealth				The Christian's Walk			
Divisions	Thanksgiving for Wealth	Wealth of Salvation		Wealth of the Church	Walk at Church	Walk in Holiness	Walk at Home and Work	Walk in Warfare
	1:1 1:23	2:1 2:22	2:23	3:21	4:1 4:16	4:17 5:21	5:22 6:9	6:10 6:24
Topics	Calling				Conduct			
	Privileges				Practicalities			
Place	Rome							
Time	A.D. 60–61							

Building the Body of Christ
Ephesians 1–6

26

📖 **Overview:** Summarizing the message of Ephesians is simple: What you believe affects how you behave. . . . Walk worthy of your calling. . . . You are rich in Christ, so live that way! But it takes a lifetime to live out the reality of those statements. The Christian's conduct should be consistent with his calling. He is indescribably rich in Jesus Christ, endowed with every spiritual blessing. But he must learn to walk in the light of that wealth. A spiritual war rages, and only those who learn to appropriate and use the full armor of God will be able to stand against Satan's wily attacks.

Heart of the Passage: Ephesians 1, 4

Chapter 1	Chapter 2	Chapter 3	Chapters 4–5	Chapter 6
Acceptance in Christ	Union in Christ	Access in Christ	Walking in Christ	Warfare in Christ
Calling			Conduct	

✍️ **Your Daily Walk:** A little child in Sunday school once misquoted Ephesians 4:1— ". . . walk worthy of the vacation to which ye are called." But the apostle Paul makes it amply clear in chapters 4–6 that the Christian's vocation is no vacation! Ephesians also makes it clear that your Christian vocation is not simply to be a doctor, factory worker, housewife, or student. Rather it's to translate the glorious realities of your position "in heavenly places in Christ" (1:3) into visible actions (and invisible attitudes) daily.

When you pray, make sure your will is in neutral so God can shift it.

Write out a brief job description of your regular work (inside or outside the home). Include an explanation of your position and the actions you perform to accomplish your job. Then as you read through Ephesians, think of it as your Christian "job description," with chapters 1–3 describing your position and 4–6 explaining the performance necessary to carry out your responsibilities.

✒️ **Insight:** A Worthy Daily Walk
In 4:1 Paul begins the second half of his book with the command, "Walk worthy of the vocation wherewith ye are called." Can you find four other commands to "walk" in chapters 4 and 5?
Walk worthy (4:1).
Walk _____ (   ).
Walk _____ (   ).
Walk _____ (   ).
Walk _____ (   ).
In which of these five areas do you need to exercise most today?

27 *One Anothering*

Step Back

Scripture Reading: Selected Verses

The New Testament Epistles are full of commands about the relationship God desires that we have with "one another." Here are just 12 of the many "one another" commands in the Epistles:

- "Be kindly affectioned one to another with brotherly love . . ." (Romans 12:10)
- ". . . in honour preferring one another" (Romans 12:10)
- ". . . able also to admonish one another" (Romans 15:14)
- ". . . have the same care one for another" (1 Corinthians 12:25)
- ". . . by love serve one another" (Galatians 5:13)
- "Bear ye one another's burdens" (Galatians 6:2)
- ". . . Be ye kind to one another, tenderhearted . . ." (Ephesians 4:32)
- ". . . forgiving one another, even as God for Christ's sake hath forgiven you" (Ephesians 4:32)
- ". . . submitting yourselves one to another in the fear of God" (Ephesians 5:21)
- ". . . teaching and admonishing one another . . ." (Colossians 3:16)
- ". . . love one another" (1 Thessalonians 4:9)
- ". . . comfort one another with these words" (1 Thessalonians 4:18)

Look Up

God calls us not to a solitary sainthood but to fellowship in a company of committed individuals.

As you can readily see, our relationships with our brothers and sisters in the Lord are intended to have a positive and lasting impact in all of our lives. Perhaps that's why God started the church in the first place. The church is God's way to have all people—regardless of race, wealth, social standing, professional position, education, etc.—to stand equally before God, to stand on level ground at the foot of the cross.

Spend some moments in prayer thanking God for establishing the church as a haven of support, growth, and encouragement. Pray particularly for your closest friends with whom you regularly fulfill the "one another" commands.

Move Ahead

Have you been obeying these "one anothering" commands of Scripture? As a special project, pick two or three of the verses above, and make a special effort to put them into practice today. It's the heart of New Testament living—putting the needs of others before your own, and having your own needs met by them.

Philippians

P aul is now a prisoner in Rome. In
spite of his difficult circumstances, he
remains joyful and writes to commend the
Philippians for their faithfulness and to
challenge them to make Christ the center of
their experience. Jesus' life and ministry,
described in 2:6-11, is the life pattern all
believers must follow so that their faith
might become evident to others. Paul
acknowledges that divisions sometimes exist
among believers but is confident that unity
will be restored as they imitate the servanthood of Christ.

Focus	Rejoice in God's Will				Relax in God's Peace		
Divisions	Paul and Philippians	Paul and Prison	Christ and Living	Timothy and Epaphroditus	Philippians and Errors	Philippians and Holiness	Paul and a Gift
	1:1 1:11	1:12 1:26	1:27 2:18	2:19 2:30	3:1 4:1	4:2 4:9	4:10 4:21
Topics	Information		Appeal	Plans	Warning	Exhortation	Thanks
	Rejoicing in Affliction		Rejoicing in Ministry		Rejoicing in Jesus	Rejoicing in Blessings	
Place	Rome						
Time	Approximately A.D. 62						

28 *Joy and Peace in Christ / Philippians 1–4*

Heart of the Passage: Phil. 1, 4

Overview: Philippians is a joyful letter, written by Paul from a prison cell in Rome to one of the churches he founded on his second missionary journey (Acts 16). In spite of Paul's adverse circumstances, Philippians is a letter of encouragement in the midst of persecution. There is much for Paul to rejoice about: the Philippians' repeated financial assistance, the hope of visiting the Philippian believers soon, the church's steadfast testimony for the gospel. Though that testimony is threatened by divisions in the church, Paul is confident their unity will be restored as they imitate the humility and servanthood of Christ. Indeed, Paul can urge with confidence, "Rejoice in the Lord always" (4:4).

Chapter 1	Chapter 2	Chapter 3	Chapter 4
Rejoicing in Affliction	Rejoicing in Ministry	Rejoicing in Jesus	Rejoicing in Blessings
"Rejoice in the Lord always" (4:4).			

Joy is the gigantic secret of the Christian.

Your Daily Walk: How many areas in your life would you consider exemplary—areas you would not be ashamed for others to imitate?

When Paul wanted to illustrate his teaching, he often used flesh-and-blood examples. He did not hesitate to set forth Timothy as a model of caring (2:19-20), Epaphroditus as a model of steadfastness (2:25), and Christ as a model of humility (2:5-8).

Do you view yourself as a personal illustration? "Oh," you say, "not me!" But it's true whether you volunteer or not. People around you evaluate Christianity by the way they see it lived out in your life.

Do *you* "rejoice always" (4:4)? Are *you* anxious and thus deny the reality and power of prayer (4:6)? Do *you* give daily evidence of the "peace of God" at work in your life (4:7)?

Your children, parents, neighbors, co-workers, relatives—even strangers—will notice whether the quality of your life is different. Select one area today where, with God's help, you will seek to be an example in all you do and say.

Insight: Christ, My All in All

Beginning with Paul's thought in 1:21 ("For to me to live is Christ"), see how many ways you can complete this sentence based on what you have read in Philippians: "To me, Christ is my . . ." Share your answers with an encouraging friend!

Colossians

P aul is imprisoned in Rome when he receives word that heretical doctrines are threatening the church at Colosse. To refute the spiritually lethal combination of eastern mysticism and Jewish legalism, Paul reestablishes the truth of the gospel and demonstrates the supremacy of Christ. As Lord of all, Jesus Christ is the giver of salvation and sufficient for every need. No rituals or legalistic practices are needed. Since Christ is all in all, Paul encourages the Colossians to pursue a godly lifestyle befitting those who are "risen with Christ" (3:1).

Focus	Christ, the Lord of the Universe			Christ, the Lord of Life			
Divisions	Prayer to the Father of Christ	Supremacy of Christ	Sufficiency of Christ	New Life	Home Life	Christian Life	Conclusion
	1:1 1:12	1:13 2:3	2:4 2:23	3:1 3:17	3:18 4:1	4:2 4:6	4:7 4:18
Topics	Transforming Relationship			Transformed Relationships			
	Consistent Doctrine			Consistent Life			
Place	Rome						
Time	A.D. 60–61						

29 Life in the Preeminent Christ
Colossians 1-4

Heart of the Passage: Colossians 1:1–2:7

📖 **Overview:** All is not well in Colossae. A dangerous heresy—that Jesus Christ is neither central nor supreme—is undermining the church. Paul's response to these false teachings is twofold. First, he upholds Christ as the preeminent Head of the church. Next, he speaks out against the rituals and man-made regulations which typify the worship of the Colossians. Instead of their present practices, Paul encourages them to pursue a godly life befitting those who are "risen with Christ" (3:1).

Chapter 1	Chapter 2	Chapters 3–4
Christ Our Spiritual Head	Christ Our Suffering Savior	Christ Our Sovereign Lord
"Christ is all, and in all" (3:11).		

Jesus' name is not so much written as it is plowed in the furrows of history.

🛠 **Insight: "Make Two Copies of This, Tychicus. . . ."**
It is quite possible Paul wrote the books of Ephesians and Colossians about the same time under the Spirit's inspiration. Notice the many striking similarities: Both letters were delivered by the same "postman"—Tychicus; both were written from prison; the salutations are similar; the structures of the books are remarkably alike; and there is an obvious correspondence between pairs of verses:

Ephesians	Colossians
1:7	1:14
1:10	1:20
1:15-17	1:3-4
1:18	1:27
1:19-20	2:12
1:21-23	1:16-19, etc.

📖 **Your Daily Walk:** Colossians 1:27 is one of the most remarkable verses in the Bible, for it makes this claim: "Christ [is] in you, the hope of glory." This statement is not merely hypothetical or psychological or potential. For the Christian, it is factual! Christ as Lord of all gives complete salvation, setting us free from sin's power and penalty, He is sufficient for every need, and He is the guarantee that we will be like Him and be with Him forever.

List the major activities you have planned for today, including the people you expect to be with. Now jot down one difference that will result in each of those activities and encounters today as you strive to be conscious of Christ in you. Why not share "the riches of the glory of this mystery" with one other person today as well!

400

Our Defense Against the Devil **30**

⬅ Step Back

Every New Testament writer teaches of the existence of Satan, the fallen angel, who even now commands legions of angels who followed him in rebellion against God (Matthew 12:24).

When Jesus Christ died on the cross, Satan was judged (John 12:31). When one puts his trust in Jesus Christ as his Savior, Satan's control over him is ended.

But that doesn't stop Satan from trying to derail the Christian's life. The Scriptures indicate that Satan accuses, slanders, hinders, and tempts the children of God in order to keep them from being as effective as possible in the world. "For we wrestle not against flesh and blood, but against principalities, against powers, against the rulers of the darkness of this world, against spiritual wickedness in high places" (Ephesians 6:12).

Even so, believers have a three-fold defense to employ against Satan:

1. *Christ is interceding on our behalf* (John 17:15). Even now, Christ is praying for believers in heaven that the evil one would be restrained.

2. *The believer should keep on guard* (1 Peter 5:8). "Be sober, be vigilant," Peter puts it. Don't take Satan lightly. He is real, he is angry, and he seeks to keep you out of God's will for you.

3. *The believer should wear the armor of God* (Ephesians 6:11-18). The apostle Paul outlines the spiritual armor of God, "that ye may be able to stand against the wiles of the devil."

Scripture Reading: Ephesians 6:11-18

⬆ Look Up

Prayerfully read through Ephesians 6:11-18, and by faith put on each piece of the armor of God. Thank Him for His provision and His protection for you.

Above all, thank Him that your destiny has been settled for all time, and that ultimately Satan will be judged and destroyed forever (Revelation 20).

Satan hinders prayer, but prayer also hinders Satan.

➡ Move Ahead

The more you know about the way Satan works, the better defended you will be against his evil ways. Using a study Bible, concordance, or Christian book on the subject, do some research about the nature and work of Satan.

But more important, keep praying for yourself and others. Keep sober and vigilant. Keep standing strong in the armor of God. As C. S. Lewis once wrote, "Like a good chess player he is always trying to maneuver you into a position where you can save your castle only by losing your bishop."

1 Thessalonians

Prosperous, prominent, and thoroughly pagan, the seaport city of Thessalonica first heard the gospel on Paul's second missionary journey. A dynamic fellowship developed there, becoming a continual joy to Paul. He writes 1 Thessalonians to encourage them. They were being persecuted; he urges them to persevere. They had heard slander about Paul; he refutes it. Their city is full of sensual temptation; he exhorts them to hold to Christian standards. Finally, he corrects some misunderstandings about the return of Christ.

Focus	Personal Relations to the Thessalonians		Practical Instructions to the Thessalonians		
Divisions	Paul's Memories	Paul's Methods	Paul's Directions	Christ's Return	Paul's Reminders
	1:1 1:10	2:1 3:13	4:1 4:12	4:13 5:11	5:12 5:28
Topics	Personal	Parental		Prophetic	Practical
	A Saving Hope	A Purifying Hope		A Comforting Hope	
Place	Corinth				
Time	Approximately A.D. 51				

The Hope of Christ's Return
1 Thessalonians 1–5

1

 Overview: Paul has many pleasant memories of the days he spent with the infant Thessalonian church. Their faith, hope, love, and perseverance in the face of persecution are exemplary, and Paul's labors as a spiritual parent to the fledgling church have been richly rewarded. His tender affection is visible in every line of his letter as he encourages the Thessalonians to excel in their faith, increase in their love, and rejoice always as they await the return of the Lord—an event which provides hope and comfort for believers both living and dead.

Heart of the Passage: 1 Thess. 1, 4

Chapter 1	Chapter 2	Chapter 3	Chapter 4	Chapter 5
Christ's Return: A Hope That Is . . .				
Saving	Rewarding	Purifying	Comforting	Sobering
Past	Present		Future	

 Your Daily Walk: "It's ten o'clock; do you know where your children are?"

That's a healthy reminder to parents that the duty of discipline and supervision of their children is a 24-hour job. And shirking that duty can only lead to heartache in the lives of the children.

If Paul were writing a letter to you today, he might begin it this way: "Here it is, December already; do you know where your spiritual children are?" Though Paul's converts were spread out in more than 20 different cities, he never "abandoned" them, but rather carried them all in his heart and corresponded with them regularly.

Check Philippians 1:3-4, Colossians 1:3, and Philemon 4, and you'll find the same kind of statement that begins Paul's first letter to the Thessalonians: "We give thanks to God always for you all, making mention of you in our prayers" (1:2). Do you pray daily for your spiritual children? Do you communicate with them periodically through phone calls, visits, or letters? If not, start today! As Paul discovered, spiritual growth is nurtured best in the soil of prayer and encouragement.

Many people pray as if God were a big aspirin pill. They only come when they hurt.

Insight: Unemployment in Thessalonica

When Paul was first planting the church in Thessalonica, he preached heavily on the imminent return of Christ. He repeats his message in the famous passage on the second coming of Christ (4:16-17). Some of the Thessalonian believers, however, had taken his earlier preaching too far by quitting their jobs (4:11-12; 5:14).

403

2 Thessalonians

As the believers in Thessalonica face growing persecution, Paul writes to encourage them that God's judgment will eventually bring about justice. He dispels the rumor that the Day of the Lord has already come, as some thought. They had concluded that they were living in the tribulation and had quit their jobs. Paul exhorts them to return to work and stop burdening the body of Christ. Instead they are to take advantage of the time they have and and "be not weary in well doing" (3:13) before Christ returns.

Focus	Commendation	Instruction	Correction
Divisions	Return of Christ	Revelation of Antichrist	Return to Work
	1:1 1:12	2:1 2:17	3:1 3:18
Topics	Strengthening the Stressful	Confirming the Confused	Disciplining the Disorderly
	Encouragement	Explanation	Exhortation
Place	Corinth		
Time	Approximately A.D. 51		

The Coming Day of the Lord
2 Thessalonians 1–3

2

Overview: Paul begins his second letter to the Thessalonians by commending them for their faithfulness in the midst of persecution and by encouraging them with the truth that present suffering will be repaid with future glory. Therefore, despite the persecution, hopeful expectation can be high. But Paul must also deal with a misunderstanding concerning the coming Day of the Lord. Despite reports to the contrary, that day had not yet arrived, and Paul recounts the events which must take place first. Laboring for the gospel—rather than lazy resignation—can be the only proper response to such truth.

Heart of the Passage: 2 Thess. 3

Chapter 1	Chapter 2	Chapter 3
Return of Christ	Revelation of Antichrist	Return to Work
Encouragement	Explanation	Exhortation

Your Daily Walk: How does the promise of Christ's return affect your daily life? Would a casual observer detect that something is different about you because of Christ's words, "I will come again" (John 14:3)?

Christ's return is a balancing doctrine. It gives both the present and the future a sense of perspective and helps us establish priorities that honor God.

Some members of the Thessalonian church viewed Christ's return as a reason to relax—withdraw from society, close down their businesses, and settle back to wait. But Paul responded sternly to such misguided laziness (3:10-14)!

Have you slipped into the same error through neglect of your family, business, or spiritual duties? What better time than today to get back on target! Call a family council this evening to discuss any neglected tasks God wants you to perform until His Son returns. You might even want to make 3:13 your family motto for the week!

The crowns we will wear in heaven must be won on earth.

Insight: Two Epistles, Side by Side

1 Thessalonians:
• emphasizes faith, hope, love
• concerns the day of Christ
• offers comfort derived from Christ's return
• commends laboring saints

2 Thessalonians:
• emphasizes faith, hope, love
• concerns the Day of the Lord
• corrects misapprehensions about Christ's return
• condemns lazy saints

3 *Letters to Two Leaders*

Scripture Reading: Psalm 23

⬅ Step Back

In the next few days you'll be reading the three letters the apostle Paul wrote to pastors whom he had trained and befriended — Timothy in Ephesus and Titus in Crete. First and Second Timothy and Titus are called the Pastoral Letters because they offer instructions to them about the pastoral care of the churches under their charge.

All three letters touch on these similar topics and themes:

1. *Acknowledge God as your Savior* (Titus 1:3; 2:10; 3:4; 1 Timothy 1:1; 2:3; 4:10). This is a theme Paul no doubt drew great personal strength from himself in the waning years of his robust ministry.

2. *Maintain sound doctrine in your teaching* (Titus 1:9; 1 Timothy 1:10; 6:3; 2 Timothy 1:13; 4:3). Sound teaching not only builds one up in the faith, it also protects against the corruption of false teachers. The word *sound* is found eight times in Paul's three letters to Timothy and Titus and nowhere else in his writings.

3. *Maintain a godly walk in the world* (1 Timothy 2:2; 3:16; 4:7-8; 6:3, 5-6, 11; 2 Timothy 3:5; Titus 1:1). Here again Paul admonishes the leaders to build godliness in their lifestyles, but nowhere else is the word "godly" or "godliness" found in his writings. Godliness means living a good and holy life, specially emphasizing a deep reverence for God, the Source of life.

4. *Deal with controversies straightforwardly* (1 Timothy 1:4; 6:4; 2 Timothy 2:23; Titus 3:9). As pastors, Timothy and Titus were required to oversee the flock under their care, which included protecting them from erroneous teaching and handling other controversies with godly wisdom.

Although Paul's letters were addressed to pastors, the strength these truths can give can also bring us strength to live holy lives that really make a difference in our world.

⬆ Look Up

A sermon's length is not its strength.

To prepare for your reading of the Pastoral Epistles, spend some time in prayer today for your own pastor and the other staff members of your church. Ask God to build in their lives the four themes Paul discussed in his letters. And as you read Psalm 23, ask that God would shepherd the one who is your earthly shepherd.

➡ Move Ahead

You'll discover as you read these three letters that both Timothy and Titus faced countless difficulties in fulfilling their crucial role as pastor. Paul's encouragement no doubt meant a great deal to them. Today, write your pastor a note of encouragement. Share with him what you're learning.

1 Timothy

Timothy, a young disciple discovered by Paul on his second missionary journey (Acts 16:1), enjoyed a unique relationship with the apostle. Referred to as his "own son in the faith," Timothy ministered side by side with Paul as a missionary, and later received the challenging assignment of pastoring the church at Ephesus. Paul's first letter to him resembles a manual for building church leadership. More generally, it is a rich mine of principles for anyone who wishes to have a spiritual impact in the lives of others.

Focus	Organization in the Church			Operation of the Church		
Divisions	Law and Grace	Worship and Women	Bishops and Deacons	Apostasy in the Church	Age Groups in the Church	Areas of Conflict in the Church
	1:1 1:20	2:1 2:15	3:1 3:16	4:1 4:16	5:1 5:25	6:1 6:21
Topics	Life of the Church		Leaders of the Church	Apostasy of the Church	Groups in the Church	Example to the Church
	Plans			Problems		
Place	Macedonia					
Time	Approximately A.D. 62–63					

4 *Protecting the Faith / 1 Timothy 1–6*

Overview: Timothy, a young disciple discovered by Paul on his second missionary journey (Acts 16:1), enjoyed a unique relationship with the apostle. Referred to by Paul as his "beloved son" (2 Timothy 1:2), Timothy ministered side by side with Paul as a missionary and later received the challenging assignment of pastoring the church at Ephesus. Paul's first letter resembles a manual for building church leadership. But more generally, it is a rich mine of principles for anyone who wishes to have a spiritual impact in the lives of others.

Heart of the Passage: 1 Timothy 2–3

Chap. 1	Chap. 2	Chap. 3	Chap. 4	Chap. 5	Chap. 6
Instructions for . . .			Problems with . . .		
Leaders	Ladies	Laity	Doctrine	Dependents	Debt
Organization in the Church			Operation of the Church		

Your Daily Walk: There is a dangerous disease spreading among Christians today.

Its name: "Backyardism."

Storms make for strong trees; testings make for strong Christians.

Its symptoms: Preoccupation with personal pursuits; ignorance (and indifference) about how God is working around the world.

Its result: A stunted prayer life.

Notice Paul's antidote in 2:1-2—"I exhort therefore, that, first of all, supplications, prayers, intercessions, and giving of thanks, be made for all men [not just those in your church, city, state, or country]; for kings, and for all that are in authority."

The cure for nearsighted vision is farsighted prayer.

When was the last time you prayed for your president . . . congressional leaders . . . Supreme Court justices . . . local officials? How about the leaders of other countries of the world? Do you know a missionary family in Africa? Australia? Asia? South America? Europe? Today as you finish your Daily Walk, step to a window that gives you a clear view of your back yard. As you gaze at what is familiar, ask God to lift your eyes above your own "back yard" to see what is unfamiliar and far away—but still near and dear to Him. Become a world-conscious Christian in your vision and prayers.

Insight: "Timothy, Take a Letter. . . ."

In addition to his duties as traveling companion and fellow missionary with Paul, Timothy is also named as co-author of six of Paul's letters. Without peeking, how many can you name?

2 Timothy

P aul's life is drawing to a lonely close in a Roman prison as he writes to encourage Timothy, whom he refers to as his "own son in the faith." Timothy has ministered side by side in mission endeavors with the apostle, but now he faces new challenges as pastor of the church at Ephesus. Paul's first letter offers instruction and advice for building strong leadership within the congregation and lays down principles for those who want a ministry of discipleship. Underlying each theme is the importance of God's Word as the foundation for living.

Focus	Be Steadfast in Your Ministry			Be Steadfast in Your Doctrine		
Divisions	Thanksgiving for Timothy	Exhortation to Timothy	Duties of Timothy	Apostasy and Timothy	Charge to Timothy	Death of Timothy's Friend
	1:1 1:5	1:6 1:18	2:1 2:13	2:14 3:17	4:1 4:5	4:6 4:22
Topics	Hold Fast the Gospel		Pass on the Gospel	Protect the Gospel	Preach the Gospel	
	Foundation		Faithfulness	Foes	Fearlessness	
Place	Roman Prison					
Time	Approximately A.D. 67					

5 *The Pastor and Coming Apostasy*
2 Timothy 1–4

Overview: Paul writes his second letter to Timothy from a Roman prison (1:8, 17). Death is imminent (4:6); Paul is cold (4:13) and lonely (4:9, 11, 21); and there is little to occupy the long, tedious hours of his imprisonment (4:13). And yet, the focus of Paul's letter is not on his own problems and needs but on the problems and needs of young Timothy. Paul, who has stood faithfully for the Lord throughout his life, now passes on that same challenge to Timothy. There is no need to fear persecution or pain, dungeon or death, when you serve the Lord of the universe and endure hardship for His sake.

Heart of the Passage: 2 Timothy 2

Chapter 1	Chapter 2	Chapter 3	Chapter 4
Call to Courage	Call to Commitment	Prepare for Wicked Days	Preach the Living Word
"Endure hardness, as a good soldier of Jesus Christ" (2:3).			

Your Daily Walk: How far back can you trace your physical ancestors? Try it! On a large sheet of paper, draw your family tree for as many generations as you have information. Now using a colored pen or pencil, transform that diagram into a spiritual family tree as well by noting each family member who has given testimony of faith in Jesus Christ.

The greatest treasure a man can leave his children is an intimate knowledge of God.

Timothy enjoyed a rich heritage of family faith. Both his mother and grandmother walked with God (1:5). From his earliest childhood he received instruction in the Scriptures (3:14-15), and that biblical heritage equipped Timothy for later fruitful service.

There is nothing you can do to influence your children more strongly for God than to expose them daily to the reality of God's Word. If you have not already done so, begin a regular program of Scripture memorization as a family. Set a family goal of two verses for each family member this month, and plan a family outing as a treat when you reach your goal!

Insight: Paul, the Persistent Student of Scripture
To the very end of his life, Paul remained a student and a learner. In 4:13 he asked Timothy to bring "the books, [and] especially the parchments." The "books" were perhaps his personal library, and the "parchments" were undoubtedly papyrus scrolls of the Old Testament Scriptures. Have you read a good Christian book lately? Discover again the richness of reading!

Titus

Titus lived on Crete, the largest island in the Mediterranean, and worked among a people who collectively had one of the worst reputations in the world. Paul had left Titus to oversee the growth of the church there and now writes to encourage him in that difficult task. In order to promote sound teaching and offset false doctrines that were on the rise, Titus is told to appoint and train spiritual leaders as elders. Paul's short letter is a summary of Christian doctrine that emphasizes holy living and encourages all to live worthy of the gospel.

Focus	Duties of Church Leaders		Duties of Church Members	
Divisions	Elders Designated	Heresy Described	Good Works Demanded	Heretics Denounced
	1:1　　　1:9	1:10　　　1:16	2:1　　　2:15	3:1　　　3:15
Topics	Servants		Service	Salvation
	Preservation of Truth		Use of Truth	
Place	Probably Written in Corinth			
Time	Approximately A.D. 63			

DECEMBER ☐ Day 340

6 *Paul's Conduct Manual / Titus 1–3*

Heart of the Passage: Titus 2

Overview: Titus, a young minister, is left on the island of Crete by Paul to begin the challenging task of organizing new converts into local congregations. Paul's brief epistle is thus a practical guide for those involved in church administration and organization. Leaders must be chosen on the basis of proven character and conduct; false teachers must be quickly detected and removed; church members of all ages must be encouraged to live lives worthy of the gospel they claim to believe. Paul shares guidelines for young and old, men and women, leader and laity. All should demonstrate the reality of their faith by being "careful to maintain good works" (3:8).

Chapter 1	Chapter 2	Chapter 3
The Person God Chooses	The Manner God Uses	The Marvels God Performs
Servants	Service	Salvation

Love is not just sentiment; it's service.

Your Daily Walk: "P.S. I love you."

Have you ever penned those words on the bottom of a letter? Perhaps the previous pages of your correspondence were so filled with current events or weighty matters that you hadn't had a chance to share the deep feelings you held for the reader. But now the substance of your letter is complete; the urgent news has been shared. Now you can concentrate on the little expressions of affection that make a letter something more than an office memo!

Paul had a habit of adding postscripts to his epistles that show the deep feeling he held for his spiritual children. The last four verses of Titus are like that. And notice how many personal names and practical steps of action Paul includes. Love is like that! It demands an object and an outlet. Follow Paul's lead by writing a short "epistle" of your own today—a newsy note to a family member or friend that is perhaps long overdue. Oh yes—don't forget the "P.S."! It could well be the most important part of the letter.

Insight: Titus's Challenge on the Island of Crete

Read Paul's commentary on the Cretans in 1:12, taken from one of the Cretans' own prophets! The classics abound with allusions to their untruthfulness—so much so that "to act the Cretan" had become a synonym for "to be a liar."

412

Philemon

O n the run after committing a wrong
against his master, Onesimus the
slave sought refuge among the masses in the
city of Rome. There he crosses Paul's path
and converts to faith in Jesus Christ.
Though he shows his gratitude by serving
Paul, he still must reconcile with his master
Philemon. Paul writes this letter to Philemon asking him to forgive Onesimus, the
bearer of the letter, and to accept him as a
brother in Christ. This short epistle reminds
believers of our heavenly Father's love and
forgiveness.

Focus	Praise for Philemon		Plea for Onesimus		Preparation for Paul
Divisions	Paul's Preface	Paul's Commendation	Paul's Intercession	Paul's Promise	Paul's Message
	1:1　　1:3	1:4　　1:7	1:8　　1:16	1:17　　1:21	1:22　　1:25
Topics	Greetings	Gratitude	Grace		Good Words
	Courtesy	Compli-ment	Counsel		Conclusion
Place	Rome				
Time	Approximately A.D. 60–61				

7 *From Bondage to Brotherhood / Philemon*

Heart of the Passage: Philemon 10-12, 15-18

Overview: Paul's "postcard" to Philemon is the shortest and perhaps the most intimate of all his letters. It is a masterpiece of diplomacy and tact in dealing with a festering social sore in the Roman Empire: human slavery. Onesimus, a slave of Philemon, had stolen from his master and had run away to Rome. There he came in contact with Paul (who was under house arrest, Acts 28:16, 30) and with the claims of Jesus Christ. After his conversion, Onesimus faced yet another confrontation—this time with his estranged master, Philemon. Paul sends him back with this letter in hand, urging Philemon to extend forgiveness. Onesimus had left as a bond servant. Now he was returning as a brother in the Lord.

Verses 1-7	Verses 8-17	Verses 18-21	Verses 22-25
Greetings and Commendation	Plea for Onesimus	Pledge to Philemon	Salutations and Benediction
"If thou count me . . . a partner, receive him as myself" (17).			

Souls are not saved in bundles.

Your Daily Walk: Here is a challenge. On your ride to work (if you carpool), over coffee with a neighbor, or on some other convenient occasion, hand the book of Philemon to an unsaved friend and ask him or her to read its 25 verses. Then lovingly ask, "Did you know that little story illustrates how to get to heaven?"

Continue: "You, like Onesimus, have been running from God. You have gone your own way, seeking fulfillment in life. But even as you were running from the Creator who made you, you were running toward the Savior who loves you . . . who died to pay sin's penalty . . . who died to reconcile you to God. The debt which you owe your Master has been paid in full, if you will but accept the provision of Christ's death. Wouldn't you like to know the joy of sins forgiven right now?"

In God's strength, share the message of Philemon with one unsaved friend this week. Follow up with a gospel tract, or make an appointment for further conversation.

Insight: An Extrabiblical Postscript on Onesimus

Whatever happened to Onesimus? How did Philemon react to Paul's plea? The Bible does not say, though tradition provides some interesting clues. Possibly Philemon freed his slave and sent him back to assist Paul (vv. 13-14). Ignatius, a second-century church father, reports that Onesimus later became a minister in Ephesus.

Hebrews

M any Jewish believers were tempted to renounce their newfound faith and return to Judaism to escape persecution. The anonymous writer of Hebrews appeals to them to pursue maturity based on Christ's superiority to the Jewish religious system. Christ is better than Moses, for Moses was created by Him; He is better than Aaron, for His sacrifice never need be repeated; He is better than the Law, for He mediates a better covenant. More is to be gained by suffering for Christ than by reverting to a system He came to fulfill.

Focus	Christ, the Better Way				
Divisions	Christ, Better Than the Angels	Christ, Better Than Moses and Joshua	Christ, Better Than Aaron's Priesthood	Christ, Better Than the Old Covenant	Christ, Example of the Life of Faith
	1　　　　2	3　　　　4	5　　　　7	8　　　　10	11　　　　13
Topics	A Superior Person		A Superior Priesthood		A Superior Power
	Doctrine				Discipline
Place	Written to Scattered Jewish Believers				
Time	About A.D. 64–68				

8 Christ, Better Than the Angels
Hebrews 1–2

Heart of the Passage: Hebrews 1:1-4; 2:1-3

Overview: God spoke in times past through the prophets, but He has reserved the greatest declaration of His glory for His Son. The Son of God is greater than any prophet. He is even greater than the angels, through whom Moses' law was communicated (2:2; Acts 7:53). In order to bring salvation He willingly became a little lower than the angels. And by His suffering and death He made it possible to lift mankind above the angels into the family of God. Because of His perfect humanity, Jesus is uniquely qualified to serve as High Priest for sinful mankind.

Chapter 1		Chapter 2	
A Better Prophet	A Better Messenger	A Great Salvation	A Great Sufferer
Christ, the Son of God		Christ, the Savior of Mankind	

Religion is man searching for God; Christianity is God reaching down to mankind.

Your Daily Walk: The book of Hebrews opens with a penetrating statement: "God . . . hath . . . spoken unto us by his Son" (1:1-2). The heart and core of Christianity—and the reason for its superiority over the old Judaic system—can be summarized in a single word: Christ. The old system was built around precepts; the new centers around a Person. The old was merely a shadow; the new supplies the substance.

On what foundation are you building your life? It is easy to substitute man-made traditions and performance standards for a growing relationship with the Son of God. Evaluate the "religious rituals" of your own life. Are they advancing your relationship with God, or keeping you from getting to know Him and His Word better?

John summarizes this crucial issue well: "He that hath the Son hath life; and he that hath not the Son of God hath not life" (1 John 5:12). Are you a have . . . or a have not? If the answer disturbs you, let John 1:12 point the way to a foundation that is unshakable!

Insight: Jesus Is Greater Than Angels, Isn't He?
Jesus' superiority over angels (Hebrews 1:4) may seem rather obvious, but to Jews angels were highly exalted beings. They were present at the giving of the Law, God's supreme revelation, to Moses at Sinai (Hebrews 1:4; Deuteronomy 33:2). Moreover, we now know from the Dead Sea Scrolls that some expected the archangel Michael to be the supreme figure in the messianic kingdom.

416

Christ, Better Than Moses and Joshua
Hebrews 3–4

9

📖 **Overview:** Those who rebelled against God in the days of the wilderness wanderings were excluded from His rest in the Promised Land. However, for the people of God today there exists an even better rest than that—the one His Son spoke about. Moses was a servant in God's household, but Christ is the divine Son over God's household. Joshua was Israel's provider of peace in the land of Canaan, but Christ will bring His people into the eternal resting place of heaven. Since the promise of entering His rest still stands, let us be careful that none of us keeps from entering in and enjoying it!

Heart of the Passage: Hebrews 3:1-6; 4:1-6

Chapter 3	Chapter 4
Past Failure Through Unbelief	Present Dangers Through Unbelief
Christ, Better Than Moses	Christ, Better Than Joshua

✔️ **Your Daily Walk:** Which is more deserving of praise:
- a house or the architect of the house?
- a servant or the master for whom the servant works?
- a leader of a nation or the Creator of a nation?

If you picked the second answer in each pair, you're on the same "wavelength" as the author of Hebrews! Moses was a faithful servant in the house of Israel . . . but Jesus Christ built the house. Moses and Aaron were the apostle and high priest of Judaism . . . but Jesus Christ is the Apostle and High Priest of the better way, Christianity. The children of Israel died in the wilderness without experiencing the rest God intended for them in Canaan . . . and the same danger exists today for the people who refuse to enter the rest made possible by the finished work of their High Priest, Jesus Christ.

"Jesus, I Am Resting, Resting" was J. Hudson Taylor's favorite hymn. Find a hymnbook, look it up, and read thoughtfully its penetrating words. It may provide just the rest you've been needing!

There may be those on earth who dress better or eat better, but those who enjoy the peace of God sleep better.

📖 **Insight:** A Handy Chart to Summarize Hebrews

Chapters	Title	Focus
1	Christ, the Son of God	Deity
2–3	Christ, the Son of Man	Humanity
4–10	Christ, the High Priest	Ministry
11–13	Christ, the Better Way	Example

417

Introduction to the
Non-Pauline Epistles

Pauline Epistles: Individuals			
1 Timothy	2 Timothy	Titus	Philemon

	Pauline Epistles: Church			Non-Pauline Epistles and Revelation
	2 Thessalonians		Hebrews	
	1 Thessalonians		James	
	Colossians	*"That which we have seen and heard declare we unto you" (1 John 1:3).*	1 Peter	
	Philippians		2 Peter	
	Ephesians		1 John	
	Galatians		2 John	
	2 Corinthians		3 John	
	1 Corinthians		Jude	
	Romans		Revelation	

Acts			
Matthew	Mark	Luke	John
Historical Books			

Many Jewish believers had been dispersed abroad for their faith. As they faced intense persecution, God provided instruction and encouragement in the form of open letters: the so-called Non-Pauline (or General) Epistles.

Hebrews portrays Christ as the better way of salvation: better than anything that Old Testament Judaism could provide. James integrates true faith and everyday experience by stressing that genuine faith "works." Peter's epistles are manuals on "How to Handle Suffering from Without and Within." John's letters encourage fellowship with God and the brethren. Jude sounds the battle cry to defend the gospel. Revelation encourages the faithful believers of all ages to stand firm in the midst of persecution, awaiting the return of Christ in power and great glory.

Christis, Better Than Aaron's Priesthood **10**
Hebrews 5–7

Overview: High priests, such as Aaron, had the divinely appointed task of building a bridge between sinful mankind and holy God. But their sacrifices had to be perpetually repeated, and sooner or later the priest died. By contrast, Jesus is the High Priest after the order of Melchizedek. His priesthood has no beginning or end; His sacrificial death is once for all time. Truly Christ is the better Priest!

Heart of the Passage: Hebrews 5:1-10; 7:1-3

Chapter 5	Chapter 6	Chapter 7
Christ, the Better Priest	Christ, the Better Foundation	Christ, the Better Priesthood
Sinless	Changeless	Timeless

Your Daily Walk: Do you understand the significance of Christ's priesthood being likened to Melchizedek's? If not, don't be disappointed. Even the writer of Hebrews admits that this is not an easily digested truth. With the help of Genesis 14:1-20, see if you can "sink your teeth" into these questions:

1. Who were Melchizedek's parents?
2. When was Melchizedek born?
3. When did Melchizedek die?
4. Who was greater, Abraham or Melchizedek?

If you answered the first three questions, "I don't know," you're right each time. And that's precisely the point! Nowhere does Scripture record that Melchizedek was born or died . . . had beginning or end. He simply appears as a timeless priest who is greater than Abraham and worthy of his honor. In the same way, Christ is eternal in His existence and worthy of honor as your great High Priest.

Tonight around the dinner table, share ways in which your High Priest is worthy of your worship. Who is He and what has He done on your behalf? What is He doing in your life right now? What can you count on Him doing tomorrow?

The head that was once crowned with thorns is crowned with glory now.

Insight: Six Foundation Stones of Faith
The first two verses of chapter 6 list six "principles of the doctrine of Christ"—that is, rudimentary truths of the Christian faith: repentance, faith, baptism, laying on of hands, resurrection, and judgment. For an excellent Bible workout, huddle with family or friends and see if you can come up with one New Testament passage that expands on each of these foundational truths. Happy hunting!

11 *The Superior Savior*

Scripture Reading: 2 Corinthians 12:9

Step Back

The book of Hebrews is a moving appeal to wavering Christians to return to the Savior. Facing great opposition from fellow Jews, and persecuted by the world, these Hebrew believers were wearying of keeping the faith. But the author encourages them to get back on solid ground—to return to the basic truths of their faith, and a closer relationship with their Lord.

Two aspects of the Savior are highlighted through the book:

1. *Jesus is superior in every way.* The first four chapters of Hebrews clearly show how Jesus is superior in His person—better than the prophets (1:1), better than the angels (chapters 1–2), better than Moses (chapter 3), better than Joshua (chapter 4), better than all the other priests (chapter 4). He is our "great High Priest"—One who knows us, understands us, and intercedes for us (4:14-16). We can turn to Him in full confidence and stop drifting. Chapters 5–10 show that Jesus is superior as a priest—better than the earthly priests (chapter 5), better than the old covenant (chapters 6–7), better than the Law of Moses (chapters 8–10). Finally, chapters 11–13 demonstrate that Jesus is superior in all of life's circumstances. No matter what we face, we can persevere in Him.

2. *Jesus is sufficient in every experience.* Jesus is all we need. His sacrifice on the cross satisfied God's requirements for the payment of our sin. Though our salvation is eternally assured, we still need endurance through the tough times on earth (10:32-36).

No matter what we face, we can be unalterably confident in Jesus. He is superior than any other way to God, He is sufficient in every need.

Remember Jesus for us is all our righteousness before a holy God, and Jesus in us is all our strength in an ungoldy world.

Look Up

The desire to give up living a life of faith and godliness may sometimes grow in us as we face a world of compromise and temptation. Rather than face opposition or disapproval, we may tend to try to "blend in" with the world, keeping our faith a secret.

If you are wrestling with thoughts like these, heed the message of Hebrews. God will give you all the strength and endurance you need, if you will turn to Him. Your Savior Jesus Christ is superior to the world's ways, and He is sufficient for your every need. Turn to Him anew in a prayer of rededication right now.

Move Ahead

In 2 Corinthians 12:9, Paul gives a promise of Jesus Christ—one he claimed when he faced trials in his own life. Read that verse carefully, and spend a few moments memorizing it. More than that, claim that promise as your own today.

420

Christ, Better Than the Old Covenant *Hebrews 8–10* 12

Overview: The writer concludes his argument for the superiority of Christ by pointing out that the heart of the human problem is the problem of the human heart. The institution of Judaism and the old covenant was ineffective and inadequate because it was unable to deal permanently with sin. But God's new method of dealing with mankind—the new covenant written in Christ's own blood which He shed on the cross—makes full provision for the forgiveness of sins. Christ's death forever accomplishes what the old covenant was powerless to do.

Heart of the Passage: Hebrews 10

Chapter 8	Chapter 9	Chapter 10
A Superior Covenant	Two Covenants Contrasted	A Superior Sacrifice
"Christ was once offered to bear the sins of many" (9:28).		

Your Daily Walk: If you truly believed your house was on fire right now, how would you respond? If you were convinced there was buried treasure in your back yard, how would you act? Would knowing those facts change your priorities and conduct?

In today's reading, 8:1–10:18 provides the doctrinal basis for the exhortations to proper behavior which follow in the rest of chapter 10. Because Christ is a better High Priest . . . because He has provided a better way . . . because "Christ was once offered to bear the sins of many" (9:28), we should respond to those truths in specific acts of obedience.

There is seldom an inner urge to preach what one practices.

As you read the final 21 verses of chapter 10, put each command in the first person singular: "Let me draw near" (10:22); "Let me hold fast" (10:23); "Let me consider how to provoke others to love and good works" (10:24). Before taking the initiative to provoke another Christian to be what God wants him to be, take stock of your own response to the truth you are about to share! Choose one of the "let us" verses in chapter 10 and make it your personal "let me" project.

 Insight: Christ, the Superior Sacrifice

Sacrifices Under the Law (10:1-4)
A shadow of things to come
Repeated constantly
A reminder of sin
Blood of animals

Sacrifice of Christ (10:5-18)
The real thing
Once for all time
The Remover of sin
Blood of Christ

13 *Christ, the Example of the Life of Faith*
Hebrews 11–13

Heart of the Passage: *Hebrews 11:1–12:2*

Overview: Hebrews closes with an appeal for a persevering faith that relies on the promises of God regardless of the circumstances. Writing to an audience whose actions were being shaped by pressure from the world rather than promises from God, the author of Hebrews urges the kind of faith-inspired walk that characterized so many Old Testament saints. These men and women were so convinced of God's faithfulness that they ordered their lives according to His Word. Follow their commendable example and walk by faith, not by sight!

Chapter 11	Chapter 12	Chapter 13
Patterns of Faith	Perseverance of Faith	Progress of Faith
Patriarchs	Persistence	Practice

Your Daily Walk: "Seeing is believing" may be a good rule of thumb when buying a used car or shopping for real estate, but it is a poor way to live the Christian life. For the one desiring to live in a God-honoring manner, the quote might better read, "Not seeing is believing," because "faith is the . . . evidence of things not seen" (11:1).

Faith is daring to do something regardless of the consequences.

Receiving Christ as your Savior was an act of faith in which you accepted the trustworthiness and credibility of God. But the exercise of faith doesn't end at salvation, as Hebrews 11 demonstrates. By faith, God's people were courageous in battle, patient in suffering, and joyful in difficulty. They acted in response to His commands and promises, even when they could not see the reason for what they were being asked to do.

Is faith the operating principle in your life today? Or is your motto "Seeing is believing"? To help boost your faith, take a piece of paper and see if you can list 10 things you know are true about God, but that you can't see with your eyes. For example, "God is loving . . . God works all things together for good. . . ." Then think through the decisions and responsibilities you will face in the next 24 hours, and determine to put your faith to work.

Insight: The Desirable Dozen
Chapter 13 lists 12 practical suggestions for the Christian who desires to live a life well pleasing to God. How many of the 12 faith-lifting exhortations can you find?

422

James

I n this epistle to Jewish believers, the
apostle James shows how faith integrates
with everyday practical experience by
stressing that true faith produces doers of the
Word. For James, a faith that produces no
change in a person's life is really no faith at
all. True faith will bear fruit in actions
and deeds. James offers many tests for
genuine faith: It endures trials, obeys the
Word, harbors no prejudice, controls the
tongue , is separated from the world, and
resists the devil. Above all, faith waits
patiently for the coming of the Lord.

Focus	Tests of Faith						
Divisions	Trials and Temptations	Test of Attitude toward Bible	Test of Social Distinctions	Test of Works	Test of Self-Control	Test of Reactions to Word	Test of Prayer
	1:1 1:18	1:19 1:21	2:1 2:13	2:14 2:26	3:1 3:18	4:1 5:12	5:13 5:20
Topics	Wisdom		Works		Words	Walk	Wait
	Faith Tested		Faith Displayed		Faith Proved	Faith Con-trasted	Faith Re-warded
Place	Probably Jerusalem						
Time	A.D. 46–49						

14 *A Gauge for Genuine Faith / James 1–5*

*Heart
of the
Passage:
James 2*

Overview: Just as a human body that fails to breathe is labeled a "dead body," so too a faith that fails to "breathe" is labeled a "dead faith." And the breath of faith in the Christian life is good works: demonstrating concern for the poor, controlling the tongue, exhibiting a spirit of humility, building up others. If you think you have faith but there is no living demonstration of that faith in your life, James has news for you: Your faith is worthless. True faith and good works cannot be divorced, for your life is the laboratory in which your faith is shown to be real.

Chapter 1	Chapter 2	Chapter 3	Chapter 4	Chapter 5
Faith Tested	Faith Displayed	Faith Proved	Faith Contrasted	Faith Rewarded
"Faith, if it hath not works, is dead, being alone" (2:17).				

*What's
true of
biology is
also true
of faith:
If it isn't
growing,
it's
probably
dead.*

Your Daily Walk: If someone tells you, "I believe there is a God in heaven," you can be sure that person is (a) a Christian, (b) a user of this devotional guide, (c) a churchgoer, (d) none of the above. (Pick one answer, then check James 2:19 for the startling answer!)

James speaks out strongly against a "faith of God" that merely *professes with the lips* without *practicing with the life*. You might summarize his book this way: "If you say you believe as you should, why do you behave as you shouldn't?" True faith is more than words; it is a vital walk that shows God has truly invaded your life. It "breathes" in unmistakable ways. And that raises a timely question. . . .

Since you trusted Christ as your Savior, how has your lifestyle changed in the troublesome areas of prejudice . . . profanity . . . gossip . . . planning for the future . . . accepting unpleasant circumstances? And what is one area where today, with God's help, you will move from being a *hearer* to a *doer* of God's Word (1:22)?

Insight: A Light, a Lamp, a Mirror . . . and More!

James describes God's Word as a mirror (1:23-25), helping you see yourself as you really are. What other word pictures does the Bible use to describe itself?

The Bible is a _____ to light my _____ (Psalm 119:105).

The Bible is like a _____ and a _____ (Jeremiah 23:29).

The Bible is the _____ of the Spirit (Ephesians 6:17).

The Bible is _____ to be sown in the world (Matthew 13:3, 19).

1 Peter

The apostle Peter writes to scattered Jewish Christians who are undergoing intense persecution for their faith. He reminds his readers that God has given them the privilege of being born again. Therefore, they shouldn't be surprised when suffering comes their way; they should expect it, prepare for it, and respond to it correctly. He also encourages them to imitate Christ through a submissive spirit toward one another. If they do, God will richly reward them when the trials of life are over.

Focus	Christian Salvation		Christian Relationships				Christian Suffering			Christian Discipline	
Divisions	Salvation	Sanctification	World	State	Home	Church	Blessings	Example	Encouragement	Church	Individual
	1:1 1:12	1:13 2:10	2:11 2:12	2:13 2:17	2:18 3:7	3:8 3:12	3:13 3:17	3:18 3:22	4:1 4:19	5:1 5:6	5:7 5:14
Topics	New Birth		New Building				Necessary Bulwark				
	Salvation		Submission				Suffering				
Place	Rome or Babylon										
Time	Approximately A.D. 63–64										

15 *Pain with a Purpose / 1 Peter 1–5*

Overview: Peter writes to scattered Jewish Christians who are undergoing intense persecution for their faith. He reminds his readers that God "hath begotten us again unto a lively hope" (1:3). Therefore, don't be surprised when suffering comes your way; expect it—prepare for it—respond to it correctly. And be sure you are suffering for doing what is *right*, not for doing what is *wrong*. Imitate Christ in your submissive spirit toward one another, and God will richly reward you when the trials of life are over.

Heart of the Passage: 1 Peter 2

Chapter 1	Chapter 2	Chapters 3–5
A New Birth	A New Building	A Necessary Bulwark
Salvation	Submission	Suffering

Your Daily Walk: Few things bring more delight to a parent's heart than a fistful of flowers picked and delivered by a small child. And few things are sadder to look at than that same "bouquet" three days later!

The brook would lose its song if the rocks were removed.

Visit your local war museum and what will you find? Old military uniforms, battle flags, artifacts—all of them discolored and disintegrating with time. Earthly glory fades with the years. *Not so with God's glorious gifts!* They never fade away (1:4), but grow steadily more glorious (2 Corinthians 3:1-18).

Now do you understand why a heavenly perspective is so important in dealing with your earthly problems? If your inheritance in heaven is eternally safe (1:4), what does it matter if you suffer the loss of a few earthly possessions? If your faith is more precious than gold (1:7), then the heat of adversity can only serve to *refine* it, not *ruin* it!

Plan to visit a local museum sometime this week. Take your family or friends along. It will be a good reminder for you that what you see *isn't* all there is!

Insight: The All-Important Cornerstone

Peter makes an obvious allusion to Christ when he quotes Isaiah 28:16, "Behold, I lay in Zion a chief cornerstone" (2:6). In biblical times a stone was put where two walls met. More than being just a foundation, the cornerstone helped align the building horizontally and vertically and held it together. Thus, Christ is the all-important One on whom we, as "living stones," are built into a spiritual house.

2 Peter

Peter's first letter taught his readers to persevere through persecution and other external trials with hope. His second letter, written to the same audience, teaches them to oppose internal spiritual struggles and attacks by Satan with the knowledge of the truth. Peter warns against apostasy within the church, moral perversions that tempt on every side, and the denial of Christ's return that false teachers propagate. He exhorts his readers to grow in grace and knowledge that come through Jesus Christ, thereby gaining strength to resist error and avoid heresy.

Focus	True Knowledge			False Knowledge			Challenge		
Divisions	Salutation	Growth in Knowledge	Source of Knowledge	Fear of False Teachers	Fate of False Teachers	Facts About False Teachers	Denial of Return	Truth of Return	Application of Return
	1:1 1:2	1:3 1:11	1:12 1:21	2:1 2:3	2:4 2:9	2:10 2:22	3:1 3:7	3:8 3:10	3:11 3:18
Topics	Growing in Grace			Growing in Knowledge			Growing in Expectation		
	"Grow Up!"			"Watch Out!"			"Look Up!"		
Place	Probably Rome								
Time	Approximately A.D. 64–66								

16 *Poison in the Pews / 2 Peter 1–3*

Overview: While Peter's audience is the same as in his first letter (3:1), his theme and purpose are different. Persecution from unbelievers can be hard for Christians to bear (1 Peter), but defection within the community of believers can be even more devastating (2 Peter). To counteract the effects of this "poison in the pews," Peter reminds his readers of the timeless truths of the faith and exhorts them to continue growing toward Christian maturity. Those who scoff at the thought of future judgment will find, like Sodom and Gomorrah, that ignoring God's Word will ultimately lead to destruction.

Heart of the Passage: 2 Peter 1:1-11; 2:1-9

Chapter 1	Chapter 2	Chapter 3
Growing in Grace	Growing in Knowledge	Growing in Expectation
"Grow Up!"	"Watch Out!"	"Look Up!"

Your Daily Walk: Find a dictionary and look up the word *cultivation*. Write the definition here: "Cultivation means

_____

_____ ."

The growing Christian must cultivate the concentrated gaze of a person living in the future.

Perhaps you never thought of it this way, but your spiritual life is one long exercise in cultivation: providing the kind of environment conducive to spiritual growth, and avoiding hindrances which might stunt that growth.

Just as you would add water, sunlight, and fertilizer (and subtract weeds and rocks) if you were serious about causing a seed to grow, so there are qualities you need to give attention to in adding to your faith in Christ (1:5-7): virtue (moral excellence), knowledge, temperance (self-control), patience, godliness, brotherly kindness, and charity (love). Notice Peter's promise: "For if these things be in you, and abound, they make you that ye shall neither be barren nor unfruitful in the knowledge of our Lord Jesus Christ" (1:8).

Select one of the seven qualities listed above and use it to complete this sentence: "Today with God's help I will seek to cultivate (what?) _____ in my life by (how?) _____ ."

Insight: Seeing Is Believing, and Believing Is Behaving
In 3:11-17 Peter uses words like *seeing*, *look*, and *looking* a total of six times to highlight the importance of watching for enemies as you walk in the truth. How many of the six can you find (and circle) in the next 60 seconds?

1 John

John, "the beloved apostle," has long known and enjoyed the Lord. He writes 1 John to help his spiritual brothers in their walk with the God who is light, love, and life. He wants them to be grounded in assurance of their salvation, experiencing victory over sin and the full joys of the Christian life. He reminds them that all these gems can be dimmed by false teaching, so he reminds the reader that belief should be based on the facts about Christ's incarnation and that every believer has the responsibility to walk like Christ.

Focus	Assurance Through Fellowship		Assurance Through Conflict			Assurance Through Love		Assurance Through Spirit	
Divisions	Basis of Fellowship	Obedience of Fellowship	Truth vs. Error	Purity vs. Impurity	Fact vs. Falsehood	God's Love	Our Love	External Witness	Internal Witness
	1:1　　2:2	2:3　　2:17	2:18　2:28	2:29　3:24	4:1　4:6	4:7　4:16	4:17　5:5	5:6　　5:9	5:10　5:21
Topics	Walking		Warring			Wooing		Witnessing	
	Abiding in Christ		Abiding in Truth			Abiding in Love		Abiding Assurance	
Place	Ephesus								
Time	Approximately A.D. 90								

17 Promoting Christian Living
1 John 1–5

Heart of the Passage: 1 John 1

Overview: The apostle John, who is enjoying a delightful fellowship with God, earnestly desires that his spiritual children enjoy that same fellowship, and writes a letter telling them, "Here's how!" God is light, and therefore to engage in fellowship with Him means walking in the light of His commandments. God is love, and thus His children must walk in love. Those who do not love do not know God, for that is His very character. God is life, and those who desire fellowship with Him must possess that same quality of life—spiritual life, which begins with spiritual birth through faith in Jesus Christ.

Chapter 1	Chapters 2–3	Chapters 4–5
Prerequisite of Fellowship	Pattern of Fellowship	Proof of Fellowship
Confession	Conduct	Confirmation

We were not converted to be introverted.

Your Daily Walk: Make a list of all the qualifications you need in order to be called as a witness in a court trial: age, sex, education, etc.

You probably came up with a very short list—one item long! "All I need to be called as a witness is firsthand knowledge of a crime." And you'd be right! Now listen to these words from 1 John 1:3: "That which we have seen and heard declare we unto you, that ye also may have fellowship with us." Being a witness for Christ is as simple as sharing the firsthand knowledge you enjoy about the Savior. Have you been a spectator to a miracle of rebirth in your life? Then you are a Christian—and a candidate to be a witness! Write in the margin the name of one person with whom you will share that firsthand knowledge today. That's how the Good News gets around!

Insight: First John, the Purposeful Epistle

Tucked away in John's first epistle are at least five statements describing why he wrote the letter (which shouldn't surprise you, since he stated his purpose so clearly in the gospel that bears his name, John 20:31). Can you complete each of these five purpose statements?

1:3— That you may have _____ .
1:4— That your _____ may be full.
2:1— That you might not _____ .
2:26— That you might not be _____ .
5:13— That you may know_____ .

430

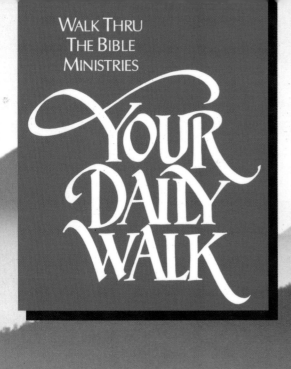

WALK THRU
THE BIBLE
MINISTRIES

YOUR
DAILY
WALK

365 DAILY DEVOTIONS TO READ THROUGH THE BIBLE IN A YEAR

2 John

Addressing this brief note to an "elect lady and her children," the apostle John stresses the importance of balance in the Christian life. Whether the recipient is an actual family or a church family makes little difference: John commends the group for standing firm in the faith. However, he cautions them to have discernment about whom they learn from and whom they aid. False teachers, who deny the true humanity of Christ, are abroad. John exhorts his readers to obey God by loving God and one another, and to abide in the doctrine of Christ.

Focus	Practicing the Truth		Protecting the Truth		
Divisions	Greeting	Exhortation	Wrong Doctrine	Right Response	Conclusion
	1:1　　1:3	1:4　　1:6	1:7　　1:9	1:10　　1:11	1:12　　　　1:13
Topics	Living in Truth and Love		Learning to Detect False Teaching		Looking for John's Coming
	Important Command		Timely Caution		Tender Conclusion
Place	Ephesus				
Time	Approximately A.D. 90				

18 Bolt the Door to Enemies / 2 John

Heart of the Passage: 2 John 4–6

Overview: In his brief letter to a chosen lady and her children, John highlights the importance of balance. It is not enough simply to walk in love and truth; you must be equally careful to discern and avoid error when it comes knocking. Warning and encouragement . . . belief and behavior . . . doctrinal accuracy and discerning love—these themes weave their way throughout the book as John urges his audience to make their daily walk with God a discerning walk, a walk that detects and avoids false teaching.

Verses 1-4	Verses 5-6	Verses 7-11	Verses 12-13
A Proud Commendation	An Important Command	A Timely Caution	A Tender Conclusion
"Whosoever . . . abideth not in the doctrine of Christ, hath not God" (9).			

Your Daily Walk: Two little girls were playing together. One pretended she wanted to rent the other's playhouse. "Have you any parents?" asked the owner of the playhouse. "Yes, two," was the reply. "Oh, I'm so sorry," replied the first, "but I never rent to children with parents. They're so noisy and destructive!"

Isn't it interesting how seldom people are too busy to stop and tell you how busy they are.

Parents are prone to give their children everything except the one thing they need most: *time.* Time for listening, time for understanding, time for helping, time for guiding. Giving of one's time may sound simple, but in reality it is often the most difficult and the most sacrificial task of parenthood.

Has God placed you in a parenting role today? Then you have been entrusted with a most strategic ministry: that of shaping young minds and hearts to be in tune with God's will. Perhaps you have been discouraged lately with the progress your children are making in learning obedience, respect for authority, or love for the things of God. (As one parent put it, "When I was a kid, everything was the kid's fault; now I'm a parent and everything's the parent's fault!") If so, take heart from 2 John: Even children can learn to walk in the truth (v. 4). But it takes time . . . your time . . . and lots of it.

Insight: A Timely Word on Time
Someone has remarked that no one seems to have enough time anymore. And yet, we have all the time there is. Are you living for time—or for eternity? That's a timely question to ask now, in light of the eons of eternity that lie ahead.

3 John

J ohn's third letter opens with an address to Gaius, a man he calls "well-beloved" and whose hospitality and love of the truth is a source of joy to John. In addition to Gaius, John holds up Demetrius as another commendable example of a saint. Both men walk in the truth, serve the church faithfully, and have good reputations both within and without the community. By contrast, John rebukes Diotrephes for his gossip, pride, and arrogant attitude. John concludes his letter by promising that he will deal with other problems during a personal visit.

Focus	Hospitality		Haughtiness	Holiness	
Divisions	Greeting	Commendation	Censuring	Compliment	Close
	1:1	1:2 1:8	1:9 1:10	1:11 1:12	1:13 1:15
Topics	Commendation of Gaius		Censuring of Diotrephes	Compliment for Demetrius	
	Helping Through Hospitality		Harming Through Haughtiness	Honoring Holiness	
Place	Ephesus				
Time	Approximately A.D. 90				

19 *Commending Christian Hospitality*
3 John

Heart of the Passage: 3 John 5-8

Overview: In 1 John the apostle discusses fellowship with God; in 2 John he forbids fellowship with false teachers; in 3 John he encourages fellowship with Christian brothers. Following his expression of love for Gaius, John voices his joy that Gaius is persistently walking in the truth and showing hospitality to the messengers of the gospel. But John cannot commend certain others in the assembly. Diotrephes, for example, has allowed pride to replace love in his life, even rejecting John's words of discipline. Everything that Gaius is, Diotrephes is not! John uses this negative example as an opportunity to encourage Gaius. Godly character and loyalty to the truth are never easy, but they bring God's richest commendation . . . and John's as well!

Verses 1-8	Verses 9-10	Verses 11-14
Duty of Hospitality	Danger of Haughtiness	Demonstration of Humility
Gaius	Diotrephes	Demetrius

Your Daily Walk: True or False: If you do not have a particular spiritual gift (such as the gift of evangelism), then God does not hold you responsible for performing that ministry (that is, the work of an evangelist).

To keep good news to ourselves would be in effect to repudiate its validity.

It may surprise you to realize the number of times in the New Testament that Christians are commanded to do something regardless of whether they have that gift or not. For example, "Do the work of an evangelist" (even if you are not gifted as an evangelist, 2 Timothy 4:5). "Teach all nations" (whether or not you have the gift of teaching, Matthew 28:19). "Use hospitality one to another" (even if hospitality is not your gift, 1 Peter 4:9). Concentrate on this last area today. How can you learn from the example of Gaius to make your home a God-honoring haven of hospitality? Invite a church leader and his family over for dinner as an expression of thanks for their labors.

Insight: Gaius, the "Mr. Smith" of the New Testament
Whereas 2 John is addressed to a woman, 3 John is addressed to a man, Gaius. It is impossible to identify exactly who this Gaius was since the name was one of the most common in John's day. Four other men named Gaius are found in the New Testament: Gaius of Macedonia (Acts 19:29), Gaius of Derbe (Acts 20:4), Gaius of Corinth (Romans 16:23), and Gaius who was baptized by Paul (1 Corinthians 1:14).

Jude

Alarmed by the presence of false teachers in the church, Jude is compelled to unmask them and their deadly ways, and to exhort the believers to stand firm for the way of truth. Contending for the faith is not just a good idea; it is imperative when the work of God is undermined by false philosophies and destructive heresies. Jude, who was the brother of James, ends his short but powerful epistle with a series of urgent commands: Remember Christ's words, remain in God's love, and seek to remove erring brothers from the fiery danger of their ways.

Focus	Emergency	Examples	Exhortations
Divisions	Announcement of Apostasy	Anatomy of Apostasy	Antidote for Apostasy
	1:1 — 1:4	1:5 — 1:16	1:17 — 1:25
Topics	Why Contend for the Faith		How to Contend for the Faith
	Contention	Condemnation	Caution
Place	Ephesus		
Time	Approximately A.D. 66–80		

20 Defending the Faith / Jude

Overview: Jude's epistle is a firm denunciation of false teachers who are infiltrating the church. Though Jude does not describe the heresies in detail (since his readers would no doubt be familiar with the targets of his verbal blasts), he spares no words in rebuking the false teachers. He condemns both the error of the teacher and the teacher of the error, promising God's swift judgment for their damaging heresies. How is a believer to resist such onslaughts? By "building up yourselves [in] your most holy faith" (v. 20).

Heart of the Passage: Jude 3-4, 17-23

Verses 1-3	Verses 4-16	Verses 17-25
Remember Your Faith	Remember God's Judgment	Build Up Your Faith
Contention	Condemnation	Caution

Your Daily Walk: Below is a list of 10 items you'll probably never find on the training regimen of an athlete preparing to compete in an Olympic competition. Can you suggest a reason why each should be avoided by a serious athlete?

Spiritual things are against the stream; heaven is up the hill.

Late-night TV	Drugs
Skydiving	Sleeping in
Rich desserts	Fast foods
All-night parties	Smoking
Alcohol	Soft drinks

If an athlete has any hope of competing (much less winning), he or she must be in top physical condition. That requires a strict regimen of proper diet, adequate rest, and regular exercise.

How is your *spiritual fitness program* coming? Are you regularly involved in activities to help you "contend for the faith" (v. 3)?

Write out your own "spiritual training schedule" for the coming week. Be sure to include the three items Jude mentions: prayer, compassion, and sharing Christ (vv. 20, 22-23).

Insight: Jude's Curious Quotations (vv. 9, 14-15)
Jude is the only New Testament author who quotes from the writings called the *Pseudepigrapha* (books which bear the names of famous Old Testament characters but were not written by them, and which scholars do not consider inspired). Paul also quoted from uninspired sources (see Acts 17:28, a Roman poet; Titus 1:12, a Cretian prophet).

Revelation

J ust as the first book of the Bible—Genesis —provides the opening chapter of God's redemptive program, so the last book— Revelation—supplies the conclusions as it describes the return of Jesus Christ and the creation of a new heaven and earth. Revelation portrays Jesus Christ as the victorious King and coming Judge. Writing from exile on the Island of Patmos, John uses a dramatic series of symbolic word pictures to capture the awesome holiness of the Lamb of God coming to defeat Satan's forces and judge the world in perfect righteousness.

Focus	Judge	Judgment					Jubilation
Divisions	Seven Letters	Seven Seals	Seven Trumpets	Seven Signs	Seven Plagues	Seven Dooms	Seven New Things
	1 3	4 6	7 9	10 13	14 16	17 19	20 22
Topics	Heavenly Vision on Earth	Horror from Heaven to Earth					New Heaven and Earth
	"... things which thou hast seen ... which are, and ... shall be" (1:19)						
Place	Aegean Island of Patmos						
Time	About A.D. 95–96						

21 *Seven Letters for Seven Churches*
Revelation 1–3

Heart of the Passage: Rev. 1

Overview: After greeting the seven churches in Asia Minor, John describes how he received his orders to write. Each church needs a particular message, and John is commanded to tailor his exhortation to fit each spiritual need. Each message begins with the expression, "I know thy works"; each contains a promise "to him that overcometh"; each concludes with the warning, "He that hath an ear, let him hear what the Spirit saith unto the churches." In short, John sends words of reproof and reassurance from Jesus Christ, the Alpha and Omega, to each of the seven churches.

Chapter 1	Chapters 2–3
Greetings to the Churches	God's Word to Seven Churches
Candlesticks	Correspondence

Your Daily Walk: Which book of the New Testament do you find the most challenging to understand?

God is not obligated to tell us everything we want to know.

Now find a dictionary and look up the word "revelation." Can you discover two synonyms?

It is ironic that Revelation (which literally means "disclosing" or "unveiling") is viewed by many Christians as the one indecipherable book of the New Testament! What makes Revelation so challenging is the more than 300 symbols contained in its pages. Just as the deaf have a sign language in which each gesture is filled with meaning, so the writer John has a purpose and meaning behind each symbol he employs. Our challenge: to interpret those symbols the way John (and the Holy Spirit) intended!

Your local Bible bookstore would be an excellent place to find a commentary or study guide on the book of Revelation. And your minister or Sunday school teacher would be delighted to suggest a few titles you might want to consider. There's a blessing in store for you during the next few days. And that's a promise from God (1:3)!

Insight: The Seven Churches

Although much of Revelation is symbolic, we do know that these churches did exist when John was seeing his visions. They were postal centers for seven geographical regions, and apparently each one received a copy of the whole book of Revelation (1:11). Flip to the map section in the back of your Bible and try to locate these seven cities. (Hint: you'll find them in the western part of modern-day Turkey.

438

God's Ministering Messengers

22

⬅ Step Back

Angels. The word brings a multitude of images to our minds, but the world's conception of angels as baby cherubs or departed souls who have "earned their wings" confuses the biblical portrait of them as glorious and powerful spirit beings whom God created for certain purposes.

Scripture Reading: Revelation 4:8-11; 5:8-14; 7:11-12; 11:15-18; 19:1-8

Basically, the good angels are servants (Hebrews 1:14). And their ministry is multifaceted.

• *In serving God,* they worship and praise Him, serving Him as He commands (Psalm 148:1-2; Revelation 5:8-13; 22:9).

• *In serving Christ on earth,* they announced His birth, ministered to Him after His temptation, and stood ready to protect Him (Luke 1:26-28; Matthew 4:11; 26:53).

• *In serving Israel,* Michael the archangel guarded the nation (Daniel 12:1). Angels also watch over the rulers of nations and influence them (Daniel 4:17; 10:21; 11:1).

• *In serving believers today,* angels have been involved in communicating God's truths as recorded in the Bible, which we benefit from today (Daniel 7:15-27; 8:13-26; 9:20-27; Revelation 1:1; 22:6, 8). The New Testament also shows that they served in:

1. Bringing answers to prayer (Acts 12:5-10).
2. Assisting in bringing people to Christ (Acts 8:26; 10:3).
3. Observing Christians (1 Corinthians 4:9; 11:10; Ephesians 3:10).
4. Encouraging in times of danger (Acts 27:23-24).
5. Caring for the righteous when they face death (Luke 16:22).

Though God's power be sufficient to govern us, yet for man's infirmity He appointed His angels to watch over us.

⬆ Look Up

In Revelation, one of the more glorious aspects of the angels' ministry is to worship God. Today, join with them in praise by using two or more of these passages to encourage you in your time alone with God: Revelation 4:8-11; 5:8-14; 7:11-12; 11:15-18; 19:1-8.

➡ Move Ahead

One of the most startling insights about angels from the Scripture is that they watch how believers conduct themselves. They may be watching you even now. Why? Perhaps since they do not personally experience salvation, they watch to see how it is worked out in human lives, to see what a difference it makes to walk with God.

Paul notes that we are watched not only by angels, but by the world (1 Corinthians 4:9). What do they see when they look at you? Are you reassured or embarrassed by the fact that you are being observed? Why not give the angels something to cheer about today!

23 *Seven Seals / Revelation 4–6*

Heart of the Passage: Rev. 4–5

Overview: John describes an amazing series of visions depicting activities in heaven and on earth. God, majestically enthroned, holds a scroll written on both sides and sealed with seven seals. No one is found worthy to break the seals and reveal the contents of the scroll except the Lion of Judah. As the first six seals are broken, calamities break forth upon the earth involving warfare, famine, death, earthquakes, and heavenly disturbances. The kings of the earth know only too well the explanation of it all: "For the great day of his wrath is come; and who shall be able to stand?" (6:17).

Chapter 4	Chapter 5	Chapter 6
A Sacred Throne	A Sealed Scroll	A Seven-Sealed Judgment
Worthy Lord	Worthy Lamb	Wrathful Lamb

Your Daily Walk: Here is a question worthy of your consideration: In your estimation, how worthy is Jesus Christ?

What you worship determines what you become.

Is He worthy of your unquestioning obedience, even when the whys and whens of His will aren't readily apparent?

Is He worthy of your worship, affection, and devotion?

Is He worthy of your trust that, as your loving Savior, He wants the best for your life?

Three times in chapters 4 and 5 the elders and angels proclaim to the Lamb of God, "Thou art worthy" (4:11; 5:9, 12). And you can join their chorus of praise today.

Use this sentence to verbalize the desire of your heart: "With God's help, today I will show the world the worthiness of my Savior by _____ ." Whatever action you consider, you can count on this: He is worthy!

Insight: Five Songs Worth Singing

When completed, the following chart will provide a concise summary of the five songs in today's section. Try it!

Passage	Who Sang?	How Many Sang?	About Whom?
4:8			
4:10-11			
5:8-10			
5:11-12			
5:13			

A Christmas Eve Celebration

24

← Step Back

On this Christmas Eve, step back today to celebrate Christ's coming to earth. Matthew recounts an angel's revelation of the Messiah's birth to Joseph, while Luke recounts the angelic announcement to Mary and then to the humble shepherds who come to worship the Christ child. Finally Matthew tells of the wise men who later come from afar to worship the newborn King.

Rich or poor, high-level or humble, Jesus comes to be Lord over all. And yet, He came facing a number of obstacles:

1. He had to be born in Bethlehem according to the prophets, and while still a child escape the murderous intentions of a mad king (Matthew 2:6, 17-18).

2. He had to be born of the line of David and grow up in Nazareth (Matthew 1:1-17; 2:21-23).

3. He had to fulfill more than 300 specific Old Testament prophecies during His life and ministry.

Yet God effortlessly brought it all to pass. His power was sufficient for the task—just as it is sufficient for any need in your life.

Keep that truth in mind as you read the Christmas story in Matthew 1:18-25; Luke 2:1-20; Matthew 2:1-12.

Scripture Reading: Matthew 1:18-25; Luke 2:1-20; Matthew 2:1-12

↑ Look Up

Just as the shepherds and the Magi came to worship the newborn King, you can too. Prayerfully, sing several Christmas carols as an act of worship. Even though you've known the words for years, consider them afresh.

Reconsider the amazing miracle of the Incarnation—God with us in the flesh. Then close your time in prayer, thanking God for the gift of His Son to the world . . . and to you.

Keeping Christmas is good, but sharing it with others is much better.

→ Move Ahead

In Christ's birth, God demonstrated that He is a God of the miraculous. Look back over the past year and think of a miracle He has accomplished in your life. Perhaps you've never even recognized it as a miracle before. What miracles would you seek from Him in the coming year?

Remember, nothing is impossible with God. No obstacles could prevent Him from sending His Son into the world, and no obstacles can prevent Him from working in your life as well. From rebuilding shattered lives and restoring broken relationships to providing the necessities of daily life, our God is a miracle worker. His power is sufficient for your need.

25 Seven Trumpets / Revelation 7–9

Heart of the Passage: Rev. 8–9

Overview: Before the seventh seal is opened, John sees four angels place a seal upon 144,000 "servants of . . . God"— 12,000 from each of the 12 "tribes of the children of Israel" (7:3-4). In contrast to this carefully numbered multitude, John next sees a great multitude "which no man could number," taken from "all nations, and kindreds, and people, and tongues" (7:9). John—who wonders about the identity of this vast multitude—learns these are "they which came out of great tribulation, and have washed their robes, and made them white in the blood of the Lamb" (7:14). The seventh seal is then broken, revealing seven trumpets. As each is sounded in turn, natural and heavenly disasters once again result: hail, fire, falling stars, death, darkness, torment— plagues which cause people to "seek death, [but] not find it" (9:6).

Chapter 7		Chapters 8–9	
A Sealed Multitude	A Numberless Multitude	The Seventh Seal	The Seven Trumpets
Interlude		Intensified Judgment	

We are often so caught up in our activities that we tend to worship our work, work at our play, and play at our worship.

Your Daily Walk: What exactly does it mean to worship God? How would you define worship for a new Christian who has never been to church, never sung a hymn, and never prayed before?

A good place to begin might be Revelation 7:11-12: "And all the angels . . . and the elders and the four beasts . . . fell before the throne on their faces, and worshiped God [how?], saying 'Amen: Blessing, and glory, and wisdom, and thanksgiving, and honor, and power, and might, be unto our God for ever and ever. Amen.'"

Take each of the seven elements mentioned in those verses (blessing, glory, wisdom, thanksgiving, honor, power, and might) and use it to complete this sentence: "Today I will worship God by bringing _____ to Him in my speech, deeds, and attitudes." At day's end, evaluate how you did. And for further insight, look up the definitions of those seven words. You might be surprised at their meanings.

Insight: Egyptian Plagues Revisited
Commentators have long noted the similarity between the judgments described in Revelation, and the 10 plagues brought against Egypt in the days of Moses. Scan Exodus 7:12–12:36 and see how many of the trumpet judgments in today's reading have a counterpart in the days of Egyptian bondage.

Seven Signs / Revelation 10–13

26

📖 **Overview:** John sees a mighty angel carrying a little book. John is not permitted to record part of the angel's message, but he is instructed by the angel to eat the book, which proves sweet to the taste but bitter to the stomach. Next John is told to measure the temple, altar, and courtyard in preparation for the arrival of two witnesses who will prophesy, perform miracles, and finally suffer martyrdom for their testimony. The seventh and last trumpet sounds, ushering in a grand chorus of praise. Then the scene shifts to heaven, where a mighty conflict takes place involving a woman, a dragon, a child, and Michael the archangel. The section closes with a description of two beasts: the first, a warring beast with seven heads and ten horns, and the second, a deceiving beast with two horns, great power, and a name whose number is 666.

Heart of the Passage: Rev. 10–11

Chapter 10	Chapter 11	Chapter 12	Chapter 13
Signs Involving . . .			
A Book	A Bugle	A Baby	Two Beasts
Second Interlude in the Judgments			

👣 **Your Daily Walk:** What is your response when confronted with a critical deadline? Do you (a) panic? (b) begin frantic activity? (c) get angry? (d) do all of the above? (Pick one.)

Did you know that Satan is no different? In his vision John heard a loud voice in heaven saying, "The devil is come down unto you, having great wrath, because he knoweth that he hath but a short time" (12:12). He is facing a deadline—a time after which he will no longer be able to roar, prowl, or seek whom he may devour (1 Peter 5:8).

Better check up on your spiritual defenses.

• Is your armor in place (Ephesians 6:10-18)?

• Do you remember the devil's schemes (he only has three, you know—2 Corinthians 2:11; 1 John 2:16).

• Are you keeping a sharp eye for his snares (1 Timothy 3:6-7)?

Satan is never too busy to rock the cradle of a sleeping saint.

📝 **Insight:** History's Most Overworked Number (13:18)

The famous number 666 has been identified with almost all the historical tyrants of the past 19 centuries. Symbolically, six has often been called the number of fallen men, and 666 an emphatic form depicting the "super fallen man." Exactly who this verse refers to, however, will not be known . . . until he is revealed.

27 *Seven Plagues / Revelation 14–16*

Heart of the Passage: Rev. 14

📖 **Overview:** Once again the 144,000 appear in John's vision, this time singing a new song before God's throne. Angels in the midst of heaven announce news that the hour of judgment is come. The Son of Man, sickle in hand, arrives to begin the harvest of the earth, and those ripe for judgment are cast into the wine-press of God's wrath. Seven angels emerge with the seven last plagues, which involve boils, blood, scorching heat, darkness, pain, earthquakes, hailstones, and a titanic confrontation at a place called Armageddon.

Chapter 14	Chapter 15	Chapter 16
Here Comes the Judge	Here Comes the Judgment	Judgment Is Here
Two Harvests	Seven Vials	

For the Christian, death does not extinguish the light. It puts out the lamp because the dawn has come.

✔️ **Your Daily Walk:** The Bible contains a number of statements about "blessed" people, statements that, at first glance, don't make good earthly sense!

"Blessed are the poor in spirit . . . they that mourn . . . the meek . . . the merciful . . . the pure in heart . . . the peacemakers . . . they which are persecuted" (Matthew 5:3-10). Clearly God's concept of heavenly "blessedness" differs from the world's concept today!

In the midst of his visions of divinely sent death and destruction, John hears a voice from heaven declaring, "Blessed are the dead which die in the Lord" (14:13). Only a Christian can look at death, not as a calamity, but as a commencement—the beginning of rest and reward for faithful service.

Paul told his spiritual children at Philippi, "To me . . . to die is gain" (Philippians 1:21). The psalmist declared, "Precious in the sight of the LORD is the death of his saints" (Psalm 116:15). And David's familiar words in Psalm 23 have provided comfort for countless thousands: "Yea, though I walk through the valley of the shadow of death, I will fear no evil: for thou art with me."

Those who view death as a blessing are those for whom death is not an end, but a beginning. Do you share that joyful hope? Have you shared it recently? Won't you share it with someone today?

🖼️ **Insight:** The "Greatest" Story Ever Told
The vividness of John's apocalyptic visions is suggested by the fact that the word "great" appears 72 times in the book!

The Business of Heaven

28

⬅ Step Back

Revelation offers some intriguing glimpses of heavenly life. Yet the mystery of heaven remains. W. E. Sangster, a British pastor of the first half of this century, wrote this about common misconceptions of heaven:

Some have regarded heaven as an interminable church service with the choir doing most of the work. Sir Walter Scott dreaded for himself "an eternity of music" and hoped for "some duty to discharge." Lloyd George confessed: "When I was a boy, the thought of heaven used to frighten me more than the thought of hell. I pictured heaven as a place where time would be perpetual Sundays, with perpetual services from which there would be no escape." The overworked, not unnaturally, have thought of heaven just as a place of rest, and would find it hard to believe that, to many of us, endless rest would become endless boredom. But there is authority in the Bible for asserting that we shall be employed, we shall develop, and we shall have unspeakable joy.

Scripture Reading: 1 Corinthians 3:12-15; 2 Corinthians 5:9-10

The Scriptures only tantalize us with a broad concept of what we'll do to keep busy forever, but at least seven heavenly activities of the saints can be noted:

1. We will worship God (Revelation 19:1-8; 22:8-9).
2. We will serve God (Revelation 22:3).
3. We will know God perfectly (Revelation 21:3; 22:4).
4. We will reign with God (Matthew 25:21, 23; Revelation 22:5).
5. We will fellowship with other believers (Hebrews 12:23; Revelation 19:7-9; 22:14).
6. We will enjoy God and our heavenly home (Revelation 19:7; 22:14).
7. We will rest (Revelation 14:13).

⬆ Look Up

As you consider these seven activities, ask the Lord how you can begin doing some of them now—such as fellowship, worship, and service. You may enjoy a foretaste of heaven right here on earth!

What we weave in this world we shall wear in heaven.

➡ Move Ahead

The bottom line is this: Our actions on earth will determine the extent to which we'll enjoy those activities. According to 1 Corinthians 3:12-15 and 2 Corinthians 5:9-10, Jesus Christ will judge the activities of each believer on earth to evaluate our works and give us rewards in accordance with them.

Take time to evaluate your use of time in light of the judgment seat of Christ.

29 Seven Dooms / Revelation 17–19

Heart of the Passage: Rev. 19

Overview: Following the catastrophic judgments of the seven vials, John sees the doom of Babylon the Great predicted and brought to pass. While Babylon is suffering a shameful demise on earth, a great multitude in heaven sings praises to God in anticipation of the marriage supper of the Lamb. A white horse emerges, mounted by the King of Kings who destroys the beast, false prophet, and their army. The "dead, small and great" are judged at the great white throne (20:11-12), setting the stage for the coming of a new heaven and earth.

Chapter 17	Chapter 18	Chapter 19
Babylon's Doom Predicted	Babylon's Doom Produced	Babylon's Doom Praised
"Almighty!"	"Alas!"	"Alleluia!"

Your Daily Walk: Doomsday. A frightening thought even to those who face crisis as a way of life. No one wants to admit that he . . . or his family . . . or his nation might be doomed.

The saddest thing from birth to sod is a dying man who has no God.

In the space of three intense chapters, John sees and records seven major events of doom which unfold in the drama of the book of Revelation: (1–3) the doom of Babylon ecclesiastically, 17:1-18, commercially, 18:1-23, and politically, 19:1-18; (4) the doom of the beast and false prophet, 19:19-21; (5) the doom of the nations, 20:7-9; (6) the doom of the devil, 20:10; (7) the doom of the lost, 20:11-15.

God's judgments are sure. Though He is a patient, loving God who is "not willing that any should perish" (2 Peter 3:9), people will perish if they do not heed His call to repentance.

How about you? Is your name written in the Book of Life? Have you experienced God's mercy through Jesus Christ—or are you in line for God's judgment? What better time than on the threshold of a new year to come to God, so that you too can sing, "Alleluia; Salvation, and glory, and honor, and power, unto the Lord our God" (19:1).

Insight: Marriages Old and New

The Bible begins with a marriage (Genesis 2:8, 21-25) and ends with a marriage (Revelation 19:9, the marriage supper of the Lamb). Christ's first public miracle took place at a marriage in Cana (John 2). And for the Christian, marriage is to be a sacred picture to the world of Christ's love for His bride, the church (Ephesians 5:25-33).

The First and the Last

30

Step Back

The book of Revelation ties the themes of the Bible together. For instance, there's an especially strong contrast between the first three chapters of Genesis and the last three of Revelation, which you will read tomorrow:

Scripture Reading: Genesis 1–3

• "In the beginning God created the heavens and the earth" (Genesis 1:1) . . . "I saw a new heaven and a new earth" (Revelation 21:1).

• "The darkness he called Night" (1:5). . . . "There shall be no night there" (21:25).

• "In the day that thou eatest thereof thou shalt surely die" (2:17). "There shall be no more death" (21:4).

• Satan appears as a deceiver of mankind (3:1). . . . Satan disappears forever (20:10).

• Initial triumph of the serpent (3:13). . . . Ultimate triumph of the Lamb (20:10; 22:3).

• "I will greatly multiply thy sorrow" (3:16). . . . "There shall be no more death neither sorrow" (21:4).

• "Cursed is the ground for thy sake" (3:17). . . . "There shall be no more curse" (22:3).

• Access to the tree of life is lost in Adam (3:24). . . . Access to the tree of life is reinstated in Christ (22:14).

• They were driven from God's presence (3:24). . . . "They shall see His face" (22:4).

In a very real sense, Revelation 21–22 is the new Genesis. But this time there will be no Fall.

Look Up

As you praise God for His wonderful plan of the future, think of a friend, family member, neighbor or co-worker whom you'd like to join you in heaven forever, but who has yet to make a commitment to Christ. Pray for that person; ask God to prepare a way for you to share with him or her the glorious truth of salvation.

Never be afraid to trust an unknown future to a known God.

Move Ahead

After your reading tomorrow, you will have completed reading through the entire Bible from Genesis to Revelation. That's 1,189 chapters and more than 31,100 verses!

You've no doubt gained great wisdom and knowledge along the way, perhaps seeing the Bible in a way you've never seen it before. Why not commit to do it again next year with *Your Daily Walk* . . . and invite someone to join with you! It's more fun to walk together.

31 Seven New Things / Revelation 20–22

Heart of the Passage: Rev. 21:1-8; 22:16-21

Overview: In one sentence John sums up the end of this present world order: "The first heaven and the first earth were passed away; and there was no more sea" (21:1). He then describes the breathtaking splendor of the new heaven and earth, God's new order in which "the tabernacle of God is with men, and he will dwell with them, and they shall be his people, and God himself shall be with them, and be their God" (21:3). Once again, God and His people live in intimate, unbroken fellowship. Revelation closes with Christ's thrice-repeated promise, "Behold, I come quickly" (22:7, 12, 20) and John's refrain, "Even so, come, Lord Jesus" (22:20).

Chapter 20	Chapter 21	Chapter 22
Doom of the Devil and Death	Delight of the New Heaven and Earth	Declaration of Christ's Coming
Lake of Fire	City of Gold	Tree of Life

Your Daily Walk: Tomorrow is an important day on the calendar as we enter a new year. But it could never compare with the glorious age Christ will usher in when He comes.

Satan never fears the Christian whose Bible is covered with dust.

By reading through your Bible with the aid of *Your Daily Walk* this past year, you have no doubt gained a greater love for God and a greater sense of anticipation for Christ's return. But the question remains: How will next year be different from this one because of the time you spent in God's Word these past 12 months? What new lessons have you learned? Where have you experienced growth in your Christian life? Take a moment right now to seal the decisions you've made this year. Ask God to help you build upon those steps of growth as you continue to walk with Him in the coming year.

C. H. Spurgeon once said, "Nobody ever outgrows Scripture; the book widens and deepens with our years." Why not make it your New Year's resolution to walk through the Bible again with *Your Daily Walk*. And why not invite one or two friends to read along with you!

Insight: A Cube in the Old, A Cube in the New

The cube has special significance in the Bible. In both the tabernacle and Solomon's temple, the Holy of Holies was a perfect cube. And the New Jerusalem is described as a perfect cube measuring 12,000 furlongs (1,500 miles) on a side.